LITERARY
BROOKLYN

LITERARY BROOKLYN

❧

THE WRITERS OF BROOKLYN

AND THE STORY OF

AMERICAN CITY LIFE

Evan Hughes

A HOLT PAPERBACK

HENRY HOLT AND COMPANY

NEW YORK

Holt Paperbacks
Henry Holt and Company, LLC
Publishers since 1866
175 Fifth Avenue
New York, New York 10010
www.henryholt.com

A Holt Paperback® and 🖪® are registered trademarks of Henry Holt and Company, LLC.

Library of Congress Cataloging-in-Publication Data

Hughes, Evan, 1975–
    Literary Brooklyn : the writers of Brooklyn and the story of American
city life / Evan Hughes. — 1st ed.
        p.   cm.
    "A Holt Paperback."
    Includes bibliographical references.
    ISBN 978-0-8050-8986-8
    1. Authors, American—Homes and haunts—New York (State)—New York.
2. Brooklyn (New York, N.Y.)—In literature.   3. American literature—New York
(State)—New York—History and criticism.   4. Brooklyn (New York, N.Y.)—
Intellectual life.   I. Title.
    PS144.B76H84 2011
    810.9'974723—dc22   2011006652

Henry Holt books are available for special promotions and premiums.
For details contact: Director, Special Markets.

First Edition 2011
Designed by Meryl Sussman Levavi
Printed in the United States of America

1   3   5   7   9   10   8   6   4   2

Grateful acknowledgment is made for permission to reprint the following published and unpublished material:

Excerpts from the letters and poetry of Hart Crane are used by permission of the Rare Book & Manuscript Library, Columbia University.

Excerpts from the letters of Marianne Moore, as published in *The Selected Letters of Marianne Moore*, ed. Bonnie Costello (New York: Alfred A. Knopf), 1997, are used by permission of Literary Estate of Marianne C. Moore, David M. Moore, Administrator of the Literary Estate of Marianne Moore. All rights reserved. Excerpts from Marianne Moore's "Poetry" and "Callot-Drecol-Cheruit-Jenny-Doucet-Aviotte-Lady" from *The Poems of Marianne Moore*, edited by Grace Schulman: Copyright © Penguin Books and Copyright © Marianne Moore, used with permission of the Literary Estate of Marianne C. Moore as well as the permission of Penguin Books.

Excerpt from an unpublished portion of a *Paris Review* interview with Bernard Malamud: Reprinted by the permission of Russell & Volkening as agents for the author. Copyright © 1957 by Bernard Malamud, renewed 1985 by Bernard Malamud.

Excerpts from the letters of W. H. Auden: Copyright © W. H. Auden, used with permission of The Wylie Agency LCC.

Excerpts from the published writings of William Styron are used by permission of the Estate of William Styron.

Excerpt from Pete Hamill's essay "Brooklyn: The Sane Alternative" is used by permission of Pete Hamill.

For my father,
Guy D. Hughes,
1934–2009

Contents

LITERARY
BROOKLYN

MANHATTAN

SEE PAGE XIV

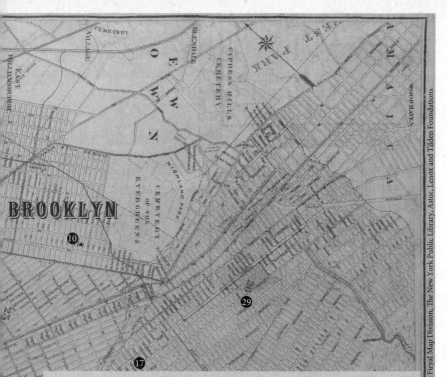

BROOKLYN

WALT WHITMAN
1) 251 Adams Street
2) 41 Tillary Street
3) 120 Front Street
4) 71 Prince Street
5) 106 Myrtle Avenue
6) 99 Ryerson Street
7) 99½ Classon Avenue
8) Rome Brothers print shop

HENRY MILLER
9) 662 Driggs Ave.
10) 1063 Decatur Street
11) 264 Sixth Avenue
    179 Cumberland Street*
    91 Remsen Street*
12) 288 Clinton Avenue
13) 180 Clinton Avenue

HART CRANE
110 Columbia Heights*
77 Willow Street*
130 Columbia Heights*
190 Columbia Heights*

JOHN DOS PASSOS
110 Columbia Heights*

MARIANNE MOORE
14) 260 Cumberland Street

*See inset on page xiv for all
Brooklyn Heights locations.*

THOMAS WOLFE
15) 40 Verandah Place
    111 Columbia Heights *
    101 Columbia Heights*
    5 Montague Terrace*

DANIEL FUCHS
16) 366 South 2nd Street

BERNARD MALAMUD
1111 Gravesend Avenue
(not shown, south of map)

ALFRED KAZIN
17) 256 Sutter Avenue

RICHARD WRIGHT
18) 175 Carlton Avenue
19) 343 Grand Avenue
20) 552 Gates Avenue
    7 Middagh Street*
21) 101 Lefferts Place *and*
    89 Lefferts Place *and*
    87 Lefferts Place
22) 11 Revere Place

WILLIAM STYRON
23) 1506 Caton Avenue

BERNARD MALAMUD
(Not shown, south of map)

ARTHUR MILLER
350 E 3rd Street
(Not shown, south of map)
For other addresses see inset

NORMAN MAILER
24) 555 Crown Street
    102 Pierrepont Street*
    142 Columbia Heights*
For other addresses see inset

TRUMAN CAPOTE
25) 17 Clifton Place
    70 Willow Street*

PETE HAMILL
26) 471 14th Street
27) 435 13th Street
28) 378 7th Avenue

ISAAC ASIMOV
29) 425 Van Siclen Avenue

L. J. DAVIS
30) 138A Dean Street

PAUL BOWLES
31) 2 Water Street

PAUL AUSTER
32) 18 Tompkins Place
33) 458 3rd Street

Manhattan

Brooklyn Bridge

Fulton Street

Manhattan Bridge

Brooklyn Heights

Doughty St.
Vine St.

Poplar Street

Middagh Street

Cranberry Street

Orange Street

Pineapple Street

Clark Street

Love Lane

Pierrepont Street

Penny Bridge

Montague Street

Remsen Street

Grace Court
Alley

Joralemon Street

State Street

Atlantic Avenue

Columbia Heights

Willow Street

Hicks Street

Henry Street

Fulton Street

Liberty Street

Clinton Street

Monroe P.

Furman Street

Heights

Columbia

Willow Pl.

Clinton Street

Stanley Pl.

Livingston

Schermerhorn

Garden Pl.

Grace Ct.

HENRY MILLER
1) 91 Remsen Street

HART CRANE
2) 110 Columbia Heights
3) 77 Willow Street
4) 130 Columbia Heights
5) 190 Columbia Heights

JOHN DOS PASSOS
2) 110 Columbia Heights
   (see Crane)

THOMAS WOLFE
6) 111 Columbia Heights
7) 101 Columbia Heights
8) 5 Montague Terrace

RICHARD WRIGHT
9) 7 Middagh Street

TRUMAN CAPOTE
10) 70 Willow Street

NORMAN MAILER
11) 102 Pierrepont Street
12) 142 Columbia Heights
13) 49 Remsen Street
14) 20 Remsen Street

ARTHUR MILLER
15) 62 Montague Street
16) 18 Schermerhorn Street
11) 102 Pierrepont Street
    (see Mailer)
17) 31 Grace Court
18) 155 Willow Street

ALFRED KAZIN
19) 150 Remsen Street

W. H. AUDEN
20) 1 Montague Terrace
9) 7 Middagh Street
   (also Gypsy Rose Lee,
   Richard Wright,
   Paul and Jane Bowles,
   Benjamin Britten)

Adapted from a 1933 map by the Garden Place Association, courtesy Brooklyn Collection, Brooklyn Public Library

Introduction

In 1965, when the writer L. J. Davis bought an eleven-room Brooklyn town house for $17,500, the neighbors laughed at him for overpaying. On the surrounding streets of his neighborhood, Boerum Hill, loose garbage blew down the sidewalk, the trees were stripped bare, and walking home meant carefully planning the least threatening route. Stately brownstones built in the nineteenth century had been converted into crumbling boardinghouses "paved with mattresses," with up to thirty people living in squalor in a space designed for one family. A neighbor slept in a tent inside his house because large chunks of the roof had caved in. Davis's literary agent told him that Brooklyn was not a suitable place for an author to live.

Davis sold his house a few years ago for roughly one hundred times what he paid to buy it. A phenomenal decrease in crime and a remaking of Brooklyn's image over the last two decades have turned neighborhoods like Boerum Hill into centers of cultural vibrancy. In recent years writers have made the move to Brooklyn in droves, and the borough has drawn new independent bookstores, a prominent literary festival, and a steady flow of readings and book parties. Brooklyn's bookish "scene" has become the talk of the literary world. There's a good chance a given American author lives in New York City, as always. But now there's an even better chance a New York City author is based in the borough of Brooklyn.

This migration from Manhattan to Brooklyn represents something of a reversal in the fraught historical relationship between the two boroughs. On the one hand, more people live in Brooklyn than in San Francisco, Washington, D.C., Boston, and Miami *put together*. Its population tops Manhattan's not by a little but by over 900,000. But when the world pictures New York City, it pictures the skyline of Manhattan.

Back when Brooklyn led the movement to build the Brooklyn Bridge, it was a thriving independent city, and the architectural marvel instantly became a source of hometown pride when it opened in 1883. But in a sense that first bridge to Manhattan spelled doom for Brooklyn's autonomy. Fifteen years later Brooklyn was swallowed into the enormous City of New York despite much reluctance and even outrage. Until then the third-largest city in the country, Brooklyn became a mere "outer borough," subject to the control of New York's elite. The consolidation proposal passed by only 277 votes in Brooklyn, where some residents hung black crepe in their windows in mourning. Consolidation conferred many benefits on Brooklyn, but the borough president still refers to it, only half in jest, as the "Great Mistake."

From early on, Brooklyn has grown up in the long shadow of its more glamorous and vertical neighbor. Manhattan has had the strongest retail trade, the grandest museums, the Ivy League, the titans of industry, the tourists, Wall Street, Broadway, the skyscrapers that symbolized power and achievement. There isn't much it hasn't had. Brooklyn has meanwhile nursed a certain grudge over its subordinate position, especially when some Manhattanites have seemed to view Brooklyn, in Ralph Foster Weld's words, as somewhere "remote as . . . Tibet, a vague and unreal land, possibly nonexistent." Even today, unlike those major U.S. cities that it dwarfs in size, Brooklyn has had no major newspaper and no major sports team for over fifty years, and indeed no independent government for twice that long. For commuters, it is more a place you start from than a place you end up.

Until recently, too, the focus on Manhattan as an intellectual beacon left little room to imagine Brooklyn as a cosmopolitan or sophisticated place, for all its size and diversity. Most of the associations that Brooklyn did call to mind—Coney Island, the Dodgers, stickball, the egg cream—had little to do with arts and letters. In fact, the Brooklyn guy in the movies always seemed to be a bit of a dim bulb with a mongrel accent—salt of the earth, good for a laugh. If you were looking for writers, you were supposed to go to Greenwich Village.

But Brooklyn has always offered a perspective that Manhattan hasn't. Saul Steinberg's "The View from 9th Avenue," a 1976 cover illustration for the *New Yorker*, famously captured Manhattan's special brand of provincialism: everything about Manhattan's west side looms large, consuming most of the picture, while the rest of the country and the world is barely worthy of a haphazard sketch. Brooklyn shares some of the same viewpoint, being after all a part of New York City. But the writers of Brooklyn have also shown that there is more to the American story than the behemoth next door.

There is no "Brooklyn school" of literature and there never has been. We shouldn't mistake a massive place for an aesthetic camp. One experience Brooklyn's writers have shared, however, is living just outside the colossal, churning center of the metropolis—across the river from what is still often referred to as "the city." Some have used all their might to make the escape from impoverished Brooklyn neighborhoods to the urbane quarters of Manhattan—the crossing Norman Podhoretz called "one of the longest journeys in the world"—but in their work they have often returned to the scene of their early Brooklyn struggles. Other writers have chosen Brooklyn as an escape from the commercial clamor of Manhattan, seeking a retreat where the rent is lower, the pulse runs slower, and the buildings don't crowd out the sky. For this group, too, the distance between the boroughs has felt greater than in actual fact. In either case, writers have tended to find more meaning and inspiration in Brooklyn itself than they might have expected.

Part of Brooklyn's richness as a site of the literary imagination, I think, lies in the very fact that it is not only a truly distinct place from Manhattan but a less exceptional one, in the strict sense of the word. More human in scale, less visually extravagant, not as wealthy or stylish, more suspicious of what is fashionable or famous, slower to hunger for the new—Brooklyn is more like America.

As such, for centuries Brooklyn has provided a revealing window onto the broader history of American urban life. And the borough's writers, casting their eyes on the same streets decades apart, have brought that history to life in vivid colors. In Walt Whitman's nineteenth-century Brooklyn, we see a pastoral scene rapidly supplanted by the wild, unchecked glories and afflictions of the frantically urbanizing North and the intense polarization of the country that led to the Civil War. In Henry Miller's reflections on his childhood, we see a jumble of European immigrant groups at the turn of the twentieth century all trying to gain a foothold on the same turf. In Hart Crane we find the fallout of the Great War giving way to 1920s prosperity and a more hopeful kind of modernity. In the narratives of Daniel Fuchs, Alfred Kazin, and Bernard Malamud, the sons of poor Jewish immigrants, we come to grips with the depths of the Depression, when families like theirs grasped at the lowest rungs of society. Thomas Wolfe, too, turned his attention to the Brooklyn streets to capture the grim 1930s. The southerner had gone there to hole up alone, but he found instead that while "young men were writing manifestos in the higher magazines of Manhattan, . . . the weather of man's life . . . was soaking in on me in those years in Brooklyn." The high-society crowd in Manhattan who thought their fingers were on the American pulse, he felt, were actually missing everything.

In his books *Native Son* and *Black Boy*, Richard Wright illuminates the Great Migration that was radically transforming northern urban centers like Brooklyn just when he was living and writing there. William Styron's *Sophie's Choice* captures a postwar Brooklyn and America where new hopes commingled uneasily with the horrors of the recent past. Arthur Miller, in *Death of a Salesman*, gives us the archetypal faltering American business-man, unable to keep up with the postwar march of capitalism. In Norman Mailer's works, we get a close-up of U.S. soldiers in Word War II; an allegory of early Cold War repression and paranoia played out in a Brooklyn boardinghouse; a view of the uninhibited impulses breaking out at the fringes of fifties society; an impas-sioned frontline report on the Vietnam protest movement. Hubert Selby Jr. shows us, in *Last Exit to Brooklyn*, an early-sixties dysto-pian picture of the looming urban crisis, which would cripple not only Brooklyn but most major American cities into the seventies and eighties. The novels of L. J. Davis, Paula Fox, and Jonathan Lethem grapple with that crisis and with the precarious and halt-ing beginnings of the return of middle- and upper-middle-class residents to inner cities weighed down by years of decline. The growing crowd of young writers in Brooklyn today are reckoning with the consequences of gentrification, which has changed many American cities but has had a particularly pronounced effect on Brooklyn.

A guiding principle of this book, a hybrid of literary biography, literary analysis, and urban history, is that literature has a special ability to offer an intimate view of a very particular place and time. It gives us history on a personal level, on a scale small enough to comprehend. A talented novelist can convey a degree of empathy and emotion that a sociologist or a historian has trouble matching. And a novel or poem or memoir needn't be overtly focused on a place to reflect something important about it. Literature brings home the way the broad forces that shape a place also come to bear on individual lives—the lives of the authors as well as their characters.

Although Brooklyn's writers are each unique in background and in artistic vision, they have walked the same streets, cast their eyes on the same neighborhoods. Over time, the terrain has shifted beneath their feet, as social change has swept over the landscape. But taken together, their impressions bring that change to life and make us understand it a new way. This is Brooklyn's story, seen through the eyes of its great storytellers.

1.

The Grandfather of Literary Brooklyn

WALT WHITMAN

Just as you feel when you look on the river and sky, so
  I felt,
Just as any of you is one of a living crowd, I was one of
  a crowd.

—"Crossing Brooklyn Ferry," WALT WHITMAN

WHEN WALT WHITMAN WAS IN HIS EARLY THIRTIES, HE HAD
already lived out the first act of his life. The son of a failing carpenter, he had been a grammar school dropout; an office boy for a law
firm; an apprentice to various printers; and, disastrously, a schoolteacher. Eventually he found a calling in journalism, moving upstairs
from the printing room to the editorial office. And at the age of
twenty-six, in 1846, he was named the editor of booming Brooklyn's leading newspaper, the *Brooklyn Daily Eagle*, where his office
window looked out on the foot of Fulton Street, by the glinting,
well-traveled East River and the Fulton Ferry. He became a prominent and eccentric man about town. To entertain people he would
shout out lines from Shakespeare and Homer from a stagecoach or

at the seashore, and he would hum arias as he walked down the street. He was talked about. He was known.

Then, in 1848, he was fired from the *Eagle* after clashing with his boss over politics. His next newspaper jobs were short-lived, and he began to slip out of view. He took on the look of a social dropout, with shaggy hair, a gray beard, and overalls. In the ensuing half decade he was a sometime freelance journalist, a sometime bookseller at a store he operated out of his house on a lot he'd bought for a hundred dollars, and a sometime carpenter. And sometimes he was plain unemployed. "There was a great boom in Brooklyn in the early fifties, and he had his chance then," his brother George later said, "but you know he made nothing of that chance." Strange and a bit rough around the edges, Whitman didn't make it easy for others to reach out to him. Things were not looking good.

But something powerful was taking hold of him from within: "I found myself remaining possess'd, at the age of thirty-one to thirty-two, with a special desire and conviction . . . that had been flitting through my previous life, or hovering on the flanks, [that] finally dominated everything else." He began composing a series of very long, unstructured poems, of a kind not yet seen by the world. Each day, he took them into the Rome Brothers print shop at the corner of Cranberry Street and Fulton Street, where he and the owners set them into type during off-hours. He would sleep late, write more, return to the print shop. It was the nineteenth-century equivalent of self-publishing out of a Kinko's. And the result was *Leaves of Grass*. "No other book in the history of American letters," Malcolm Cowley has written, "was so completely an individual or do-it-yourself project."

Where *Leaves of Grass* came from no one will know. But as Whitman said, his masterpiece drew breath from the people of Brooklyn, his literal and spiritual home. Walt Whitman, as much as he was "one of a crowd," was America's first great bard and the keystone of Brooklyn's literary tradition.

It requires a considerable feat of imagination today to picture Brooklyn as it was when Whitman first arrived as a child of three, in 1823. It was a place so different from the huge urban mass of today, with its population of 2.5 million, that it is scarcely possible to hold it in the mind's eye. Then a separate entity from the city of New York, which was restricted to the island of Manhattan, Brooklyn was a placid little town of low-slung houses topped with billowing chimney smoke, tucked in close to the shore of the East River; the surrounding area later incorporated into Brooklyn consisted of large farms of rolling hills and a handful of even smaller hamlets. What is now the borough of Brooklyn boasted about as many residents as today's Wasilla, Alaska.

Across the water, Manhattan was beginning to become a central place in American commerce and in the American imagination, but its tallest building was only four stories high. You could stand in Brooklyn Heights and see clear across Manhattan and the Hudson and well into New Jersey. From that spot you could watch a great crowd of high-masted ships carrying goods up and down the East River and especially the Hudson.

In Brooklyn in 1823 there was no regular police force, no public transportation, and flickering gas lamps were just being introduced to help light the eerily quiet, unpopulated nighttime streets. Families had to gather round the fireplace to cook or stay warm. Some had horses and a carriage, but they contended with rutted, narrow dirt roads, and there was no organized stagecoach service. Residents kept pigs and chickens that roamed in the streets in daytime, rooting through the garbage alongside open sewers. Water was drawn from street wells and carried home. Taverns and stables stood among houses and shanties. The odors were rank. To the east of the village—on land now densely packed with multistory apartment buildings—were sprawling green fields still owned mostly by the Dutch. They kept a firm hold on their properties, assured of a market for their produce and livestock in the village of Brooklyn and in Manhattan.

Many slaves worked the land and tended to houses. In 1800, before slaveholding was abolished in New York State, in 1827, about 60 percent of the white households within Brooklyn's current borders owned at least one slave, the highest proportion in the North. The nationwide battle over slavery would shadow Whitman's life as it grew to be the foremost threat to the country.

But America was a young nation in Whitman's childhood, and the Civil War was still far off. Whitman's father, also named Walter, was born the same year as the federal government, in 1789. Whitman's great-uncle fought and died in the Revolutionary War's first major battle, the Battle of Brooklyn, in 1776. That rout by the English cost twelve hundred American lives in a matter of hours, with at least another fifteen hundred wounded, captured, or missing. With defeat clearly at hand, George Washington, standing where Court Street now crosses Atlantic Avenue, is said to have cried, "Good God! What brave fellows I must this day lose!" But acts of valor on the American side would live on—particularly in the story of the Maryland forces who sacrificed themselves almost to a one in challenging and delaying the much larger British contingent at the Old Stone House, near today's Fourth Avenue and Ninth Street in Brooklyn. That stand allowed Washington and his men to make an overnight escape across the East River to Manhattan, whispering to one another in the fog to avoid alerting the British. If it weren't for this getaway, the war could easily have ended in a brutally swift British victory. According to the historian Kenneth Jackson, one observer later said, "The Declaration of Independence that was signed in ink in Philadelphia was signed in blood in Brooklyn." Both the heroism and the tragedy of the Battle of Brooklyn and its aftermath would become a touchstone of Whitman's work.

Between 1790 and 1810, Brooklyn's population nearly tripled, as Irish, Yankee, and Manhattanite new arrivals crowded out the Dutch. The Brooklyn Navy Yard gave rise to other shipyards and maritime trades, providing work for carpenters and craftsmen. Wooden market stalls stood by the water, and small manufacture spread out from the river. Whitman's father moved to Brooklyn to be a carpenter and builder, in the hopes of capitalizing on the town's population boom. Although the boom continued, he didn't succeed, perhaps because he favored old ways of building and because he lacked the gift for self-promotion, though his son would soon possess it in spades. The Whitmans moved at least ten times in the space of a decade.* Walt attended Brooklyn's single elementary school, District School No. 1, which had been established in 1816 on Concord and Adams Streets, for about five years. That would remain the only formal education for the man about whom the venerated critic Harold Bloom has written, "No comparable figure in the arts has emerged from the last four centuries in the Americas." Before Whitman, American literature was largely for Harvard men, like Emerson, Thoreau, and Henry James. It called to mind men of leisure, with crisp white collars and hired help. Then Whitman barged in.

Walt's family's finances forced him to leave school at age eleven and go to work, and for the decades to follow he would have the kind of extraordinarily varied and checkered work history shared by many writers since. In his childhood and adolescence, Brooklyn offered very little in the way of literary and cultural life. Few residents wanted to give money for a proposed Apprentices' Library in 1824, so library representatives took a wheelbarrow door to door to collect cast-off pamphlets and books. The literacy rate was low and the media hadn't extended a very meaningful reach into Brooklyn, or indeed much of the nation. The stodgy and relatively expensive political newspapers had not yet met with the competition of the mass-oriented "penny press," whose pioneers were the New York *Sun* (founded in 1833) and the *New York Herald* (1835).

Soon Whitman would enter the burgeoning journalism trade, beginning his apprenticeship in the laborious work of typesetting and printing at the Brooklyn-based Long Island *Patriot.* He bounced from publications of one political stripe or another in Brooklyn,

---

* Their known addresses at this time were on Front Street, Cranberry Street, Henry Street, Johnson Street, Adams Street, Tillary Street, and Liberty Street (no longer in existence). In later years Whitman lived on Prince Street, on Myrtle Avenue, on Cumberland Street, at 99 Ryerson Street (the only one of his homes that still stands), on Classon Avenue, and on Portland Avenue, on the site of today's Walt Whitman Houses, a public housing project.

Manhattan, and Long Island, picking up writing and editing skills along with the craft of printing. In the 1830s, as New York slid toward a depression, the newspaper business ran into trouble, and Whitman fled to Long Island and became (at about seventeen) a schoolteacher. An itinerant and miserably unhappy five years followed. "O, damnation, damnation!" he wrote, "thy other name is school-teaching." He also attempted, with little success, to publish his own Long Island paper, but he moved to Manhattan in 1841 and joined its revived journalism industry. Tired of living in one Manhattan boardinghouse after another for short stints—a pattern that many writers in their early twenties would follow—he moved back to Brooklyn in 1845.

That was Whitman's last time living in Manhattan. He always took to Brooklyn more heartily. A great deal of his learning and cultural exposure came from Manhattan, but he saw it as an over-crowded place and the center of the kind of commerce he considered vulgar. In "Brooklynania," a series of articles he published in his forties, his lasting pride in his hometown is evident. Brooklyn's "situation for grandeur, beauty and salubrity is unsurpassed probably on the whole surface of the globe," he wrote, "and its destiny is to be among the most famed and choice of the half dozen of the leading cities of the world." He would remain in Brooklyn for the next seventeen years, his longest stay in one place and the period when he came into his own.

He drew energy from Brooklyn, absorbing, as he said later, the immense and moving power of everyday lives. Striking a chord that echoes down through the last century and a half of Brooklyn literature, he relished Brooklyn's position at an arm's length from the mass of humanity and the incessant rattle of business in Manhattan. Near the end of those seventeen years, he wrote of Brooklyn with evident pride, "It may not generally be known that our city is getting to have quite a worldwide reputation." He added: "With much greater attractions than our neighboring island of New York, Brooklyn is steadily drawing hither the best portion of the business population of the great adjacent metropolis, who find here a superior place for dwelling." Indeed, since before Whitman's birth wealthy businessmen and merchants had begun building fine homes in the Brooklyn Heights neighborhood, which overlooked the East River and offered a short commute on the ferry to their jobs in lower Manhattan. Whitman put his finger, then, on a trend that would drive Brooklyn's history: many people reliant in their professional lives on Manhattan would find Brooklyn a more pleasing place to live.

But it wasn't the home-owning class that most interested Whitman. He identified more, as writers tend to do, with those who had something of the countercultural in them—those who were, in a favorite word of his, "agitators." In his mind he was always allied with the common and even lowly man, the one who was spurned by others. He would sometimes be coy about the extent of his reading because he didn't want to be associated with the snobbery he saw among the learned. Such views can be traced back to his father, who "believed in resisting much, obeying little," in the words of Whitman biographer Justin Kaplan. He trained his sons "as radical Democrats, on the side of the farmer, the laborer, the small tradesman, and the 'people.'" The poet and aesthete James Russell Lowell once warned a foreigner against paying a visit to Whitman after he had become famous. Lowell pegged him as "a rowdy, a New York tough, a loafer, a frequenter of low places, a friend of cab drivers!" Whitman would have liked the description.

⁓

The changes that have occurred in Brooklyn in the last forty years are truly momentous, but they cannot compare to those of Whitman's first decades, the era that preceded and influenced the early editions of *Leaves of Grass*. Brooklyn evolved from a quiet village of about five thousand at Whitman's arrival to the third-largest city in the nation by the time of the Civil War, when Whitman was in his mid-forties. In his twenties alone the population tripled. Part of what spurred the growth was Brooklyn's investment in an industrial waterfront that competed with Manhattan's. In the 1830s,

Williamsburgh, then a separate town from Brooklyn (and spelled with an *h*), built large wharves along the East River and, much to New York's dismay, a new ferry line to Manhattan, which transported commuters both ways. By the 1850s the waterside factory district stretched from Greenpoint and Williamsburgh in the north, down past the Navy Yard, and on to the southern edge of South Brooklyn, where the Atlantic Basin, a new forty-acre shipping terminal in today's Red Hook, drew much Erie Canal traffic away from Manhattan. Along this corridor, iron foundries flourished, as did breweries, distilleries, sugar refineries, and drug companies (Pfizer started up in Williamsburgh in 1849).

These developments did little to glamorize Brooklyn or increase its prestige. The tourists were still over the river, promenading on Broadway. Brooklyn was becoming a boiler room belowdecks of the region's economic ship. And who was stoking the boiler? Immigrants, in large part. Williamsburgh was turning into a version of Manhattan's Kleindeutschland: by 1847 it was two-thirds German. Irish and British were also arriving in massive numbers, bringing the foreign-born proportion of the population to roughly half in 1855. Joining the immigrant working class, though, were members of the middle class—young professionals, clerks, and shop owners—who migrated from Manhattan while holding on to their jobs there. The place of choice for the most affluent remained Brooklyn Heights. Others spread southward into the more affordable area that incorporated today's Cobble Hill, Boerum Hill, and Carroll Gardens. The frontier neighborhoods to the east, land of bargains, were Fort Greene and East New York.

As Brooklyn rapidly urbanized and became more commercially active, it also gained something of a cultural foothold—developments that don't necessarily go hand in hand in the growth of cities. Whitman had no true local literary equals, but around him there emerged an intellectual ferment, and in particular a multiplicity of voices that swam against the current of mainstream society. He befriended activists in the women's rights movement, wrote in the papers in defiance of economic injustice to women, and embraced women as equals in poetry. Striking a note that was characteristically both inclusive and controversial, he wrote, "I am the poet of woman the same as man, / And I say it is as great to be a woman as to be a man." Although he was not a Quaker—he attended many churches, but never a single one for very long—Whitman venerated the iconoclastic Quaker leader Elias Hicks, whose radically democratic version of the faith, denying any special sanctity of Christ, had gained ascendancy quickly in Whitman's childhood. Whitman lived in an age when orators achieved widespread popularity and whipped up a great stir—nowhere more so than in Brooklyn, where a more accessible pulpit style took root. At one point he wrote regular columns reviewing local sermons and speeches. Whitman didn't align himself with any religion or political perspective but gave due attention and credit to the art of speaking out—the American religion, you might say, in his eyes.

The most famous local orator was Henry Ward Beecher, who packed the house beginning in 1847 at the Plymouth Church, still active today, on the corner of Hicks and Orange Streets in Brooklyn Heights. So many Manhattanites came to see him that on Sundays the Fulton Ferry came to be called "Beecher's Ferry." With his informal manner, his rousing voice, and his defiance of the norms of religion, Beecher offered a combination, it was said, of Saint Paul and P. T. Barnum. Not surprisingly, he became Whitman's favorite Brooklyn minister. Beecher's sister was Harriet Beecher Stowe, whose 1852 novel *Uncle Tom's Cabin* energized the abolitionist movement. After early objections to freeing existing slaves, Henry Ward Beecher, for his part, turned Plymouth Church into a center of antislavery activity and held "auctions" where church members bought the freedom of particular slaves. Brooklyn became a vibrant center of abolitionism, and Beecher grew to be a national and even international figure. Fierce division over this most fundamental issue of the day marked the whole period of Whitman's intellectual coming-of-age, a tumultuous era in national politics.

The newspaper business held a place in the thick of it all.

Where Whitman himself stood on slavery would be made clearest when he served as editor of the *Brooklyn Daily Eagle*, his most prominent journalistic position. Although he was still in his twenties when he was hired as the editor, he had become a man of considerable experience in journalism and seemed a natural for the position. He had been trained and, more to the point, had trained himself for the role. In *Walt Whitman: Song of Himself*, Jerome Loving writes, "If a whaling ship was Melville's Harvard and Yale, Brooklyn and newspaper work were this poet's university." The *Eagle* was the leading paper of Brooklyn, and Whitman possessed not only a deep familiarity with the life of the city and its surroundings but a formidable grasp of the national scene. In Brooklyn, the political forces shaping the nation were intensified and writ large, and he appeared more than happy to play a central role. The paper was steeped in a sense of Brooklyn pride that pitted itself against Manhattan, a pride that exists to this day, and it was a fitting place for Whitman to give unbridled voice to his populist views.

Although he adopted neither extreme in the debate over emancipation, he was anything but indifferent. An undeniable strain of racism ran through his thinking, yet he objected to slavery. He famously wrote, in the preface to *Leaves of Grass*, "The attitude of great poets is to cheer up slaves and horrify despots." But his main preoccupation was not the slaves themselves but the danger of the nationwide crisis over their fate. In the *Eagle* he came out firmly in support of the Wilmot Proviso, which proposed a ban on slavery's expansion into the new territories of the West, in a dispute then on everyone's lips. He wrote, "*We must plant ourselves firmly on the side of freedom, and openly espouse it.*" The owner of the *Eagle*, Isaac Van Anden, fell into line when Democratic leaders dropped their support for the proviso. Whitman, never one to back down and always a proud heretic, wrote an editorial in defiance of his boss's views, and weeks later he was out of a job.

When he turned to writing verse, Whitman found himself stirred by the same fondness for the common people that had motivated his journalism. Whitman had shown little promise in his formulaic earlier poetry, but he let loose in 1855 with a shot across the transom of American literature and America itself—a shot that almost no one initially heard—in the first edition of *Leaves of Grass*, a series of verses that he would rework and add to for the rest of his life. Nothing in his past would lead a reader to expect the ingenuity and majesty of this work. *Leaves* was immensely idiosyncratic and original but, as is the case with many drastic artistic departures, it went largely unnoticed—until it began to be widely disparaged. Loving writes that while Whitman was alive, "his poetry was generally reviled, condemned by reviewers as obscene in content, deficient in diction, irregular in rhythm, and absent of rhyme." The *New York Times*'s final review of *Leaves of Grass*, published just after his death, argued that Whitman could not be called "a great poet unless we deny poetry to be an art."

Whitman, confident though he was, knew he was out on a limb in *Leaves of Grass*, courting rejection. No imprimatur, no publishing company, no mentor or mainstream advocate lent support to the book. It was "a call in the midst of the crowd," in Whitman's own words, written by a journeyman journalist whose career had run aground. It was a profoundly eccentric piece of work, and it was incredibly egotistical. Describing "the greatest poet" in the almost ecstatic preface, Whitman writes, "If he breathes into anything that was before thought small it dilates with the grandeur of life and of the universe." Whitman's writings leave no doubt as to who "the greatest poet" was meant to be. The first lines of "Song of Myself," which opens *Leaves of Grass*: "I celebrate myself, / And what I assume, you shall assume, / For every atom belonging to me as good belongs to you." It is crucial to see in *Leaves of Grass* that the tone is both grandiose and inclusive. It invites us into its grandeur, elevating all: "I am the mate and companion of people, all just as immortal and fathomless as myself; / They do not know how immortal, but I know."

Leaves of Grass also represented an alliance forged with the downtrodden and an affront to mainstream mores and art, inaugurating a new, less lofty strain in American poetry. Whitman's decision to go it alone, his eschewing of rhyme and meter, and his bawdy, indecent material were all of a piece with this resolutely democratic and radical project. The preface advised the reader with disarming directness: "This is what you shall do: Love the earth and the sun and the animals, despise riches, give alms to every one that asks, stand up for the stupid and crazy, devote your income and labor to others, hate tyrants, argue not concerning God, have patience and indulgence toward the people, take off your hat to nothing known or unknown or to any man or number of men." Whitman's explicit treatment of sexuality and prostitution and other vulgarities invited and received a steady drumbeat of controversy. One early reviewer called *Leaves of Grass* a "mass of filth," and the Boston district attorney suspended publication of the 1881 edition on the grounds that it was illegally obscene. But most brave of all was Whitman's embrace and exaltation of those explicitly cast off by the world around him.

> *Through me many long dumb voices,*
> *Voices of the interminable generations of slaves,*
> *Voices of prostitutes and of deformed persons,*
> *Voices of the diseased and despairing, and of thieves and*
>   *dwarfs,*
> *Voices of cycles of preparation and accretion,*
> *And of the thread that connect the stars—and of wombs,*
>   *and of the fatherstuff,*
> *And of the rights of them the others are down upon,*
> *Of the trivial and flat and foolish and despised,*
> *Of fog in the air and beetles rolling balls of dung.*

Literature was supposed to be a high and dignified cultural product and thus far in America poetry had restricted itself largely to verses rife with pretty lyricism, sentiment, and pastoral scenes. Major writers nearly all had good educations and came from moneyed backgrounds, and they generally stayed away from "low" subject matter. But here, in *Leaves of Grass*, was an unstructured, bizarre, vast poem that gloried in baseness: "The scent of these arm-pits is aroma finer than prayer." The frontispiece of the book featured a now famous lithograph of Walt Whitman dressed in disheveled workingman's clothes, his hat tilted, his hand jauntily placed on one hip—Brooklyn's first literary hipster. Long after Whitman's death, his friend William Sloane Kennedy would wrinkle his nose at the picture: "It is to be hoped, nevertheless, that this repulsive, loaferish portrait, with its sensual mouth, can be dropped from future editions." Whitman's name appeared only twice in the book—once, as Walter Whitman, on the copyright page, and again as the more informal Walt, on page 29, in a delayed introduction to the "I" who has been narrating the poem.

> Walt Whitman, an American, one of the roughs, a kosmos,
> Disorderly fleshy and sensual . . . . eating drinking and
>   breeding,
> No sentimentalist . . . . no stander above men and women or
>   apart from them . . . . no more modest than immodest.

"One of the roughs"—Whitman and Henry David Thoreau regarded each other warily, but Thoreau privately told a close friend that Whitman was "the greatest democrat the world has seen. Kings and aristocracy go by the board at once."

In the second edition of *Leaves*, Whitman first published "Sun-Down Poem," later to be called "Crossing Brooklyn Ferry." At the time it was written, with no East River bridges yet built, the ferry connecting Brooklyn and Manhattan was at the center of thousands of dull commutes, and the poem recounts the mundane trip. But "Crossing Brooklyn Ferry" is a work of celebration— not only of the vista of the cityscape above and the sparkling water below, but more crucially of the city's men and women, of all men and women. The poem is addressed at first to the commuters aboard the ferry, and the voice is eager and full of wonder: "Crowds of men and women attired in the usual costumes, how curious you are to me! / On the ferry-boats the hundreds and hundreds that cross, returning home, are more curious to me than you suppose."

And quickly the poem moves to embrace not only those people around Whitman but those who populate the future, whose lives will take place on this same spot on earth, the trace of their movements like overlays on a map: "And you that shall cross from shore to shore years hence, are more to me, and more in my meditations, than you might suppose." Harold Bloom has written, "How could [this poem] change so radically the immemorial covenant of intimate separations between reader and poet? . . . Whitman's urgent power is *immediacy*." The idea and sentiment of oneness is repeated like an incantation, and magnified. Aboard a ferry that connects Manhattan to Brooklyn, Whitman connects present to future, and above all people to other people. The words of "Crossing Brooklyn Ferry" are today cut into sheets of steel that surround the Fulton Ferry Landing, at the end of Brooklyn's Old Fulton Street, where the ferry once departed and arrived.

Whitman wrote that *Leaves of Grass* amounted to his observations of New York and Brooklyn and the ordinary people who made up the bulk of their populations. Even more so than it is today, Brooklyn, with its increasing confluence of people of all stripes, was then a microcosm of the nation—a jumble of ethnicities struggling and thriving through the era of industrialization. This confluence would only grow more lively but also more fractious and unforgiving. The character of the place was churning through change in the years following the first editions of *Leaves*, and Whitman grew concerned. He had generally failed so far to earn the respect of the world of arts and letters through poetry, so he returned to journalism in 1857, at about thirty-eight, assuming the editorship of the *Brooklyn Daily Times*. He was soon speaking out in editorials against the direction the nation seemed to be taking, and more particularly against the changes afoot in Brooklyn and New York. Manhattan he had referred to ten years earlier as "the vast Gomorrah across the water," but now Brooklyn, too, came under more criticism. Its main thoroughfares had grown to be home to nearly constant cacophony, at least during the daytime. Crime had become a problem, as had rowdiness and public drunkenness, all of which Whitman decried.

In his *Eagle* editorials in the 1840s, Whitman had presciently campaigned nearly daily for the creation of a park in Brooklyn—a "lung" to allow it to breathe as it stretched eastward, spreading away from Manhattan across the old farmland, and a place for people of all walks of life to enjoy together. Within a couple of years, what is now Fort Greene Park—Brooklyn's first, and a predecessor to the great Prospect Park—was established. But crowding continued, and construction struggled to keep pace with the population. Whitman, who retained some of his father's attachment to the old-fashioned and artisanal, spoke out against the unchecked growth. Brooklyn life had been greatly altered and modernized in 1844 by the arrival of the Long Island Rail Road, which then connected Queens and Brooklyn to Boston and which still runs from Brooklyn's Atlantic Avenue out to the tip of Long Island. Whitman lamented, typically, the railroad's rapid replacement of the wooden farm wagon. Sentimental about the past, he cast a skeptical eye on redevelopment and bemoaned the real estate developers' "pull-down-and-build-over-again spirit," the spirit that proclaimed, "Let us level to the earth all the houses that were not built in the last ten years; let us raise the devil and break things!" In the early 1860s he wrote, "Our city grows so fast that there is some danger of the events and incidents of more than ten years gone being totally forgotten."

He wanted history, and particularly local history, to be recognized and honored. Whitman contended that August 27, 1776, the day his great-uncle and so many other Americans were killed in the Battle of Brooklyn, should be as venerated a day as July 4. He was obsessed with the "Wallabout Martyrs," the title of one of his late poems and his term for the estimated twelve thousand American prisoners who subsequently died as captives aboard British ships moored off of the Wallabout section of Brooklyn—in Kenneth Jackson's words "the greatest American tragedy of the eighteenth century." Whitman wrote:

> *Greater than memory of Achilles or Ulysses,*
> *More, more by far to thee than tomb of Alexander,*
> *Those cart loads of old charnel ashes, scales and splints of*
>   *mouldy bones,*
> *Once living men—once resolute courage, aspiration, strength,*
> *The stepping stones to thee to-day and here, America.*

During his tenure as editor of the *Eagle*, Whitman had argued for a memorial to the lost, and his efforts eventually led, after his death, to the Prison Ship Martyrs' Monument, the world's tallest Doric column, which stands today in Fort Greene Park.

Around him Whitman increasingly saw corruption and "a general laxity of morals" that "pervades all classes." His empathy for the masses was being stretched to the limit by the increasingly chaotic nature of urban life. The political battles in the metropolitan area were fierce enough to explode into physical violence, as they did in Manhattan in 1857 when the Dead Rabbits, a gang allied with the Democratic Party, clashed with the nativist Bowery Boys, leaving eight dead and thirty wounded. Later that year, Whitman would write, "Mobs and murderers appear to rule the hour." Whitman sought, in *Leaves of Grass*, to channel all voices, to encompass all things—"I am large, I contain multitudes"—and thus, as biographer David Reynolds has suggested, to apply a kind of unity and a healing balm to the republic. If Whitman could say, "I am all people," implicit was that *we* were all one people. It was a belief and hope that would be put to the most severe test within a decade of the first *Leaves of Grass*.

The social ills of the city echoed a looming national crisis. In the late 1850s, Whitman, in a gloomy period, wrote the elegiac poems "Out of the Cradle Endlessly Rocking" and "As I Ebb'd with the Ocean of Life," both of which he added to the 1860 edition of *Leaves*. In that year, Whitman, ever a self-appointed "seer" and often a very good one, also wrote this line in a poem called "Year of Meteors (1859–60)": "O year all mottled with evil and good—year of forebodings!" New York was divided over slavery and over Abraham Lincoln, but when the Civil War finally broke out, many Brooklynites, New Yorkers, and northerners generally, including Whitman, welcomed what they saw as a coming cleansing of the nation. At the outset, Whitman watched exultant, blue-clad troops marching through Brooklyn, near where he and his family now lived, on Portland Avenue. The men had ropes tied to their muskets, in his words, "with which to bring back each man a prisoner from the audacious South, to be led in a noose, on our men's early and triumphant return!" Walt's brother George went off to war at once. In 1863, writing for the *Brooklyn Daily Eagle*, his old paper, Walt wrote an article about George's regiment called "Our Brooklyn Boys in the War." Full of local pride, it said that in fourteen months the regiment had been in seven pitched battles, "some of them as important as any in American history." Vague word of George's injury at Fredericksburg in 1863 drew Walt to the front to find him. The wound was minor, but the sight of the war dead left a strong impression. Soon after, Whitman moved to Washington and, while serving in government jobs, tended to the wounded as a hospital volunteer. Although he envisioned a short stay, he would remain in Washington for ten years.

Over the course of the war, Whitman, who had been opposed to Lincoln's candidacy in the Illinois Senate race of 1858, emerged as a devout convert. Lincoln became his political hero and probably his utmost hero of all. Whitman felt that Lincoln supplanted George Washington as the true democratic father of the country. Whitman rejoiced at the rise of a man who embodied, he felt, "the commonest average of life—a rail splitter and a flat-boatsman!" Whitman devoted four poems to the president and called him "the greatest, best, most characteristic, artistic, moral personality" in American life. Whitman's two most famous Lincoln poems are the celebratory "O Captain! My Captain!" and the grave "When Lilacs Last in the Dooryard Bloom'd," both published after the president's death, and added to late editions of *Leaves of Grass*. Each is bold and emotionally raw, perhaps too much so, moving away from the incantatory hymns of his earlier verses into a tone of exaltation and almost rapturous grief—"But O heart! heart! heart! / O the bleeding drops of red."

David Reynolds has suggested that Whitman saw not only something of himself in Lincoln but something of the healing "I" that Whitman created in *Leaves of Grass*, a man who absorbed all and brought union. What Whitman also found captivating was that Lincoln was "essentially non-conventional," that he embodied the American spirit by taking unpopular positions. He didn't care if he was the underdog. Often he liked it. And so, too, did Whitman.

After his time in Washington, during which he visited Brooklyn only for short periods, Whitman moved to Camden, New Jersey, where his brother George had settled, taking a room in his house. Now distant both physically and temporally from his farmhouse roots and his father's working-class struggles in Brooklyn, Whitman became in a certain sense more conservative, as some do in old age. At times he granted that the raffish youth pictured in the lithograph from *Leaves of Grass*—a thirtysomething firebrand who wrote, "I sound my barbaric yawp over the roofs of the world"—was no longer the same man. As his work slowly gained some acceptance and acclaim, he enjoyed the fruits of his work, giving speeches, granting audiences, and generally curating his legacy.

Back home in Brooklyn, the workings of the American republic, though often crooked and halting, were bringing more and more newcomers and an ever-greater frenzy of activity. A bridge was being built, not only a grand bridge across the East River but a bridge to modernity. The Brooklyn Whitman knew as a child was long gone, and the Brooklyn of his pre–Civil War adulthood was fading from memory, too. Yet the democratic spirit Whitman had given voice to and the urge to capture the whole of America would echo down through the decades, continuing to breathe life into the place and its literary tradition.

2.

The Street Was Everything

HENRY MILLER

My concern was always for the nobody, the man who is lost in the shuffle, the man who is so common, so ordinary, that his presence is not even noticed.

—from *Sexus* (1949), HENRY MILLER

IN A SCENE FROM HENRY MILLER'S *SEXUS*, THE FIRST-PERSON narrator, also named Henry Miller and nearly indistinguishable from the author, has a run-in with a group of young southern men in New York. They're friends of a friend who have come to town with their "trim racing cars" and jugs of peach brandy. One of them makes a crucial mistake: a "stupid remark" about Walt Whitman. "So when the cultured young gent from Durham tried to cross swords with me about my favorite American writer," Miller writes, "I was at him hammer and tongs." The group laughs at Miller's fury, enraging him further. "I accused them of being a bunch of drunken sots, of being idle sons of bitches, ignorant, prejudiced, the product of good for nothing whoremongers."

The reaction is typical of Miller, whose reverence for writing he loved was coupled with the attitude of a hotheaded brawler. Like

Whitman, Miller lurked in the corner of the literary cocktail party, alarming guests with his bawdiness. He didn't belong.

In an earlier novel, *Tropic of Cancer* (1934), Miller expressed more lyrically his admiration for Brooklyn's first laureate and "the greatest man America ever produced":

> In Whitman the whole American scene comes to life, her past and her future, her birth and her death. Whatever there is of value in America Whitman has expressed, and there is nothing more to be said.

"There is nothing more to be said," Miller writes, but he would further Whitman's project, in a sense, and create his own unique portrait of Brooklyn and America. Although he found his legs as a writer in Paris, Miller's deepest roots were in Williamsburg, the North Brooklyn neighborhood where he lived as a child—a home less than three miles from where Whitman spent his Brooklyn days. Miller wrote numerous and sometimes lengthy works of fiction, but he freely admitted that they were very closely based on his own life, so much so that sometimes he didn't bother to change names. He is particularly well known for writing *Tropic of Cancer* and *Tropic of Capricorn* (1939) and even better known for writing, as Whitman did, in flagrant, happy violation of the prevailing attitudes and guidelines about profanity and obscenity.

Customs officials banned *Tropic of Cancer* and *Tropic of Capricorn* from entering the United States for decades after they appeared in France, and no one dared publish them in the States until the sixties, when *Tropic of Cancer* went on trial for obscenity charges in fifty-three separate courtrooms across the country. Indeed, in 1962, rather late in the historical day for this sort of thing, a Brooklyn court issued a warrant for Miller's arrest, citing a conspiracy between him and his publisher Barney Rosset, of Grove, to "prepare and author" a work of pornography, *Tropic of Cancer*.

By then, though, Miller's works were underground classics, and they were already on the way to outstanding sales. Courts couldn't very well put a stop to George Orwell's widely read 1940 essay about Miller, "Inside the Whale," two decades after the fact. William Carlos Williams, Edmund Wilson, Cyril Connolly, T. S. Eliot, and John Dos Passos, too, had engaged in spirited debate over Miller in the thirties and forties. To them, Miller's work was a jolting bolt from the blue. "We need a blood transfusion," Anaïs Nin wrote in a preface to Miller's debut. "And it is blood and flesh which are here given us." Like Whitman, Miller chose to speak in an entirely different tone and register than his serious contemporaries did. He wanted, in his words, "to get off the gold standard of literature" and reject all that contentedly bobbed along in the cultural current: "What is not in the open street is false, derived, that is to say, *literature.*" Miller was a writer engaged with the body more than the mind—"a really great book starts in the midriff and works outward," he said—and he devoted his work to base realities. Unfortunately for his many critics, it was very difficult to dismiss him as merely a crank or a peddler of smut, though in a way he was both.

⚜

Miller was born in 1891 on the Upper East Side of Manhattan, but his family moved soon after his birth to Williamsburg, just across the East River from Manhattan's Lower East Side. Miller would be deeply preoccupied with his Brooklyn childhood for all of his writing life, devoting pages and pages to his early days. Miller lived in Brooklyn almost exclusively until he moved to Paris in his late thirties. In many respects, for Miller as for Whitman, to see Brooklyn was to see the essence of the American experiment and to watch its evolution.

When Whitman published *Leaves of Grass* in 1855, he recognized that New York, across the river, was already becoming a bitterly divided place, in ways that the war's end would not heal. In 1857 the genteel *Harper's* magazine noted with alarm, "What was then [1827] a decent and orderly town of moderate size, has been converted into a huge semi-barbarous metropolis—one half as luxurious and artistic as Paris, the other half as savage as Cairo or Constantinople—not well-governed nor ill-governed, but simply not governed at all." In the five-day draft riots of 1863, opponents of the first American conscription law grew wildly violent, targeting and lynching blacks and also killing many whites. The rioters set fire to the mayor's residence and were turned back by police and the military with artillery and bayonets. Staffers at the *New York Tribune*, a strong proponent of abolition and the subjection of the Confederacy, fired Gatling guns to defend the building from attack.

In the wake of the Civil War, New York was prosperous and growing, but it was so riven by conflict that it risked falling into a kind of chaos unknown in the city today. Organized crime and gang violence struck heavily. Ethnic tensions tipped over into street crime and roiled New York.

The nation was undergoing a period of rapid and transformative industrial formation. And industry, especially massive industry like railroad construction, relied for its growth on financing that came from Wall Street banks. As is often true today, cycles of boom and bust in the national economy were magnified in New York, the undisputed financial capital. In the depression of 1873, 25 percent of the city's workers were unemployed. Those who had jobs were saddled with workdays of ten hours or longer after the failure of a massive 1872 strike in New York—the city's largest to date—involving a hundred thousand workers seeking an eight-hour day. That standoff, among others, left a bitter taste all around.

By the time Miller was born, Brooklyn had become something of a release valve, a place where New Yorkers came in search of a haven, but also a place where troubles tended to follow them. Middle-class families continued to migrate from Manhattan to Brooklyn, spreading beyond Brooklyn Heights. In Manhattan, apartment houses for the middle class—as distinct from town houses (for the wealthy) and tenements (for the poor)—were not yet plentiful, which helped to spur the relocation, as demand for town houses outstripped supply. As Edwin G. Burrows and Mike Wallace write in *Gotham: A History of New York City to 1898* (1999), many New Yorkers associated apartment living, with its limited privacy, with a lower standard of living than they were willing to accept. They wanted houses, but Manhattan was running out of affordable places to put them. It is largely for this reason that "brownstone Brooklyn" exists today.

In the 1860s, '70s, and '80s, people of means spread deeper into Brooklyn as transportation options improved. They moved into neighborhoods such as Fort Greene, particularly the area immediately surrounding Fort Greene Park, the realization of Whitman's hopes. There the prosperous contractor and public figure William Kingsley was a pioneer. The well-to-do also found a place in Clinton Hill, where oil baron Charles Pratt built a mansion in 1875, still standing at 232 Clinton Avenue, amid a crop of other large and distinguished homes. Clinton soon became "the most fashionable avenue in Brooklyn," according to the *Real Estate Record and Guide*, though Miller was anything but fashionable when he lived there for a time in his thirties. Less costly housing could be found in Boerum Hill, Carroll Gardens, and, most affordably, lower Park Slope, which some thought too close for comfort to the industry (and smell) surrounding the Gowanus Canal. Brooklyn had developed a vibrant cultural life of its own, anchored by institutions such as the still-thriving Brooklyn Academy of Music (which was then in Brooklyn Heights, until it relocated to Fort Greene after a catastrophic fire in 1903). The Mercantile Library and the Long Island Historical Society (now called the Brooklyn Historical Society) afforded opportunities for study. Green-Wood Cemetery, one of the grandest in the entire region, offered a place for contemplation. Prospect Park, designed by Frederick Law Olmsted and Calvert Vaux, who preferred it in some respects to their own Central Park, was new and hugely popular, the crown jewel of the city. Brooklynites began to boast, as some do now, that their city was a New York without problems, free from its raucous conflict and other urban troubles.

But this notion was well wide of the mark. The new middle and

upper-middle classes didn't mingle easily with those working at
the wharves and factories that stood between them and the river.
The immigrant groups of laborers were settling into ethnic enclaves
within Brooklyn and pitting themselves against one another, too,
often clashing over jobs. In 1877 Joseph Pulitzer's New York World
declared that the "uncivilized classes in Brooklyn are quite as murderous as the savage in Montana."

Transportation infrastructure, always the engine of Brooklyn's
development, rapidly grew, particularly in the 1880s, with the fast
proliferation of elevated train lines, precursors to today's subway
system. These trains took workers close to the East River, where
they could board ferries to Manhattan, like the one that Whitman
mythologized. Beginning in 1883, cable car service, and then electri-
fied trains, would take you all the way to lower Manhattan without a boat ride. How? By crossing a brand-new edifice, the Brooklyn
Bridge. These transportation improvements tied the city ever more
tightly to New York, contributing immensely to Brooklyn's growth
and prosperity. Not everyone was pleased, however. People with
lower incomes could now move to Brooklyn without giving up
Manhattan jobs, a development not welcomed by all the Brooklynites who were building elegant brownstones. Now Brooklyn
business owners could happily draw on a larger pool of workers,
especially those who lived in Manhattan's squalid Lower East Side,
famously documented in Jacob Riis's 1890 book How the Other
Half Lives. As the bosses saw it, the problem with these immigrants
coming to Brooklyn for the workday was that they might decide
to stay.

The 1883 opening of the Brooklyn Bridge, the culmination of
an immense and sometimes fatal undertaking that lasted for
decades, brought into being what was and remains the greatest
landmark and symbol of the deep connection between Brooklyn
and Manhattan, both physical and social. Some thought the bridge
would be impossible to build. Its two towers would have to be
about as high as the tallest buildings in New York. Political obstacles were considerable as well. Some Brooklyn residents saw it as

too tight a connection to unruly Manhattan. And some Manhattan commercial and political interests feared—quite rightly, it turned out—an outflow of business and of home buyers. The bridge's first engineer, John Augustus Roebling, died following an accident that crushed his foot, and his son Washington took over. Workers toiling in caissons—watertight chambers—on the river floor to lay the foundations of the bridge's towers developed a painful disease, called "the bends" for the way cramps contorted its victims, and it cost many their lives. (The cause is nitrogen bubbles in the blood, and it remains the greatest danger of scuba diving.) Washington Roebling contracted the illness himself on-site, and thereafter oversaw construction from his sickbed in Brooklyn Heights, which afforded a bridge view. His wife, Emily, relayed instructions to the building crew and played a significant role in finishing the project.

The opening of the bridge, the first East River crossing, presaged the consolidation of Manhattan and Brooklyn and the other three boroughs into one huge metropolis, the City of New York, in 1898. (Whitman had predicted the merger of Brooklyn and New York twenty years before.) The two towers, the arc of the enormous cables that linked them, the crisscross of thinner cables below that dazzled from all angles—these sights would be forever linked to the world's image of Brooklyn and to its own image of itself. A powerful symbol for writers and artists both, the bridge has been a literary subject and icon since its conception. Whitman was an older man and living in New Jersey by the time it was finished, but he described seeing it under construction from a sailboat in a rhapsodic passage from his autobiographical book, *Specimen Days*: "to the right the East river—the mast-hemm'd shores—the grand obelisk-like towers of the bridge, one on either side, in haze, yet plainly defin'd, giant brothers twain, throwing free graceful interlinking loops high across the tumbled tumultuous current below."

❧

The Brooklyn Bridge and the train system made it more practical for people like Henry Miller Sr. and his wife, Louise, to move to

Brooklyn while working in Manhattan. Both husband's and wife's parents were German (Henry's original last name was Mueller) and had arrived with that influx of German nationals to the area in the middle part of the nineteenth century. Henry Sr. followed his father-in-law into work with a tailoring firm in Manhattan. But shortly after his son, Henry Valentine Miller, was born on December 26, 1891, he and his wife joined the heavily German community in Williamsburg, accepting a longer commute in exchange for more space at a lower price.

In the 1890s, 662 Driggs Avenue, where the family lived for eight years, was on the edge of the dirty industrial Brooklyn that lined the waterfront. (This is still the case today on that block, though there is not as much active industry, and very nearby is an area lined with bars, restaurants, and the college-educated classes.) Dwellings like the Millers' abutted loud factories and dusty warehouses. A passage from *Black Spring* depicts the surroundings and illustrates how Miller expressed a kinship with the downtrodden even at times when he was neither starving nor an artist.

> Where others remember of their youth a beautiful garden, a fond mother, a sojourn at the seashore, I remember, with a vividness as if it were etched in acid, the grim, soot-covered walls and chimneys of the tin factory opposite us and the bright, circular pieces of tin that were strewn in the street, some bright and gleaming, others rusted, dull, copperish, leaving a stain on the fingers.... I remember the black hands of the ironmolders, the grit that had sunk so deep into the skin that nothing could remove it, not soap, nor elbow grease, nor money, nor love, nor death.

Miller's family was more prosperous than was typical in the neighborhood. It was an overcrowded, provincial place. In the most insular and remote areas of Williamsburg, there were people who hadn't seen the Brooklyn Bridge ten years after it opened. But Henry lived in comfort. Sometimes his parents dressed him in elaborate, showy getups that brought jeers and taunts from other children. Miller later wrote that he felt guilt over being more privileged than many of his friends. He once gave away his gifts to other kids, but his infuriated mother made him retrieve them.

Miller was happiest when he participated in the street life around him. People like his parents shared the territory with unhinged preachers, drunks, and beggars. In the north side of Williamsburg, his section, you could find, he said, "the morgue, the slaughterhouse, the gas tanks, the fish market, the Democratic club." On North First Street and on Fillmore Place the boys played games out in the street—marbles, Red Rover, tops—and hung around, teasing girls. Down at the East River end of Grand Street was the beer hall where Henry's grandfather went to hear Socialist speeches and the syncopated German songs of his youth.

Miller wrote in *Black Spring*, with a certain pride, that "no one seemed to notice that the streets were ugly and dirty. If the sewer mains were broken you held your nose." North side kids—"some of the gang had truly murderous instincts"—squared off against the fancier south side, often with their fists, and Henry gladly got involved. He later wrote, "Our pleasure was to invade the swankier South side, beat up a few helpless sissies and return with a few captives whom we tortured to the best of our ability." This meant swiping a pocketknife or a watch or the shirt off the kid's back, maybe leaving him with a black eye. Sometimes Alfie Melta had to be held back, since he was keen to take it too far. Most of Miller's heroes of the time, who would appear repeatedly in his writings, were part of this local crew. "Napoleon, Lenin, Capone—all fiction," he wrote. "Napoleon is nothing to me in comparison with Eddie Carney, who gave me my first black eye."

One or two members of Henry's gang were headed in the direction of serious crime, but in his youth the general tenor of the streets was not as dire as that would imply. In *Henry Miller: A Life* (1991), Robert Ferguson writes of Miller's Driggs Avenue childhood, "It was a life with all the cheerful violence of a cartoon film," a world where boys brawl with one another, "are chased down the street with razor blades by drunken uncles, whack each other over the head with Christmas trees, have rock fights and snowball fights." In *Tropic of Capricorn* (fiction, but only technically) and in *Book of Friends* (nonfiction), Miller described how he and a cousin accidentally killed a boy in a rock fight, but at some point he retracted the story. Friends were beaten at home with razor strops and had the marks to show it. Insults, often of the ethnic kind, were thrown back and forth, and no doubt Henry did some of the throwing.

It was not your typical childhood idyll, though that was precisely how Miller viewed it. He considered his childhood to be the happiest time of his life. The scrappy spirit of the north side, at war with the richer kids to the south, gave rise to an enduring attraction to the underdog. The vitality of the street proved far preferable to life at home with his parents, whom he later portrayed with little affection or even mercy. However he may have distorted the picture, it seems clear that they were not very cultured people, that his mother was erratic and sometimes abusive, and that his father drank too much. On top of that, Henry would come to find their aspirant values appallingly bourgeois. Out in the neighborhood, Henry felt that he and his friends were living a more honest life, performing on a larger stage, and becoming a part of local lore. Fighting it out for the turf, Henry felt powerful.

In 1900, when Miller was about nine, his family moved to another heavily German area, Bushwick, a respectable neighborhood not far away. Sensing a decline in Williamsburg, they wanted a home farther inland that suited their middle-class taste, and they found a row house with a little patch of grass in front and a garden in the back. Henry was deeply unhappy with the move, finding the new area dreary and boring compared to Williamsburg. The boys around, he wrote later, "seemed to be replicas of their parents who were dull, strict and extremely bourgeois." His home during this period (and his parents' home for the duration) stood at 1063 Decatur Street, and again and again Miller would refer to Decatur as "the street of early sorrows." At school, Henry was already embarking on a long career of intellectual rebellion. He learned very quickly and had a great appetite for books, as well as a talent for the piano, but he learned only what he wanted to and became a disciplinary problem.

Miller insisted on going to high school back in his old neighborhood, at Eastern District High School on Wythe Avenue, but by then Williamsburg had changed. The wave of new, lower-class immigrants that the Millers had moved to escape had displaced much of the prior population. Many of the newcomers were Italian. Even more were Jewish. The Williamsburg Bridge, the second span between Brooklyn and Manhattan and the world's largest suspension bridge to date, had opened in 1903. Jews who were living in the crushingly overcrowded tenements of Manhattan's Lower East Side saw the bridge as the path to a better life in Williamsburg. So many made the move that the *New York Tribune* dubbed the bridge "Jews' Highway." Williamsburg was at the vanguard of a broad shift in Brooklyn demographics that led to a borough population that was 35 percent Jewish in 1927. More than 40 percent of New York City's Jews lived in Brooklyn by 1930, a proportion that has remained nearly intact ever since.

Henry's mother didn't like Jewish people, calling them "sheenies," and now Henry, too, began to blame them for what he saw as the deterioration of his cherished old turf. Decades later he wrote, "After the Williamsburg Bridge was thrown open, and the Exodus commenced, even the cats were ashamed to remain in the old neighborhood." His teenage years planted the seeds of an obvious, if increasingly complicated, anti-Semitism. Miller cruised through high school and Cornell offered him a scholarship, but even with the financial help his family couldn't afford it, so he headed to City College of New York. That lasted six weeks. He had no use for what was being taught, or how the school was teaching it, and he found the place "intolerably Jewish." From this point on, he would be his own teacher, inhaling the books and authors he loved and chucking the others aside. He would also go on disliking Jews, at first without equivocation and then with some ambivalence and shame, even as he grew close to a few Jewish people.

⚶

His growing anti-Semitism was just one indication that Miller was becoming an angry and alienated person. Failures of love at every turn played no small role. Henry never felt safely cared for by his mother, as his writing made only too clear. In his adolescence he became obsessed with a girl at school named Cora Seward, obsessed even for a lovesick teenager. He claimed that every evening for three or four years—can this possibly be true?—he left the house after dinner and walked three miles to the neighborhood of Greenpoint just to pass by her house at 181 Devoe Street in the hopes of catching a glimpse of her. Not once did he see her there, he said. Despite signs at school of mutual feeling, no romance ever developed, which Henry furiously blamed on his own cowardice. At seventeen or eighteen he began an intensely sexual affair with a thirtysomething divorcée named Pauline Chouteau, whom he met while giving piano lessons to her close friend's daughter. When Henry once broached the subject of marrying Pauline to his mother, she went after him with a kitchen knife. Pauline's age caused him increasing discomfort, as did his enjoyment of the sex. In Mary Dearborn's biography *The Happiest Man Alive* (1991), she writes that Miller felt that sex was "a sign of manhood" and "not to be censored . . . but neither was it beautiful nor, in fact, very nice at all."

After years of odd jobs of shorter and shorter duration, Miller got married, at age twenty-five, to Beatrice Wickens, a beguiling young amateur pianist and a cultured person Henry's mother could approve of. It was a disaster. Beatrice had been educated in a convent; she was even more conflicted about sex than Henry was. They married in 1917, despite Henry's reservations, partly to get him a draft deferment. The couple moved to 244 Sixth Avenue in Park Slope, to an apartment, wrote Miller in *Tropic of Capricorn*, with a "lugubrious parlor on the third floor of a respectable brownstone house in the dead center of the most respectable neighbor-hood in Brooklyn." He didn't mean "respectable" as a compliment, and we can read the word "dead" both ways. Middle-class life and conventional romance were not for him. To him, the real Brooklyn was the Williamsburg of his childhood. The marriage quickly dete-riorated. He felt suffocated and rebelled in all manner of ways, often staying away for long nights. When Beatrice got pregnant by acci-dent, it was unwelcome news for both of them, but despite consid-ering an abortion they had the child, a daughter named Barbara.

As sex-obsessed and as worshipful as he could become about women, Miller saw them mainly as a source of unhappiness, and often he preferred male company. In his father's tailor shop, where he grudgingly worked at times in his twenties, he found the male fellowship reassuring. The kind of male institutions and male pur-suits that fascinated him were in plentiful supply in New York at the time, and particularly in Brooklyn, where life on the urban-ized, industrialized street had a coarser edge. He became inter-ested not only in bedding women but also, from a distance, in gambling, boxing, and crime—the underworld action he and his Williamsburg crowd daydreamed about as kids.

It was as if he wanted all his life to remain a boy, to be the kind of local-kid "failure" he depicts admiringly in *Tropic of Capricorn*. Of one man he writes:

> He was very much a product of the North Side, too, and that
> was one of the reasons why I liked him. The way he talked,
> out of the corner of his mouth, for instance, the tough air he
> put on when talking to a cop, the way he spat in disgust, the
> sentimentality, the limited horizon . . . , the contempt for
> the rich . . . , the respect for learning, the fascination of the
> dance hall, the saloon, the burlesque, talking about seeing
> the world and never budging out of the city.

Miller never quite stopped making trouble on the streets, skewer-ing the bourgeois, answering to no one. These impulses made him something of a lifelong adolescent, and he grew tiresome to many people, including readers. But his desire to adopt an outsider attitude reflects the Brooklyn he knew.

Reading Miller's novels is like watching him beating against a door from the outside, screaming out of anger, or passion, or just a desire for attention. He wrote his unpublished first book, *Clipped Wings*, at thirty, while living in Brooklyn. Miller was then holding down his first serious job, though he would laugh to hear it called serious. He worked at Western Union with a corrosive unhappiness for nearly five years. Miller depicted his Western Union job in some detail in several of his books—notably *Tropic of Capricorn*. There the "Cosmodemonic Telegraph Company" is a house of capitalistic horrors, a machine that spits out any traces of humanity it doesn't flatten into submission. Miller worked out of several offices, one of them on Fulton Street in Brooklyn, another in Manhattan's Flatiron Building. The job involved hiring and firing hard-up messengers at a furious pace, which took its psychological toll when he wasn't in a sadistic mood, and he had to be on the phone nearly constantly from 8:00 a.m. to 6:00 p.m. Miller wrote *Clipped Wings* in the span of a three-week vacation. The novel consists of largely nonfictional and spiteful portraits of twelve messengers who worked for him. Its author is clearly a man "filled with bile," Dearborn writes, "and it is evident in every descriptive phrase."

In the summer of 1923, when Miller was thirty-one and still very unhappily married to Beatrice, he met and fell in love with a young woman who was coy about her background and even her real name (June Smith); she asked to be called June Mansfield. Ten years younger than Miller, she worked at a "taxi-dance" hall in Times Square, where female employees danced with whoever paid the ten-cent fee. Times Square had an air of tawdriness at the time, as it did for most of the twentieth century, and these dance halls were even tawdrier—just Miller's kind of place. A precocious, intemperate, and dangerously seductive young woman who would become a touchstone of his life and work, June garnered the following Whitmanesque description in *Tropic of Capricorn*: "America on foot, winged and sexed. . . . Whatever made America made her." He pursued her without relent, and they began a passionate and well-chronicled romance. June had aspirations to be an actress but it became clear over time that she was collecting more than ten-cent fees from customers and other men, and doing so in mysterious ways. Henry tried to hide himself, with varying success, from the reality that she was a "golddigger," a subtler kind of prostitute. But despite his occasional bouts of anger over the ways she made a living, he was too besotted to be deterred. His marriage to Beatrice was soon in ruins. Henry married June months later, in 1924, at a judge's office, with witnesses hired off the street.

After stays with friends in the Bronx and Manhattan, Henry and June moved back to Brooklyn, to an apartment at 91 Remsen Street in Brooklyn Heights. The place was far too expensive, but what was money in the face of reckless love? In *Plexus*, the middle volume of Miller's late expansive trilogy, *The Rosy Crucifixion*, he depicts the living situation on Remsen: "We occupied the front half of the first floor, looking out onto the most sedate, aristocratic section in all Brooklyn. Our neighbors all had limousines, butlers, expensive dogs and cats whose meals made our mouths water." A wry exaggeration, but it was true that Brooklyn Heights was a pocket of unusual wealth, as it had been since its early days and remains today. We can picture Miller wandering around the fringes of the neighborhood in the flush of a new marriage as he takes in the scene.

> A short walk in any direction brought me to the most diverse districts: to the fantastic area beneath the fretwork of the Brooklyn Bridge; to the sites of the old ferries where Arabs, Turks, Syrians, Greeks and other peoples of the Levant had flocked; to the docks and wharves where steamers from all over the world lay at anchor; to the shopping center near Borough Hall, a region which at night was phantasmal. In the very heart of this [on] Columbia Heights stood stately old churches, club houses, mansions of the

> rich, all part of a solid, ancient core which was gradually
> being eaten into by the invading swarms of foreigners, der-
> elicts and bums from the outer edge.

There's a gleeful irony in the observation about the "invading swarms"—which had a grain of truth in this period—because the incursion of misfits was the kind of development he and his new wife welcomed; in a way they were part of it.

Still working in his bizarre Western Union job, Miller would always get in late, often having stayed up into the early morning hours to escort June back from the dance hall. He would arrive to a ringing phone and a waiting room of sorry-looking messengers and interviewees. June, knowing of his literary ambitions and nothing if not a dreamer, encouraged him to quit his job to write. Finally, despite doubts and debts, he did.

But before he would come to write his second unpublished novel, *Moloch*, he would be battered into the rocks more than his fair share, and some of the anger in the book can be attributed to the circumstances in which it was written. Money ran dry, several times over, causing them to lose the Remsen Street place and move into a small apartment in Clinton Hill at 288 Clinton Avenue. It was on the same block as the Charles Pratt mansion but a world apart. They were soon behind on the rent there, too. Still, Henry and June refused to look for work; it seems they had both decided that a respectable job was a sign of failure, a capitulation to a social order they resisted with all their will. They tried running a speakeasy out of a basement at 106 Perry Street in Greenwich Village. They didn't draw the literary crowd they were hoping for—Brooklyn poet Hart Crane hung out at a place down the block—and the venture failed, as did Henry's 1925 trip to Florida to try to capitalize on a real estate boom that was no longer booming. Henry and June decided to each live with their parents to save money, the last thing Henry would have decided if he had other options. As he describes it in *Plexus*, at his parents' house he tapped away rather fruitlessly at his typewriter, but hid away in shame when guests dropped in.

He was thirty-five years old. It was one of several low points when Miller very deeply despaired. In his notes, he wrote, "No more hopes . . . Complete failure and submission—absolutely licked." But still he held on to an essential arrogance—or an essential grit, to look at it another way. In his view, to sacrifice comfort, to struggle, to lower his station in society so far that he was panhandling in grungy pool halls—this was what it was to be an artist. He would persist. Henry and June moved back in together in Brooklyn, first in an apartment on Hancock Street and then back on Remsen, but in a cheap room this time. Henry did swallow pride enough to take a job selling encyclopedias to survive—anything to stay out of his parents' house—and June took a gig as a waitress at the Pepper Pot in Greenwich Village. By now she had begun to lose some respect for Henry, as her encouragement of his writing (and quitting work to do so) had failed to pay off, either financially or in any other way. In the Village she was drawn into circles of eccentric and bohemian types who spent their time in speakeasies. She dressed increasingly provocatively (a strip of velvet in place of underwear was one touch); she smoked more; she attracted more gifts from mysterious men; she stopped in at a lesbian bar now and then. And finally she began an affair with a bizarre, possibly disturbed woman, a young artist she called Jean Kronski (an invented name).

For Henry the affair was torture, most of all because it threatened his manhood, which cut very close to the bone of his identity. As his writing makes clear, his self-image was tied to a few, predominately masculine fundamentals: being "born in the street" and brawling with boys as a kid; sticking it to authority and a phony society; forming bonds with certain men and scorning others; distrusting many women but falling hard for some and then conquering them. He never banked on being conquered by the one he loved the most. In this period he made an attempt at suicide; it's unclear whether he truly intended to succeed. Soon June and Jean got an even drearier apartment for all three of them to live in, on Henry Street near the corner of Love Lane (the irony of the name would not be credible in fiction). This Brooklyn Heights address is four blocks from the print shop where Whitman worked nights to set *Leaves of Grass* into type. That Henry agreed to the living arrangement can only be a sign of despondency. He later described to Nin the scene in the apartment: "Using soiled shirts for towels. . . . Washing dishes in bathtub, which was greasy and black-rimmed. Bathroom always cold as an icebox. . . . Shades always drawn, windows never washed, atmosphere sepulchral." On one occasion the three burned chairs in the fireplace for heat. For years Miller had welcomed the life of a common man, a lowly man. But this, this was humiliating.

Henry lucked into a job at the New York City Parks Department when he ran into an old rival and friend from the Fourteenth Ward who worked there. In his first week of work, he came home one day to find neither June nor Jean home. The electricity had long ago been cut off, so he had to light a match to see a note from Jean, who always used his nickname, Val. According to Miller, it read: "Dear Val, we sailed this morning on the *Rochambeau*. Didn't have the heart to tell you. Write care of American Express, Paris. Love." He broke every piece of furniture in the apartment.

But Miller seems to have hit bottom and bounced off the floor. Quite soon after, at his office at the Parks Department, he began to make some notes at his desk after work, and by 5:00 a.m. he had thirty-odd pages that represented a plan for a lifetime's work. He would tell the story of his life leading to his fateful attachment to June and the devastating arrival of Jean. As Ferguson remarks, a great deal of Miller's later work hews very closely to these notes, which suggests how profoundly his writing and his persona were shaped by his Brooklyn years.

June returned a few months later, without Jean, claiming dubiously that she had become close to Jean Cocteau, Pablo Picasso, and Marcel Duchamp. Miller always had trouble holding anything against her, and they soon moved back in together in another overly costly Brooklyn apartment, at 180 Clinton Avenue near Myrtle Avenue. In the height of the 1920s boom on this elegant and broad avenue, around Henry and June were signs of wealth: well-tended gardens and shrubbery in front of houses set back from the street, Ford Model Ts and Buick touring cars, finely dressed women pushing elaborate strollers. The couple didn't exactly fit the mold.

Inadvisably, Miller quit his job again with the intention to write. This time there was a break. June had met another male admirer who said he liked some of her writing that she had shown him—it was Henry's writing—and the man offered to pay her to produce a novel in weekly installments. So Henry wrote the serial novel that June delivered, wrestling with it mightily on Clinton until he needed a rest, when he would climb to the top of Fort Greene Park to read.

Miller centered *Moloch*, the novel-for-hire, on his life during the Western Union years, including his ugly marriage to Beatrice. Dion Moloch, when he isn't at work at the barely disguised telegraph company, rambles around the streets of New York and Brooklyn, avoiding his wife and sleeping around without remorse, including with wives of his employees. The style and tone are very inconsistent, but throughout people say things like "Look here" and "Make it snappy!" and "Hell no!" and "Gee." Other people look up to the protagonist, but the reason why is not evident. *Moloch* shows stray glimpses of literary promise, but as with *Clipped Wings,* to read it is to be cast down a river of spite and resentment. Both the author and the main character throw anger in every direction (though particularly at Jews), and the defiant, almost savage pose the novel adopts could be described in brief as anti-everything.

Moloch reveals a man contending with his scattershot rage and impotence, his sense of alienation, and his feeling that all his struggles had yet to lead to any victories. That its most memorable quality and subject is anti-Semitism is remarkably striking in light of the whopping irony that June was Jewish, which Miller had not known for sure until some time into their relationship. Miller had a number of other Jewish friends by now and he knew his anti-Semitism was deplorable, so perhaps he viewed *Moloch* as an attempt to purge it or "work it out." But the book also could have served as a channel for the rage he felt toward June. In any event, it is a depressing novel even when it doesn't intend to be, and more so when it does. It ends with the protagonist, Dion Moloch, "in midnight mood," wandering around the waterfront beneath the Brooklyn Bridge, looking up at its "towers of steel and masonry . . . sea-forms glistening in moonfire and spume"—shades of Whitman. The ferry-house of the Fulton Ferry, which Whitman famously wrote about, is "more ghastly than Caesar's gutted corpse." Moloch walks a dark street tucked below "the dreary mansions of the rich" on Columbia Heights and next to the waterfront lined with warehouses and refuse. In this "fugitive backyard of Brooklyn," what, he asks rhetorically, does the grand view reveal? "A dump heap." Even with his beloved borough in sight, the view through Miller's eyes at this point can only be bleak.

When *Moloch* was done, Henry and June took a trip to Paris, paid for by the exceedingly generous sponsor of the novel, who clearly had fallen for June. The book would go unpublished in Miller's lifetime, appearing only after its discovery among his papers by Dearborn. But Miller didn't know that, of course, and he was now feeling more justified in calling himself a writer. He wanted a taste of the expatriate artist scene that included writers he admired, such as Sherwood Anderson and John Dos Passos. He took to Paris, though he did not write during this trip. Back in Brooklyn, he set to work on a novel about June and Jean and himself, and his working titles exemplify Miller's fondness for shock value. He first called it "Lovely Lesbians" and then "Crazy Cock." As with his first two efforts, no one published the book. Finally, in 1930, June suggested he return to Paris without her. She would continue to support him and herself with her golddigging and eventually she'd join him. It isn't clear how much faith either of them had in the plan, but he accepted.

In Paris, Miller held odd jobs and began experimenting with a guttural approach to writing, "direct as a knife thrust," often profane, and less populated by high-flown words than *Moloch*. A racy story he published in the *New Review* drew some attention, and to friends he began referring to his plans for "the Paris book." In its opening paragraphs, he wrote, "This is not a book. This is libel, slander, defamation of character. This . . . is a prolonged insult, a gob of spit in the face of Art, a kick in the pants to God, Man, Destiny, Time, Love, Beauty . . . what you will." And then he echoed Whitman's "I Sing the Body Electric" and his direct address to the reader: "I am going to sing for you, a little off key perhaps, but I will sing." This was a "barbaric yawp" written under the sign of Whitman. This was *Tropic of Cancer*.

While working on it, Miller embarked on an affair with Nin, who would eventually chronicle episodes in Miller's life in her diaries. Nin was a married artist who had just written a study of one of Miller's new favorites, D. H. Lawrence. The relationship between Miller and Nin was torrid, and so were the pages Miller was turning out. The sexual exploits of the narrator are considerable in number (more so than the author's), and they are described directly and graphically, without the slightest appearance of discomfort on Miller's part. Running through the book is a strain of misogyny that depicts the Junes of the world as mere vehicles of male enjoyment. A dam seems to have opened and a river let free in the opening paragraphs, which find the stand-in for Miller in his first days in Paris, far from June: "I have no money, no resources, no hopes. I am the happiest man alive." The novel, which relates the story of Henry's first year or so in France, in which he cadged from various friends and lovers to survive, is as intentionally undisciplined as the author's own life. In a letter, he described, before he began, his intentions for "the Paris book: first person, uncensored, formless— fuck everything!"

In keeping with his new boldness, Miller gave the narrator his own name, just like Whitman, even though he fictionalized some episodes and shined a harsh light on himself. He felt energized by the sense that he had freed himself from the desire to be "literary" and found his voice in writing without restraint. "First I want to be read by the ordinary guys, and liked by them," he wrote in another letter. Here was a book for the boys back in the Fourteenth Ward, he seemed to think.

Miller's marriage to June was deteriorating during the writing of *Tropic of Cancer*, in part because of Nin, but June did join him in Paris several times and at some length, occasioning a love triangle whose tortured complexity stands out even in that crowded field. (The awful movie *Henry & June* dramatizes the events.) After a visit lasting a couple of rocky months in 1932, June punctuated her departure with another concise note to Miller tacked to the wall: "Will you get a divorce as soon as possible." Miller was distraught, swinging wildly between hatred of a nemesis and grief over a great love lost, but at least he had a book to believe in.

Tropic of Cancer, known to so many for how low it's willing to go, also spirals into great heights in marvelous passages whose words add up to much more than their sense. Orwell wrote that in the novel "the drunks and dead-beats of the cafes are handled with a feeling for character and a mastery of technique that are unapproached in any at all recent novel." The novel, he added, served as "a kind of bridge across the frightful gulf which exists, in fiction, between the intellectual and the man-in-the-street." Miller portrays his artistic aim in *Tropic of Cancer* as a kind of insurrection, carried out on behalf of the losers and misfits he willfully placed himself alongside. He writes that "the task which the artist implicitly sets himself is to overthrow existing values . . . , to sow strife and ferment so that by the emotional release those who are dead may be restored to life." In *Leaves of Grass*, Whitman had channeled with almost religious fervor the experience of those rejected by society.

> *Through me many long dumb voices,*
> *Voices of the interminable generations of slaves,*
> *Voices of prostitutes and of deformed persons,*
> *Voices of the diseased and despairing, and of thieves and*
> *   dwarfs.*

Now Miller, in *Tropic of Cancer*:

> The man who raises the holy bottle to his lips, the criminal
> who kneels in the marketplace, the innocent who discovers
> that *all* corpses stink, the madman who dances with light-
> ning in his hands, the friar who lifts his skirts to pee over
> the world, the fanatic who ransacks the libraries in order to
> find the Word—all these are fused in me, all these make my
> confusion, my ecstasy.

Jack Kahane of Obelisk Press in Paris greeted *Tropic of Cancer*
with the enthusiasm that Miller had so long been denied. Kahane
specialized in publishing English-language books that would have
run afoul of obscenity laws in America or England (and probably
also in France, had they been published in French). In his autobiography he recalled, "I had read the most terrible, the most sordid, the
most magnificent manuscript that had ever fallen into my hands."
    Miller, past forty, was finally on his way.

⅋

In the lag before *Tropic of Cancer* was published, in 1934, he worked on
two books. One of them, eventually published as *Black Spring* (1936),
was not really a novel but a collection of semi-autobiographical
pieces. Some of them tell of his time in Brooklyn, beginning with
his fond memories of early childhood. Miller's impressions of New
York and Brooklyn from later in life have a distinctly gloomier cast,
reflecting his darkening attitude toward the country that had not
recognized his gifts. Miller himself referred to the pages of *Black
Spring* as being populated with "hallucinating stuff . . . and cracked
ideas," and in fact it is something of a peculiar hodgepodge, jumping
between barely connected topics and digressing into much more
inaccessible territory than does *Tropic of Cancer*. Orwell remarked
about *Black Spring*, amusingly, that "the written word loses its power
if it departs too far . . . from the ordinary world where two and two
make four."

In the other work in progress, a more sustained and larger project, Miller planned to begin to tackle the material he had outlined so many years ago at the typewriter at the Parks Department: *Tropic of Capricorn* was to begin to chronicle his life with June. And it would be "a tomb of June that will live for several centuries to come. That's what comes of injury and insult. The Jewish cunt will twitter!" In actuality *Tropic of Capricorn* is not chiefly about June, for it focuses on Miller's childhood, his adolescence, and his Western Union days. Mara, the June character, enters only near the end. The sex scenes in *Capricorn* are even more extended and unflinching than in *Cancer*. To Frances Steloff, the prominent woman of letters and founder of New York's legendary Gotham Book Mart, Miller wrote of his new book, "I think they would hang me for it if they could." The novel continues in the vein of *Black Spring* in its use of impressionistic techniques and unsettling disjunctions in time and setting.

The political situation, new works of art, local or even global news—none of these play any important role in *Capricorn*, which was published, mind you, in the year 1939. This same goes for any other Miller work; he was truly apolitical, almost shockingly so, often bragging of his hatred for reading the newspaper, which, he said, was no match for his own thoughts. Orwell: "I should say that he believes in the impending ruin of Western Civilization much more firmly than the majority of 'revolutionary' writers; only he does not feel called upon to do anything about it."

To Miller, family life was *his* family life; New York and Paris were *his* versions of them, colored beyond all proportion by his unique experiences and moods there. And above all Brooklyn was *his* Brooklyn, most vividly the Fourteenth Ward of his early childhood, the home of so many self-defining days on the street. His way of telling the news was to get down to street level, to the human level. To show what it was like to be in Paris or in Brooklyn was far more important to him than to tell us what it meant. Miller also writes in *Tropic of Carpricorn* that nobody understood what he was writing, and indeed he was an iconoclast with few supporters or peers. But it's important to note, too, that he takes pride in that fact (now that he has found a publisher and a bit of recognition): "I was so lucid they said I was daffy," he writes.

Miller's ego had grown to the point that he was swearing off writers left and right, including those he had once admired. One he did fear as competition for a time was a man who also spent some of his writing life in Brooklyn, Thomas Wolfe. But after reading Wolfe's *Of Time and the River* (largely written down the block from Miller's old place on Remsen), Miller declared, "I am beyond that and beyond all Americans writing here [in Paris] in my native tongue." But Miller was protesting too much, for as his confidante Nin remarked, he was very sensitive to hints of rejection or even silence from the literary establishment. He was still an outsider looking in. This fate he had brought upon himself, through the borderline pornographic style that kept him from being published in the United States for decades, and through his rejections of all things intellectual—a word he came to view with disdain.

Having come into his own in Paris, Miller turned even more decisively against America, New York, and even Brooklyn, all of which now stood, apparently, for the suffering and humiliation he had endured there. The Fourteenth Ward still held out as a beacon in his memory, but he found the present reality very different on a 1935 visit back to the neighborhood, recounted in a pessimistic little volume he wrote called *Aller Retour New York*. He took Nin on a tour on a snowy night, and it left a sour taste. Now the Depression was on, but the real problem for him was that time had done its customary work. His elementary school had been demolished; the tin factory across from the family house had burned down; the saloons were long gone; no ferries ran from the end of Grand Street; the Presbyterian church building had become a synagogue. To a friend he wrote, "The street itself has changed tremendously. I can't get over it." Thereafter, he would spend little time in Brooklyn or New York, and, as Dearborn puts it, "New York City would become the place to which Miller repaired to do his dirt: to raise cash, to procure women, work scams. It brought out the worst in him."

It wasn't until the middle of World War II (which typically entered little into his thinking) that Miller returned to the long-planned big project of documenting his relationship with June. He conceived of an extended bildungsroman built on the foundation of his formidable memory. It would be what Ferguson has called "a working-class Proust, a Brooklyn Proust." The pages emerged in fits and starts, and it was 1947 before he had finished *Sexus*, the first volume of what he called *The Rosy Crucifixion*.

Sexus begins essentially where *Capricorn* leaves off, with the meeting between Henry and June. The book also details his increasingly bitter relationship with his first wife, Beatrice, already anatomized in *Capricorn*, and concludes with the suggestion that, having lost much of himself to Beatrice, he was now being dragged down further by June. With *Sexus*, Miller once again steps up the sexually explicit material, as if unsatisfied by the level of outrage he has so far received. All euphemisms or terms of art are chucked overboard. Miller no doubt saw this as unvarnished honesty, but it comes across as almost ludicrously puerile, as if he was still trying, in his fifties, to shock his mother and his teachers by piling one "cunt" or "prick" on top of another. The book raised a ruckus when it was published in France, and it was banned even there. His publisher, Maurice Girodias, got a jail sentence.

Miller appears to have written the book partly as an act of revenge against Beatrice and June. Near the beginning Miller writes, revealingly, "A man writes to throw off the poison which he has accumulated because of his false way of life." Well, this man did. Probably the more conventional Beatrice would have found his vengeance most wounding. We get all the way to page 6 before Henry thinks, "Choke on it, you bitch," after she expresses disappointment that he won't be coming home for dinner. His thought continues: "At least I know that I don't want you, any part of you, dead or alive." (Miller later expresses guilt about leaving her, but the damage is more than done.) In *Sexus* and throughout the trilogy, the virulent anti-Semitism of *Moloch* is generally absent but, as Ferguson notes, in its place is a rather suspect *pro*-Semitism, wherein the narrator's favorable and generous attitudes seem to be brandished whenever possible, in the manner of a showy deathbed conversion.

With the twin aims of putting the sword in both the "respectable" society he loathed and the two leading women, *Sexus* sacrifices much of its energy and appeal. In some quarters it was better received than the two *Tropics*, but from this distance it is difficult to see why. However, for Lawrence Durrell, later to be the famous author of *The Alexandria Quartet* but at this point a young acolyte and friend of Miller's, the book spelled catastrophe. When he finished reading it in manuscript, he wrote what is surely one of the great succinct hatchet jobs of all time, telegraphing from Corfu: "SEXUS DISGRACEFULLY BAD WILL COMPLETELY RUIN REPUTATION UNLESS WITHDRAWN REVISED LARRY." Miller was undeterred and replied with equanimity, going so far as to tell Durrell, typically, that his criticism brought a smile to his face.

Plexus, the second and longest volume, is written with a freer hand. It covers the early part of Henry's marriage to June, when all was "just ducky," but digresses into other periods of his life, most often, and once more, his Brooklyn youth. As in *Moloch*, written so many years before, the style sometimes slips into the worn grooves of the cheerily faux-gritty hard-boiled detective novel. The dialogue, never Miller's strength, is often horrible, as if the author merely wanted to lay out the gist of a plot-moving conversation— rat-a-tat-tat—and hustle along.

A decade passed between the writing of *Plexus* and the completion of the much shorter *Nexus*, which was originally meant to be augmented by its own second volume but never was. During most of the interval, Miller lived in the relative isolation of a cabin in Big Sur, California, the state where he would spend much of the rest of his life. *Nexus* is a short, painful account of the entrance of the interloper Jean Kronski into the marriage of Henry and June.

June's cold abandonment of him to go to Paris with Jean figures centrally. Miller's own departure for Europe, marked by a series of good-byes to America, several of them of the gleeful "good riddance" variety, closes the book. (The second volume was to have detailed Miller's trip to Europe with June, and perhaps would have brought Miller's story up to where *Tropic of Cancer* begins, but Miller gradually lost the energy and memory, he said, to write it.)

The rapidly and sloppily written *Nexus* speaks to Miller's long, slow decline as a writer. Immediately after finishing it, he felt himself in a sort of crisis, which he confessed to Durrell in a letter, whose youth and energy he admired: "Writing seems so foolish, so unnecessary now." Miller wrote nothing publishable until he was in his forties, then wrote two startlingly original and necessary American classics in the *Tropics*—and then failed to match them in quality from that point on, despite living nearly to ninety years old. The signal events of the second half of his life were not artistic per se: they were the publication in America in the sixties of the books he had written three decades before. At the time, Barney Rosset had published the first American edition of Samuel Beckett's *Waiting for Godot*, works by the leading Beat Generation writers, and an unexpurgated version of D. H. Lawrence's *Lady Chatterley's Lover*, the last involving a long legal battle. Rosset was the man for the job. In publishing Miller in the States, he took a tremendous risk and invited the trials that followed. But the sales and publicity and above all the significance justified all. It was but one product of Rosset's bravery that Henry Miller became a literary celebrity.

Miller met this fate with mixed feelings, for it threw into question the underdog status that was so central to his own self-understanding—a status that was central to Whitman, too. Ferguson takes note of the fact that as an older man Miller wrote of his upbringing, "I did not belong to any environment." Ferguson disputes the notion: "Miller was the product of a very definite environment, the immigrant Brooklyn which he captured with such impressionistic brilliance." But couldn't both be true? During his time, and in some ways today, Brooklyn was a place for the unsettled and uprooted, for the people who landed there by accident or because it was very close to the heart of the legendary metropolis—but definitely outside it. The outsider's resentment commingled with the outsider's pride. Miller didn't only record this essential aspect of Brooklyn. He helped define the scrappy, uncouth, and rebellious image. Very late in his life, in *Book of Friends*, he put his finger on his own role, though he credited it, characteristically, to the whole childhood gang he loved and idolized.

> Once I wrote that I was born in the street and raised in the street. . . . Today I prefer to think that we who lived in the street, we for whom the street was everything, created these streets, created these homes, created the very atmosphere we breathed. We did not come into our world ready-made; we invented our world.

3.

Out of the Fray

HART CRANE AND MARIANNE MOORE

BEFORE SHE SPENT DECADES LIVING IN BROOKLYN, THE POET Marianne Moore served as the editor of the prestigious New York literary magazine the *Dial*, in the 1920s. During that time she published a number of Hart Crane's poems and helped establish his place in the literary world when he was still in his twenties. But he grew angry when Moore rejected some of his work, and even the poems she accepted caused friction. Crane had not yet produced his highest achievement, *The Bridge* (1930), the epic poem about the Brooklyn Bridge that he published at age thirty, and she was older and had more professional stature. The larger issue was a clash not only of aesthetic viewpoints but of temperament and personality. To friends Crane often painted Moore as an uptight scold, referring to her as the "Rt. Rev. Miss Mountjoy." (He was not the only one to adopt this opinion of her.) She in turn found him to be emotionally ungoverned, an attitude he probably sensed. In a letter to James Sibley Watson, co-owner of the *Dial*, she called Crane "vapid and pretentious, not well-reefed." Moore was an upright woman, private and proper and uninterested in romance or drink; Crane was the opposite in every respect.

In a widely discussed incident that sealed the enmity between them, Moore agreed to take Crane's "The Wine Menagerie," but gave it a thorough once-over with the red pen and changed the title to "Again." Crane agreed to the changes but ranted about it to anyone who would listen. He visited a friend and cried himself to sleep on his bed about the humiliation of the experience. To another couple he complained, "*The Dial* bought my Wine Menagerie poem—but insisted (Marianne Moore did) on changing it around and cutting it up until you would not recognize it." Crane was in no financial state to fight—"I would never have consented to such an outrageous joke if I had not so desperately needed the twenty dollars"—and probably resented not only the editing but the powerlessness of his position. Kenneth Burke, who worked with Moore at the *Dial*, sided with Crane on this point. He quipped that Moore had succeeded in taking all the Wine out of the Menagerie.

Moore had the last word when she spoke of Crane to Donald Hall in an interview for the *Paris Review*, nearly thirty years after Crane's death: "Hart Crane complains of me? Well, I complain of *him*." Her biographer Charles Molesworth surmises that perhaps she had heard of Crane's remark, referring to her *Dial* and Margaret Anderson's *Little Review*, that poetry was in the hands of two "hysterical virgins."

Despite the antipathy and the considerable differences between Moore and Crane, a strain of commonality lay beneath their testy relationship. From the beginning, they both held fast to their aesthetic principles in the face of conflict, sometimes to a fault. They were proud and very particular artists who had high ambitions but were not motivated primarily by approval. And there was some admiration between them as poets, as Moore's decision to publish him suggests. Speaking about Crane, Moore added in the Hall interview that he had "so much intuition, such a feel for things, for books—really a bibliophile—that I took special interest in him" and that "we [at the *Dial*] liked him—friends, and with certain tastes in common." For his part, Crane told a dear friend, even after the "Wine Menagerie" fiasco, that "one goes back" to Moore, as one does to Whitman, Poe, Melville, and Frost, "with renewed appreciation of what America really is, or could be."

The writer Crane drew from the most was probably Brooklyn's original bard, Walt Whitman. Echoing Henry Miller, he said of Whitman, "No other American has left us so great a heritage." When Crane was twenty-three and living in Ohio, the conception of his signature work was already taking shape in his mind. He wrote to a friend, "The more I think about my Bridge poem the more thrilling its symbolic possibilities become, and . . . I begin to feel myself directly connected with Whitman. I feel myself in currents that are positively awesome in their extent and possibilities." When the poem came to fruition, it would speak directly to Crane's forebear, bridging the years between them and trying to find him on the very territory they shared. "Walt, tell me, Walt Whitman, if infinity / Be still the same as when you walked the beach / Near Paumanok—your lone patrol." (Paumanok was once the name of Long Island, which included Brooklyn, as geographically it still does.) This section of the poem, its literal and conceptual center, goes on to close by suggesting an answer—that yes, the same infinity that ran through Walt outlived his death and runs through Hart.

> yes, Walt,
> Afoot again, and onward without halt,—
> Not soon, nor suddenly,—never to let go
> My hand
> in yours,
> Walt Whitman—
> so—

New York City has always attracted those who feel they will never fit inside the confines of their hometowns, and so it was with Crane. In the last decade of his short life, Crane moved in rarefied New York literary circles and lived an extraordinary life while barely scraping by financially. But his upbringing had the outlines of a typical upper-middle-class existence. He was born in 1899 and raised in Ohio by a hardheaded father, a successful businessman called C.A., and a mother, Grace, who loved her son with perhaps too much intensity. (C.A.'s company made candy, and for a time he held the patent on Life Savers, but he sold it off too soon to get truly rich.) Crane mystified his father, who had designs on bringing him into his business, by taking an interest in piano, dancing, and fashion, and above all by spending hours alone with books and a pen. In his youth, a growing antagonism between his parents left Crane in the middle of a bitter situation he neither created nor understood. At fifteen he twice attempted suicide—once by slashing his wrists, then by swallowing all his mother's sleeping powders. But at seventeen he would rejoice at publishing poems in two serious New York magazines, having announced at age ten that he wanted only to be a poet. He convinced his father and mother to allow him to go to New York by saying he would get himself admitted to Columbia University (despite having quit high school). He never went. Walt Whitman, Henry Miller, and Hart Crane together had not one semester of college.

The single-minded pursuit of art called out to Crane in a frequency his parents couldn't hear. For a young man who had gone through considerable difficulties at home and at school, he showed remarkable optimism about his prospects. To a friend more than ten years older he wrote, "I have had tremendous struggles.... Thank God, I am young, I have the confidence and will to *make* fate." This kind of self-assurance could be considered a characteristic shared by all successful writers, if not all high achievers. But for Crane, as for Whitman and Miller, it played a particularly essential role, allowing him to withstand the resistance and even hostility of the literary establishment. In the eyes of contemporaries, Whitman had no business self-publishing a lewd "barbaric yawp" and sending it around to dignified men of letters. Henry Miller, raised among the rabble on the filthy streets of Brooklyn, had no business crashing the gates with sexually graphic autobiographical romps. Hart Crane had something a bit nearer to the right pedigree, but by all rights he should have become a Cleveland company man with a nice wife and a nice car. Instead he became a gay New York City poet, forever short of money, writing verses that even many of his close friends found hopelessly out of fashion.

In his twenties, Crane lived mostly in New York but flitted elsewhere, often for financial reasons. In the early New York years, while sporadically holding various jobs he didn't care about, he began cultivating an aesthetic and intellectual identity in unsteady steps, largely through correspondence with writers he had come to know. He would single out a certain author for ardent admiration, be it Joyce, Eliot, or Wallace Stevens, and then, with that phase over, move on to another. A magazine that he'd much admired and that had published him early on, the *Pagan*, became a "fetid corpse." He would seek to reconcile somewhat with his father and maintain a stable relationship with his domineering mother, but again and again they would disappoint him—or the other way around. In a brief period back in Ohio he had his first brief gay affair, telling almost no one about it. He was becoming his own person. To look at it another way, though, he was becoming more and more alone.

Crane continued to publish in his early twenties and produced one major work, the three-part poem "For the Marriage of Faustus and Helen," later included in his debut collection, *White Buildings* (1926). In the first section of "Faustus and Helen," Crane's deep affinity with Whitman reveals itself in the combination of a litany of earth-bound, everyday particulars and a soaring, myth-making lyricism. The details that ground the poem are unmistakably urban, and certain of them unmistakably New York: "the memoranda, baseball scores, / The stenographic smiles and stock quotations"; the "druggist, barber and tobacconist"; an invitation to "suppose some evening I forgot / The fare and transfer." This cataloging of urban ephemera leads to the discovery of Helen of Troy, figure of history and legend, now sitting within reach in a place that calls to mind Times Square: "There is some way, I think, to touch / Those hands of yours that count the nights / Stippled with pink and green advertisements." An eroticism enters with the sight of Helen's "deep blush, when ecstasies thread / The limbs and belly, when rainbows spread / Impinging on the throat and sides . . ."

At the time that he was writing "Faustus and Helen," Crane, like many of his fellow poets and writers, was coming to grips with Modernism, and in particular with the immense influence of T. S. Eliot, eleven years older than Crane and now achieving widespread recognition. W. B. Yeats, a generation older, had captured in his poem "The Second Coming" (1920) something of the grim spirit that prevailed in the wake of the rending of body and mind brought about by the Great War: "The blood-dimmed tide is loosed, and everywhere / The ceremony of innocence is drowned." Eliot took Yeats's despair and enriched it, deepened it; he as much as announced the end of Romanticism, to anyone who doubted it. All those involved in poetry had to reckon with the bomb Eliot had dropped, especially after *The Waste Land* appeared in 1922.

In Crane's view, Eliot deserved the utmost respect, for he represented the ultimate expression of a certain worldview. But it was not a worldview he shared. "I take Eliot as a point of departure toward an almost complete reverse of direction," he wrote to his friend the poet Gorham Munson. "His pessimism is amply justified, in his own case. But I would apply as much of his erudition and technique as I can absorb and assemble toward a more positive, or (if [I] must put it so in a skeptical age) ecstatic goal." Committing himself to a hopeful aesthetic project—and he did remain committed—constituted a considerable act of rebellion at Crane's historical moment, particularly in poetry. To sound the death knell in art, to shock and awe with destruction, is often considered brave, clear-eyed, but at times it is far braver to open oneself to the charge of naïveté by trying to build a bridge rather than burn it behind you. Walt Whitman and Henry Miller defied the prevailing norms by inviting revulsion, outrage, and censorship. Hart Crane defied them by stepping out of the fashionable depths of despond. To the poet Allen Tate he wrote, "Perhaps this is useless, perhaps it is silly—but one does have joys. . . . Let us invent an idiom for the

proper transposition of jazz into words! Something clean, sparkling, elusive!"

All the draining jobs and poverty of Crane's early career kept
his output low—he was never very prolific—and sometimes left him
deeply dispirited. But he held on to his belief in his own vocation,
keeping that Whitmanesque "ecstatic goal" in view. From Cleveland he wrote a wild midnight letter to Gorham Munson with
"Apologies later!" scrawled in massive letters across the top.

> At times, dear Gorham, I feel an enormous power in me—
> that seems almost supernatural. If this power is not too dis-
> sipated in aggravation and discouragement I may amount to
> something sometime. I can say this now with perfect equa-
> nimity because I am notoriously drunk and the Victrola is
> still going with that glorious Bolero.

When he was invited to read his work at a party along with a number of luminaries, he saw a chance to make an impression, and
even terrible food poisoning couldn't keep him from attending.
Marianne Moore read first, in her quiet voice, and Crane followed
her, having cured himself with five whiskey and sodas that left him
"the picture of health," he said. Crane's fondness for alcohol, which
for long stretches he viewed as a requirement for a night of writing,
would come to play a troublingly central role in his life. Like Whitman and Miller, he valued the body and its pleasures. As for the
"sins of the flesh," well, were they sins? None of them was sure about
that.

Crane was twenty-four when he began the great affair of his
life with Emil Opffer Jr., a merchant seaman who had connections
to the intellectual world. His father, who brought his family from
Holland to America, worked as a journalist and as the editor of a
Brooklyn-based newspaper for Dutch émigrés. Emil's brother was
a member of the Provincetown Players, a mainstay of the Greenwich Village artistic scene. Crane had a weakness for sailors, and
this one had a foot in Crane's circles. Falling for Emil, Crane wrote

a rapturous letter to the novelist Waldo Frank: "I have gone quite dumb with something for which 'happiness' must be too mild a term."

The meeting of Hart and Emil led Crane not only to Brooklyn but to an uncannily perfect spot. Crane was unhappily living in a cheap Manhattan apartment at the time they met, but Emil had a thought: a room for rent had opened up in his father's building. Emil Sr. lived and had his newspaper office in Brooklyn Heights, at 110 Columbia Heights. It was the westernmost street in the neighborhood, so it had the choicest views of the harbor and the Manhattan skyline. According to Crane biographer Clive Fisher, the house was one of three, 106–110, that were owned by the same man, and he had turned them into an artists' colony of a kind. The buildings were connected on the lower floors, with an art school in the basement. One observer described the atmosphere as that of "the 'arty' middle class," who liked the company but also appreciated the quiet in the "non–Greenwich Village surroundings." Another young writer of promise was already renting a room at 110 Columbia Heights. He was on the mend from rheumatism and arthritis and recovering, too, from a minor scandal involving his overt objection to World War I while serving as a soldier on the front. His name was John Dos Passos. While living there, he would begin work on a landmark novel that would put him on the map, *Manhattan Transfer.*

Crane moved in, relishing the thought of a perch outside Manhattan and in close range of his great subject. He soon told his mother about "the finest view in all America. Just imagine looking out your window directly on the East River with nothing intervening between your view of the Statue of Liberty, way down the harbor, and the marvelous beauty of Brooklyn Bridge close above you and on your right!" As it happened, Crane was now living in the very building from which an ill Washington Roebling oversaw the construction of the Brooklyn Bridge. Crane eventually took over the same room Roebling had occupied, positioning his writing desk near the very same window where Roebling had positioned his telescope forty-odd years before. Roebling had built the bridge. Now Crane would rebuild it in words.

Years after conceiving of *The Bridge*, Crane felt himself in a kind of waking dream. The structure he had spent so long thinking about was right there in front of him. "Imagine my surprise," he wrote, "when Emil brought me to this street where, at the very end of it, I saw a scene that was more familiar than a hundred factual provisions could have rendered it!" The feeling was immensely powerful, bringing out in Crane an almost religious tone: "I believe I am a little changed—not essentially, but changed and transubstantiated as anyone is who has asked a question and been answered."

❦

"This section of Brooklyn is very old," Hart told his mother, "but all the houses are in splendid condition." The first part of the sentence was certainly true. The Brooklyn Heights of his time featured the oldest and some of the most elegant houses in Brooklyn, a legacy of its status as "America's first suburb." A number of town houses dating to the mid-nineteenth century still stand—along with a handful from even earlier, as far back as 1820—and the exteriors of most of them are more or less unaltered. The patchwork of streets, elevated on a bluff above the harbor (hence the name), did and still does enjoy a tranquillity occasioned by being a kind of cozy, neighborhood-size cul-de-sac. Bordering it to the east is the distinctly less classy downtown area, where in Crane's time an elevated train rumbled through what is now Cadman Plaza. The tracks were demolished in the thirties and early forties, and more than three hundred buildings were destroyed to make way for the plaza. Now the imposing slabs of the courthouses, the post office, and Borough Hall surround an often unpopulated and windswept space. Robert Moses, the exceedingly powerful official and builder who changed the face of New York City in the twentieth century, made the spectacularly wrong prediction that Cadman Plaza would "be as much the pride of Brooklyn as the Piazza San

Marco is the pride of Venice and the Place de la Concorde the cynosure of Paris." Walking around there now, you could be in any city
of some note but little attraction.

To the north of the Heights is Dumbo; the name is an acronym
for Down Under the Manhattan Bridge Overpass, though the neighborhood lies below both the Manhattan and Brooklyn Bridges. Now
a land of very pricey high-rise condos, in Crane's time it showed a
lowlier face. It was and remains quite distinct from the Heights
geographically and architecturally. Crossing between the two
means descending or scaling a daunting hill that separates the
Heights from the dockside streets and ferry landing that Whitman
wandered around and looked upon from the Fulton Street offices
of the *Eagle*.

To the south, the Heights gently slopes down to the busy thoroughfare of Atlantic Avenue, getting a bit less fancy on the way
down until Atlantic, the southern boundary of the neighborhood,
brings the peaceful feel to an abrupt halt. Cobble Hill, to the south
of Atlantic, now resembles the Heights in socioeconomics, but in
Crane's era it was far less exclusive. It housed some of the huge
population that relied on Red Hook's shipyards for work and a
Middle Eastern immigrant community, mainly Syrian. (These
were the "people of the Levant" that Henry Miller referred to, and
their presence is still felt in a cluster of Middle Eastern restaurants
and groceries on Atlantic.)

And finally, to the west of Brooklyn Heights is of course the
East River, and across it the expanse of Manhattan, laid out per-
pendicularly as if it positioned itself to afford the Heights the ideal
view: *Have a look at this*. Brooklyn Heights can't spread, then—
there's nowhere for it to go—and so it retains an exclusive feel; to
get in, someone else has to relinquish her spot. Crane was lucky to
gain entrance, and, once in, he was outnumbered by those of a higher
station in society.

The part of the Heights closest to the river, where he lived, was
not as quiet as it is now, because active warehouses and piers lined
the water's edge. Much of the commerce of the Midwest, via the

Erie Canal, flowed through the area. Nevertheless, the Heights stood at a remove from the noise, demographically a world away, since it literally overlooked all the action below the bluff it stood upon. The houses were relatively small, three or four stories, mostly, with some elegantly miniature two-level carriage houses as well. Even at a remove from the river view, the streets offered a wide, refreshing view of the sky. The novelist Paula Fox recently described making this discovery upon moving to Brooklyn from the Upper West Side: "As I looked up at it I realized, as I seldom did in Manhattan, that it was limitless, not a roof for a city, not a part of a stage decor, but the heavens." The houses in the Heights, though, were densely packed together and the streets were narrow, which created an intimacy not unlike what you would find near a town green with a steepled church, in the densest part of a small village. Here you are in America, not "the city."

Despite the continued existence of fine housing stock, the citadel of white-gloved gracefulness had been showing cracks during the preceding two decades, as Miller suggested with his remark about the "invading swarms." Since the middle of the nineteenth century, the Heights and Brooklyn at large had resisted the most efficient, and disruptive, modes of transportation. Officials had balked at permitting steam trains, with their noisy churn, belching smoke, and occasional runaway cars, to go right into Brooklyn's heart, which forced produce and freight to be offloaded to wagons at Jamaica Station in Queens. While Manhattan remade itself to stay at the vanguard of all trends, Brooklyn eyed change warily, to the pleasure of Heights residents.

But in 1908 Brooklyn, now a borough rather than a separate city, saw its subway systems connect up with Manhattan's. The logical move eased commuting and spurred growth but also brought more and more people to Brooklyn. The hotels in the area filled up and new ones were built. A series of additions made the Hotel St. George the largest in the nation by 1929, with 2,623 rooms. F. Scott Fitzgerald would visit the bar there and also the top-floor restaurant and nightclub at the Hotel Bossert on Montague Street, built in 1909. Brooklyn had become a destination.

Not all the newcomers were up to the usual Heights snuff. But the diversity encroaching on the Heights didn't put Crane off at all. Just a short walk down the hill to the north and east were the bars his mother wouldn't hear about in letters home. The infamous Sands Street offered up all-hours iniquities hidden from most of the city's view. Al Capone, born the same year as Crane, had gone to school a few blocks away, at P.S. 7 at 85 Jay Street, and in his teenage years he was known to stop by the Sands Street bordellos; a persistent rumor has it that it was here he contracted the syphilis that eventually killed him. This was no ordinary red-light district. Locals called it "Hell's Half Acre." John Kobler describes the place (with exaggeration?) in his biography of Capone.

> Sands Street at night, all night, catered to more robust tastes, as droves of sailors piled ashore, clamoring for liquor and women. It was one of the roughest haunts in the country, the Barbary Coast of the East, where mayhem and murder constantly threatened the unwary. . . . There were tattooing parlors, gambling dives, dance halls, fleabags with rooms for rent by the hour, and a galaxy of bangled, painted whores, known by reputation in every port of the seven seas, like the Duchess, and Submarine Mary, who had a mouthful of solid gold teeth.

With Emil away at sea a lot and their relationship intermittent, Crane walked down to Sands Street to look for sex, searching for sailors to share in a rendezvous meant not to last. In *The Broken Tower: The Life of Hart Crane* (1999), Paul Mariani writes that despite Crane's high-flown social life, as with "Whitman before him, it was among the city's vibrant teeming masses that he felt most at home." Cruising was a dangerous pursuit for Crane in a time of rampant homophobia. More than once he came home beaten and bloodied.

Homosexuality did not torture Crane to the extreme degree that it did many others in that era, in part because he moved among the relatively accepting circles of liberal literary New York. Still, it is revealing that he often sought out lovers not among the chattering classes but among men that his friends would never meet. Crane and Dos Passos shared mutual acquaintances, and now as neighbors they occasionally dined together. When Crane was seriously drunk, Dos Passos would try to talk him into turning in for the night. Crane would pretend to be persuaded and then sneak out to the bars. There was a certain shame in it, he thought, and it seems likely that for Crane, the danger of Sands Street felt somehow right; seeking romance ought to be difficult, secret, and capable of ending with a bruised face.

⁊

When Crane was living in Brooklyn, and indeed for much of his brief adult life, New York was experiencing an unprecedented economic boom. Money seemed to "roll in the gutters," he once said. Crane's twenties were the 1920s, and what a time and place to be that age. It remains true today, I think, that this was New York City's most glorious decade. The population increased by 1.3 million, to nearly 7 million. (In the eight decades since, it has increased by only about a million more.) Driven by speculation and the proliferation of margin buying, Wall Street generated untold riches. Its denizens lived in blissful ignorance (or denial) of the coming crash. Between 1920 and 1925, F. Scott Fitzgerald published his phenomenally successful debut, *This Side of Paradise*, followed by *The Beautiful and the Damned* and *The Great Gatsby*. Along the way he popularized the term "Jazz Age" in the middle of its short but incandescent life. (*Gatsby*'s warnings about the perils of wealth didn't resonate at the time; the book didn't find a large readership until decades later.) New York City's mayor for the second half of the decade, Jimmy Walker, drank heavily, barely showed up for work, wrote pop songs, and moved in with his mistress at the Ritz-Carlton. He was reelected.

The Ziegfeld Follies captivated Broadway audiences, and the fashion in the shows filtered out onto the streets. Prohibition drove New York nightlife into new underground cabarets, and they welcomed women more than legitimate saloons had—a happy development for all involved. The cabarets drew the jazz scene from Chicago, and Louis Armstrong, Duke Ellington, and company provided a truly American-born soundtrack to city living. Stravinsky's *Rite of Spring*, a major cannon shot of Modernism, came across the Atlantic for a Carnegie Hall American premiere, and George Gershwin's *Rhapsody in Blue* made its worldwide premiere in midtown. The Great Migration brought a generation of black artists and writers to Harlem, transforming it into the new center of black culture. The poet Langston Hughes looked on the city's rapidly changing face and wrote, in 1926, "New York is truly the dream city—city of the towers near God, city of hopes and visions, of spires seeking in the windy air love and perfection." Indeed, skyscrapers were climbing impossibly high in a dazzling competition, the abstract concept of macho capitalism made into edifices forged out of steel. After a frenzied decade of building, three New York behemoths—the Bank of Manhattan Trust Building, the Chrysler, and the Empire State—claimed the mantle of world's tallest building one after the other, all within a year. (By the time they were finished, between 1930 and 1931, they were late to the party; the economy had gone to pieces.)

Amid all this hyperactivity, Crane looked on with the classic excitement of the boy from the provinces but also with a great measure of financial and emotional exile. All the dazzle and swing of the twenties jibed with his affirmative vision, his hope of transposing jazz into words. But he couldn't seem to complete his long-planned masterpiece, *The Bridge*, and money was a constant problem. Poetry, which rarely paid, was the only thing in life that really mattered. He frequently had to write to his father to hint obliquely that a "loan" would be helpful, a painful task. Sometimes he lacked the subway fare to travel outside the neighborhood.

At a crucial moment he found a very wealthy patron to support the writing of *The Bridge*, but Crane had no trouble burning through the money, not least on drink. Although he sampled the pleasures of Jazz Age New York—attending concerts of the new music, meeting Charlie Chaplin, taking in the new plays of Eugene O'Neill (a friend he had pursued), visiting exhibitions, and drinking at Village speakeasies—he felt marginalized by his limited bank account. And during his first Brooklyn stint he was still earning his stripes in the literary community, published in prominent magazines but yet to produce a first book.

The most substantial and accomplished work in *White Buildings*, though, was begun in that lovesick spring of 1924 when he moved to Brooklyn. "Voyages," a six-part poem, is clearly in large part an outgrowth of Crane's saving love for Emil Opffer. It is rife with images of swimming and drowning, and its gauzy, undulating style and diction create a disorienting difficulty for the reader. We are at sea, in more than one sense, and so is the young lover whose voice permeates the verses: "Upon the steep floor flung from dawn to dawn / The silken skilled transmemberment of song. / Permit me, voyage, love, into your hands . . ."

While living on Columbia Heights, Crane was developing a very sensuous relationship to Brooklyn, recorded mostly in numerous letters. In these writings, which find him exploring the streets in all conditions and seasons, we see a joy in a beloved place but also the shadow of a fertile melancholy (particularly in Emil's absence). Here, in a representative passage, we get a clear sight of the view from his window.

> Everytime one looks at the harbor and the NY skyline across the river it is quite different, and the range of atmospheric effects is endless. But at twilight on a foggy evening . . . it is beyond description. Gradually the lights in the enormously tall buildings begin to flicker through the mist. There was a great cloud enveloping the top of the Woolworth Tower, while below, in the river, were streaming reflections of myriad lights, continually being crossed by

the twinkling mast and deck lights of little tugs scudding along, freight rafts, and occasional liners starting outward. Look far to your left toward Staten Island and there is the Statue of Liberty, with that remarkable lamp of hers that makes her seen for miles. And up to the right Brooklyn Bridge, the most superb piece of construction in the modern world, I'm sure, with strings of light crossing it like glowing worms as the Ls and surface cars pass each other going and coming. It is particularly fine to feel the greatest city in the world from enough distance, as I do here, to see its larger proportions. When you are actually in it you are often too distracted to realize its better and more imposing aspects.

Work continued, in fits and starts, on *The Bridge* in the ensuing years, when he shuttled between disparate places: there were long stays in the countryside in and around Pawling and Patterson, New York; a sojourn on the Isle of Pines off of Cuba (now called the Isle of Youth), where his mother had property; some months in Hollywood ("this Pollyanna greasepaint pinkpoodle paradise"); a visit to Paris that ended badly, due to a worsening alcohol problem; and more city living on a shoestring, with stops in Brooklyn. His emotions about the grand poem vacillated widely and frequently. As he wrote in a letter, his optimistic vision was becoming embattled. All seemed constricted, sterile, contented with a pragmatism that masked futility.

The bridge as a symbol today has no significance beyond an economical approach to shorter hours, quicker lunches, behaviorism and toothpicks. . . . If only America were half as worthy today to be spoken of as Whitman spoke of it fifty years ago there might be something for one to say—not that Whitman received or required any tangible proof of his intimations, but that time has shown how increasingly lonely and ineffectual his confidence stands.

Crane stayed at 110 Columbia Heights again for a short while in 1927, but the next time he spent a substantial period in Brooklyn came in 1928, after he told Malcolm Cowley, "Tomorrow afternoon I may find a room over on Columbia Hts. if the patron saint of rooming houses (St. Anne, I believe!) is feeling commodious." He ended up one block away at 77 Willow Street, which was close enough: again he had a view of the river and the bridge. (Truman Capote would later live at 70 Willow, across the street.) The first piece of mail Crane received at his new address was a telegraph from his mother informing him of his grandmother's death. It was sad news, but not unexpected, and Crane well knew that a five-thousand-dollar inheritance was coming to him—enough to put aside job hunting and finish *The Bridge*.

Before the money came through, though (it ended up taking some time), he had to take a job. This one came about through help from a friend. After Crane got his foot back in the door of 110 Columbia Heights, in the fall of 1928, he was walking one day down under the Brooklyn Bridge when he came across a young man with a small camera who seemed as interested in the bridge as he was. It turned out their fathers knew each other back in Cleveland. Crane started spending time with the photographer, who had bought his first camera that year and who took a room on Columbia Heights himself. Together they went for walks around the neighborhood, pointing out the sights to each other. Crane's new friend was Walker Evans, later among the most famous photographers of the century. Evans got Crane hired at the brokerage firm where he had a day job. Crane couldn't stand "sorting securities of cancelled legions ten years back" while around him executives reaped the market's 30 percent returns. In a few weeks he made a showy exit scene after arriving at the office at around noon, still drunk and wearing the same clothes as the day before. What reaction Evans had to this outburst is unclear, but he did consent to having one of his remarkable Brooklyn Bridge photos grace the Paris edition of *The Bridge*.

Stalking out of the job exemplified Crane's increasingly erratic behavior, driven by booze and an intermittent but severe frustration. One night, after a bout of drinking, he caught a cab back to Brooklyn with Sam Loveman, a writer and friend who was a neighbor. The driver mistakenly took the Williamsburg Bridge and Crane ordered him to stop so he could urinate on the bridge. Back on Columbia Heights, Crane discovered he lacked the money for the fare, leaving it to Loveman to pay. After the driver pulled away, Crane began shouting that he was finished, all used up, and he took off at a run toward his apartment. Loveman gave chase and bounded up the stairs by twos all the way to the roof. Crane had almost reached the edge when Loveman grabbed him and pulled him back, enraged. I'm not writing, Crane explained to Loveman after he'd calmed down, so why live?

But the following year, 1929, Crane finally did finish *The Bridge*, despite the rough half year in Paris in the interim. As he made the final changes back in Brooklyn (at 130 Columbia Heights now) on the day after Christmas, exhausted by the effort, he must have felt a good deal older than thirty, but thirty he was. Waiting for the book to come out, he moved into a tiny place in the basement at 190 Columbia Heights. Again he found himself penniless, and now, in the wake of the massive stock market crash of October 1929, the hopes of finding a job were even slimmer.

⚘

As the title suggests, *The Bridge* is an expression of the act of connection, not least the connection between the past and the present. One strand running through the verses, often artfully hidden, is the record of one man's day, beginning with a crossing from Brooklyn to Manhattan, and ending after a crossing in reverse and another look back on the bridge and the river. But this day is surrounded and overwhelmed by the forces of centuries of history. The poem begins with a gorgeous section called "To Brooklyn Bridge" (originally published by Marianne Moore in the *Dial*) that consists of eleven stanzas, all essentially riffs on a series of images of the great structure, seen from different angles. It is directly addressed to the bridge, as if offering up as tribute a record of years of watching "Thee, across the harbor, silver-paced / As though the sun took step of thee, yet left / Some motion ever unspent in thy stride,—." The moment of the poem is contemporary: the "I" speaks in present tense and refers to the modern workplace, to "Some page of figures to be filed away; / —Till elevators drop us from our day . . ." And the cinema, subways, and traffic lights, the visual commerce of the modern city, make appearances. So does a lone man in distress, high on the bridge's deck: "Out of some subway scuttle, cell or loft / A bedlamite speeds to thy parapets, / Tilting there momentarily, shrill shirt ballooning."

Soon, in the "Ave Maria" section, we are plunged back into America's dawn, as Crane lays out a scene of Columbus returning to Spain, battered by a storm but bringing word of a new land of Indians: "It is morning there—." Then we are on the trail of Pocahontas, in a multipoem section called "Powhatan's Daughter." But we are awash in this section in a timeless place, as the continuity of the natural world underlies the link that binds together long-separated eras. Crane describes a dawn, viewed through a frosted window, that finds the harbor shrouded in fog, emanating the sounds of foghorns and gongs, until "Cyclopean towers across Manhattan waters" alight—skyscrapers meet ancient myth. And in the next playful poem, Rip Van Winkle turns up on the twentieth-century streets: "*And Rip forgot the office hours / and he forgot the pay; / Van Winkle sweeps a tenement / way down on Avenue A,—.*" In "The River," as in the section about Columbus, there is a celebration of journeying not only across time but across space. Crane retraces the steps of the pioneers, traversing the Mississippi, the Ohio, Cheyenne, the Dakotas, but he does so "on the 'backs' of hobos," as he explained in a letter, who are riding the rails of freight trains.

From those marginalized and lowly hobos, the roving eye of the poem, sloshing again into the present, swings to a drinker in a bar by South Street. (South Street Seaport in Manhattan is now a riverside outdoor mall, but in Crane's time South Street was a gathering spot for sailors and toughs, like Sands Street in Brooklyn.) And then, in "Cape Hatteras," the South Street drunkard seems to morph into Whitman himself, who once walked the same soil, "our native clay . . . eternal flesh of Pocahontas." Whitman is the man to whom "Cape Hatteras" is "a kind of ode," in Crane's words, the man he most wants to reach out his hand across time to touch, the man who tended to the nation's wounded, as the poem suggests. And in *The Bridge* he is also a lowlife on a bar stool. The dark everyday of the present intrudes again in "The Tunnel." The subway, the dominant mode of New York's "to and fro," is depicted explicitly as "the Daemon," a wicked, dehumanizing expression of industrial modernity.

> *The phonographs of hades in the brain*
> *Are tunnels that re-wind themselves, and love*
> *A burnt match skating in a urinal—*
> *Somewhere above Fourteenth TAKE THE EXPRESS*
> *To brush some new presentiment of pain—*

The Bridge has by now built its way, though, to "Atlantis," and here again Crane captures the Brooklyn Bridge, this time at night, with an almost overpowering cascade of words. Now the wires and cables across its span are imagined as an instrument, perhaps a harp, "As though a god were issue of the strings . . ."

The Bridge is an extremely difficult work. The bridge at its center is made to bear a lot of weight. It stands in for a massive array of connections, accumulated by the poet's mind over many years. What kept him going over that time was his desire "to handle the beautiful skeins of this myth of America." Like Whitman, Crane saw in the Brooklyn Bridge a reflection of the nation's history and ideals and the promise of a new America just now being born. He viewed it as not merely the product of an enormous technical endeavor but the product of an outsize dream. For those who felt alienated by the inexorable advance of technology—the machinations of machines, the defining legacy of the twentieth century—Crane's answer was to turn a marvel of technology into a metaphor, to make the concrete abstract, to cast the inanimate object as an expression of humanity.

The greeting party for *The Bridge* in June 1930 did not provide the unanimous praise that Crane might have hoped for. In reviews, Herbert Weinstock, Louis Untermeyer, and especially Granville Hicks bestowed important laurels, but others, including friends, spoke with qualifications. More than a few, like Percy Hutchinson in the *New York Times Book Review,* were dismayed by the "lack of intelligibility." Words like that made Crane wince, for he viewed himself as a "social poet." But Crane could hardly be surprised that he was not taken into open arms, so idiosyncratic and even anachronistic was his vision, and he defended that vision mightily. The poet Allen Tate, in a letter to Crane, laid out an exemplary criticism: "Your vision of American life comes from Whitman, or from the same sources in the American consciousness as his. I am unsympathetic to this tradition, and it seems to me you should be too." A review Tate wrote went further, calling *The Bridge* not only incoherent in structure but a "sentimental muddle" of Whitman and "pseudo-primitivism." Most damningly, Tate cast it as naively romantic and therefore outmoded, dead on the page. "In his rejection of a rational and qualitative will, Crane follows the main stream of romanticism in the last hundred years," Tate wrote, and he characterized that stream as "dying out."

We can imagine how sharp the barb must have felt, for what Tate was saying was that Crane had spent years in worship of a false hope. Crane penned a fair but pointed rejoinder in a personal letter, questioning whether it really could be true that he was something like the last romantic, and, more revealingly, whether that in fact represented a criticism: "I shall be humbly grateful if the Bridge can fulfill simply the metaphorical inferences of its title. . . . You will admit our age (at least our predicament) to be one of transition." Perhaps, he added, the poem could serve as "a link connecting certain chains of the past to certain chains and tendencies of the future." In the landmark Crane biography *Voyager* (1969), John

Unterecker notes that some have read Crane's letter as an admission of certain weaknesses in *The Bridge*. Unterecker chalks up the concessions to politeness. I hear a different subtext: Crane seems to me to be saying, gently, that if Tate could not see the role and importance of his aesthetic project, then so much the worse for Tate. Crane would hold fast to his viewpoint, even if it cost him acceptance.

In the two years after *The Bridge* was published, Crane's personal decline became more and more evident. He did win a Guggenheim Fellowship, which he used to live and work in Mexico, but there the drinking became worse. Late-night arguments landed him again in jail. Friendships ended. He began to feel distant from New York, partly because his fellow writers there were enlisting in the new political wars of the early thirties, while he remained happy to be the apolitical exile artist. A highly unlikely love affair soon arose in Mexico with Peggy Cowley, who was on her way to a divorce from Crane's friend Malcolm Cowley, the literary editor of the *New Republic*. It felt preposterous at first but she inspired him and took care of him when he needed it, which was often. Waldo Frank once wrote, imagining a kind of sine curve of Crane's moods, "The periodicity of his excesses grew swifter; the lucid intervening times when he could write were crowded out. Crane fought death in Mexico." And he was losing control of the battlefield. After he wrote a will and tried to kill himself by swallowing a bottle of Mercurochrome, Peggy Cowley decided they needed to leave Mexico.

They caught a ship bound for New York, the *Orizaba*. Crane got drunk and found trouble on the ship overnight, apparently propositioning a male member of the crew. The following day, just before noon, he walked into Peggy's cabin in pajamas and a topcoat and said, "I'm not going to make it, dear. I'm utterly disgraced." Accustomed to such remarks, she told him to go get dressed. He agreed and said good-bye, then walked to the stern of the ship, churning off the shore of Florida, and vaulted himself over the rail.

In a life touched by the uncanny and blessed by ironies, here was the darkest irony. Crane's potent imagery of the overpowering sea in "Voyages," written during the relatively happy times of the romance with Emil, brings a shiver in light of Crane's fatal plunge. So, too, does the bedlamite standing on the edge of the bridge, considering a leap.

Hart Crane was thirty-two years old.

In his personal life, Crane was probably too well aligned with the New York City of the 1920s. Of that time in the city, Fitzgerald wrote, "The catering to dissipation set an example to Paris; the shows were broader, the buildings were higher, the morals were looser and the liquor was cheaper; but all these benefits did not really minister to much delight. Young people wore out early." So it was for Crane, who crashed along with the twenties when the dark thirties came. In his work, however, Crane bucked the tide of his times. The roar of the capitalist economy held no appeal for him, and he set himself against "shorter hours, quicker lunches, behaviorism and toothpicks." But rather than embrace the pessimism of the poetic age of Eliot, he embraced an "ecstatic goal." His dramatic death, often mined for meaning, obscures his wider significance; he grew into greatness in an era that was out of step with his ideals.

Marianne Moore spent the twenties surrounded by the same maelstrom of excess, and she was living in the middle of the action, in Greenwich Village. When she had visited Manhattan as a college student, she was enchanted by the breakneck pace. "Dear Family," she wrote in a letter, "Art is long, but life is so fast I wonder it does not catch up to it." Becoming editor of the *Dial* years later pulled her right into the whirl of the literary and artistic community. But in 1929, the year Hart Crane finished *The Bridge*, his last book, and the year the stock market crash ripped the needle off the phonograph, Moore left Manhattan behind when the *Dial* folded. It was after that break away from the frenzied center of the literary world that her talent as a poet fully bloomed. Those years were spent in Brooklyn.

Born in 1887, Moore earned a far better education than did

Crane, Henry Miller, or Walt Whitman, despite the obstacles women faced at the time. She graduated from Bryn Mawr College in Pennsylvania in 1909. She had written steadily for the college literary magazine, and though she found writing to be a struggle, she pursued its quiet rewards with determination. Professional publishing interested her, but she knew little about it and was advised to seek secretarial work. (If publishing work represented a somewhat impractical choice for a man, for a woman it was thought to be beyond reach.) So Moore moved back to Carlisle, Pennsylvania, the town where she was raised by her mother, Mary Warner Moore. Marianne's mother had split with her husband in Missouri before Marianne ever met her father. Marianne would choose to be close to her mother, figuratively and literally, for the duration. Her mother died at Brooklyn Hospital in Fort Greene in 1947, a few blocks from their shared apartment.

After college, Moore took classes in typing and shorthand; worked at a summer camp set up by Melvil Dewey (of the decimal system) in Lake Placid, New York; and taught at the Indian School in Carlisle, an institution set up for the benefit of largely impoverished students of American Indian origin. (One of the students was the legendary athlete Jim Thorpe.) She was never happy there, however, and poetry exercised a stronger and stronger pull, even when it went badly and left her in what she called a "black frenzy." (In a college short story of hers, the narrator feels that "there are times when I should give anything on earth to have writing a matter of indifference to me.") She continued to place work in a Bryn Mawr magazine, but now Moore was also submitting poems, rather brazenly, to professional publications, several of them in the upper echelon in sales or prestige: the *Smart Set*, edited by H. L. Mencken; *McClure's*; the *Atlantic Monthly*; the *Century*.

As Charles Molesworth notes in *Marianne Moore: A Literary Life* (1990), Moore rejected certain prevailing aesthetic models with remarkable assuredness even in this amateur period. Her comments about contemporary literature of the time reflect a proclivity for the new and untraditional and a point of view growing ever more pointed. There emerged in her work a gently mocking, wry tone with an identifiable ring to it. Asked in a late interview whether her writing style had any literary antecedents, she answered, "Not so far as I know."

The breakthrough would come on her terms, then, from a somewhat new journal edited by Harriet Monroe called *Poetry*, which in 1914 snapped up four of her more conventional, rhyming poems and ran them the following year. In 1915, there came an acceptance of three of her more unique verses from the *Egoist*, where Ezra Pound, living in London, was throwing his weight around as "foreign editor." The *Egoist* soon took more of her work, and joining the group were the *Lantern* and the cutting-edge magazine *Others*, which also published early poems from Hart Crane within a few years. The editor of *Others*, Alfred Kreymborg, praised her work as "an amazing output and absolutely original" and quickly became a staunch supporter and mentor. She still "had met no writers," she later recalled, but against the odds, at twenty-seven she was well on her way.

Flush with her newfound success, in 1915 Moore made another visit to New York, more magical still than the first. This time she came in contact with the Greenwich Village creative community and she toured Alfred Stieglitz's gallery, 291, which showed the very latest art. By now Moore no longer quite stood in awe of New York. (In fact, at twenty-three she had expressed that she had no desire to settle there.) She came to it, as Molesworth indicates, with a precocious sensibility and with a reputation already secured, albeit among a relatively small group. She did not fit the mold of the provincial type making a wide-eyed pilgrimage, as Hart Crane did in the same period. Prepared perhaps for an unvarnished talent from the sticks, the mainstays of the New York scene encountered someone else entirely. Kreymborg described her as "an astonishing person with Titian hair, a brilliant complexion and a mellifluous flow of polysyllables which held every man in awe."

A good job offer for Moore's brother, a Presbyterian pastor, in Chatham, New Jersey, nudged her and her mother closer to New

York, as they all moved to New Jersey to be together. Moore's valuable, eccentric, and wonderfully written letters, a selection of which were finally published in 1997, reveal a family trio so intimately connected that they shared what you might call their own private dialect. Moore was a biology enthusiast and famously an ardent lover of animals, and she, her brother, and her mother used odd, animal-inspired nicknames for one another—among them "Fangs," "Gator," and "Fish." Moore cared deeply about her brother's and mother's views of her work, and the two often played some role in her writing process or at least gave her comments after publication. Warner, as her brother was called, remarked about two of her poems from the *Dial*, "I was . . . greatly impressed with the fundamental grasp of 'Life' in them and expressed too in our own special 'language' but so marvelously handled that the 'aliens' could and can understand them & enjoy them." When friction at home did inevitably arise, she was quite capable of holding firm. Her mother noted in a letter to Warner that while many women needed to be loved, her daughter was not one of them.

In fact, Moore had written to her brother from the Lake Placid camp that she had received the attention of some suitors—seven, she said with precision—but they were all decisively rebuffed. In a lifetime of copious published correspondence and poetry, this is one of only a few references to even the possibility of romantic love, let alone marriage.

The stay in Chatham was short-lived; Warner took a commission as a chaplain in the navy and then got engaged to a woman from the Bronx. He found Marianne and her mother a place in New York to stay for a time, at 39 Charlton Street in Manhattan, and then an apartment nearby at 14 St. Luke's Place, in 1918. This was Greenwich Village, a neighborhood that had already become a hotbed of radical left politics. It would also become, for decades, synonymous not only with a profusion of art and literature but with a burst of what Moore might tactfully have called creative living. During Moore's time at that address, Theodore Dreiser would live two doors down, at No. 16, while working on *An American*

Tragedy, and Sherwood Anderson would live two doors in the other direction, at No. 12. (Moore seems to have liked Anderson, but called his wife "a crude, undignified curtain-tassel-swinging woman, well meaning but impossible.") At the time that Dreiser lived there (1922–23), he was still battling the censors over *Sister Carrie*, published decades before, and a group of his supporters, including Fitzgerald, Mencken, Horace Liveright, and Carl Van Vechten, held at least one meeting on the parlor floor of his house.

Elsewhere in the neighborhood, the Provincetown Players were shaking up the theater scene, providing a more adventurous and less commercial alternative to Broadway; Mabel Dodge's salon had been serving as a focal point for colorful counterculturalism; obscenity laws and the New York Society for the Suppression of Vice provided a target of widespread ire and ridicule; and Edna St. Vincent Millay skipped around town, flaunting her new sexual freedom with her sister in tow, the two of them the talk of all the men in the Village. Millay was beginning her ascent into a kind of renown almost unprecedented for a poet, as readers responded to her beauty and the devil-may-care abandon she famously expressed: "My candle burns at both ends; / It will not last the night; / But ah, my foes, and oh, my friends— / It gives a lovely light!"

In her early thirties, Moore was now in the thick of the action. But she was never quite *of* the action. She lived with her mother; she was suspicious of liberal politics and the rejection of mainstream morality; she took a job at the dowdy local branch of the public library, and enjoyed it; she thought the Provincetown Playhouse ought to have been called "Plague House." About Millay, her field's leading light, Moore had not a word to offer in print, which, in Molesworth's words, "seems much more a judgment than an oversight." Not long after Moore's arrival, she wrote to Pound in early 1919, embracing the Village on very different grounds than many of her contemporaries did: "I like New York, the little quiet part of it in which my mother and I live. I like to see the tops of the masts from our door and to go to the wharf and look at the craft on

the river." Writers all around were diving into the fray; she was
looking past it, to the ships in the sea. She enjoyed the energy of the
city, but only when it pointed in the direction of general improve-
ment rather than individual pleasure or power. To Pound she
added, "I sometimes feel as if there are too many captains in one
boat."

The literati were beginning to celebrate the unusual voice now
living in their midst, but she wasn't sure how she felt about it. In a
poem written around this time, Moore wrote:

> *when you*
> *See a light and mothlike want to*
> *   Go in, this is to be said in favor of staying out—*
> *There is danger in being appre*
> *Ciated*

It was also in this period that she published the most famous lines
of her career, and they, too, show her keeping a wry distance from
the art she had chosen. The title of the poem was "Poetry" and the
first line, amusingly barbed, was "I, too, dislike it: there are things
that are important beyond all this fiddle." But the lines that follow
point to the elements of poetry that called out to her: "Reading it,
however, with a perfect contempt for it, one discovers in / it, after
all, a place for the genuine." Thirty years after the poem was published, she maintained that she still disliked poetry "with all my
heart: I fear and dread it, and we are estranged from it by much
that passes for virtuosity—that is affectation or exhibitionism."
(She didn't like to call her works poems, preferring the term "observations.") She hastened to add, though, that sometimes "talent
comes to the rescue . . . and automatically we are helplessly interested."

Moore was drawn into the tight circle of the *Dial* in the early
twenties, particularly after she met one of its young co-owners,
Scofield Thayer, an aesthete and heir whose art collection was valued at $40 million when he died in 1982. The publication was, in

Donald Hall's estimation, "without doubt the most prestigious of the literary periodicals in this country and, many would say, the world." In earlier decades it had been a forum for socially engaged writers like John Dewey and Thorstein Veblen, but under this new ownership it was becoming more aesthetic and less political. It did not fall into any existing camp, leaving it vulnerable to criticism from all comers, as Molesworth points out. Some blamed its eventual demise on its lack of a distinct point of view, but Moore admired that quality. A 1917 *Dial* manifesto announced that it would "try to meet the challenge of the new time by reflecting and interpreting its spirit—a spirit freely experimental, skeptical of inherited values, ready to examine old dogmas, and to subject afresh its sanctions to the test of experience." The words were well suited to Moore.

She published many of her poems in the *Dial* during this period, and she came to be well known in the literary world—while maintaining a marked artistic independence. To the writer Bryher she wrote, "I must tell the truth and admit that friends are continually writing what I resist, but that fact in no way lessens the keenness of my interest." In *Marianne Moore: The Cage and the Animal* (1970), Hall writes, "At a time when American writers were casting about uncertainly for a distinctive new mode of expression, Miss Moore, by virtue of her independent spirit, was pointing the way." One poem she published in the *Dial*, in 1921, was "New York," whose first line, "the savage's romance," evokes something of the drama of the place. The poem draws lines of connection between the present and a pre-urban New York, an island with a thriving trade in fur pelts, a land where "the ground [is] dotted with deer-skins." This harkening back to an untamed past echoes Whitman, who wrote with awe of walking the same ground as Indians who saw only wilderness. Crane showed the same instinct, fixing his attention in *The Bridge* on Pocahontas and Columbus. Moore's poem suggests that the essence of New York is not commerce but, as the closing words have it, "accessibility to experience," a phrase from Henry James. Despite her reclusive streak and her opposition to Village mores, Moore did much to make herself accessible to experience. In a 1922 letter to her brother, she wrote of a single day when she saw the actress Yvette Guilbert in a matinee, went to a tea in honor of the Benét family, attended a reading by Amy Lowell, and visited the studio of Gaston Lachaise.

In 1924 Moore received the Dial Award and in 1925 the magazine hired her and soon made her its editor. Now the demands on her time and energy ramped up even more, as she both took on a full-time job and saw her social and professional cachet rise. As editor she had to contend with satisfying both Watson and Thayer, the two co-owners, even as Thayer was becoming difficult to handle. (At one point Sigmund Freud was consulted about Thayer's attempts to abruptly fire several employees.) Meanwhile, Moore made a significant mark on the publication. She didn't yank it in a new direction and she was not authoritarian with her staff—that wasn't in her nature—but she exercised great control and kept the magazine fresh. She often made surprising editorial choices based on which written work grabbed her and her colleagues with its "intensity," a favorite word around the office. When Hall asked her what made the *Dial* so good, she answered, "Lack of fear, for one thing." About the criteria for publication, she added, "I think that individuality was the great thing. We were not conforming to anything." Her decision to keep publishing Crane despite their many differences proves the point. Unconventionality sometimes meant rejecting established figures with perhaps too much explanation as to why. This led to an argument by mail with the writer Maxwell Bodenheim, then a star of the avant-garde, who finally wrote to her, "God how I hate you and your mean, unfair, half-blind, apprehensively arbitrarily, literary group."

While residing in one of the most bohemian zip codes in America and editing an artistically adventurous journal, Moore attended church without fail. She was greatly influenced by her even more religious mother, who felt that her daughter's writing should serve a larger purpose: "You have a vivid and expanding imagination; see that you put it to the right use." Moore sought to fulfill this aim and shared little in common with Village creative types who treated faith and decorum as the bourgeois enemy. She always supported the bold and new in art but held the line against the onrush of coarse or sexually explicit content. "Judging by our experimental writing," she wrote in 1936, "we are suffering today from unchastity, sadism, blasphemy, and rainsoaked foppishness." At times she crossed the line into prudishness. She took exception to her close friend and protégée Elizabeth Bishop's use of the term "water closet" in a poem, which she found vulgar ("the heroisms of abstinence are as great as the heroisms of courage," she told Bishop). But for the most part she took it in stride that she was fighting an uphill battle, and she listened to opposing views. In a remembrance of her *Dial* years published in 1940, Moore reprinted with admiration a letter she had received from D. H. Lawrence after she turned down some poems among a batch he had sent, while accepting a few others. The letter read in part, "I knew some of the poems would offend you. But then some part of life must offend you too, and even beauty has its thorns and its nettle-stings and its poppy-poison."

In 1929 the *Dial* folded. Along with some sadness and regret, Moore felt considerable relief, drained as she was by the stress of running the show. Now she could do things that earlier she could do only by guiltily slipping out of the office on a Friday afternoon, like seeing Charlie Chaplin (also a favorite of Hart Crane's) in the circus. The end of the *Dial* was a chance to take a breath, to spend more time with her mother and brother, and of course to write; having published not one of her own poems during her tenure at the magazine, she wanted to return to composing her eccentric, compressed, and careful verses. It was a good time to move to Brooklyn.

Moore had never liked the lack of fresh air and sunshine in her Greenwich Village apartment on St. Luke's Place, which she felt contributed to the fragility of her mother's and her own health. And the small-scale charms of the neighborhood were under growing threat as the Roaring Twenties roared and commerce and construction made their boisterous din. The crowds on the sidewalks, the alcohol-drenched parties, the writers new and old seeking her attention—it was like swimming in a river that had once refreshed her but now pulled her in its current too rapidly for comfort. With the *Dial* years over, she didn't have to be here. She could step ashore. In the summer of 1929 she vacationed with her mother in Maine, a favorite place, and on August 13 her brother found them a Brooklyn apartment just a ten-minute walk from the Navy Yard, where he was stationed. Moore soon moved in and would live there, at 260 Cumberland Street in Fort Greene, for all of her many years in Brooklyn, an era of tectonic change that spanned from the 1920s to the 1960s. The neighborhood was a bit deeper into Brooklyn than where Crane lived, though within range of a long walk. For a writer at the time, it was a more unusual choice than Brooklyn Heights.

Her apartment building on Cumberland, limestone with a parapet ornamented by lions' heads, still stands (with an additional story added to the original five). It is less than a block from Fort Greene Park, the sloping green space that Whitman campaigned for and that Henry Miller used as an afternoon reading spot. Miller was probably visiting the park in the first months after Moore arrived. Had they become acquainted, they no doubt would have hated each other. Moore was attending services with her mother at the church around the corner every Wednesday and Sunday. Miller was trying to publish a novel called *Crazy Cock*.

Miller commented on the gentility and the well-preserved character of the area during his time there, spent mostly a few blocks away, on Clinton Avenue. Now Moore took in the same sights as she settled in, even with the Great Depression descending; the long-standing prosperity of the neighborhood was not so quickly dispatched. Great wealth did not predominate, but the legacy of Pratts, Kingsleys, and Pfizers still made itself felt—in proper modes of dress, for instance, with hats for men and broad skirts for women, and in the ivy climbing the walls of houses whose architecture bespoke solidity. The blocks surrounding Moore's ornamented limestone building on Cumberland were, then as now, lined with Italianate and Anglo-Italianate row houses, most of them with facades made of brownstone that had been quarried in Connecticut or New Jersey and transported at great expense. Where it meets Dekalb Avenue, Cumberland Street becomes Washington Park, which overlooks the green expanse of Fort Greene Park. Washington Park became one of the most desirable addresses in Brooklyn after the park was rebuilt in 1867 under the direction of Olmsted and Vaux. (The two had completed Central Park, and their already beloved Prospect Park in Brooklyn had recently opened while still under construction.)

Moore and her mother's expenses were covered mainly by Warner's support, by the generosity of some benefactors who admired Marianne's work, and by income from property that her mother had inherited. They lived modestly, in the kind of affordable multi-unit building that had been built more recently than the grand brownstones nearby. The church Moore attended, Lafayette Avenue Presbyterian Church, was built in the early 1860s and later supplemented by an extraordinary set of Tiffany stained-glass windows. It was the site of her memorial service in 1972, and it remains in operation.

From the beginning, the move to Brooklyn was a welcome change for Moore and her mother. Compared to the narrow and crowded streets of the Village, the new neighborhood provided far more sunlight and breezes and a sense of space. Marianne liked to play tennis in Fort Greene Park with local kids. Often she would take in the sun from the roof of her building, which afforded a view of treetops and a few scattered pedestrians. As Manhattan became colossal, Brooklyn offered a human scale. Molesworth notes that she remarked to George Saintsbury in 1930 that Brooklyn "seemed to her decorous and leisurely, as the outside world did to her as a child." She later wrote that in the wake of the move, "Anonymity, without social or professional duties after a life of pressure in New

York, we found congenial." "Decorum," "anonymity," "an atmosphere of privacy with a touch of diffidence"—these words that Moore chose to describe her new surroundings she never would have chosen for her Manhattan home.

Brooklyn breathed new air into Moore's fascination with the natural world. Although hardly a pastoral or even suburban place, her part of Brooklyn was not the massive sculpture of concrete, steel, and tarmac that much of Manhattan was becoming in the era of the race to build the world's tallest skyscraper. Moore remarked that Brooklyn, often nicknamed "a city of churches," "might also be called a city of trees." Time spent in Fort Greene Park yielded an admiration for "the massive branches of elms with the anatomy of oaks"; in one of her typically exact images, she described those branches "emerging black after a shower through a mist of incipient emerald leaves." Even closer to home, "a linden at our corner diffused in spring just enough perfume, not too much; in autumn dropping its seeds, two on a stem from the center of each leaf." Birds came to her window and drew her eye. She once wrote a personal essay for *Harper's Bazaar* in which she imagined that a crow from Fort Greene Park had adopted her hat for a perch and that she had adopted the bird in return. In the essay, she named the crow Pluto and took him on errands, "although he attracted attention in a drugstore or store like Key Food."

Moore liked to visit the Prospect Park Zoo and watch nature documentaries at the Brooklyn Institute for Arts and Sciences, today's Brooklyn Academy of Music. The Brooklyn Institute, where she attended talks and performances by, for example, Thornton Wilder, W. B. Yeats, Igor Stravinsky, and a snake-wielding zoo curator, gave her such enjoyment that "I was pitied at home for not being able to sleep in the building." The Brooklyn Institute had grown out of the original Apprentices' Library, founded in Whitman's childhood with cast-off books collected in a wheelbarrow. Brooklyn had come a long way as a cultural center. In another magazine essay, Moore saw fit to mention not only an "eminent stationer" and "a really literary bookstore" nearby where the young saleswoman "knows what the wanted thing is and where to find it," but also a particularly fine florist among several "meriting a compliment." These are the remarks of a woman finding pleasures away from the main stage, in a life of vibrant but smaller proportions.

After moving to Brooklyn, Moore spent a couple of years working in private on her verses and writing criticism, making frequent use of the Pratt Institute's then public library, before she began to publish her "observations" again. Beginning in 1932, there emerged a slow stream of them, largely written under the sun on the roof of 260 Cumberland. As Hall writes, compared to her earlier work they "seem to come from a gentler hand, more self-assured." Among these were a number of nature poems, several of them among her most well-received works: "The Jerboa," "The Plumet Basilisk," "The Frigate Pelican," and "The Pangolin." Each of these is a study, written with occasional delight but constant precision, of an exotic creature. These are very rewarding and also difficult poems. She once wrote, "When an author writes as if he were alone, without thought of an audience . . . it is this which makes a masterpiece." But Moore's reserve and restraint played a role, too. Her desire for the poems to be unmuddied and clear—and she did have that desire—was at war with a fear that she herself would be too readily understood. In these nature poems, self-protection is a central theme, as Moore delineates how her animal protagonists shield themselves against a threatening world. "The Pangolin" begins self-consciously: "Another armored animal—." So, too, did she armor herself in her writing. In 1951 she wrote in an unusually revelatory letter, " 'Society' is intolerable—so decadent and pleased to be decadent, that one's heart fails one. However, since our life depends on immunizing ourselves to externalities that are destructive, we can do it."

Hall suggests that Moore's animal studies and other poems from the thirties demonstrate a turn inward that coincided with the changing times and also with the new phase of her life that began with her move to Brooklyn. In the midst of the Depression, as men who had worked furiously in the effort to build the Empire State

Building now stood in breadlines, Moore declined to address contemporary social trends. Instead she admired the trees and the
birds—timeless subjects—and the slow feel of her neighborhood.

But the literary establishment increasingly responded, no matter how much she tried to put it out of mind. In 1933 she won a
major prize from *Poetry* magazine, and Warner's words of joy and
congratulations must have pleased her greatly: "The *Poetry* award
affects me to the very soul. . . . Perhaps, the best of it is the reliving
of the moments of my den in '260' [Cumberland] when we gathered to read Rat's po'ms & listen to Mole read them while I gazed at
the steeple [of the Presbyterian church] with its star slightly tilted
awry & watched pigeons circle the spire, against an azure sky." In
1935 Moore's *Selected Poems* appeared, along with a laudatory
introduction by T. S. Eliot. His words did little to sway Moore's
detractors, however, many of whom now found both her and Eliot
guilty of standing aside as the world came apart. In the pages of
the *New Republic*, the *Nation*, *New Masses*, and other magazines
(almost all of them in Manhattan), writers were sounding a call to
arms for a more socially engaged poetry in Depression-era America. Ezra Pound, in spirited correspondence, took her to task directly
for avoiding politics. While Moore may have felt some pangs of
guilt—"I confess . . . to writing a poem about a persimmon let us say
instead of . . . handing out the dole"—she held firm in this period,
as Miller and Crane did, in supporting the value of art that stands
outside the fray.

In the forties her work took a more outward-looking turn,
speaking more directly, and with more straightforward articulations
of private feeling. In 1943 she published "In Distrust of Merits," an
antiwar poem that is often quoted and anthologized. It conveys an
anguish over the speaker's intentional lack of involvement: "I
inwardly did nothing. / O Iscariot-like crime!" Moore later dis-
avowed the poem in a sense, granting that it was "truthful" but
saying that it was haphazard and even shrill: "It is just a protest. . . .
Emotion overpowered me." This battle between public expression and
engagement on the one hand and reticence on the other continued

throughout her career. In 1965 she said she was "much more aware of the world's dilemma" than she had been early in her career, and in the 1961 *Paris Review* interview she spoke against obscurity: "I don't approve of my 'enigmas.'" Yet she remained committed to withholding, and to studying rather than teaching.

A poet who wrote of the danger of appreciation, she began to experience quite a bit of it. Acclaim for Moore reached its pinnacle after her *Collected Poems* was published in 1951. She swept the Bollingen Award, the National Book Award, and the Pulitzer Prize in the same year. The forties had brought her a number of difficulties—a slowing of poetic output, the failure to publish a novel she worked on for years, and, what was worse, her mother's decline and eventual death in 1947. After these struggles with adversity, Moore was not too saintly to be gratified by this remarkable outpouring of applause. Interview requests accumulated, and invitations to conferences and colleges and teas; she was asked in a letter from the Ford Motor Company to help come up with a name for a new model of car, beginning a correspondence that was published in the *New Yorker* (Ford called it the Edsel, not one of her suggestions); a devoted Brooklyn Dodgers fan, she published a bit of light verse in support of the team on the front page of the *New York Herald-Tribune* on the day the 1956 World Series began; she turned up in magazines such as *Vogue* and *Seventeen* and was called on for fashion advice; she took up the cause of saving an ailing grand tree in Prospect Park in her poem "The Camperdown Elm," and so the tree, "our crowning curio," was saved; George Plimpton invited her to a World Series game so he could write it up for a national magazine; she appeared on the cover of *Esquire* and even on Johnny Carson's *Tonight Show*.

In short, Moore became a living legend, which brought some of the dangers she had feared. She continued writing, and she remained a poet of originality and independence, but the public flattened her into a charming, eccentric grandmother figure—"a kind of declawed and adorable poetic mascot," in the apt words of Jeredith Merrin. This distorted view was especially unfortunate because it misrepresented her essential self as a poet. Her sharp aesthetic was eccentric, yes, but not at all in the quaint and grinning way that her new admirers imagined. She was a challenging and uncompromising poet.

Moore likely would have honed her unique voice and held fast to it even if she had never moved to Brooklyn, and the same is true of Hart Crane. But the place did suit them both as artists and as people, as different as they were. Crane found his secret pleasures in the tawdry world of Sands Street, a social universe far removed from his friends. More significantly, he found his perch, in the same building where the Roeblings lived, to write about the great subject and metaphor of his life's work, the Brooklyn Bridge. From that place in the Heights, just on the outside of the awesome skyline, he deemed it "particularly fine to feel the greatest city in the world from enough distance, as I do here, to see its larger proportions." To be right in the center of the metropolis, he added, was to be "often too distracted," and Moore would have readily agreed. For her, the fresher air and the smaller scale of the pleasures she knew in Brooklyn made a ready match not only for her way of writing but for her way of being. In 1960 she wrote, "Brooklyn has given me pleasure, has helped to educate me; has afforded me, in fact, the kind of tame excitement on which I thrive."

4.

A Long Way from New York

THOMAS WOLFE

IN THE SUMMER OF 1931, IN THE BROOKLYN NEIGHBORHOOD now called Cobble Hill, a man who sweated the days away, half dressed, in his ground-floor apartment regularly drew stares from passersby. From the sidewalk across from 40 Verandah Place, they could look past the bars on his window, which had no shades or curtains, and see him scribbling on loose typing paper or in a massive bookkeeping ledger—not sitting at a table but standing up, using the top of an old Frigidaire as a desk. If this posture made any sense, it was only because the man was enormous, about six feet six, "or maybe a little more" in his estimation, and no dieter either. While he concentrated on his work his big, sulky lower lip puffed out and his eyes widened. If one of his stubby pencils wore down, he chucked it to the side and picked another one out of a coffee can. When he finished with a page—sometimes only twenty sprawling words would fit—he would push it to the floor with a meaty hand and go on. In the afternoons a young typist would come and pick the sheets off the floor, then try to put them in order and make some sense of the handwriting, which generally consisted of a first and last letter for each word, with a wavy line between the two (why waste time with the other letters?). All the while the writing continued, so that the typist would have to keep shuttling between the typewriter and the floor around the writer's feet.

The apartment cost sixty-five dollars a month including utilities and it contained barely more than a few busted-up pieces of furniture and haphazard piles of papers and books, with coffee cups and ashtrays dotting the landscape. It was a federally declared intellectual disaster area.

Looking at this giant who worked deep into the night, who paid no attention to personal comfort or social decorum, who drank sludgy coffee and lit cigarettes off the burning butt of the one before, those people on the sidewalk must have thought they were beholding the very image of the writer, the artist.

If they did, they were right. Thomas Wolfe fit all the stereotypes just about to a tee. (And if you believe that myths about the artist tend to be reductive and damaging, reading about Wolfe can be troubling, because he only reinforces them.) Wolfe drank too much, spoke with great volume and abandon, and recklessly dove into and out of love affairs. He could make you feel like the most fascinating, wondrous person in the world in conversation and then call you in the middle of the night to berate you in slurred words for a tiny or nonexistent transgression. He brought down emotional destruction on people close to him, not only by shunting them aside out of the (usually mistaken) belief that they were standing in his way but by creating scathing portrayals in his work. "You have crucified your family and devastated mine," a teacher named Margaret Roberts wrote to Wolfe in 1929 after reading descriptions of her husband and herself in Wolfe's *Look Homeward, Angel*—and her character is one of the book's few heroes.

Wolfe also oscillated, true to cliché, between elated arrogance and self-hating despair. At twenty-two, before he'd ever published a book, he wrote to his mother, "I know this now: I am inevitable, I sincerely believe. The only thing that can stop me now is insanity, disease or death. . . . And I intend to wreak out my soul on paper and express it all." But while *Look Homeward, Angel*, his debut novel, garnered exalted praise, including Sinclair Lewis's remark that he didn't see why Wolfe couldn't become "one of the greatest world writers," Wolfe reacted to a few poor reviews by saying, "Life is not worth the pounding I have taken from public and private sources these last two years." He informed his publisher from Europe, where he was on a Guggenheim Fellowship, "I have stopped writing and do not ever want to write again." Within weeks of this resignation notice, he telegraphed his editor, Maxwell Perkins, with a brief update: "WORKING AGAIN. EXCUSE LETTER."

※

Published in 1929, when Wolfe was not yet thirty, *Look Homeward, Angel* is a sprawling outpouring from a troubled soul. It portrays Wolfe's coming-of-age and turbulent family life in his hometown, Asheville, North Carolina, which serves as the rich and seamy backdrop and sometimes the main character. Like nearly all of Wolfe's work, the novel is a roman à clef (literal meaning "novel with a key") that might as well have had the key printed on every page. "It would be hard to find a character, a building, a street, or a scene in *Look Homeward, Angel* for which there was not a real-life prototype," David Herbert Donald writes in his biography of Wolfe, the most doggedly researched and definitive so far, *Look Homeward: A Life of Thomas Wolfe* (1987). Where Wolfe did distort or invent, it was often to the detriment of the person or place depicted, as if publicly airing the sordid truths about Asheville were not enough. Publication touched off an immediate uproar in the town, where the book was widely regarded as an obscene, malicious betrayal.

The epic novel has no plot in the conventional sense; in essence it is simply a record of one boy's experience in a vivid setting, re-created by a prodigious memory and striking descriptive powers. The tumult of Wolfe's youth sprang mostly from the life of his large and volatile family. His father was a stonecutter who, in Wolfe's telling, "saw the passionate fullness of his life upon the wane, and he cast about him like a senseless and infuriate beast." Wolfe's mother clamped down on her husband's wanderer's spirit with a "terrible will" and drove a stake into the ground with the steady acquisition of Asheville real estate, looking to profit from a booming market. She opened a boardinghouse near the center of town and brought her youngest child, Tom, to live there with her, meanwhile hoarding money with an austere thrift. All the kids found themselves caught in the parents' crossfire. Neither camp offered a true shelter for the young Wolfe, called Eugene Gant in the book. He found his solace in "the full delight of loneliness" and thoughts of an undefined but radically different future. Wolfe writes in a lovely passage that Eugene "sank deeper year by year into the secret life, a strange wild thing bloomed darkly in his face, and when [his sister] spoke to him his eyes were filled with the shadow of great ships and cities."

The novel is best when it stays closest to the ground, recording with a discerning eye the particularities of American life and the rough terrain of one boy's inner landscape. In its strongest passages, the book resembles reportage and showcases Wolfe's talent for re-creating a telling moment with such fidelity that reading it amounts to being forcefully plunged into bracing water.

Some detractors noted right away that *Look Homeward, Angel* is overlong, shapeless, and often bombastic and grandiose. In one review Frank Swinnerton bemoaned Wolfe's "over-excited verbosity" and lamented that in the book he keeps suddenly "crying 'O this' and 'O that,' as if he were parodying the Greek Anthology." This kind of critique, complete with sarcasm, has evolved over time from a minority view to the prevailing response to Wolfe. His reputation has suffered a long and deep decline since its heyday in the thirties and forties. Even where he dials back the rhetoric, Wolfe's excesses are jarring, out of step with the value accorded to subtlety, form, selection, and concision. He takes giant strides along the line between the marvelously grand and the disastrously overwritten, veering drunkenly to either side, sowing confusion as to whether we are witnessing a tour de force or an epic failure. In 1987 Harold Bloom wrote, "There is no possibility for critical dispute about

Wolfe's literary merits; he has none whatsoever." But in 1929 the preponderance of critics and readers could hardly have disagreed more. Notices everywhere heaped praise on Wolfe and compared him to Dostoyevsky, Rabelais, Melville, Joyce, and, naturally, Whitman, the original unbuttoned American voice. The reviews in the influential *New York Times* and *New York Herald-Tribune* were so over-the-top that his publisher, Scribner's, ordered a second printing. The British writer Hugh Walpole—"America had better wake to [Wolfe], for he has the making of greatness"—and the novelist James Boyd—"I have an uneasy feeling that the little fellows had better move over for this bird"—aptly conveyed the sense that Wolfe was a kind of storm that had come out of nowhere to plow into the literary world.

Wolfe was hardly the southern rube he sometimes made himself out to be; he had graduated from the University of North Carolina at age nineteen and got a master's at Harvard, where he laid siege to Widener Library in his voracious appetite for knowledge. But he did come from an unsophisticated background and from a family, he once said, to whom "a 'writer' was a very remote sort of person . . . , very far away from any life or any world that *we* had ever known." When he began *Look Homeward, Angel,* he was unfamiliar with much of the canon. Having long been fixated on becoming a playwright, he was also unacquainted with major contemporary novelists like Fitzgerald, Hemingway, and Faulkner (whose novel *The Sound and the Fury* garnered lesser reviews and sales the same fall that *Look Homeward, Angel* appeared). Like Whitman and Henry Miller, Wolfe made his start as something of an autodidact, observing no trend or "method." The novelistic conventions of the day had as little effect on him as the social ones. "Less than any other writer of his generation was he affected by the anxiety of influence," Donald argues.

Partly for this reason, his writing had a direct, unmediated vitality. For many, to read Wolfe was to feel that a man was looking into your eyes and inviting you into a very intimate and momentous conversation. The response was personal and powerful, and untroubled by critical objections. At the time of his early death in 1938 and well beyond, he was a worshipped figure. The poet and novelist James Dickey, author of *Deliverance*, tells of first reading Wolfe in 1943, when he was in the air force: "Like many another young person I was shocked and released; I felt that I was reading about myself, or, really the self that I contained but had never freed. Wolfe made me understand that I was settling for too little of life, and far too little of myself."

In the fall and winter of 1929, after *Look Homeward* was published, the fan letters to Wolfe poured in. In New York everyone wanted to meet him, especially women. The phone wouldn't stop ringing with invitations to speaking engagements, signings, and particularly dinner parties. Word was getting around that Thomas Wolfe *was* Eugene Gant, that readers could meet the man they felt they already knew. Sometimes they were disappointed, since Wolfe could be quiet and sensitive, and he took it badly when he felt he was being treated like some kind of circus animal: "Oh, isn't he *charming*?"

But more often he won over his audience, whether it was one person at a party or a hundred at a speech or thousands reading at home. He didn't express himself with a knowing tone or with the protective coat of irony and self-deprecation in fashion today. As a consequence he said and wrote some very clichéd things, proclaiming without embarrassment his sometimes naive views about Art and Life and Greed and America. But he was always sincere. He wrote to a friend, "I can't help it if it sounds melodramatic—it is the simple truth." Often his remarks began with phrases like "By God" and "Listen here" and "I must now tell you." His words conveyed the whole force of his character, and encountering them could make the stuff of ordinary conversation seem like terribly weak tea. Surely he can't be serious, a listener or reader might think, but he was—he was desperately serious. And coming to understand that often proved completely disarming, for who is the childish one, the person who pours his heart out or the one who rolls his eyes in response?

In the wake of his debut, Wolfe reveled in the attention for a time, but within a few months he grew tired of literary celebrity. He could barely get any work done. But there was a more fundamental problem, too. All these members of the chattering classes who were calling him up, hanging on his words, marveling over him—well, he hated them. The Manhattan intelligentsia were just the same as the people he recoiled from at Harvard—pretentious, full of frauds and hangers-on.

In his second book, *Of Time and the River*, which picks up his autobiography where *Look Homeward, Angel* left off, with his departure for graduate school, Wolfe mercilessly satirizes the sophisticates he encountered in George Baker's famous Harvard playwriting workshop, which had a record of launching careers in theater. Among this crowd, a show of enthusiasm for the wrong writer—just about any writer, really—met with a reply along the lines of "I simply can't read him. Sorry." Remarks like this emerged, Wolfe said, in a "not of this world accent which might be English but isn't. 'My dear fellow' and so on." Wolfe was too green at first to resist. By his own account much later, he became tied up in a "niggling and over-refined aestheticism, which, it seems to me, was not only pallid and precious, but too detached from life to provide the substance and the inspiration of high creative work."

The artists and intellectuals he met in his first years in Manhattan had left no better impression, though his own bitterness over his early failures clearly colored his view. He had gotten a limited entrée into the upper echelons of the New York theater set largely through the great love of his life, Aline Bernstein, an accomplished designer of sets and costumes who was married and eighteen years older than Wolfe. They had met aboard a ship when Wolfe was twenty-four. Theirs was a magnificent love affair before it was a horribly troubled one. *Look Homeward* emerged from the earlier, happier days, and it is hard to imagine, as Bloom says, that Wolfe could ever have pushed through to complete *Look Homeward, Angel* without her emotional and material support. But Wolfe had no patience with her circle of creative friends, no matter how admired they were, and even less affection for the elements of high society she mixed with. (She came from a prominent family and was married to a wealthy stockbroker.)

When Wolfe finally got his break with the acceptance and publication of *Look Homeward, Angel*, he grew more confident in his rejection of the Manhattan cultural establishment. In his youth he had dreamed of gaining entrance to a mysterious and glamorous world far from Asheville. In his notes he had captured the view from outside the imposing door: "I have wanted a key to enter, not a key to set me loose." But now he was inside, and he no longer wanted to be there. In *You Can't Go Home Again*, Wolfe's posthumously published fourth novel, he ridiculed the "cognoscenti" for what he saw as an above-it-all rejection of all that he found vital. This crowd, he wrote, greeted ecstatically the artist Alexander Calder and his whimsical miniature circus acts but dismissed Wolfe's creative heroes as a bunch of "stuffed shirts": "The chemises of such inflated personalities as Goethe, Ibsen, Byron, Tolstoy, Whitman, Dickens, and Balzac had been ruthlessly investigated by some of the most fearless intellects of the day and found to be largely filled with straw wadding." This kind of fashionable boredom infuriated him. To give in to it was to fail to grapple with the stuff of life. Enough parties of "the literati, actorati, and plain rotty-rotty," he thought. He applied for the Guggenheim Fellowship, got it, and left New York for Europe alone, breaking with Aline along with Manhattan.

His ten months abroad brought mixed results—spates of profuse and enthusiastic writing along with less productive wanderings, both literal and psychological. He got together with F. Scott Fitzgerald for the first time in Paris at the suggestion of Max Perkins, editor to them both. The two had a good time, but they never became close. Fitzgerald dressed sharply and wrote lean, well-plotted stories; Wolfe threw on whatever rumpled clothes were spread on the floor of his closet, spat when he spoke, and could not stop rambling. In this period in Paris, they got into an argument when Fitzgerald disagreed with Wolfe's claim that Americans are deeply tied to the land. Fitzgerald professed that he himself had no great feeling for the country. That comment outraged Wolfe. The fact of the matter was that Wolfe was acutely homesick, as he often was abroad—not for New York, not for Asheville, but for America, the place he wanted somehow to capture in its entirety. He wrote to a friend from a Paris hotel that the book he was writing was filled with an "unspeakable" love of country: "Dear Jack, I *know* that I know what some of our great woe and sickness as a people is now, because that woe is in me."

Toward the end of his time in Europe he was pouring out pages, and he felt ready to come back to the States to work more; "the 'going abroad to write business' is the bunk." Back on home turf, he thought, he would correct a literary injustice: "No one has ever written any books about America—I mean the real America."

Exactly where in America he would go took some time to decide. "Most of the people I like, and a great many I dislike, are in New York," he wrote in the same letter in January 1931, "but I can't go back there: it would be like walking around with perpetual neuralgia at present: the place is one vast ache to me." Another reason he didn't want to go back was Aline, who would not accept the end of their affair and wrote him telegrams so desperate that he began reading the obituaries in the New York papers. Soon he decided that his hideout would be "the quaint old town of Brooklyn," a place to hole up cheaply and write extravagantly. Cobble Hill was closer to Manhattan's "little sneering Futility People" than was ideal, but it was also close to one Manhattanite he relied on and respected to the fullest: Max Perkins. Perkins had accepted *Look Homeward, Angel* when Wolfe was down to his last twenty-seven cents and had given up hope of ever being published. Perkins had led him firmly and carefully through a difficult editing process, but when Wolfe moved to Brooklyn, he was not ready for collaboration on his second book. He cabled Perkins before sailing from Europe, "NEED NO HELP NOW." What he needed, he said, was six months to work alone.

Writing to the secretary of the Guggenheim Foundation, Wolfe emphasized that though Brooklyn may be just across the river from New York, to him it represented another world entirely: "Brooklyn is a fine town—a nice, big country town, a long way from New York. You couldn't find a better place to work." As he settled in at 40 Verandah Place, he found his life of solitude and anonymity congenial, not because it offered comfort and pleasure but, in a sense, because it didn't. It suited his self-image to live in an apartment that, as he put it, "may seem to you more like a dungeon than a room that a man would voluntarily elect to live in." In *You Can't Go Home Again*, Wolfe's protagonist, again a mirror of himself, also chooses a hovel in a Brooklyn alleyway: "George Webber has . . . here holed up with a kind of dogged stubbornness touched with desperation. And you will not be far wrong if you surmise that he has come here deliberately, driven by a resolution to seek out the most forlorn and isolated hiding spot that he could find."

Isolated though he may have been for most of his day, he soon found that, as he'd hoped, Brooklyn was putting him in touch with America again. In that spring and summer of 1931, Wolfe was confronted not with the "nice, big country town" he'd imagined but with the brute reality of the Great Depression. A dreadful pall had descended, and men in ragged clothes rode the subway in silence, all color drained from their faces. The stock market crash of '29 struck an instant blow to some, particularly in the investor class, but the Depression itself (which was not caused by the crash alone) settled in over a grinding period of several years. With a dramatic drop in demand, workers slipped down the employment ladder. Those who had already been stationed near the bottom, including countless working-class Brooklynites who manned the wharves and distilleries and factories, slipped off the bottom rungs; unemployment climbed to about one in four in the winter of 1932. Wolfe had never been much for politics and economics, but now, now the human toll was plain to see, and for him it could not be ignored. "Shipwrecked men" were begging for a cup of coffee, "huddled in doorways or squatting in the foul congestion of public latrines," and the flat analyses Wolfe heard would not suffice, "because for the first time in my life I wanted to know, in the name of God, why?"

The question brought no straight answer, but the years in Brooklyn did provide that measure of understanding, so necessary to the novelist's art, that comes only from casting about with a hungry eye.

> Young men were writing manifestos in the higher maga-
> zines of Manhattan, but the weather of man's life, the sub-
> stance and structure of the world in which he lives, was
> soaking in on me in those years in Brooklyn, in those count-
> less days and hours spent in my room, above my table, look-
> ing out the window, walking the endless jungle of the
> streets, talking to men all night in all-night coffee shops, in
> subways, along the waterfront, upon the bridges, in South
> Brooklyn, upon trains.

Staggering from the fatigue of many hours at his desk, he would head out on nighttime rambles to escape the suffocation of his apartment and of his own mind. The first stop was a local diner for a heaping meal on the cheap. Seeing the waiter make the counter dirtier by wiping it with a grimy rag made him smile; a man who often stirred his drink with his finger, Wolfe felt at home where the niceties didn't much matter. Wolfe stalked over the Brooklyn Bridge and back, often after one in the morning. En route, on the emptying, darkened streets, he passed the grand building on Montague Street that had been the Mercantile Library, where Beecher and Emerson had lectured, and that now served as the main branch of the Brooklyn Public Library. His path took him near the offices of the *Eagle* as well, and the former apartments of Henry Miller and Hart Crane. Wolfe's descriptions, many of them unpublished, of the smells and sights of the harbor and of the sounds of ship horns are eerily similar to both Whitman's and Crane's.

To the east of the Heights, in downtown Brooklyn, Wolfe would come upon a disquieting scene. In the twenties, the area had offered a vibrant urban bustle. Department stores like Abraham & Straus, Loeser's, and Martin's and the women's store Oppenheim & Collins all anchored a hugely popular shopping district along Fulton Street. (Abraham & Straus became Macy's, which remains on Fulton.) On weekends, suburbanites would come in via the Long Island Rail Road to shop, then perhaps stop for a bite at Gage & Tollner restaurant (which opened in 1879, before the Brooklyn Bridge, and lasted all the way until 2004). They might also take in a movie at one of the three magnificent theaters near the corner of Fulton Street and Flatbush Avenue: the Brooklyn Paramount (which screened its first film in 1928 and had a staggering 4,400 seats in its sole theater), the RKO Albee, and the Fox. In the thirties all these elements of lively city life remained, but like the Empire State Building and other markers of the twenties boom they seemed like relics of a bygone prosperity. The stores were too often near empty, the waiters too often waiting for someone to arrive. Wolfe looked around and saw worry on all the faces.

He also explored the dockyards of Red Hook, not far from home, where Italians and Irishmen controlled the flow of freight, trading favors and bribes and insults across the river from the Statue of Liberty and Ellis Island. The Erie Basin, which drew business from Manhattan beginning in the nineteenth century, still employed thousands, and the nearby Atlantic Basin employed thousands more. *The WPA Guide to New York City*, which put writers to work in the thirties under the auspices of the Works Progress Administration's Federal Writers Project, remarks on Red Hook: "Sailors from a hundred foreign ports fill the bars and rooming houses, and the prevailing atmosphere of a great international seaport is increased by the Syrian shops and coffee houses and their Arabic signs, on Atlantic Avenue." There quickly follows, though, an acknowledgment that a great seaport is not necessarily a clean one, in any sense of the word. "The residential blocks are squalid and overcrowded," it goes on, and in crookedness "the district rivaled Manhattan's Hell's Kitchen for years." Wolfe lived on the margin of this territory, which kept the rent low and the atmosphere shabby. In a Wolfe short story called "Only the Dead Know Brooklyn," the Brooklynite protagonist is incredulous when he meets a man who tells him he walked around Red Hook just to see it. He tells the wanderer, "It's a good place to stay away from, dat's all."

Red Hook was a tough world, or really an underworld, rife with the racketeering and corruption that would be boldly documented in Malcolm Johnson's huge, Pulitzer-winning series of investigative reports for the New York *Sun* the following decade. The series, called "Crime on the Waterfront," detailed the heavy mob influence in the ports of New York. (One of those implicated was Charles "Lucky" Luciano, who made trouble with Al Capone in Brooklyn in their early years of crime.) In the thirties the city's Board of Health gave out free milk to impoverished immigrants from a building on nearby Second Place that would be called the Milk Station for years afterward. When the *WPA Guide* was written, the public Red Hook Houses, which are still in operation, were being built to accommodate some of the low-income masses working on and around the docks. The project offered more than twenty-five hundred apartments, to be rented for about six dollars a room.

During Wolfe's time, after the stevedores and sailors got off work, they filled the kind of bars Wolfe liked to visit, similar to the ones Crane frequented on Sands Street. "When you enter a saloon and feel that wet bar under your hand," Wolfe once remarked, "you've got something." Here and throughout the Brooklyn streets, Wolfe found truth and beauty in the down and dirty, as he had in *Look Homeward, Angel*, becoming lyrical about what others found ugly or beneath notice: "Suddenly I would see a gaunt and harsh and savage webbing of the elevated structure along Fulton Street, and how the lights swarmed through in dusty, broken bars, and I could remember the old, familiar rusty color, that incomparably rusty color that gets into so many things here in America."

It wasn't affection, really, that Brooklyn brought about in Wolfe. He wrote of its grayness, its misery, its "shacks, tenements and slums." He went on about the "huge symphonic stink" of the Gowanus Canal, which smelled of "deceased, decaying cats" and "prehistoric eggs." But as he walked the Brooklyn streets and "saw, lived, felt, and experienced the full weight" of the Depression, "that horrible human calamity," he sensed that he was closer than ever to understanding the shared life of America, a life that was nowhere to be found at penthouse soirées in Manhattan. Aline and her high-flown friends thought they were at the center of things, Wolfe felt, when in fact they were completely out of touch. In an interview where he was asked about his impressions of Brooklyn, he said:

> All the underdogs in the world live here. The dishwashers, the fellers who run the subway trains, the fellers in cafeterias, the elevator operators, the scrubwomen, the fellers who work in chain grocery stores—they all live here.
>
> But it's a great place, too. I've seen stuff out here in great uncharted places that nobody in New York ever heard of.

Wolfe's raw, visceral energy and his penchant for mining the beauty in the everyday, the lowly, and the profane made him a direct heir to Whitman. His novels were fed by the same democratic and unvarnished yearning that animated Whitman and Henry Miller. When Wolfe moved to Brooklyn, Marianne Moore had been in Fort Greene for a year and a half, but their circles—if Wolfe could be said to have one—did not overlap. Their personalities and aesthetics could hardly have been more different, given Moore's tendency toward restraint and decorum. But they each moved to Brooklyn to escape the bright lights of literary Manhattan and to find a quiet place to work, a place a bit more in keeping with the American towns they came from. When Wolfe moved near Hart Crane's old apartment, Crane had recently left Brooklyn and his suicide was soon to follow. After Wolfe's own death, John Peale Bishop pointed out that Wolfe and Crane both embraced the grandeur of America and espoused a romantic individualism that ran against the grain of the times: "Both came too late into a world too mechanic; they lacked a wilderness and constantly tried to create one as wild as their hearts."

＄

In the course of writing a book, there often comes a time when a writer sinks into grave doubt, when the path through the woods hits a dead end and no way out presents itself. For Wolfe, everything was bigger than normal, so for *Of Time and the River* that dark moment lasted for years. He had been tapped as a writer of great promise, but there in Brooklyn, as he wrestled with a manuscript that had "no ordered narrative, no planned design," he looked around at his disheveled room and his ordinary shirts and his ordinary bed, and he felt himself an impostor. He had broad themes in focus, chiefly the inexorable march of time—often symbolized, rather tritely, by the flowing waters of a river—and man's search to find a father, not merely his actual father but "the image of a strength and wisdom external to his need and superior to his hunger." Yet without a blueprint and without the discipline to restrict himself, much of his mad scribbling was wasted, months of life and reams of pages lost to "blind alleys" and false starts. "It was a black time," he later said. "I was a creature stumbling with fatigue, almost bereft of hope, almost ready to admit defeat, to admit that I was done for as a writer, and could not possibly complete the work I had set out to do." The "giant problem of my own work," as he put it, paradoxically forced him into a less self-obsessed mode; although it did not mitigate his suffering at the time or even make his later memories of the period less painful, being brought low made him more attuned to the misery around him in Brooklyn, he said.

He later called the experience invaluable, saying that every artist must reach a state of "utter, naked need, utter, lonely isolation" to do his best work. Studying at the feet of other artists, he thought, represents a real mistake. Just as he felt he must escape those high-society types whose "favorite sport is trapping literary lions," so, too, must he stand apart from the contemporary literary establishment. In *You Can't Go Home Again*, Wolfe writes with admiration of the fictional version of Max Perkins that "he had no part in the fine horse-manure with which we have allowed ourselves to be bored, maddened, whiff-sniffed, hound-and-hornered, nationed, new-republicked, dialed, spectatored, mercuried, storied, anviled, new-massed, new-yorkered, vogued, vanity-faired . . . and generally shat upon by the elegant, refined, and snobified Concentrated Blotters of the Arts."

But the confidence in that passage threatens to obscure what Wolfe really felt while writing *Of Time and the River*: hopelessness. Money ran short as royalties from *Look Homeward, Angel* petered out, with advance royalties for the second book already spent. (Wolfe had no bank account and managed his finances so badly that Scribner's eventually took over, holding his royalties in a company account and filing his taxes. The company explained to the government that Wolfe was "not so constituted that he is able to look after matters of this kind.") Wolfe had moved into a roomier apartment by the water in Brooklyn Heights in November 1931. The new place was in a brownstone at 111 Columbia Heights, across the street from the building where Crane and Dos Passos had lived several years before, and where, decades before that, Washington Roebling had overseen the completion of the Brooklyn Bridge. But Wolfe couldn't really afford the place, and he began to sell off chunks of his manuscript as short stories, once selling a piece when he had just seven dollars left. After less than a year he moved to a smaller apartment at 101 Columbia Heights that saved him fifteen dollars a month, while the world wondered where Thomas Wolfe's second book was, sometimes within his earshot.

Finally Max Perkins stepped in and he and Wolfe came to an agreement to make the book a straightforward narrative and to ground it more firmly in Wolfe's experience. This spurred a boost in Wolfe's productivity but did not have a lasting effect on his morale. Despite a further advance from Scribner's, he ran short of money again in 1933 and moved into an even cheaper apartment, a four-story walk-up at 5 Montague Terrace (an extension of Columbia

Heights) with a "miserable makeshift" kitchen, one of his typists said. (This brownstone building is the picture of elegance now and bears a plaque dedicated to Wolfe.) The apartment's furnishings included a Victorian sofa bereft of stuffing, a lounge chair whose springs had fallen onto the floor, a rusty iron bed with a thin mattress, an unused icebox in the bathroom, and undifferentiated piles of books and clothes. At the end of the year Perkins, fearing that Wolfe would continue to write and spiral downward indefinitely, called him to his house in Manhattan and told him that the book was finished, no matter what Wolfe thought.

There began a collaboration–cum–battle of the wills unlike any in publishing history. Wolfe reluctantly delivered to Perkins nearly a million words of manuscript—the length of about twelve typical novels at the time—and told his editor that he needed his help now more than ever. For most of 1934, the two met for editing sessions at Perkins's office every day, including Sundays and holidays, usually in the evening, after each had put in a day's work. Perkins first convinced Wolfe that he had really written two (huge) books, and the second, covering the affair with Aline, could be set aside for later. (Perkins also feared that Aline might sue.) Then the laborious cutting began. Perkins mostly left Wolfe's language untouched but suggested the removal of paragraphs, pages, whole chapters. "My spirit quivered at the bloody execution," Wolfe said later. Numerous arguments ensued, as did standoffs where each man sat in silence waiting for the other to break. But at the end of the evening they would have a drink, often at the outdoor bar of the Hotel Chatham, and by midnight Wolfe would walk Perkins to his home on East Forty-ninth Street. Then he would head for home, usually on foot across the Brooklyn Bridge.

In the late morning Wolfe began work again, crafting transitional passages to cover the splices in the manuscript, and often these ran to such dizzying length and digressed so far from the main narrative that Perkins, a genteel and decorous man, became enraged. At one point, Wolfe wrote a very long set piece about the death of his father that violated the limited point of view that he and Perkins had agreed on. Despite being at wit's end, here Perkins relented, saying later, "What he was doing was too good to let any rule of form impede him." And indeed the father's death brings out some of Wolfe's finest writing in *Of Time and the River*, with "numberless touches in it showing that his eye penetrated to secrets," as Edgar Lee Masters put it, "to understandings that are hidden from all except those gifted with the eye of imagination." Eventually Perkins took over the driver's seat, going so far as to return corrected proofs to the printer without consulting Wolfe, who was dithering over changes.

Wolfe was trying now to give the story more social content and universal import. He had become drawn to left-wing ideas, spurred by the suffering of the Depression poor, which he would expend much energy and care depicting in *You Can't Go Home Again*. In that novel, he describes wretched homeless men fighting for the stalls in public bathrooms for a place to rest, while there within view "blazed the pinnacles of power where a large portion of the entire world's wealth was locked in mighty vaults." Perkins, a mainstay of publishing gentry, was far more conservative and resisted these revisions, though in part he was simply trying to get the book into print before Wolfe's name fell off the map.

When all the work was done and there was little to do but wait for the 912-page book to appear in stores, an interview in the *New York Herald-Tribune* produced an embarrassing portrait of Wolfe and of his slovenly quarters, right down to the alarm clock that functioned only when set down on its face. The article even gave his address, which attracted unwanted visitors. Soon after, he decided to let go of his place and move out of Brooklyn. The borough served as a daily reminder of the great trial of the spirit he had undergone there: "I have lived here long enough and finished a big job here, and it's time to go." With the intention of missing the publication date, he traveled again to Europe. As America receded behind the ship, he felt a profound sense of loss over his book that he compared to the grief of losing a brother. The big day passed while Wolfe was out of communication with the States, but in Paris he finally screwed up the courage to retrieve a tantalizing telegram from Perkins: "MAGNIFICENT REVIEWS SOMEWHAT CRITICAL IN WAYS EXPECTED, FULL OF GREATEST PRAISE." Wolfe's initial euphoria faded in minutes, for in his grim mood he began to think that Perkins was telling him in his tactful way that the book was "an utter and colossal failure." Several bleak, drunken days later, Wolfe responded and asked Perkins to give it to him straight and be brutal if necessary. Perkins's reply was a writer's dream: "GRAND EXCITED RECEPTION IN REVIEWS, TALKED OF EVERYWHERE AS TRULY GREAT BOOK, ALL COMPARISONS WITH GREATEST WRITERS, ENJOY YOURSELF WITH LIGHT HEART."

Of Time and the River had met with prominent rave reviews and exceptional sales, and it would become the literary phenomenon of the year. Harsh assessments appeared, too, as the book polarized public opinion, garnering the most votes in a *Saturday Review* poll for the best novel of 1935 and for the worst. But now there could be no doubt that Wolfe was more than a writer of promise; he was a literary giant. As Andrew Turnbull puts it in his very fine *Thomas Wolfe: A Biography* (1967), part of what launched Wolfe into wider recognition was that *Look Homeward, Angel* "had been a North Carolina book, but in *Of Time and the River* he widened his canvas." Behind Wolfe's style—his lyricism about the seasons and the masses and the view from train windows—was, Turnbull writes, "an urge to body forth the whole of America which only Whitman could rival."

In *Of Time and the River*, Eugene Gant has a very personal conversation by the banks of the Charles River with a midwestern friend from his Harvard drama workshop called Francis Starwick (who is based on Wolfe's classmate Kenneth Raisbeck). The dialogue is unrealistic, as is typical of Wolfe, with each man setting out too directly, too articulately, and too dramatically his own views on the meaning of life, all of which have the distinct smell of being in fact the author's views. But there is something very stirring in the essence of the scene. Starwick confides that his overwhelming fear is that he has an artistic talent and soul but will not have the power to bring true art into being: "Oh, God! Eugene! is *that* to be my life—to have all that I know and feel and would create rot still-born in my spirit." He asks Eugene to do what he himself believes he cannot—to describe the tremendous river he grew up beside, "the unceasing Mississippi," and by extension the country: "Speak one word for a boy . . . who once stood above a river—and who knew America as every other boy has known it." In *Of Time and the River,* Wolfe fell short in the attempt to capture the American experience, and he knew it, but *by god*, you might say, he was trying.

For the next three years he went on trying, until tuberculosis spread to his brain and killed him at thirty-seven. Not long before his death he wrote to Perkins, in his last letter, about "the impossible anguish and regret of all the work I had not done." Wolfe left behind roughly a million and a half more words of writing and a rough outline for another epic piece of work, this time entrusting the work to his new editor, Edward Aswell of Harper & Brothers; Wolfe had parted ways with Perkins and Scribner's in an attempt to assert his independence. Taking large liberties with unfinished and disorderly material, Aswell shaped this mass of pages into three posthumous novels that Wolfe of course never revised or approved, *The Web and the Rock* (1939), *You Can't Go Home Again* (1940), and *The Hills Beyond* (1941). None of these fulfilled Wolfe's promise or ambition. Probably no book ever could have.

In retrospect, the peak of Wolfe's life had come three years before his death, in the summer of 1935, when he returned to America after his long depressive period. While he was gone, *Of Time and the River* had been published. During the crossing of the Atlantic, on board the *Bremen*, Wolfe received a triumphal cable from another Scribner's editor: "DEAR TOM YOU RETURN A CONQUEROR." On a gloriously sunny day, he found reporters waiting for him on the docks in New York, along with Perkins. Wolfe had left Brooklyn as a promising but unproven writer, beset by fears, and now returned to New York indisputably famous. That night he and Perkins painted the town red. They even broke in to the unheated

Manhattan loft where Wolfe had written *Look Homeward, Angel* so that Perkins could see where it all began. At sunset they made a visit to the roof of the Hotel St. George in Brooklyn Heights, the neighborhood where he had toiled over his book for years that seemed to last for centuries. The rooftop offered up that vista that Hart Crane called the finest view in the country, with Manhattan and New York Harbor spread out in a vast panorama. Wolfe looked out on America, cured of homesickness. It was the Fourth of July.

5.

The Longest Journey

DANIEL FUCHS, BERNARD MALAMUD, ALFRED KAZIN

"ONE OF THE LONGEST JOURNEYS IN THE WORLD IS THE JOUR-
ney from Brooklyn to Manhattan—or at least from certain neighborhoods in Brooklyn to certain parts of Manhattan."

So begins Norman Podhoretz's brash but thoughtful book
Making It (1967), which charts his own voyage from a poor and
marginalized section of Brooklyn to a place that to anyone who
stayed behind was "a country as foreign to him as China and
infinitely more frightening. That country is sometimes called the
upper middle class." But Podhoretz didn't have it as bad as those
who made a similar journey a decade or two earlier. He was born
in 1930, too late to be fully aware of what the Great Depression cost.
Like him, Daniel Fuchs (born 1909), Bernard Malamud (1914), and
Alfred Kazin (1915) were Jewish writers raised in Brooklyn by
immigrant parents. But they had to make their way into adulthood
and success in the thirties, just as the land of opportunity reached
a brutal low ebb.

While Hart Crane, Marianne Moore, and Thomas Wolfe chose
to exile themselves from Manhattan to Brooklyn as adults, a crowd
of other writers were clamoring to get out of the poor, seemingly
hopeless Brooklyn neighborhoods where they grew up. Fuchs,

Malamud, and Kazin were all children of the huge wave of Jewish immigrants that transformed New York in the early decades of the twentieth century. Many of these newcomers were reeling from ruthless persecution in Eastern Europe, and they heard the call of those lines inscribed on the Statue of Liberty, from the Jewish poet Emma Lazarus's sonnet "The New Colossus": "Give me your tired, your poor, / Your huddled masses yearning to breathe free."

During this period, Brooklyn increasingly held out the promise of something marginally better than miserable Manhattan slums like the Lower East Side, now bursting at the rotten seams. But before long, the influx filled and overfilled places like Williamsburg and Brownsville, too, leaving the huddled masses still yearning to breathe free. Brooklyn grew to have a very sizable Jewish presence, a significant element of the character of the borough to this day. The immigrant Brooklyn that Fuchs, Malamud, and Kazin knew as they came of age felt far removed from the dreamlike spires of Manhattan's skyline. As they grew up to acquire an understanding of the world where ideas flowed, where achievement happened, they also came to appreciate that they lived outside of it. And they wanted badly to get in.

All three managed to gain admission to "City," the City College of New York, a cherished goal of so many impoverished Jewish parents of the era. City College was the first free public institution of higher education in the nation and is the alma mater of nine Nobel laureates. An extraordinary number of the Jews who shaped intellectual life in the mid-twentieth century graduated from City, including Irving Howe, Daniel Bell, Irving Kristol, Sidney Hook, and Nathan Glazer, all of them central players among the "New York intellectuals." Almost to a one, they traveled by subway from immigrant homes to the upper Manhattan campus to debate the political issues of the day in the renowned Alcove One. The school was "famous, awesome, severe," in the words of Kazin, who attended City College in the thirties. In that decade in particular, if you were mired in the slums of New York, this was the ticket up and out. For Fuchs, Kazin, and Malamud, great literary accomplishment followed. But to reach those heights from the depths of Depression-era Brooklyn, they had to undertake and undergo an almost violent passage that Malamud described in a rare moment of self-revelation: "I beat myself into shape with a terrible will."

Fuchs wrote a trio of Brooklyn novels in the thirties that have since gained a small cult following. He was one of six children raised in a tenement with six families per floor and an upstairs brothel. A seventh child had been killed when he was pushed off the roof of a building on the Lower East Side at age five. Fuchs's father, whose family had brought him to America from Russia, had developed lung disease from working as a furrier and had become incapacitated and penniless before Fuchs was born. He later sold papers from a newsstand so small that his foot wore a groove in the wall as he sat cross-legged on a stool day after day.

They lived in Williamsburg, the neighborhood Miller had adored as a child. By Fuchs's adolescence, in the 1920s, the streets had gained a harder edge. Fuchs's Williamsburg, in fact, is precisely the one that Miller's anti-Semitic parents wanted to escape when they left for Bushwick two decades earlier. Now it was more crowded, much more, and a "sweaty dinginess" clung to the aging tenements. The neighborhood had different pockets of immigrants, including German families like the Millers and Irish ones like the Nolans in Betty Smith's *A Tree Grows in Brooklyn*. But the residents were more and more likely to be Jewish, and they were often badly struggling.

Walking around as a youth, Fuchs took in the place with curiosity and wonder. He would see bums lingering by the garbage cans, couples grappling each other in the street with nowhere else to go, and regular fistfights. One day after school, in daylight, he saw two men get out of a car with pistols in hand, walk into a corner candy store on South Third Street, and execute a man sitting at the counter where they sold malted shakes and sodas—a gang murder. A cop watched the whole thing, but when the shots rang out he bolted in the opposite direction.

The thirties, when Fuchs came to be a writer, gave rise to a rash of autobiographical fiction about the urban poor, much of it shot through with the radical-left politics and militancy that was gaining currency during the Depression (particularly at City College). Kazin pointed out that whereas many of the essential male writers of the twenties had come "from 'good' families"—Dos Passos, Hemingway, Fitzgerald—the thirties were "the age of the plebes," of "those whose struggle was to survive," those who "wore a proletarian scowl on their faces as familiar as the cigarette butt pasted in their mouths." Henry Roth, James T. Farrell, Michael Gold, and, in film and theater, Clifford Odets and Elia Kazan—trailblazers like these, disproportionately Jewish, "moved the streets, the stockyards, the hiring halls into literature," in Kazin's words.

This movement provided an enlivening shot in the arm of fiction, but much of its output has fallen into obscurity; political outrage played such a central role that it dated and often distorted the work. Although Roth was a Communist and painted a dark picture of his harsh New York upbringing in *Call It Sleep* (1934), one of the most successful and lasting novels of its kind, the Communist party line was that the book was too aesthetic and bourgeois. Gold hewed closer to the right views. He served as editor of the Communist magazine *New Masses* and wrote the autobiographical novel *Jews Without Money* (1930), which gained international attention in leftist circles for its own grim portrayal of the Lower East Side—a place that could as easily have been, in Gold's view, "a hundred other ghettoes scattered over all the world." An influential essay of Gold's, calling for a commitment to "proletarian realism," suggests some of the strident extremism that animated his work.

> The worst example and the best of what we do not want to do is the spectacle of Proust, master-masturbator of the bourgeois literature. . . . Proletarian realism is never pointless. It does not believe in literature for its own sake, but in literature that is useful, has a social function.

Fuchs had his own stories of hardship to tell. But in the thick of this political atmosphere and fresh from City College, he proved to be a remarkably apolitical writer. He documented with a discerning eye a cold and claustrophobic environment—the Jewish Brooklyn he knew—but he pointedly declined to hold out the prospect of a revolution or even an escape. For him it was enough to show what happened in a small world with invisible walls. *Summer in Williamsburg* (1934), *Homage to Blenholt* (1936), and *Low Company* (1937), all published when Fuchs was in his twenties, have sometimes been misleadingly called his "Williamsburg Trilogy." The books do not form a real trilogy in terms of character or plot, and the last work takes place in a different section of Brooklyn, a fictional grim seaside area resembling Brighton Beach, where he was living at the time. Three decades later Fuchs recalled his approach in his first book: "I was determined to write fairly. I wanted to be like the man from Mars. I wanted to examine everything with an absolutely clear view, unencumbered and unaffected." For many of Fuchs's contemporaries at City College, ideas represented the only salvation from the rock-hard reality they encountered. Fuchs flipped this arrangement on its head, putting reality first. Discussing his Brooklyn novels late in life, he wrote:

> I had "ideas" for each of these books, but I soon tired of them, ideas being—for me, at any rate—unsatisfactory. I abandoned them . . . and devoted myself simply to the tenement: the life in the hallways, the commotion at the dumbwaiters, the assortment of characters in the building, their strivings and preoccupations, their troubles in the interplay of the sexes.

Life, in other words, became Fuchs's subject—but life as it is lived in very close quarters, where people are forever bumping up against things and turning down hallways that lead nowhere. Wealth and possibility might be just across the river, but here, where old women peddle pretzels all day on Havemeyer Street, they might as well be fairy tales.

Near the beginning of *Summer in Williamsburg*, Philip Hayman, the stand-in for Fuchs, seeks to gain some understanding of a local suicide. An old man counsels him to simply observe, to compile "a dictionary of Williamsburg." The dictionary Hayman/Fuchs creates would be unrecognizable to the young, hip residents of Williamsburg today, who come to live among other creative people, talking of blogs, bistros, and farmers' markets, day jobs in web design. If they harbor any nostalgia for the neighborhood's rough-and-tumble days, these novels would take little time to disabuse them of the feeling.

In Fuchs's portrayal, the place is "a closed-in canyon" where everyone is flushed into the hallways and into the fetid summer streets by the suffocation of tenement apartments. The dramas of a life lived close to the bone play out in the open, and privacy and often dignity disappear. A fight between two women in *Summer in Williamsburg* brings out a crowd to see one rip the other's kimono— something to break up the doldrums. The streets are a shabby stage, but a stage nonetheless, and Fuchs lends a vibrancy to sidewalk theater, particularly in *Homage to Blenholt*. But in all three of the Fuchs novels, ideals give way to a coarse fight to thrive where only the corrupt can thrive. Virtue leads to continued poverty, vice is sometimes rewarded, and dreamers give up hope. A father in *Blenholt* ends up seeing "the exact point at which his son had changed from youth to resigned age." As Boris Fishman wrote in the *New Republic*, Fuchs's books are "cumulatively a counterhistory to the official triumphant *bildungsroman* of modern American Jewry." In other words, the trilogy could be called "Not Making It."

Bernard Malamud's father bore a strong similarity to the good guys in Fuchs's work: Max Malamud, too, got little for being good. He came from Russia to America, fleeing the pogroms, in 1905 or 1906, at the height of the immigration boom, first settling on Flushing Avenue in Williamsburg a few years before Fuchs's parents arrived. He had very little education, as the surviving letters to his son make poignantly evident. After relocating for good to 1111

Gravesend Avenue (now called McDonald Avenue), he worked an endless succession of days in a foundering little grocery store he ran. "He used to get up at six a.m. and work seven days a week, until about ten or eleven p.m., apparently the kind of life he was used to and the only kind he would respect," Malamud wrote. (The store was located near the Washington Cemetery, about halfway between Prospect Park and Coney Island, in a place that has fallen under various neighborhood names over time.) The relatively few Jews who lived in the area when the Malamuds did were mainly shop-keepers, who struggled along quietly before struggling along des-perately. "It was not very good anywhere until the Depression," Malamud said, "then it was bad."

In his family "nobody starved," Malamud said, but financial anxiety hummed steadily as the business drifted downhill, particu-larly in the 1930s, when Malamud was in his teens and twenties and still living at home. The family made their home above the store, but the place they really lived was behind the counter, where Malamud's mother and Malamud himself also did their time. The parents spent days climbing up and down the stairs in their own "closed-in canyon," in a box that essentially defined the limits of their hori-zons. They had no social life to speak of and little time for Bernard and his troubled younger brother, Eugene. "There were no books that I remember in the house, no records, music, pictures on the wall," Malamud once said. "On Sundays I listened to somebody's piano through the window."

Private troubles entangled themselves with the economic woes. Malamud helped save his mother's life at thirteen by getting help after she attempted suicide by swallowing a bottle of disinfectant, a scene re-created in his novel *Dubin's Lives* (1979). But he couldn't save her when she died mysteriously in a mental hospital two years later, on Mother's Day 1929. Eugene dropped out of high school within a few years and later entered a never-ending loop of psychi-atric care. Malamud faced very long odds.

His father's belief in education, along with Malamud's own intelligence and drive, helped propel him out of the canyon—the family's lone escapee. When Malamud was nine, he caught a serious pneumonia, "and when I was convalescing my father bought me *The Book of Knowledge*, twenty volumes where there had been none." Around that time, Bernard made his way into an exceptional new elementary school well outside his district, P.S. 181 in Flatbush; his parents may have used their prior address. (The school is still in operation but, like the surrounding district, it has a radically different demographic makeup. Malamud ran with a crowd of fellow Jewish boys there; in 2009 the school had 1,088 black students and 14 white ones.) From there it was on to Erasmus Hall High School, something of a legendary institution in the annals of the American dream; it was sometimes called the "mother of high schools." Dutch settlers founded it in 1786, with funds contributed by such men as Alexander Hamilton and Aaron Burr. After the school became public in 1896, the city expanded it in the early twentieth century to house an exploding immigrant population hungry to climb the social ladder; in Malamud's era, enrollment stood at around eight thousand. The new buildings were designed in the Collegiate Gothic style and, in both appearance and massive scale, the main quadrangle resembles Yale University's residential colleges. (Today, alas, a huge Rite Aid stands across the street.) At Erasmus, a first-rate school during his time, Malamud excelled and began to apply himself to writing. Next stop City College, of course.

As he crossed the river to Manhattan and moved into the more cosmopolitan realm he had longed for, growing pains soon set in. Malamud came from immigrant Brooklyn, and his father came from a shtetl. In the eyes of cocktail-party New York, Malamud came from nowhere. And unlike his parents, he gained enough worldliness to fully understand that perception. In an unprinted portion of a 1974 *Paris Review* interview, he told of being in college and looking in at his father through the window of the store and seeing him with fresh eyes.

> I felt, my God, here's this man sitting here 16 hours a day, waiting for someone to come in to the place, what a shame-

ful waste of life, and existence, and all that, and why does he do it? Why does he allow himself to be victimized in this particular way, and you know, it's a form of imprisonment, and I was conscious of that, and I wanted better for him, you know, I felt a really strong sympathy for him. He was a good man, he was a nice man, he was a kind man, and I feel, you know, just eternally grateful to him.

In this passage, Malamud's appreciation and empathy come on strong at the end, as if to correct a discernible exasperation earlier on. Malamud clearly regrets that his father suffered but also suggests that he was complicit in the suffering, using the word "shameful" and adding, "Why does he allow himself to be victimized." It's a conflicted attitude familiar to many children of immigrants, but it is particularly emblematic of the experience of early-twentieth-century Jewish sons, who traveled so far so fast. (In this era and milieu, it was the sons, more than the daughters, whose success was paramount.) Irving Howe expertly addresses the phenomenon in his landmark book on Jewish immigration, *World of Our Fathers* (1976). The men who had come through Ellis Island, Howe writes, knew that circumstance and a lack of learning trapped them—"in the awkwardness of their speech, in the alienness of their manners"—in a very tight space. They determined, then, "that everything would now be staked on their sons, a decision any Jewish father could share without even being aware of it, so deeply had it come out of the reserves of common desire. In behalf of its sons [this generation] was prepared to commit suicide; perhaps it did."

The process placed a heavy burden on the shoulders of the young people it was supposed to help. In his memoir *A Walker in the City*, Kazin writes, "It was not for myself alone that I was expected to shine, but for [my parents]—to redeem the constant anxiety of their existence. I was the first American child, their offering to the strange new God; I was to be the monument of their liberation from the shame of being—what they were." To prove yourself, then, was to put a great distance between yourself and the people who loved you and gave you the chance. And what if you did so? Certainly Fuchs, Malamud, and Kazin all did. Then the psychological strain merely took on a different form. Howe writes that the high achiever in this position, beginning even in childhood, felt "a half-acknowledged shame before the perceived failings of one's parents, and both embarrassment and shame mounted insofar as one began to acquire the tastes of the world. And then, still more painful, there followed a still greater shame at having felt ashamed about people whom one knew to be good." This was in many ways the measure of that immense journey from Brooklyn to Manhattan that Podhoretz describes. It was not only an intellectual and material challenge; it was an emotional crucible.

Podhoretz goes so far as to say that if he had known what was involved, if the voyage had not been blind, he would not have wanted to make it: "There was a kind of treason in it: treason toward my family, treason toward my friends. In choosing the road I chose, I was pronouncing a judgment on them, and the fact that they themselves concurred in the judgment makes the whole thing sadder but no less cruel." When someone tells you, "Go on ahead and leave me behind," and you do it, you can choose to look back or you can choose not to. Either way it pains you.

❧

City College did not propel Malamud quickly into success. He found it disappointing after Erasmus Hall, where he had thrived, and the intense political atmosphere did not ignite his interest. After graduating he worked as a public-school teacher in training, twice failing the exam that would have made him eligible for a permanent substitute job like Fuchs's; he earned $4.50 a day, while lucky Fuchs took in $6.00 the same decade. Malamud enrolled in a master's program at Columbia in 1937, which he called "close to a waste of time." He took odd jobs at factories and department stores, and in the thick of the Depression he often visited the miserable job agencies on Sixth Avenue. For long stretches in the late thirties he was unemployed and not doing much writing. His priority was to try to earn; he was part of that new crop of writers whose back-ground meant that "there was nothing to go back to," as Kazin put it. In 1940 he took a mindless job in the U.S. Census Bureau in Washington. He found he could complete his tasks in half the day and spend the rest writing at his desk. His sketches of real life began to appear in the *Washington Post* and later he placed short stories in little magazines for no pay, but the entire forties passed before Pearl Kazin, Alfred's sister and an editor at *Harper's Bazaar*, made him a professional fiction writer. In 1950 she published "The Cost of Living."

In this short story and in several others—notably "The Grocery Store" (written in 1943, published only posthumously), "The Place Is Different Now" (1943), "Take Pity" (1956), and "The First Seven Years" (1950)—Malamud used many of the brushstrokes that would find their way into his second published novel and one of his best, *The Assistant* (1957). Each prefigures elements of the longer work's plot, and each derives its setting and subject from Mal-amud's Brooklyn youth, exploring not his own life so much as his father's. By the time Malamud's first paid writing appeared, he had relocated to Oregon to take a college teaching job. Malamud had used education to vault himself out of Brooklyn, to surpass by miles his father's social standing, to become that foreign being, a writer. And now, after some years of searching for his footing, he was finding it back in his homeland. Back in the world he had worked hard to escape, he found everything he needed. "Brooklyn you are the universe," he once wrote.

Before publishing *The Assistant*, Malamud wrote his fanciful and mythic baseball novel *The Natural* (1952) and sold it to the leg-endary editor Robert Giroux, then at Harcourt, Brace, and later the chairman of Farrar, Straus and Giroux. Giroux would remain Mal-amud's editor his whole life. *The Natural* is probably now Malamud's most famous book, due mostly to the 1984 Robert Redford movie, which strays far from the novel. When Giroux bought the manu-script, he did so partly on the strength of "The Magic Barrel," a Mal-amud story that later appeared to widespread praise in *Partisan*

Review. He found it "wholly unlike" *The Natural* and "also unlike anyone else's writing anywhere." Sealing the deal, he told Malamud, "I greet you at the beginning of a great career." Malamud caught the reference instantly, replying, "Emerson to Whitman."

"The Magic Barrel" became the title story for a 1958 collection, which draws so much from the author's roots that Malamud's biographer Philip Davis aptly says it is "like a Jewish Brooklyn version of Joyce's *Dubliners.*" As Joshua Cohen puts it, Malamud's work is "a map of the world with Brooklyn as its capital, a tenement as the silver crown of the cityscape." *The Magic Barrel* won the National Book Award. Malamud took the honor again in 1967 for *The Fixer*, which also won the Pulitzer Prize. *The Assistant* sold well over a million copies in its first twenty years. Malamud became widely recognized as a member of a powerful triumvirate of American writers who transcended the "Jewish writer" label and gained widespread fame: Saul Bellow, Philip Roth, Bernard Malamud. Bellow took to calling them literature's Hart, Schaffner & Marx, after the clothing business founded by three Jewish men.

The slices of Brooklyn life in some of Malamud's stories crystallized into a much fuller portrait in *The Assistant*, but Malamud still did not offer a wide shot or a long view of Brooklyn and its history, at least not at first glance. *The Assistant* shows us Malamud's father's world, and it is simple, unromantic, and painfully small. The rest of the country and its news barely intrude, Manhattan is an overseas nation, and little occurs outside the dark hovel of a barely visited grocery store operated by Morris Bober. As Kazin points out, Morris and Malamud's Jews generally are not connected to the wider Jewish working class and its place in history, "its unions, its collective strikes, its dreams of socialism." A dreary loneliness reigns. For just that reason, though, the novel provides a truthful portrait of Brooklyn life and American life in the thirties. The Depression fostered a spiritually damaging sense of living in a shrinking sphere. As Arthur Krystal has written, "The Thirties were not just about a lack of opportunity; they were also about hopelessness." Even Morris's gifted college-age daughter, Helen, fears that she is trapped. As she eloquently puts it, "I feel that every day is like the day before, and what's worse, like the day after. . . . I want the return of my possibilities."

For all its faithful re-creation of hard times, *The Assistant* often has the feel of a parable, with schematic moral conflicts and an atmosphere that feels obscurely a bit unreal. But it's no fairy tale; as in Fuchs, honesty, poverty, and industriousness don't add up to much, and sometimes perversely get punished. Two hoodlums rob the store and can't believe how little money there is to take. In an instance of Malamud's faintly comic but dark irony, one of them knocks Morris out cold, thinking he's hiding cash. If only he were. One day an Italian Gentile named Frank comes to the store and begins doing a bit of work for no pay. Gradually he insinuates himself into the place, despite opposition from Morris and his wife. In a poignant broken English that became a Malamud trademark, Morris tells Frank he isn't interested in his arguments, and continues: " 'Interests me what you can learn here. Only one thing'—he pressed his hand to his chest—'a heartache.' "

We learn that Frank was one of the men who robbed the grocery, the reluctant accomplice, and he has returned incognito to do penance. A simple ethical setup—but complexity mounts, as is typical in Malamud, when Frank begins to steal from the store even as he brings an increase in business. He also falls for Helen. In spite of all obstacles and flaws (and his religion), Frank seems the better choice for her, sentimentally, than the slick law student who took her virginity. But Frank's increasingly serious transgressions incline in a different direction. *The Assistant* is about suffering, and the question at its center is whether enduring pain, or at least the kind in the novel, is worth it—whether it earns you grace or simply turns your life into a depressing waste.

Malamud was not religious and neither, really, were his parents, but in *The Assistant* he seems to be coming to terms with the unique identity of immigrant Jews like his father and what they left to their sons and daughters, so many of whom grew up in Brooklyn. Malamud had become a success, but "almost without understanding why," as he said much later, he had begun thinking about his parents, about his father's "meager living and what he paid for it": "I thought of him as I began *The Assistant* and felt I would often be writing about Jews, in celebration and expiation, though perhaps that was having it both ways. I wanted it both ways."

Malamud has fallen well out of the company of Bellow and Roth in reputation, but the point Bellow was making with his quip about Hart, Schaffner & Marx still applies. In the time of the three writers' midcentury ascendancy, Bellow said, minority groups were staging cultural challenges to the WASP establishment, and the rise of a supposed "Jewish mafia" was greeted as an "unwelcome eruption." The absurdity of it was that these three men wanted only "to add ourselves to the thriving enterprise we loved; no one wanted to take over." As with Bellow and Roth, Malamud's stories were Jewish stories and outsider stories, but the resonance in them was American. To immigrate, to work and endure, to raise your children above your own shoulders—what is this but the American story?

☙

Alfred Kazin also lived that story and bore unique witness to it, with all the verve and gusto of the recently arrived, the recently transformed. Kazin rose from a Brooklyn ghetto to become one of the leading literary critics during a golden age of criticism. When *On Native Grounds*, his elegant and authoritative book on modern American literature, appeared in 1942, he was twenty-seven years old and he turned overnight into a highbrow superstar. The *New Republic* hired him as the next literary editor, a mountaintop previously occupied by Malcolm Cowley and Edmund Wilson. He became probably the foremost critic in the nation in the forties, when the cachet of the profession was still in ascent. Even with small circulations, the "little magazines" that made a home for the circle of writers Kazin joined wielded a big stick. Fewer than fifteen thousand read *Partisan Review*, the most prestigious of them all, but as Sam Tanenhaus has written, "Who cared? Every initiate knew that revolutions are created not by the untutored mob but by the vanguard, who see with clarity 'what is to be done.'" The word "revolutions" is instructive. These magazines proudly published radical material, and the unabashed ambition was to change things from what they were to what they ought to be.

Kazin had walked into the offices of the *New York Times* at nineteen to challenge John Chamberlain over one of his columns, and Chamberlain admired his chutzpah and his mind enough to scribble a recommendation note that called him "an intelligent radical." But Kazin's pieces didn't aim to incite any overthrows. As Bellow said of Malamud, Roth, and himself, the intention was to join a great tradition rather than overturn it, and the country was just now making it possible and even propitious for young men like them to succeed. The story of that potent combination of talent and history became Kazin's great subject, as Jed Perl has argued. Kazin's trio of personal histories, *A Walker in the City* (1951), *Starting Out in the Thirties* (1965), and *New York Jew* (1978), together form a powerful collective memoir of a generation of thinkers.

Kazin's family's experience and his early poverty made him an unlikely believer in the American experiment. Like Malamud's parents, Kazin's emigrated from Eastern Europe early in the century and found themselves barely scraping by in the Depression. They lived at 256 Sutter Avenue in Brownsville, near the end of the IRT line at New Lots. It was "the margin of the city," Kazin remarked, "the last place, the car barns where they locked up the subway and trolley cars." Here there was plenty of space, at least on the edges, but most of it, Kazin observed, was "dead land, neither country nor city, with that look of prairie waste I have so often seen on my walks along the fringes of American cities near the freight yards." Here is where Jews were welcome, and here is where they came in multitudes. Developers reeled them in with promises of more room than could be had on the Lower East Side. The Kazins joined the migration, leaving a Lower East Side boardinghouse for the Brownsville apartment they occupied for the next forty years. "When I was a child," Kazin wrote in *A Walker in the City*, his unusual and moving memoir of his early years, "I thought we lived at the end of the world."

The wave of new residents, many of them in the garment trade, grew massive after the subway was extended into the neighborhood in 1920–22. A dizzying conversion made Brownsville "the Jerusalem of America." In 1925 it was 95 percent Jewish, split up into mini-neighborhoods housing those who had emigrated from the same part of "the old country." *Landsmanschaften*, associations organized by immigrants from the same area or even the same village, sprang up and provided both a social life and an ad hoc safety net, paying for personal emergencies out of the pool of membership dues. Halfway down the block from the Kazins' synagogue was another they never set foot in; "it belonged to people from another province." More than seventy Orthodox synagogues lined the streets by the end of the thirties. A hush fell on Friday nights for Shabbos, with candles lit in windows all around, and the peace remained through sundown Saturday. On other days, on Belmont Avenue, a pushcart market attracted housewives with bargains on a jumble of household goods, on pickles, on kosher meats. The saleswomen harangued the passersby with a pidgin Yiddish-English. They conducted business year-round, huddling around wood fires in oil drums in the winter. By the late thirties, Brownsville was the most densely populated part of Brooklyn, surpassing even Williamsburg and its slums, with two hundred thousand residents in 2.19 square miles.

Kazin's parents, both of them Poles from the Minsk area, endured the neighborhood's typical travails. Alfred's father, Charles, who had been placed in an orphanage by his mother after his father died, worked as a house painter, which was enough to subsist in the twenties but not enough when the thirties came. A signature memory and motif of Kazin's youth was seeing his father arrive daily at the front door from the labor pool by the Municipal Bank and hearing his mother, Gita, ask him, "*Geyst arbeten?*"— "Will there be work?" For nearly the entire thirties, there was not. Gita held the family together with the stitches of the dresses she

made for other women in the neighborhood. (She had been a seamstress for a time in the Triangle Shirtwaist Factory and was lucky to
no longer be there when its devastating 1911 fire killed 146 workers
and brought to light management abuses and grossly negligent
safety standards.)

Charles Kazin dissolved into a spectral presence, emasculated
by unemployment, "the loneliest man in the world, more like a son
than a father." This kind of diminution was typical of men in the
Depression, perhaps particularly poor and Jewish ones, as Richard
Cook points out in *Alfred Kazin: A Biography* (2007). The world
expected them to provide, and they expected it of themselves; their
spirit and identity crumbled as that demand went unfulfilled. The
humiliation of it, and the resulting imbalance of the family as the
mother emerged as the head of household, left a mark on the children of the era. Young Alfred lacked a lot of things, sleeping on
three chairs by the country stove in the kitchen in winter, but
above all he lacked a dependable father. When Alfred helped haul
blocks of ice from a vendor two blocks away to the icebox in the
hallway, he carried them with his mother. "To anyone who grew up
in a family where the father was usually looking for work," Kazin
wrote in a 1980 book review, "every image of the thirties is gray,
embittered."

For Kazin, elementary school proved to be a trial, not least
because he had a stutter so embarrassing that he sometimes pretended not to know the answer rather than try to spit it out. The
pressure to excel weighed on him. Even in his teens, at Franklin K.
Lane High School, Friday morning tests (and the school obsessively
tested the students) "were the terror of my childhood," he writes.
"It was never learning I associated with that school: only the necessity to succeed." The revealing word there is "necessity."

Meeting that requirement was a daunting task. It was a tough
school, and whispers of boys being sent off to reform school or
even the notorious Sing Sing prison made an impression: "Anything less than absolute perfection in school always suggested to
my mind that I might fall out of the daily race, be kept back in the

working class forever, or—dared I think of it?—fall into the criminal class itself." That last notion seems absurd, but during this
period Brownsville carried the stench of crime, including, notori-
ously, the organized variety. By 1940 the police declared that
Brownsville was "spawning more gangsters and criminals than
any other section of the city." The ones who generated the most
press—and "heat"—based their operations out of Midnight Rose's
candy store, a little headquarters on the corner of Saratoga and
Livonia Avenues, in the shadow of the Saratoga Avenue station
on the elevated train. This group, almost entirely Jewish, carried
out hits on behalf of national crime figures (many of them also
Jews, like Bugsy Siegel and Meyer Lansky). A journalist gave the
outfit the name Murder, Inc., and it stuck.

For young men trying to make good, a sense of belonging
came from the activist politics that surrounded them. Brownsville
was radical enough to have sent eleven Socialists to the New York
State Assembly and the city's Board of Aldermen between 1915 and
1920. Men shouted slogans and speeches from the street corners
along Pitkin Avenue, celebrating the worker and decrying not only
the corrupt man in Washington but the landlord down the block, a
popular target of scorn. Daniel Bell—like Kazin a New York intellectual in the making—delivered an address written by Eugene V.
Debs to a welcoming street audience at age thirteen. Kazin himself became a Socialist almost unconsciously; the suffering of the
Depression seemed to call for a systemic change, for one, but also
"everyone else I knew in New York was a Socialist, more or less."
But he didn't find his true calling in "the movement."

Even at City College, the ultimate political hotbed, a sixteen-
year-old Kazin found his home not in the debates in Alcove One,
but in reading literature. Although family pressure had driven him
to study, by now he took great pleasure in the company of writers: "I
could swim out from the Brownsville shore to that calm and sunlit
sea beyond where *great friends* came up from the deep." Unlike
many contemporaries, Kazin held no fondness for City, even in retrospect. "The radical ambience was fanatical, arrogant, quite violent

at times," he said later. He preferred his literature class, where he and Malamud sat in the same room, each disenchanted with the school, each knowing next to nothing about the other.

But college did give him access to the world beyond the old neighborhood's horizons. As a youth he "saw New York as a foreign city" and wanted to escape the confines of his environment to get to the wider American country, to a place "where there was nothing to remind me of Brownsville." He loved the America of the paintings in the Metropolitan Museum, of skaters in Central Park (New York's imitation of Norman Rockwell), of the Midwest, of the rugged country that Theodore Roosevelt, an early hero, admired and symbolized. City College did not offer as wide a canvas as that, and it had plenty of reminders of the neighborhood. Eighty-five percent of the students were Jewish and many of them were there for the same reason he was: it was the best place you could go without paying. (Columbia University tuition cost six hundred dollars, and anyway they capped Jewish enrollment, as did the other Ivy League schools.) And yet, on the Convent Avenue campus, in the library or the Great Hall, Kazin glimpsed a life his parents had never known—the life of intellectual pursuit—and got in touch with the revolutionary power not of Marxism but of literary excellence, which outlived those who possessed it: "I looked to literature for strong social argument, intellectual power, human liberation. . . . Salvation would come by the word, the long-awaited and fatefully exact word that only the true writer would speak." Kazin would never quite shed a certain insecurity and alienation, but in the early thirties there persisted a subterranean hope and confidence that was just as Malamud evocatively described it: "The thing was there. I had it. It came with me—an almost mystical feeling proclaiming my worth. I felt it when I washed alone."

After Chamberlain's note to the *New Republic* resulted in Kazin's print debut when he was still in college, a growing number of pieces appeared in several publications after he graduated in 1935. As he writes in *Starting Out in the Thirties*, through his reviews, Kazin gained an introduction to the city's circle of editors

and writers, particularly those surrounding the *New Republic*.
During this time he met Richard Hofstadter and his wife, Felice
Swados, who hosted lively gatherings at 134 Montague Street in
Brooklyn and befriended him, to his lasting pleasure: "The bril-
liance of this young couple seemed to lie like a fine gold over the
staid brownstones of Brooklyn Heights." In the fall of 1937, he
enrolled in a master's program at Columbia, perhaps influenced by
Hofstadter's having started the previous term. As it happened,
Malamud enrolled at the same time; like him, Kazin had little good
to say about the place.

Not long after Kazin left the program in 1938, the prominent
former Columbia professor and editor Carl Van Doren suggested
that he ought to write a book the world needed, a literary history
focusing on the Americans of the last several decades. Sensing his
moment and spurred by the prospect of being published, Kazin
took on the project and wrote steadily for over four years about
American books and American democracy—and the powerful
interplay between the two. Some of *On Native Grounds* was written
at the kitchen table in a two-room apartment at 150 Remsen Street,
down the street from one of Henry Miller's places and around the
corner from the Hofstadters and other of Kazin's friends. (Norman
Mailer would soon be living on Remsen as well.) Kazin had finally
left his parents' home and moved there when, at twenty-three, he
married a woman he'd known a very short time, Natasha Dohn.
But most of Kazin's book was written in the cavernous main reading room of the New York Public Library—where Henry Miller
liked to study, where Marianne Moore first met Elizabeth Bishop,
where Thomas Wolfe met up with Aline Bernstein the day they
became lovers. Kazin read and wrote day and night, taking breaks
in nearby Automats and pool halls with Hofstadter, who was working on his own book; in the Depression era, the library, a refuge
and resource for many, opened early and didn't close until ten at
night.

Kazin was at work in the kitchen on Remsen when he heard on
the radio in August 1939 that Russia was to sign a nonaggression

pact with Germany. "No!" he shouted at the radio, echoing a widespread feeling of outrage, particularly among left-wing Jews. "It's not true!" Within a week, Hitler invaded Poland and the war was on. Now the world was at a crossroads, and Kazin's book, which addressed head-on the sweep of history, the advance and retreat of ideas, seemed ever more urgent to him. *On Native Grounds* spoke hopefully of the headway of progressive American principles, of the persistent democratic strain in American literature. In writing it, Kazin said decades later, "I felt what I have never felt since 1945—that the age was wholly with me, that I was appealing to what Hazlitt called 'the spirit of the age.'" And in fact, when the book made its big entrance in 1942, the reading public saw the significance of a young and rising Jew seizing his opportunity to write in praise of the democratic idea just when Hitler's army was wreaking its destruction.

Brooklyn writers like Kazin and Malamud confronted serious hardship as they grew up and as the Depression struck. But as Malamud's daughter, Janna Malamud Smith, notes in her memoir, *My Father Is a Book,* when they reached their prime, they found that history was on their side. Coming into their own at midcentury, they embodied a powerful combination of alienation and assimilation, and their work resonated more widely than they might have anticipated. Readers saw themselves in it. They saw the national experience.

In some ways these writers remained outsiders from the Manhattan establishment even after they made that long journey from Brooklyn to Manhattan. Malcolm Cowley noted with a wry condescension young Kazin's "heavy Brownsville voice" and his too-naked striving. For his part, Kazin held to an old class resentment brought from home and nursed a long and bitter grudge against Lionel Trilling, who in his view epitomized the Jew who snobbishly turned his back on Jewishness. Meanwhile, a plainly dressed Malamud found himself temporarily excluded from the National Book Awards dinner in his own honor by a confused waiter. Fuchs met a stranger fate. After contentment and success in Hollywood saved him from near-poverty in New York, literary types condescended to him as either a victim of American ignorance or a willful sell-out. (As Adam Kirsch memorably remarks about this treatment of Fuchs, "It is easier to shun materialism when you already have the materials.")

As separate and alienated as they might have felt, though, these writers powerfully did what they set out to do: they made vivid contributions to the flowing current of American literature. And for all of them, the source of their power, the deep reverberation of their created worlds, came from their times in Brooklyn. They had done everything to escape, and yet what ultimately made their success was the return trip. Rendering their Brooklyn days in writing put them in touch with the American narrative they had epitomized almost without knowing it. In their youth they thought everything was happening elsewhere. In fact it was happening all around them from the earliest days.

What makes Kazin's *A Walker in the City* his best-known and most read book is that everyone can somehow share in its moving look back on youth. That broad resonance, so evident in the following gorgeous passage, is bound up in the particular experience of seeking out the true beginnings of one's own searching spirit.

> I could never walk across Roebling's bridge, or pass the hotel on University Place named Albert, in Ryder's honor, or stop in front of the garbage cans at Fulton and Cranberry Streets in Brooklyn at the place where Whitman had himself printed *Leaves of Grass*, without thinking that I had at last opened the great trunk of forgotten time in New York in which I, too, I thought, would someday find the source of my unrest.

For the Depression-era writers of Brooklyn, the borough was the source of their unrest, and that unrest made their books essential.

6.

The Great Migration

RICHARD WRIGHT

MOST DAYS, RICHARD WRIGHT WOULD RISE AT SIX O'CLOCK. With the summer sun blooming in the sky, he walked a short block west from Carlton Avenue to Fort Greene Park, entering at the intersection of Willoughby Avenue and tony Washington Park. On this short street, prosperous Manhattanites had resettled in the mid- to late nineteenth century. They built a row of elegant brownstones overlooking the green space that Walt Whitman had championed and Olmsted and Vaux had overhauled. Wright climbed to the top of the hill, with a legal pad under his arm, and sat down near the Prison Ship Martyrs' Monument to work. A decade earlier, in the 1920s, Henry Miller had made this very place his reading spot when he was writing a bad serial novel under his wife's name and barely making rent on his apartment nearby. Marianne Moore would have often been in the park at the same time as Wright; her apartment was around the corner and she loved touring the greenery and playing tennis on the courts there.

But for passersby, Wright made for a more curious sight than Miller or Moore. In 1938, when Wright spent mornings in the park scrawling in his pad, black people (or Negroes, in one of the era's least derogatory terms) constituted less than 4 percent of Brooklyn's population—a strikingly low number in retrospect. (The current figure is roughly 35 percent.) Blacks did live in greater numbers in areas relatively close to the park, in Fort Greene and downtown Brooklyn, in Bedford-Stuyvesant, and in northern Crown Heights. Apart from those spots and a pocket in Brownsville, the map of Brooklyn was lily white, with microscopic dots where black servants boarded in the homes of their employers. Nearly all of Brooklyn's working black adults were engaged in menial labor—as domestics, porters, messengers, chauffeurs, or perhaps as longshoremen and factory workers if they were lucky enough to find a listing that didn't specify "whites only." And of course, in 1938, many blacks filled no job at all. It's possible that not one black man in Brooklyn was being paid to write a novel, except Richard Wright.

Today Fort Greene Park features a bench dedicated in Wright's honor. Of the novel Wright labored over there in longhand, James Baldwin would write, over a decade after its publication, "Now the most powerful and celebrated statement we have yet had of what it means to be a Negro in America is unquestionably Richard Wright's *Native Son.*"

Without the benefit of hindsight, Wright himself likely couldn't have fully grasped the historical significance reflected in his life and work. His experience and talent put him in a unique position to capture one of the central stories of twentieth-century American life: the "Great Migration" of black Americans from the rural South to the urban North and the painful adaptation that followed. As he recounts in his landmark memoir *Black Boy* (1945), Wright, born in 1908, grew up in the South in very trying circumstances. Also written during his Brooklyn days, the book originally bore the title "American Hunger," which referred to not only a metaphorical condition but a physical one. By the time Wright was four, the father who provided for him had left. Early in *Black Boy* comes this passage, which I have remembered since I first read it in high school: "Hunger stole on me so slowly that at first I was not aware of what hunger really meant. Hunger had always been more or less at my side when I played, but now I began to wake up at night to find hunger standing at my bedside, staring at me gauntly." Wright spent his childhood being shunted around the South, mostly in Mississippi. He was housed by various relatives, willing and unwilling, and even spent a terrible time in an orphanage when his mother lacked the means to support him.

Twenty-five years passed before Wright saw his father again, "standing alone upon the red clay of a Mississippi plantation, . . . smiling toothlessly, his hair whitened, his body bent, his eyes glazed by dim recollection." The sight brought home how far the younger man had come. By his late twenties, his "mind and consciousness had become so greatly and violently altered" by avid self-education, while the father remained in a life that still resembled enslavement. "I stood before him . . . feeling how completely his soul was imprisoned by the slow flow of the seasons, by wind and rain and sun, how fastened were his memories to a crude and raw past." Like the Depression-era Jewish writers who were his contemporaries, Wright survived a brutal upbringing that emerged from the even more brutal experiences of his parents and grandparents. Wright's grandparents were slaves.

When *Black Boy* appeared in 1945, others had documented the early-twentieth-century Jim Crow South, but most of them were white and almost none had Wright's raw voice, which had the resonant ring of authenticity. What is more, Wright had already made his mark and become famous with *Native Son*. His established reputation gave *Black Boy* an arresting imprimatur, for the reader knew already how high he had climbed but did not yet know just how humble were his beginnings. That Wright was known for a novel about interracial crime and suffering in Chicago, rather than his life of southern hardship, made the memoir all the more remarkable. It underlined just how typical his past really was. Pick any black man from the South, it seemed, and the song was more or less the same. An accomplished man could show you the same scars borne by a prisoner; the same neighborhoods that "swarmed with rats, cats, dogs, fortune-tellers, cripples, blind men, whores"; the same childhood apartment houses next to a sewage ditch and across from a locomotive repair depot that sent cinders floating into beds and living rooms and plates of food. On top of the physical conditions were the humiliations wrought by Jim Crow. Wright was only a skilled chronicler, rather than a unique victim, of growing up beneath a low ceiling that seemed utterly arbitrary to a rational child. Why are white people's lives so different, and why am I supposed to agree to whatever they demand?

Young Richard resisted the hard facts more than most. In the parlance of the whites around him (and some of the blacks), he didn't "know his place." At sixteen, he submitted a short story to a black weekly, which printed it. According to Hazel Rowley's fine biography *Richard Wright: The Life and Times* (2001), his schoolmates widened their eyes; they didn't study literature, and to them there was no such thing as a Negro writer. Wright's grandmother, a devout woman, upbraided him, calling made-up stories "devil's work." No countervailing voice supported him. After he cycled through odd jobs that ended badly, his black friend gave him a talking-to: "Dick, you're black, black, *black*, see? Can't you understand that?"

Much as Wright despaired over "what kind of life was possible under that hate" of racism, though, his reading gave rise to an inchoate yearning that could not be contained. In his mid-teens, "I was building up in me a dream which the entire educational system of the South had been rigged to stifle. I was feeling the very thing that the state of Mississippi had spent millions of dollars to make sure that I would never feel." Like Norman Podhoretz, Wright claims, in *Black Boy*, that "pushing against the current of my environment" required a certain ignorance of the consequences. Otherwise fear would have stopped him cold.

> The locomotive of my heart was rushing down a dangerously steep slope, heading for a collision, heedless of the warning red lights that blinked all about me, the sirens and the bells and the screams that filled the air.

The locomotive analogy is appropriate, for *Black Boy* leads us to the train ride that much of black America was taking almost as one—to the cities of the North. In the months before publication, the Book-of-the-Month Club, which had played a key role in Wright's success by selecting *Native Son* five years before, considered Wright's memoir as well. In a revealing debate surrounding the book, the board applied pressure on Wright and his editor—Edward Aswell, also the editor of Thomas Wolfe's late works—to make the ending more positive and to give some credit to Americans who were not racist. Wright rather pointedly resisted thanking white America. His response: "Frankly, the narrative as it now stands simply will not support a more general or hopeful conclusion. The Negro who flees the South is really a refugee."

Part of what lay beneath this disagreement was not only a concern about anti-Americanism on the left and among black men but also a debate about what was causing the Great Migration. Board members of the Book-of-the-Month Club, mainstay of the northern establishment, had a bit of investment in the idea that blacks who came north were setting out for a land of prospects and leaving behind a legacy of degradation. They preferred to think that the North was pulling black America in, with not only its economic climate but also—and this was more crucial to northern moral vanity—its enlightened attitudes on civil rights. To a substantial degree, they were right. The early to mid-twentieth century presented many southern black men with an almost startling opportunity. In his superb book *The Promised Land: The Great Black Migration and How It Changed America* (1991), Nicholas Lemann writes, "That moment in the black rural South was one of the few in American history when virtually every member of a large class of people was guaranteed an immediate quadrupling of income" for simply relocating. And the legacy of the Underground Railroad and the slavery-era notion that the North Star led to a place of freedom meant that for some the North symbolized liberty. More concretely, transplants who came back to visit reported that in places like Chicago, the number one destination of the time, "a black person could go anywhere, and could vote, and was not required to step off the sidewalk so that whites could pass, and was not called 'boy,' and did not have to sit in the back of the bus." The southern police didn't like these returnees, calling their new assertiveness "The Attitude."

However, most black southerners knew better than to believe in a land of real equality. You could also easily find a migrant explaining that, despite the paycheck, in Chicago he was scrubbing floors and living with several others, as Wright himself did, in a tiny kitchenette apartment in the teeming, dirty South Side. Landlords created these crude hovels by cutting an apartment into tiny pieces. They were squeezing out profits any way they could, and they didn't cut into those profits by doing repairs. Toilets were located in the building hallways and shared by several families.

As Wright argued, the South was pushing blacks out more than the North was reeling them in. Besides the poverty, which sufficed to make things miserable, lynchings and other wicked abuses occurred almost routinely, especially for perceived sexual offenses like looking at a white woman in the street. Complaining led nowhere good. For Wright, the indignities were more mundane and depressingly typical. The South offered less and less to blacks to counterbalance its many injustices.

Wright himself moved to Chicago at age nineteen, after his mother had a stroke and became unable to work. Hopes of a good job were better there, and he wanted to support his mother and other relatives. That was important. But he got on a train north from Memphis—where by then he had already been living a city life and working city jobs—largely to escape an intolerable feeling of repression: "The safety of my life in the South depended upon how well I concealed from all whites what I felt."

Part of what makes *Black Boy* such a powerful book—more powerful, I think, than *Native Son*—is that Wright does not lean heavily on his stories of hardship; that is plainly unnecessary. And he does not celebrate his own victory over circumstance, explaining only that to do other than what he did "was impossible." We come to understand that his ambitions actually made life more difficult.

Wright's decision that he could no longer stay in the South and accept his "proper place" was but one man's version of a choice that became a widespread phenomenon. One by one, men and women made this quiet resolution to head north, perhaps late at night while staring at the ceiling or smoking a cigarette on the porch. In the process they forever changed the nation. Modern-day Brooklyn would be unrecognizable were it not for the hundreds of thousands who arrived because they made this decision. Scholars have devoted much attention to pre–World War II black migration, but the fact that Brooklyn was only 4 percent black at the war's inception illustrates one of Lemann's points: the Great Migration's prime period began in roughly 1940, when 77 percent of black Americans still lived in the South, and ended around 1970. In those three decades, 5 million black people moved to the North, or about 3,200 a week, one of the most rapid internal migrations in world history. This era created the black Brooklyn neighborhoods we know today. In those three decades, the borough saw an increase in black population exceeding 600 percent, or over half a million people, while the total Brooklyn population actually fell.

§

After Wright got off the train in Chicago on a cold December day in 1927, he soon found himself shocked and discouraged. Nearly the entire black population was squeezed into a section of the South Side that was hazardously overcrowded, rife with disease, and stricken by petty crime. It very much resembled the slums of the Lower East Side and Williamsburg, but with black people rather than immigrants as the newcomer underclass. The policy of the city's white establishment appeared to be: contain and ignore. White home owners established contractual agreements called racial restrictive covenants, which constrained owners from renting, leasing, or selling to black people. Courts enforced these covenants. Closer to the poor parts of town, such contracts did not take hold; there was money in housing "the Negroes" who couldn't go elsewhere. Block by block, the dangerously simmering black ghetto spread, but not fast enough to keep up with the influx of people.

Despite their numbers, ghetto residents were kept in check politically all over the North, partly by the clout of pre-existing and opaque patronage machines. (Richard J. Daley–era Chicago is the pre-eminent example.) A people accustomed to powerlessness exercised little power. As David Bradley puts it, "Who would complain about police brutality and biased justice when in the South any group of white men could be cop, judge, jury and executioner?" All around Richard Wright, the lure of heavy drinking and illicit quick cash was dragging people under. In a cruel irony, freedom from southern subjugation brought a new sense of license that led many people astray.

Even the most savvy and ambitious met with closed doors. Low-level work in the North began to dry up as the Depression pushed white immigrant groups back down into that job market. This held true in New York City and especially in Brooklyn, where white desperation spelled the end to "the old preserve of 'Negro jobs,'" as the historian Craig Steven Wilder explains in *A Covenant with Color: Race and Social Power in Brooklyn* (2000). Twenty-four unions barred blacks entirely in 1931, with work becoming scarce. The New Deal helped matters, as President Franklin D. Roosevelt devoted WPA money to projects in black areas and put some locals on the federal payroll. Still, the northern sky no longer seemed so wide as it once had. "The only difference between the North and the South is, them guys down there'll kill you," one Wright character says, "and these up here'll let you starve to death." The nearness of prosperity, generally absent in the South, fostered "a taunting sense of possible achievement," in Wright's words, that paved the path to chronic resentment. Income stagnation brought with it a close relative, the loss of hope. In the poem "Harlem," Langston Hughes later posed the devastating question: "What happens to a dream deferred?" The poem famously closes with an ominous suggestion: "Or does it explode?"

In the case of Bigger Thomas in *Native Son*, it explodes. But the reasons why are complicated.

When Richard Wright wrote his breakthrough novel, making him the country's first black literary celebrity and among the most famous black men in the country, he had spent over a decade in the urban North. In that time he had not only done all he could to absorb a whole people's experience; he had also gained a deep familiarity with the literary canon (overwhelmingly white though it was) and had become embroiled in the intense political storms of the era. Among nonfiction writers, the gadfly H. L. Mencken topped his personal pantheon. Wright also found inspiration in writers like Zola, Dreiser, and Stephen Crane (whose novel of the New York underworld, *Maggie: A Girl of the Streets*, was a lodestone). Wright felt a desire to bring a naturalistic realism to bear on the lives of people more like him. It was an instinct shared by many of Brooklyn's writers, including Whitman, Henry Miller, and those products of the thirties who moved "the hiring halls into literature," as Kazin put it.

But Wright's literary aspirations subsisted on little in the way of money or time, as he cycled between bad jobs and the welfare rolls. Like Thomas Wolfe, he had been cynical about politics and had remained uninvolved in his youth, but the Depression gave him a newfound sense of how widely shared was the suffering of certain segments of society. A sense of kinship grew. When the relief system sent him to dig ditches in Cook County, he wrote, "I rode in zero weather for miles in open trucks, then spaded the frozen earth for eight hours, only to ride home again in the dark, in an open truck. A strange emotional peace had come to me now. I knew that my life was cast with the men with whom I worked, slow, plodding, inarticulate men, workers all." For all of Wolfe's financial woes, he had been merely a sympathetic observer of the Depression underclass; Wright was living in it, and his color meant that he was likely to stay there.

In the autumn of 1933, at age twenty-five, Wright discovered to his shock that several of his white friends from his job at the post office (the only white friends he had) were members of the Communist Party. But when one introduced him to an organization of "proletarian" writers and artists, the John Reed Club, he grew intrigued, badly in need of intellectual company. The members introduced him to publications that gave voice to the concerns of the kind of common men not generally found in the gentlemanly pages of the leading magazines; one was *New Masses*, which was regularly publishing Langston Hughes and later published Wright. So began Wright's tangled relationship with Communism, which lasted into the forties. It helped lead him to New York and made its presence felt in the ideas running through *Native Son*. Abe Aaron, the man who introduced Wright to the John Reed Club, was twice taken to task by his employers for having a black man, Wright, visit him at the hotel where he lived and worked. Aaron didn't back down or keep Wright away and he soon found himself fired and evicted, but for decades he hid the real reason. "I would never have told Dick," he said in an interview in the 1980s. "He would have been furious that I lost my job over him."

Many of the people in Wright's Communist circles were Jews, often with an extremely similar social profile to young Depression-era intellectuals like Kazin, Malamud, and Fuchs. They had grown up in "low company," as Fuchs's book title had it, and were now putting their education to use. Wright's upbringing had left him with an "antagonism or distrust toward Jews," as he frankly admits in *Black Boy*, adding that this attitude was "part of our cultural heritage." Now, as he grew close to Jews both male and female, a sea change in his thinking was under way, just as it was in so many other areas of his mental life.

Wright first visited New York City in 1935 and attended a stirring, interracial May Day rally he re-created in his story "Fire and Cloud." Back in Chicago, Wright got himself hired by the Federal Writers' Project, a creation of the WPA, and was appointed as a supervisor—probably, Rowley says, the most prestigious job for a black man in the whole city. On the South Side, he formed a black writers' group that distanced itself from the Harlem Renaissance and—despite an embrace of left-wing ideas—from Marxist dogma as well. "No theory of life can take the place of life," Wright said, sounding a lot like Daniel Fuchs. This group, with Wright as a keystone, produced a great deal of literature over the next fifteen years. Nevertheless, one year in, Wright was itching to join the fray in Harlem, the hot center of black culture, and saying of Chicago, "Most of the young artists and writers with a tinge of talent flee this city as if it were on fire." A year later, he did, too.

Harlem, when Wright came to live there in June 1937, at the age of twenty-nine, was crowded with a huge proportion of New York City's black population. Yet it had not a single public high school. Police brutality ran rampant. The ground was fertile for protest culture, and Wright plunged back into the life of the Party, using its network to get his feet on the ground. He began working as the Harlem correspondent for the Communist newspaper the *Daily Worker*. He soon tired of the demanding job and of Harlem, which for all its cultural and intellectual life was still a place, he felt, that specialized in entrapping the poor. Wright penned an essay called "Blueprint for Negro Writing" that dropped a bomb on the Harlem Renaissance, which he considered "parasitic and mannered." Its authors, he wrote, had "entered the Court of American Public Opinion dressed in the knee-pants of servility. . . . For the most part these artistic ambassadors were received as though they were French poodles who do clever tricks." These were not the words of someone who wanted to join the club, whether the club was Harlem, the Communist Party, or even the black literary tradition in its existing form.

Success helped fortify his position. In 1937, *Story* magazine was seriously considering his short-story collection in a nationwide competition for a book contract with Harper & Row. At this point, two men who played pivotal roles in the life of Thomas Wolfe fatefully entered Wright's. Sinclair Lewis, the Nobel winner whose fulsome praise helped launch Wolfe into fame, served as a judge on the magazine's panel and came down firmly against Wright's work, calling it "dreadfully repetitive" and "essentially false." Edward Aswell of Harper sided with several others in over-ruling Lewis without hesitation. It was a bellwether moment in Wright's life. The black man from the South made a great impression on Aswell, who was often, in his daughter's words, "quite conservative politically and rather narrow minded." According to his biographer Hazel Rowley, in 1941, the year after Aswell published *Native Son*, he wrote in his class report to Harvard's alumni association, "The best-read man I have ever met, the most thoughtful and courageous, and the one who seemed to me most truly 'educated,' was not a college professor, nor even a college graduate, but a young Negro, son of an itinerant day-laborer, whose formal education was limited to the grade schools in—of all places—Mississippi." The respect ran both ways. In 1957 the author wrote to Aswell, "I would rather die than let you down."

Soon Wright impetuously got engaged to his landlady's daughter, making an unromantic decision that it was time he got married. (He had very recently proposed to a black woman in Brooklyn and been roundly rejected by the father for having poor prospects.) Getting a marriage license involved blood tests at the time, and when Wright's fiancée tested positive for syphilis, he became enraged and coldly cut off the relationship. He left the Harlem rooming house to move in with a couple he was close to, Herbert and Jane Newton. Prominent Communists whom Wright had known in Chicago, they lived in Fort Greene, in an apartment in a charming house that still stands at 175 Carlton Avenue, a stone's throw from Fort Greene Park. Herbert had been the only black member of the "Atlanta Six," who were jailed in 1930 for distributing anti-lynching leaflets. According to Rowley, Newton faced a possible death penalty if convicted. Long before the nation was calling for civil rights, the Communist Party showed a willingness to break down color barriers, a fact that plays a role in *Native Son*. Jane Newton was a white woman. She and her black husband were a very early progenitor of the many interracial couples now living in Fort Greene. It hardly needs saying that it caused problems. When they were arrested in Chicago for resisting eviction, her race put an unusual spin on the couple's case; an attorney recognized her and told the judge she came from a "good family." The judge put her husband in jail and sent her to a psychiatric hospital.

Wright took a liking to Brooklyn immediately, writing to a friend, "I'm staying in Brooklyn for good now, that is, as long as I'll be in New York." The recent release of his award-winning collection *Uncle Tom's Children*, in March 1938, had launched him and spurred him to new achievement. He applied immediately for the "creative work" program of the Federal Writers' Project, and approval now allowed him to write full-time. Even before coming to Brooklyn he had begun working at night on a novel set in Chicago. This was *Native Son*, which was soon coming into its own in Fort Greene Park. After writing in the morning hours, he would return to the house and ask for Jane's opinions about the book. Frequently they disagreed, raising their voices over the din of the Newtons' children. Jane warned him about how some scenes would be received. Usually he stubbornly stuck to his approach.

☙

Although Wright was now a rising star and could feel justified in a more optimistic outlook, *Native Son* bears the stamp of "the full weight of his anger," as Irving Howe put it. It was an anger that stretched back to Wright's fatherless childhood, to poverty and humiliating jobs, and to the frustration of a northern promised land that reneged on its promises. The uneducated and bitter protagonist is a young black man in Chicago named Bigger Thomas. To Bigger, Wright later said, America and the South Side "contained no spiritual sustenance, had created no culture which could hold and claim his allegiance and faith, had sensitized him and had left him stranded, . . . a hot and whirling vortex of undisciplined and unchannelized impulses." Something old-fashioned and even conservative underlies that thoughtful sentence. It is a strain of thinking that runs through Kazin and Malamud and

Wolfe and all the way back to Whitman. For them, a belief that survives all anger is the belief that culture is a life-changing force, that the shared struggle for meaning, accreting over decades and centuries, provides an irreplaceable "spiritual sustenance." Wright, buoyed by this idea, created a novel about his rage instead of turning his back on the country in disgust.

In *Black Boy*, Wright offers a thought that might be surprising from a man who could so easily have rejected the nation's cultural heritage: "Whenever I thought of the essential bleakness of black life in America, I knew that Negroes had never been allowed to catch the full spirit of Western civilization, that they had lived somehow in it but not of it." The sentiment is just the same as Saul Bellow's when he spoke of the rise of midcentury Jewish writers: we only want to join a great tradition.

Nevertheless, for Richard Wright, to join the tradition meant providing a shock to it. After *Uncle Tom's Children* appeared in print, he once said, "I found that I had written a book which even bankers' daughters could read and weep over and feel good about. I swore to myself that if I ever wrote another book, no one would weep over it; that it would be so hard and deep that they would have to face it without the consolation of tears."

And indeed *Native Son* is a hard and unconsoling book. It opens with Bigger Thomas coldly laying waste to a rat in his family's filthy apartment. Bigger, a young man adrift in the South Side, hates his family because "he knew that they were suffering and that he was powerless to help them." He is known for being "always in trouble" and has been in reform school. His only plan is to pull another burglary with his buddies, but struck by fear he punches one of his would-be accomplices to escape committing the crime. At his mother's incessant urging, Bigger goes to see about a job possibility arranged by the relief system. Somewhat improbably, a Mr. Dalton, a wealthy man who likes helping the poor, decides to hire him as a driver. Bigger's first task is to chauffeur for the man's daughter, Mary. Unbeknownst to her father, Mary asks Bigger to take her to see her Communist lover, a man named Jan. Then Mary and Jan begin to make out in the backseat, plying each other and Bigger with alcohol all along as he drives them round and round a park. Bigger winds up carrying a senselessly drunk Mary up the stairs to her room back at her home. In a moment of panic that he'll be discovered in her bedroom, he puts a pillow to her face to quiet her and accidentally kills her. This sets off a grizzly and unnerving attempt to get rid of the body and escape the consequences Bigger knows he will suffer.

On one level the book is a crime novel that becomes a court-room drama, moving along speedily, imbued with a stomach-churning anxiety and a dark feeling of inevitability. On another it is a social novel about the place of the black man in northern urban life, and the climax comes with an impassioned speech about the moral forces that create the Bigger Thomases across America. We can imagine Wright creating the world of the novel as he sat at the peak of Fort Greene Park. On two sides were lovely brown-stones with entrances for servants, while spread out nearby was a five-block slum nicknamed the "Jungle." The slum was a potent symbol of the decay that was beginning to spread through Brook-lyn's black community. After the drafty rooming houses and seeth-ing poverty of Harlem, Fort Greene had won him over in part because in general it was not a ghetto, as Hazel Rowley told me. He could find a good black barber there. While Harlem had much the same character as the "black belt" of the South Side, Fort Greene remained multicolored and therefore less condemned to neglect. The black population was not as segregated in Brooklyn and was still relatively small, though Bedford-Stuyvesant was gaining a sig-nificant black presence.

Integrated neighborhoods would soon become a rarity in Brooklyn, too. During precisely the period when Wright moved to Brooklyn, the New Deal–created Home Owners' Loan Corpora-tion made a simple but highly influential map of the borough, similar to others drawn up nationwide. The object was to codify the relative risk of giving out mortgages in various neighbor-hoods, in order to stem the Depression tide of foreclosures and bank failures. The methodology behind the map contributed to disaster for many communities in Brooklyn, which is to say many families, many children. The grading scale explicitly took account of an area's ethnic and racial makeup in assessing its suitability for investment, as Wilder writes. Jews were derided as "Communistic type of people"; Italian neighborhoods were downgraded for their "mixture of low grade races"; but, most of all, the creators of the map put up a wall around black areas, neighborhoods that already faced an uphill struggle. Fort Greene, though mixed, escaped a failing grade as HOLC staff approved of its "British" ancestry. Bedford-Stuyvesant of course garnered the lowest grade, a D, and Clinton Hill was judged harshly despite a relative lack of problems. Not one of the eighteen neighborhoods that received a B– or better had any black presence.

To receive a D grade was to be judged unfit for mortgage investment. Grade D places were often colored red on these maps, a practice that gave rise to the term "redlining" for the resulting financial boycott. The federal government had officially approved the notion that it was safer not to take any chances on aiding black neighborhoods.

When Wright was working on *Native Son* on the eve of his thirtieth birthday, the lives and hopes of black men in Brooklyn were festering in grim areas that saw few police or social services. Craig Steven Wilder tells us that at the edge of Wright's neighborhood, on Fleet Street (which today skirts the edge of Long Island University), the Brooklyn Urban League went house to house and found among them a single one with an indoor bath. Meanwhile, as Marianne Moore once described, in the brownstones of Fort Greene the lives of whites and blacks intertwined in an arrangement that could be seen as mutually beneficial but that cast a dark shadow of historical familiarity: wealthy home owners had whole staffs of domestic servants, many of them black. What went on between owner and servant inside those houses? What might happen if things went badly? Enter Bigger Thomas.

Native Son is more valuable as a document and a literary landmark than it is as a fully realized novel; Wright said while working on the book that plausibility was not as important as getting across what he wanted to say. But black literature has resonated ever since from the force of *Native Son*'s example. Among the notable books to follow in its footsteps was Claude Brown's hugely popular autobiographical novel *Manchild in the Promised Land* (1965). It chronicled without self-pity Brown's Harlem youth in the forties and fifties, when he racked up a rap sheet beginning before his tenth birthday and got himself kicked out of numerous schools before dramatically turning himself around. In Wright's time, it took a lot of temerity to create as his "hero" a black man who is violent and unlikable. Viewed from that perspective, *Native Son* flies in the face of political correctness. In writing it he had to "steel himself to go against accepted ideas," as Rowley writes. Many black readers were outraged by how closely Bigger Thomas resembled a racist's view of a young Negro man. Wright had vigorous arguments with people who read the manuscript in progress and wondered if Bigger had to be so hard to respect. Many whites wished that the book had not skewered even those whites who meant well, as the Daltons do in the story. Wright said, "The average moral-minded American simply does not want to believe that his attitude toward others can breed personalities so thwarted and twisted."

Native Son also sounded an alarm about the worsening conditions in the black ghettoes and suggested that not all young men trapped within them would simply lie down and accept their fate. Such a notion now appears unremarkable but was a prescient and needed warning at the time. Granted, racial troubles had already been brewing, including in New York. A serious race riot shook Harlem in 1935 and by the 1940s Bedford-Stuyvesant, where most of Brooklyn's blacks lived, was a known problem area with very poor health and housing conditions. But comparison with the South was a convenient way to make the bad look good. As Nicholas Lemann poignantly illustrates, few people of any color could see that with the Great Migration would come such crippling urban problems nationwide—that the "inner city" would become a phrase with such dispiriting connotations. Northern cities were objects of black desire. A saying among young southern boys, Rowley says, was "Lawd, I'd rather be a lamppost in Chicago than the President of Miss'sippi." The common perception was that northern industrial centers would mean less bigotry and better access to solid jobs—in infrastructure projects, in stockyards and the post office (Chicago), in auto factories (Detroit), and on the dockyards and in manufacturing plants (Brooklyn). Many blacks believed that life in the North represented a huge step up and would keep getting better—and in many respects that was true. Aside from higher wages, with the migration came the Harlem Renaissance; the flourishing of jazz; black-owned companies and cultural organizations; black political leaders like Brooklyn's Shirley Chisholm, the first black woman elected to Congress; and a black middle class. According to Harold X. Connolly's *A Ghetto Grows in Brooklyn*, by 1970, 43 percent of Brooklyn's blacks were employed in white-collar fields. Success began to spread to the South, too. Well-meaning whites focused on such advances and didn't pay much attention to more ominous developments.

As late as 1962, twenty-two years after *Native Son*, when Michael Harrington woke up readers with his book on poverty called *The Other America*, a persistent denial was keeping America from taking a hard look at urban slums. (The 1963 Dwight Macdonald review in the *New Yorker* that put the book in the spotlight was aptly titled "The Invisible Poor.") At that time, as Lemann says, hearing the word "poor" would cause most Americans to form a rural white image, probably from Appalachia. Even in *The Other America*, black poverty takes up only one chapter. When the federal government began battling entrenched poverty in the cities during the John F. Kennedy and especially the Lyndon B. Johnson administrations, insiders committed themselves to it because they felt they could win. Senator Robert F. Kennedy spearheaded an important project in 1966 to rehabilitate Bedford-Stuyvesant, which created a model for many other programs and inspired hope. With the country in a prosperous postwar run and liberalism in ascendancy, the government felt strong. In the ensuing decades, reality proved stronger.

Chicago's South Side; Gary, Indiana; downtown Detroit; Harlem; and Brooklyn's Brownsville, East New York, and Bedford-Stuyvesant—these places were supposed to offer a promising future. By the seventies or eighties, for many they were synonymous with crime and social breakdown, despite attempts at government intervention. Numerous success stories happened, but as Lemann points out, success often meant leaving the ghettoes rather than improving them, just as it had in Kazin's Brownsville and Fuchs's Williamsburg.

After his time on Carlton Place in Fort Greene, Wright moved several times along with the Newtons, who'd become very dear friends. He lived with them at 552 Gates Avenue in Bedford-Stuyvesant and 101 Lefferts Place in Clinton Hill in 1938–39, all the while revising *Native Son*. These neighborhoods were more dark-skinned, and the interracial makeup of the household caused trouble from various quarters; Rowley writes that the landlord on Lefferts Place, a West Indian black man, asked them to move out because he didn't like all the "mixing" going on in their apartment. Wright joined the Newtons again at 343 Grand Avenue in Clinton Hill in 1940 after a peripatetic year in which he impetuously married a dancer named Dhimah Meidman. They quickly separated. Soon he reconnected with Ellen Poplowitz, a lovely woman he had met through the Newtons. She dropped by one day, ostensibly to see Jane, and everything changed. Richard appeared at the top of the stairs and called Ellen's name. Suddenly there wasn't any question what the future held. "It was a really eerie thing," Ellen said. "I knew immediately that my family counted for nothing. . . . I just moved in with Dick right in that house."

Ellen came from difficult beginnings in a Jewish family who

lived on Brooklyn's Eastern Parkway, and her upbringing carried echoes of the Jewish writers emerging at this time. Studying at P.S. 178 and at Girls' Commercial High School left her isolated from her uneducated and distant parents. At seventeen she ran away from home and soon joined the Communist Party, eventually heading the branch on Fulton Street in Brooklyn. Ellen's parents disapproved of Richard, famous or not, but the young couple moved together to 467 Waverley Avenue, married very quietly in March 1941, and later settled in a four-room apartment at 11 Revere Place, in Crown Heights. A daughter, Julia, was born at the Jewish Hospital in Brooklyn in April 1942, and Ellen heard nurses gossiping that, as Rowley puts it, "somebody had had a *black baby*." Immediately enveloping his child with love and worry, Richard sought out a new, more desirable place to live.

Wright soon moved his family into a house on Middagh Street in Brooklyn Heights that was chock-full of well-known writers. George Davis, a magazine editor who had published Wright's story "Almos' a Man," had invited him to join the household. The Wrights' time there brought its own difficulties, and after about a year they moved back to Clinton Hill, to 89 Lefferts Place, where they lived for two years. It was there that he finished writing the autobiography that became *Black Boy*. While living on Middagh, Wright took a trip to Nashville, Tennessee, to give a speech to a racially mixed audience at Fisk University, a historically black school. He spoke informally about his experiences with race in both the South and the North, and in the middle he noticed that the audience was "terribly still." It became clear to him that no one there had heard someone talk so frankly about race. Wright knew he was on to something. Making people uncomfortable was a specialty. At the end of the debate with Dorothy Canfield Fisher of the Book-of-the-Month Club the following year, Wright would write to her, "I think it is significant that those American writers who influenced me were all rebels of a sort."

Wright also told her that he was much influenced by the "springs of thought" found in foreign countries. Within two years, Wright and his family moved to Paris for what was supposed to be a temporary stay, but there he felt an acceptance of blacks that gave him pause. Soon the family moved to Europe permanently. Wright published a number of books thereafter, including the novels *The Outsider*, *Savage Holiday*, and *The Long Dream*, and the nonfiction books *Black Power*, *The Color Curtain*, and *White Man, Listen!* None of these was as well received as *Native Son* and *Black Boy*, and the reviews, particularly in the States, were mixed and sometimes even hostile.

Many of Wright's followers believed then, and believe still, that in Europe he declined as a writer because he had removed himself from the environment that had stoked his best material. The problem of race in America was no longer so near at hand, which was, of course, part of the reason he made the move. In any case, it is regrettable for American literature and for Brooklyn literature that Wright did not stay. Very much like Fuchs, Malamud, and Kazin, who grew up in the same era, Wright dramatized what happens when the American desire for better comes up against a wall built by others. For those who could not understand it or did not want to, they showed what happens in a "closed-in canyon," where suffering becomes accepted, where dreams get deferred.

7.

The Birth of Brooklyn Cool

"FEBRUARY HOUSE" AND TRUMAN CAPOTE

THE BROOKLYN HEIGHTS HOUSE THAT RICHARD WRIGHT MOVED into in 1942 with his wife and newborn was already famous in New York's literary and artistic circles. A strange old three-story house whose wedding-cake architecture resembled nothing else on the short, narrow lane, it stood at 7 Middagh Street, just off the corner of Columbia Heights. This was the ragged northernmost section of the neighborhood, at the precipice of a relatively steep drop where the Heights came down from its heights, quickly giving way to a more commercial and seedier neighborhood below. That low-lying area, beginning near the landing of the old Fulton Ferry immortalized by Whitman and spreading north and east, is now called Dumbo and is no longer seedy at all. But there, in Wright's time, stood the notorious brothels and sailor bars of Sands Street that Hart Crane had so loved. Just as the storied old Heights and the scruffy Fulton Ferry area almost literally met at Middagh Street, so, too, did the noted dwelling there reflect a strange blend—or was it a clash?—between middle-class respectability and *la vie de bohème*.

When the Wrights arrived, the house on Middagh Street had been home to a rotating ensemble cast of writers and other artists for nearly two years. During that span it hosted not only nightly dinner parties of a kind but frequent all-hours house parties where the guest list doubled as a Who's Who of twentieth-century creative and intellectual life. Sherill Tippins gives an engaging account of this literary hothouse in her 2005 book *February House*, to which I owe a debt for many of the facts in this chapter. (Anaïs Nin dubbed the Middagh Street ménage February House because many of the tenants had birthdays that month.)

The experiment had all been the larky idea of George Davis, the enterprising and ebullient magazine editor. Davis served in the late thirties as the literary editor at *Harper's Bazaar*, but "served" is a misleading word, and the name of the publication, too, now conjures up the wrong connotations. Armed with an expense account for boozy lunches and a tongue for biting gossip, Davis was flagrantly insubordinate and turned his section of the magazine into a fiefdom where he presided over the boldest and riskiest work from talents he expertly identified and wooed. The latest surrealist coup, or an Elizabeth Bishop verse, or a Christopher Isherwood story that sketched life in Berlin during the rise of the Nazis appeared alongside fashion spreads and ads for cosmetics in what was ostensibly a mainstream glossy. After a time, everyone wanted to write for Davis's section, and the boldface names he attracted justified his salary and behavior, right up until they didn't.

One of Davis's fresh targets, in the summer of 1940, was Carson McCullers, the tiny young woman who had just unleashed a storm with her debut novel about freakish outsiders in a southern small town. *The Heart Is a Lonely Hunter* was "a sit-up-and-take-notice book for anyone to write," Clifton Fadiman wrote in the *New Yorker*, "but that a round-faced, Dutch-bobbed girl of twenty-two should be its author simply makes hay of all the literary rules and regulations." McCullers snapped to attention when she received a note from an editor with a formidable reputation and she quickly accepted a lunch invitation. She was surprised to find a pudgy, mischievous young man, George Davis, awaiting her at the upscale restaurant in his usual secondhand clothes. He had a special fondness for her book, he told her, as it captured something of his own upbringing in little Clinton, Michigan, where he wandered around failing to fit in. Insisting that they both eat and drink heartily, the young man whom the poet Ben Hecht called "the funniest man in America" regaled her with tales of living in his twenties in 1920s Paris, when "*tout le monde* was there," making art and mischief on the cheap. He had written a novel at that time called *The Opening of a Door* (1931), a critical success now long forgotten. Soon Davis was visiting McCullers's apartment and excavating a disturbing story she'd written about a gay military man—risqué stuff under any conditions, particularly suspect while a war brewed. He gave her a generous contract for it, when she had barely any money. The odd couple of sorts, he gay and she bisexual, hit it off from day one, holding hands and talking into the night at cheap restaurants.

She confided to him about the troubles in her marriage, to the young man she'd moved with to New York, and, come September, he confided in her after another disagreement with his boss left him out of a job. The two began talking half seriously about living together, without McCullers's husband, in a kind of do-it-yourself writers' retreat. They considered the countryside but swiftly rejected it; Davis said he could never stand the isolation, and that a running brook sounded to him like a rumbling subway train. But an atmosphere of quiet and the feel of a getaway seemed attractive.

McCullers joined Davis in seeing the promise in the crumbling grandeur of 7 Middagh Street. The house had been converted to a boardinghouse and fallen into disrepair before being offered for rent. By this time, Brooklyn Heights, particularly at its edges, had slipped from its status as an exclusive domain of the wealthy families whose leading men commuted to skyscrapers downtown. When McCullers and Davis came on the scene in 1940, Brooklyn was just now emerging from a brutal decade. Thomas Wolfe had lived just a few blocks away in the early to mid-thirties when he wandered the streets surveying the Depression's toll. On Middagh Street in 1940, a reputedly rich old woman shared her house with a dozen stray dogs and a monkey. Another neighbor sometimes delivered coal. The principal driving force of local decline, as the genteel locals viewed it, was the subway, whose expansion in Brooklyn always brought both development and a leveling effect that left the wealthier population disconcerted. The subway had come to the Heights in 1908, binding Brooklyn and Manhattan more tightly together. The Brooklyn Bridge opened in 1883, the Williamsburg Bridge in 1903, and the Manhattan Bridge in 1909, all to the same effect. Where mass transportation came, neighborhoods changed. Coney Island, for example, was a getaway beach resort for the relatively well-to-do before the train pulled into the station packed with anyone able to buy a token. Now it's a crowded egalitarian carnival of exposed flesh and fried dough, and nearby are some of the poorest housing projects in the five boroughs.

The Heights came to have a bit of a bustling and diverse feel, more familiar to Manhattan than to this tranquil oasis. Some of the houses nearest to the subway were split into apartments—the horror—and then into boardinghouses, like 7 Middagh. A few bordellos even opened—genuine horror. Davis and McCullers were, in effect, looking to take advantage of this downward slide. For Davis in particular, whose taste ran to sailor bars and decorative bric-a-brac, part of the appeal of 7 Middagh was that it seemed the perfect place to slum it. Nevertheless, at seventy-five dollars a month, the place was beyond the pair's collective range. Undeterred, Davis decided they should recruit more writer-tenants to take the plunge with them. There was more than enough space, and why couldn't their retreat be more of a salon than a hiding place? Davis immediately set out to try to draw Wystan Auden to Middagh Street.

In 1940, W. H. Auden was already among the best-known poets in the world at thirty-three. He would seem an unlikely candidate to join a kooky commune in a ramshackle house. But he was quite fond of Davis, who had served as his generous guide on his first real visit to New York. Auden had described him, echoing a theme, as the wittiest man he knew. More to the point, Auden had grown dissatisfied with his current living situation and was desperately short of money. After arriving in America in 1939, he had settled at

1 Montague Terrace, only six blocks away in the Heights. (Around the corner, Alfred Kazin was writing *On Native Grounds* at the same time, and often visiting with Richard Hofstadter nearby on Montague Street. Two doors down from Auden, at 5 Montague Terrace, was Thomas Wolfe's apartment from 1933 to 1935, where he gave the unfortunate interview that exposed his slovenly ways, his lack of media savvy, and his address.)

Brooklyn agreed with Auden. "Really, it's all as quiet here as the country!" he once said. To a friend he wrote, "For the first time I am leading a life which remotely approximates to the way I think I ought to live." Auden's top-floor apartment was located in a splendid town house and offered a panoramic vista of the harbor and skyline that rivaled Hart Crane's view the previous decade. Auden had previously lived for a while in a hotel in Manhattan. His description in a letter of the view from Brooklyn echoes Crane's impressions, touching on the same idea that Manhattan is better appreciated when seen from across the river: "This house has the most beautiful view in New York: looking out over water at the towers of Manhattan. The skyscrapers with the exception of Radio City which is one of the architectural wonders of the world, are ugly close to but lovely from a distance."

As much as he liked the apartment and location, staying there began to feel untenable. Auden's apartment would now be in reach only for the very wealthy. He had thought it would be in reach for him, but a ban on the exportation of British money during the war made the English profits on his books unavailable, and income from American sources couldn't compensate. Auden, unlike most poets, relied solely on his work for income, which consistently put him in a vulnerable position. What is more, the landlord at 1 Montague Terrace was impossibly nosy; she admitted to Auden that she had staked out problematic tenants and watched their comings and goings for entire nights. Auden would not have taken this lightly, for he was living more or less openly as a gay man at a time when homosexuality was illegal. He had come to the States with Christopher Isherwood, his collaborator on several plays, and in the spring of '39 he fell hard for a considerably younger man, an eighteen-year-old named Chester Kallman.

When George Davis walked Auden to Middagh Street, the poet raised his eyebrows, or perhaps lowered them, when he saw the condition of the house Davis had been extolling. Nevertheless, he signed on. The rent was the same as his old apartment. For the whole house. At most he'd be paying a third. Apart from that, what attracted him was the prospect of a household arranged around the life of a writer working at his craft. It was the only role he wanted to play.

Auden liked to keep to strict routines, which made him potentially an odd fit for this new arrangement. "The surest way to discipline passion," he once said, "is to discipline time: decide what you want or ought to do during the day, then always do it at exactly the same moment every day, and passion will give you no trouble." He would sometimes proclaim irritably, "Sorry, my dear, one mustn't be bohemian!" But perhaps his fledgling love affair with Kallman had injected a feeling of youth and a skip in his step. Auden invited his friend Benjamin Britten, a British composer destined for renown, and Britten's lover, Peter Pears, to move in as well, upping his own stake in the success of the experiment. Auden's besotted fascination with the much younger Kallman reflected his lack of attention to certain social norms. The young man was the son of a Jewish Brooklyn dentist who had remarried twice after Kallman's mother died. Chester spent much of his time with his grandparents in Coney Island, and Auden would visit him there, scribbling in a notebook on the long ride. Auden, famous and respected, seemed not only undeterred but attracted by the differences between them. "It is in you, a Jew," he wrote to Chester, "that I, a Gentile, inheriting an O-so-genteel anti-semitism, have found my happiness."

Davis launched into the Middagh spirit by spending time scavenging in Brooklyn's junk antique shops, growing fond in particular of a store run by a "haggard" and dirty woman who allegedly slept on a couch in the shop wrapped in a Persian rug, according to McCullers. Drinking became a favored activity, and a friend of

Auden's was taken aback upon visiting to find "George naked at the piano with a cigarette in his mouth, Carson on the floor with half a gallon of sherry, and Wystan bursting in like a headmaster, announcing: 'Now then, dinner!'" The place initially had no heat nor hot water, and the toilets proved unreliable. Auden sent a note along with a poem to a friend working at the *New Yorker*: "Dear Harry, PLEASE sell this to the New Yorker as I am VERY VERY VERY poor . . . I STILL HAVE NO HOT WATER I STILL HAVE NO HOT WATER. I shall go crazy." Davis frequented the rowdy sailor bars down on Sands Street when he was on the prowl. The rest of the gang needed no excuse to join him on an excursion to a place that at three in the morning was "as vivacious as a country fair," as McCullers put it. "There is a saying among sailors that when they die they want to go to Sands Street," she added. At Tony's Square Bar, a fistfight or two always brought the crowd to its feet. Afterward a nightcap or four back at the house was in order. (The Hotel St. George in the Heights, where Wolfe looked out on the city that triumphal Fourth of July in 1935, hosted naval officers and a more upscale crowd; that proved uninteresting.)

Auden saw the need to step in and set some things in order, to keep chaos at least a little at bay and above all to ensure that he got some good work done. He nominated himself as a kind of father to the house, and thereafter began collecting rent with a very firm hand and handling bills and upkeep. He also made sure that food got on the table at specified times—if you missed breakfast, your bad luck—and enforced some quiet during the workday. At dinner he presided over the table, and as the war in Europe escalated, he took to announcing at the beginning of the table not only the menu—"we've got a roast and two veg, salad and savory"—but also the cardinal rule: no political discussion.

Everyone broke the rule. The atmosphere in Europe was rapidly deteriorating as Hitler fast extended the reach of his brutality. This cohort had taken over 7 Middagh Street in the middle of a stretch of seventy-six days in which at least a hundred planes bombed London every night but one. The rapidly unfolding events ramped up the pressure on prominent cultural figures, particularly British ones, to take a strong stand, and Auden and Britten were both widely criticized for remaining in America and staying out of the wartime fray. As Tippins remarks, detachment seemed a difficult position to defend when a rising tide of demoralized European exiles circulated through the Middagh Street house. Three of Thomas Mann's children, Klaus, Erika, and Golo, became a consistent presence, with Golo eventually taking up residence in the unfinished attic. The Manns didn't take kindly to Auden's disengagement in particular. Erika was Auden's wife, technically speaking, from 1935 until her death in 1969; he had agreed to marry her, a lesbian, sight unseen, so that she could get British citizenship. The marriage came five days before her German citizenship was revoked over her acts of artistic dissent against the Nazi regime. She was the most strident of the three Manns, but all were by now well-known dissidents who spoke out against what was happening in 1930s Germany, earlier and more forcefully than their father did.

The dinner-table disagreements and Auden's antibohemian gestures failed to deter a striptease artist with a marquee name from moving in. It was Davis who brought her into the fold. Gypsy Rose Lee, born Rose Louise Hovick, had been a girl of thirteen when she crept away from her family to browse every day in a little bookstore in Detroit, where they were visiting. She would never buy anything in the store, and yet she drew offers of kindly help from the manager, who was still in his teens and working to save money for an escape from Michigan. The manager was George Davis, who had a knack for befriending interesting people. With a raconteur's relish and charm, Gypsy loved to tell this story of their chance meeting. When she started joining the Middagh Street crew on jaunts to Sands Street, invariably creating a stir, Gypsy had already, in her mid-twenties, pulled in the staggering sum of four thousand dollars a week for her star turn in a sexy show at the World's Fair. She drew talk everywhere she went with her sassy attitude, her gift for both burlesque and publicity, and her sparkling bon mots. After a police raid on her performance she said, "I wasn't naked. I was completely covered by a blue spotlight." She played up her connections to the literary and intellectual world, persuading journalists to call her "the bohemian stripper," and in fact she was an intelligent and creative woman. She moved to 7 Middagh Street in order to work on a novel, a mystery called *The G-String Murders*, under the paid tutelage of Davis, who had a need for the money. Before she arrived, though, she took unlikely, Auden-like steps to rein in the disorder in the house, insisting on bringing in a cook and a maid and offering to loan cash for necessary repairs.

The house began to function more as it was envisioned, with creative work in solitude upstairs balanced by a constant and fertile crosstalk downstairs. Tippins quotes a passage from an Auden poem written soon after he moved in: "Where am I? Metaphysics says / No question can be asked unless / It has an answer, so I can / Assume this maze has got a plan." The plan was starting to work. For evening enhancements to the conversation, interested and interesting visitors multiplied to excess, particularly after the arrival of Gypsy Rose Lee—that "whirlwind of laughter and sex," as Louis MacNeice called her. One of the lucky early invitees was Richard Wright. Davis invited him over to a dinner party at the urging of McCullers, who was touched by a warm review from Wright for *The Heart Is a Lonely Hunter* in the *New Republic*. He had written that for the first time a white writer in southern fiction had been able "to handle Negro characters with as much ease and justice as those of her own race." Wright couldn't come that night, but he would be back.

The dinner party he missed was held on Thanksgiving for the kind of people who made their family away from home. It proved memorable, as drinking and conversation by the fireplace led to charades, other parlor games, and an impromptu talent show. At nearly dawn, the sound of sirens came from a fire station, and Gypsy and McCullers ran shrieking outside, hand in hand, to chase the bright red trucks. Something broke free inside McCullers, who had been struggling with her work, and she grabbed Gypsy's arm and, out of breath, said, "Frankie is in love with her brother and his bride and wants to become a member of the wedding!" Gypsy hadn't the slightest clue what she was talking about and was baffled when Carson burst into tears, but Carson had found the key to the plot of her novel in progress, six years before it was published as *The Member of the Wedding.*

In the interim, another story seized hold of McCullers. What many judged to be her best work arose from a concept very much born in Brooklyn. "Ideas vibrate, pulsing against each other . . . ," she once wrote, describing the feeling of hitting your artistic stride, "and there are a thousand illuminations coming day by day as the work progresses." On one of her visits to Sands Street with Davis and Auden, shortly before she returned to the South for some time, she noticed that one dive they visited was run by a massive woman who worked alongside a hunchbacked midget. The duo provoked nothing but laughter from most of the alcoholics in the place. But, as Tippins frames it, to the young borderline alcoholic McCullers, something immensely touching arose from the odd couple's evident intimacy, their practiced way of accommodating and complementing each other as they moved about the bar. It was absurd to imagine there could be love between the two. Or was it? In *The Ballad of the Sad Café*, McCullers places the towering woman and her hunched little companion in a café located, instead, in a decaying building in a cotton mill town in the South.

McCullers seems to have developed the most interest in Brooklyn of any of the housemates. Happy in her perch with its Manhattan skyline view from the back of the house, she also became absorbed by lore about the neighborhood closer at hand. As she described in her notes, the talkative corner druggist across the way let her in on the hearsay, telling her the provenance of Love Lane, which was a few steps down from the miserable Henry Miller apartment that he shared with his wife June and her mistress. The alley bears the name because a young woman once lived there with her two uncles, and she was so beautiful that her suitors regularly "mooned in the alley half the night," or so the druggist said. McCullers also heard the more widely known story that Middagh

Street took its name from a Miss Middagh, a direct descendant of a Dutch family who operated a mill there dating back to the early eighteenth century. An egalitarian woman, she didn't like that Brooklyn Heights streets were named for prominent residents (most still are) and she kept tearing down signs on the streets until the city renamed several of them after fruits: Pineapple, Cranberry, and Orange.

McCullers relayed the Love Lane anecdote in a colorful but slight essay for *Vogue* called "Brooklyn Is My Neighbourhood," the only piece of writing by the Middagh Street crew to be devoted entirely to Brooklyn. McCullers's piece shows an outlook on Brooklyn that's a bit tinged with condescension, an aren't-you-sweet attitude her housemates shared. The most quotable (and quoted) line is, "Comparing the Brooklyn I know to Manhattan is like comparing a comfortable and complacent duenna with her more brilliant and neurotic sister." The words "complacent duenna" probably did not go down well locally, and they are not as accurate as the sentence that follows: "Things move more slowly out here (the streetcars still rattle leisurely down most of the main streets), and there is a feeling for tradition."

Yes, "a feeling for tradition," but it's not clear that the Middagh housemates really engaged with that tradition, nor with the current place and its ways of being. For them, as for Thomas Wolfe, Brooklyn was an escape from Manhattan, but unlike Wolfe they liked to bring highbrow Manhattan to them almost as often as possible, which hardly makes for a great escape. The Middagh house residents regarded Brooklyn mostly as a treehouse with a Manhattan view. They ushered in a new trend in the literary history of Brooklyn. What Brooklyn offered them, above all, was not a legacy tracing back to Whitman, nor a nourishing connection with the broader American life. It offered cheap rent. Which isn't nothing, for in their case affordability meant an opportunity to live at a semi-reasonable standard in the kind of community where art and ideas thrive. Davis, McCullers, and Auden were all in an unhappy living situation before starting up the Middagh experiment, and in each case money played a role. Banding together posed an answer, and it also lent their house, their neighborhood, and their borough a new cachet as a fashionable place for literary types, however poor they might be.

❧

The wait list for a spot at 7 Middagh Street was growing longer by the day. Late to the game was an odd couple named Paul and Jane Bowles. Paul, now thirty, was a composer fast on the rise who had spent relatively happy times in Brooklyn during his peripatetic and unhappy childhood, according to Virginia Spencer Carr's *Paul Bowles: A Life* (2004). In his teens he swore off the lifestyle of his middle-class parents and left college to make his way in Paris on a shoestring. He wrote a note to a friend that showed the worldly perspective he was already growing into. He was looking forward to leaving New York, he said, even though he loved America: "The only trouble is that I have always had to live in New York, which is not the same thing at all." He ended up spending most of the 1930s in France, Mexico, and, most fatefully, Morocco, much of it with male companions and lovers. Late in the decade he was back in the States and renting two rooms for a time at 2 Water Street in Brooklyn, down by the Fulton Ferry Landing, where he held rehearsals of his music for a 1938 fund-raising concert for *New Masses*. Even while living in different New York apartments during this period, he used Water Street as his address to collect public assistance; the relief official had found the place suitably grim upon paying a visit, so why mess with success? Bowles liked to operate slightly outside the lines.

Perhaps it was that attitude that attracted him to 7 Middagh Street in 1941. Three years earlier he had married twenty-year-old Jane Auer, after an unlikely and loopy courtship. She, too, was bisexual but primarily gay. By 1941, the two had been living in New York in temporary situations here and there for months (sometimes separately) and were now in the famous Chelsea Hotel on Twenty-third Street, inveterate home to artists, musicians, and misfits. Paul couldn't have a piano there and found it impossible to concentrate, particularly because of Jane's odd hours and partying ways, including much casual sex, mostly with women. (When they were briefly in Paris in 1939, a proposition from "an obscene and lecherous man" had been too much for her. It was some months later, looking at a large photograph in the window of a Fifth Avenue bookstore, that she realized the lech was Henry Miller.) Lincoln Kirstein, a wealthy heir and patron of the arts who had initially helped Davis to pay the rent at 7 Middagh Street, recommended that Paul and Jane join the group. Davis could hardly say no to Kirstein's proposal, given his debt of gratitude. In early 1941, Paul took Gypsy Rose Lee's room, complete with a six-foot cutout of the burlesque queen. With only two chapters of her novel finished, she had relocated to Chicago to take a gig in a new nightclub show, and she was unsure if she'd return. (She didn't, but she did finish writing her book, which became the most popular murder mystery in years.) Jane took McCullers's space, since Carson was now spending a lot of time in Georgia. Lee's departure had been a blow to McCullers, who liked her greatly, and to Davis, who had become invested not only in her friendship but in her writing. He gave up his own novel-in-progress at this time, putting in for more freelance work at *Harper's Bazaar*.

Paul and Jane brought an even wider circle of creative types into the house's social whirl, including several mainstays of the surrealism movement, like the outrageous Salvador Dalí. Benjamin Britten didn't take to having a fellow composer in close proximity, and Paul ended up working at a piano in the cold subbasement. For his part, Auden became close to Jane, who helped to do his typing and drew inspiration from him to work on her new novel. But he glowered at the increasing chaos of the place and grew less and less fond of Paul, who dressed better and sometimes *acted* as if he were better than his already established housemates. Paul got angry when Auden tried to get him to vacate his room for a weekend, which would have left him to sleep in an unheated studio he kept on Columbia Heights. Soon he and Jane, now flush with some money from his new Guggenheim Fellowship, moved out, just four months after moving in.

Back they went to Mexico, where Jane, with considerable help from Paul, eventually finished her book. Their relationship had become nonsexual along the way, but they still meant a great deal to each other. Her commitment to her eccentric novel—her first and only, *Two Serious Ladies* (1943), to be followed by stories and a play—was more intense than her casual friends might have imagined. The book received mixed coverage, with many readers unable to make head or tail of it, but it gained an underground following, particularly among writers. John Ashbery, reviewing her *Collected Stories* in 1967, called her "one of the finest modern writers of fiction, in any language." Her work on *Two Serious Ladies* had an effect on Paul, who had been focusing almost all his energy on composition rather than literature for some years. By 1949 he would make his biggest mark not with music but by writing the classic novel *The Sheltering Sky*, about his adopted home for the decades to come, Morocco.

When the Bowleses departed in the early summer of '41, February House was fast losing its vitality. On top of the usual unpleasantness of New York City heat, a tense wartime atmosphere was gripping the city even though America hadn't yet entered the war. Within sight of the house, warships traveled up and down the harbor, where plans were under way to string underwater nets to defend against potential attack from German submarines. Brooklynites who lent their support in "Brooklyn for Britain Week" could visit Coney Island to see a German plane that had been shot down over London. As for the Middagh Street household itself, things began to break up. After Gypsy Rose Lee had gone, McCullers had taken ill in Georgia, stricken by what was later diagnosed as the first of a series of strokes. When she did come to New York, she was generally in the care of her estranged husband in Manhattan. Britten and Pears had left, off to California in search of a bit more peace. Golo Mann had given up his spot to take a teaching job (on his way to becoming one of Germany's leading historians), and with him went some of the international exile circuit. Auden was bereft over an affair Chester Kallman was having, and he had not written poetry for months. One night in the house, which now had an emptied-out feeling, he and Chester, now twenty, had a shouting argument that ended when Chester vowed that the relationship was over and stomped up the stairs to bed. In Tippins's recounting, after an hour of smoking and brooding, Auden climbed upstairs and stood over his sleeping unfaithful love. The poet put his hands around Kallman's neck and tried to strangle him. Chester awoke and escaped, and somehow he put the moment to rest. Auden, though, was horrified at what he had done. Years later he said to a friend, "It's frightening how easy it is to commit murder in America. Just a drink too much—I can see myself doing it." The incident is a footnote to Auden's long life now, but how easily everything could have been ruined there, at age thirty-four, on a quiet lane in Brooklyn Heights. At the end of that miserable summer, Auden pushed off from February House, taking a post as a visiting lecturer at the University of Michigan.

George Davis, the original tenant-in-chief, stayed on at Middagh Street, fixing things up and serving as the glue as visitors and residents came and went. The twenty-three-year-old Oliver Smith, who had used his manual skills and designer's eye to make the attic livable, now became a mainstay. A painter and aspiring set designer, he was taken in because he was likable and was living in terrible conditions nearby on Water Street—and because he was Paul Bowles's cousin. The rest of the population was transitory. McCullers came and went, seeking refuge from her marriage in her friendship with Davis and her burgeoning one with Smith, the new baby of the house. Colin McPhee, at the time more a composer than a writer, stayed at the house for a time. While he was there, Davis, ever the artistic nurturer, prodded him to try his hand at a memoir of his time in Bali, which he did (*A House in Bali*). And then, in 1942, Richard Wright arrived, moving into the parlor floor and basement with his family improbably in tow. Anaïs Nin, who had gotten herself ensconced in the love triangle with Henry and June

Miller the previous decade, periodically dropped by at Middagh to bat her eyelashes at Wright. She was taken with him and with the place. By now, though, the house had become less a collective than a boardinghouse with a smart-set clientele. The Wrights did meet the luminaries Davis still liked to gather, including the musical talents Leonard Bernstein, Aaron Copland, and Kurt Weill and his wife, Lotte Lenya, whom Davis would later marry, oddly, after Weill died. But the Wrights kept mostly to themselves.

The other residents of the street were not so quiet in return. "Middagh was a white man's street in white Brooklyn Heights," said Ben Appel, an acquaintance of Wright's who lived around the corner. Stones struck the window of 7 Middagh Street. And the coal deliverer, a black man, refused to serve a black man who had married a white woman. (Paul Muldoon, who was a friend of Davis's decades before becoming poetry editor of the *New Yorker*, relates this incident in his poem "Carson.") The irony is that the goings-on at the house had been far more outré and subversive for the preceding two years, with little complaint from the neighbors. And in fact Wright moved out after a year because he had a hard time coping with McCullers's drinking and the inveterate Sands Street cruising that repeatedly landed Davis in the hospital. According to Constance Webb's biography, Wright said to his wife that February House was "not a proper environment in which to raise a child." The house's hip status didn't much suit the new family man.

In 1945, five years after Davis established February House, the house at 7 Middagh Street fell to the wrecking ball, to make way for a signal event in midcentury Brooklyn history, the decades-long construction of the Brooklyn-Queens Expressway. The highway was another of Robert Moses's controversial bold strokes in his campaign to remake the city. Unlike the mayors and governors who purportedly held more sway, Moses, the "master builder" of twentieth-century New York, was not subject to elections or term limits. Over the course of a career beginning in the 1920s and spanning close to fifty years, he amassed unprecedented power as a public official in numerous posts, at one point holding twelve simultaneously. He had a gift for securing public funds for large-scale projects, and in the Depression era, when the government was pumping money into the economy, this proved especially useful.

Moses ended up building more than six hundred playgrounds, untold acres of parkland, and thirteen bridges, but his hundreds of miles of highways drew the most attention and ire. His vision involved bringing New York City, kicking and screaming, into the era of the automobile, and that meant blasting through settled neighborhoods with centuries of history. Moses met his most effective opponent in a woman with no college education, Jane Jacobs, author of *The Death and Life of Great American Cities* (1961), who led the successful campaign to kill the plans for the Lower Manhattan Expressway. Robert Caro's magisterial biography of Moses, *The Power Broker* (1974), both raised Moses's name to a new level of prominence and secured his reputation as an arrogant and power-hungry man who made his valuable contributions but dealt a heavy blow to New York's special history and character.

In the case of the Brooklyn-Queens Expressway, it cut a scar through the area south of Atlantic Avenue. But much of Brooklyn Heights was spared from demolition, largely due to local activism. A compromise allowed the highway to wrap around the Heights, mostly along two cantilevered roadways beneath the public esplanade built at the same time. But 7 Middagh Street still had to go. Moses thought it an added benefit that the new highway and the subsequently built Farragut Houses, a "towers in a park" public housing complex, spelled doom for the sordid adult hangouts and substandard buildings on Sands Street. Hart Crane would have seen it quite differently. And so did George Davis.

☙

Davis, who first found the curious house on the little side street, stayed till the last. (Although Auden ruled the roost during his time on Middagh, Davis was the keystone of February House. As in his career, others get much of the credit he deserves.) But his life and work had to roll on just as so many of his housemates already had. The same year that 7 Middagh Street fell, sending Davis back to Manhattan, a blond young stranger visited his office uninvited. Davis now served as the fiction editor at *Mademoiselle*, which like *Harper's Bazaar* was publishing vibrant fiction. The tiny twenty-year-old southerner, who looked like a child, told the receptionist he had a story to submit. "I'll wait while they read it." Davis rejected the manuscript, but he soon accepted another from the nervy kid, Truman Capote.

After publishing the story that made Capote a hot commodity ("Miriam") in 1945, Davis became a mentor of sorts to Capote. The following year, Capote took a page from Davis's book and moved to Brooklyn. In his first of two stints in the borough, he holed up in Clinton Hill for a few months in 1946–47. At the time, he was likely the most famous and connected writer never to have published a book. He wrote to his friend John Malcolm Brinnin from a rooming house at 17 Clifton Place, on a one-block street where he rented two rooms for the rock-bottom price of ten dollars a week.

> As you can see, I have changed my address and have moved to a little lost mews in darkest Brooklyn . . . for various reasons: I wanted most to get away from hectic, nerve-racking influences, to escape and get on with my work. I had reached a point where I was so nervous I could hardly hold a cigarette, and my work was not going too well.

As Brinnin probably would have understood, Capote was escaping his mother and her alcoholic fits of rage. He had been staying in the apartment she shared with Truman's stepfather on Park Avenue. Capote's parents made a hash of his upbringing in Monroeville, Alabama, and their divorce didn't much improve matters. At least his mother's next marriage brought him to New York, where the new husband was making his way in business. Capote once called his mother "the single worst person in my life." At this point, though, money for his own place was in short supply, and again

Brooklyn seemed an answer. Like Wolfe before him, Capote felt that Brooklyn offered not only affordability but an obscure and isolated hideout. "Truman regards the trip to Brooklyn about as Livingstone must have his trip to Africa," a friend drolly remarked. Capote told Brinnin he did not want anyone else to know his phone number, including his mother.

Capote was living within a half mile of the mansion once owned by Charles Pratt, and the house at 17 Clifton Place sold in 2005 for nearly a million dollars, but when he was there the neighborhood was in dubious condition. The thirties had wrought their damage, and, in the wake of the war, jobs in the war economy, for instance at the nearby Navy Yard, were on the way out. The middle-class flight to suburbia was beginning to take hold, enabled by Robert Moses's highways. Capote's 1946 essay about his time on Clifton paints a chilly but vivid picture of Brooklyn. It reads as though he is trying to brag to his high-flown friends about how low he is living, but the attitudes behind the writing are themselves rather obnoxiously high-flown: "In despair one views the quite endless stretches of look-alike bungalows, gingerbread and brown-stones, the inevitable empty, ashy lot where the sad, sweet, violent children, gathering leaves and tenement-wood, make October bon-fires, the sad, sweet children chasing down these glassy August streets to Kill the Kike! Kill the Wop! Kill the Dinge!" Of a neigh-boring abandoned church, he writes, "Definitive in its ugliness, the church for me symbolizes some elements of Brooklyn."

Capote cruelly portrays the sorry widow who owns the house where he lives, calling her a "waddling, stunted woman with a red bulldog face." She operates with her daughter a telephone answering service out of the basement. He tells of her coming up the stairs in "a sleazy sateen kimono" to lament that "the whole neighborhood's turning into a black nightmare; first Jews, now this; robbers and thieves, all of them." (Richard Wright had been living within a ten-minute walk the year before.) Also made to look unpleasant, ridic-ulous, and representative is a woman living in a nearby apartment hotel who puts on aristocratic airs and slathers on lipstick and rouge that "look rancid on her narrow, shriveled face." To the other elderly residents, Capote tells us, "she is the last souvenir of those faraway days when Brooklyn, too, supported an altitudinous society." The essay does contain some more balanced and tender description, singling out Brooklyn Heights for admiration. Capote compares its stately evocation of the past to Charleston, South Carolina, New Orleans's French Quarter, and Boston's Beacon Hill, calling the Heights "the less contrived, and certainly the least exploited" of the three. However, he adds with typical hyperbole, "it is condemned, of course; even now a tunnel is coming through, a highway is planned; steel-teethed machines are eating at its palisades." He spoke too soon, as we know; though 7 Middagh Street fell, no tunnel came through, and modernity spared the historic core of the Heights, allowing Capote to move there a decade later, in the flush of fame.

The year after leaving Clinton Hill, Capote made a splash with his debut novel, *Other Voices, Other Rooms* (1948). Its back cover depicted the slight blond author reclining on a divan, gazing at the camera like a teenage seductress. Even before the publication date, he optioned the book to Hollywood and was pictured in a full-page photo in the star-making *Life* magazine. *Other Voices* tells the Gothic tale of a thirteen-year-old boy's summer visit to the remote southern plantation house of his father, whom he's never known. The place, peopled by grotesques and misfits and depicted in a quasi-fantastical style, brings him into a more adult understanding of the world that includes a recognition of his own homosexuality. In Gerald Clarke's absorbing biography *Capote* (the basis of the fine 2005 movie of the same name), Clarke suggests that George Davis, who had given Capote his start, grew to resent somewhat Capote's outsize success because Capote was a younger alternative version of himself: a gay youngster from the sticks who came to New York to make it big. It couldn't have helped that Capote was hugely narcissistic and demanding—at once arrogant and needy. Clarke writes that Davis was silent about *Other Voices, Other Rooms* after Capote sent him a copy. When the two met for dinner, the twenty-three-year-old could no longer stand it and pressed Davis for his opinion. "Well," Davis replied, pausing. "I suppose someone had to write the fairy *Huckleberry Finn*." (Capote, an expert at holding a grudge, had his revenge for what he called Davis's "guillotine tongue." He used him as the model for a completely unlikable character two decades after Davis died.)

Capote came to know other tenants of 7 Middagh Street, which he called "a hell of a household" and a "historic ménage." (Of course, he came to know everyone.) He and McCullers, both regarded as southern prodigies and both eccentric in looks and behavior, developed an intense friendship very early in his career; she helped him land an agent and a first book contract. But she turned against him bitterly as he gained acclaim. Whoever's fault it might have been, Capote had a way of making enemies. Capote and Jack Dunphy, the man who would become a lifelong companion, spent several months in 1949 on a small Italian island, Ischia, where Auden and Kallman were also living. (Capote frowned upon Auden for coming to a rooftop party of his only to sit gloomily in a corner, and he deemed Kallman mean.) After Ischia, Capote and Dunphy spent a few months in Tangier, where Capote found life enlivened by the presence of their friends Paul and Jane Bowles. Capote held Jane's work in high esteem. He referred to her as a "modern legend" in his admiring introduction to her *Collected Works*.

His friendship with Oliver Smith had a more tangible effect on his life. Smith, who had happily done the menial chores for his older, more successful housemates on Middagh, quickly grew into a highly sought after Broadway set designer and producer. Tippins says that Carson McCullers giddily wrote to her husband about her dear friend in 1945, "Oliver Smith has *produced* a show called On the Town, which is the most successful comedy in many years. . . . Two weeks ago he couldn't pay George the rent." Smith won ten Tony Awards, for musicals and films such as *My Fair Lady*, *Hello, Dolly!*, *Oklahoma!*, *Guys and Dolls*, and *The Sound of Music*. He once said that *West Side Story* was inspired by his walks with

Jerome Robbins down at the docks by Sands Street. The set for the show, he told a reporter, was actually "more Brooklyn than Manhattan—but don't tell anyone."

Smith took in enough money from *On the Town* to buy a yellow mansion a few blocks from Middagh Street, at 70 Willow Street. Capote said it had twenty-eight rooms, and every bedroom had a working fireplace. Built in 1839, when Brooklyn's population was under fifty thousand, the house still stands, and was recently available for $18 million. When Capote and Dunphy were looking for a place to settle down in 1956, after years of a nomadic existence, they came to visit their friend Oliver, and Capote became "exceedingly envious." Capote marveled at the grandeur of the mansion's proportions, the "swan-simple curves" of the staircase, the garden in back. In an anecdote that might have showed a little of Capote's chronic fibbing, he wrote that he had won over his friend with charm over drinks on the huge rear porch. "He began to see my point: Yes, twenty-eight rooms *were* rather a lot; and yes, it seemed only *fair* that I should have some of them." According to Clarke, Smith was already turning the large basement into a garden apartment. Soon, Truman and Jack moved in.

The house on Willow Street served as Capote's primary home for nearly ten years. He and Dunphy hung dark green wallpaper and decorated the place with an eclectic array of curios culled from barn sales in the country and a beloved, multi-storefront shop in Brooklyn called Knapp's. Brinnin remembered visiting him and being served a bourbon and some Ritz crackers straight from the box. He took in the sights: draperies from Andalusia, a black and gold ashtray nicked from the Rainbow Room, and a photo of Capote himself that leaned against an unabridged Webster's dictionary. Capote quickly fell for his apartment, or at least for the mansion as a whole. He had Jackie Kennedy over for a meal in his landlord's dining room more than once. He failed to mention that it wasn't his house, and it took her some time to figure it out.

Capote's novella *Breakfast at Tiffany's*, partly written in Brooklyn, arrived with fanfare in bookstores in 1958. The beautiful and coquettish main character, Holly Golightly, glides through life among the jet set, shunning practicality and making her living cadging from men who fawn over her. Very few of her admirers know that she's really a child bride from the rural South, real name Lulamae Barnes. But as with Capote himself, her background as a have-not is key to her aspirational character. *Breakfast at Tiffany's* was a big hit, and it sold a boatload of additional copies with the 1961 release of the Audrey Hepburn movie (which Capote hated). Norman Mailer, a Brooklyn-raised tough who'd had his friction with the effeminate Capote, loved this book. Capote, he wrote, "is as tart as a grand aunt, but in his way he is a ballsy little guy, and he is the most perfect writer of my generation, he writes the best sentences word for word, rhythm upon rhythm. I would not have changed two words in *Breakfast at Tiffany's*, which will become a small classic."

High on the fragrance of praise, Capote turned his powers of observation on his Brooklyn surroundings in a 1959 essay that begins with a well-known quote: "I live in Brooklyn. By choice." "A House on the Heights" sings an ode to the neighborhood he described in an interview as "the only place to live in New York." Here he depicts the Heights as a place on the rebound from a dereliction more severe than it was in reality. First the problem was that "the immigrant tribes, who had first ringed the vicinity, at once immigrated en masse." Then, during World War II, the military "requisitioned many of the more substantial old houses"—this is true—and "their rural-reared, piney-woods personnel treated them quite as Sherman did those Dixie mansions." Now the Heights is once more "that safe citadel, that bourgeois bastion." Capote is making, sporadically, a tongue-in-cheek attempt to mimic the viewpoint of the highborn natives of his little enclave. And in fact part of the piece lampoons at length the snobbishness of a neighbor. Yet it does come through, even amid the essay's clever turns, that Capote is reveling in the altitude of his adopted perch. The piece doesn't range much beyond the outer walls of the citadel, for what would be the point? After all, "taken as a whole, [Brooklyn] *is* an uninviting community. A veritable veldt of tawdriness where even the *noms de quartier* aggravate: Flatbush and Flushing Avenue, Bushwick, Brownsville, Red Hook." The Heights is the "purest example" of the "oases" in this desert.

It was also in 1959 that Capote, in his Willow Street apartment, read in the *New York Times* a short wire story reporting the shotgun killing of a farmer, his wife, and two of their children in a remote farmhouse in Kansas. He told *New Yorker* editor William Shawn that he had found his next subject: the Clutter family slayings in Holcomb, Kansas. So began a well-documented, obsessive six-year odyssey. Returning again and again to the Kansas plains, Capote insinuated himself into the lives of not only the investigators and the community but also the two men who confessed, particularly Perry Smith, an extraordinarily intelligent murderer. After Capote served as a witness to their execution, the *New Yorker* published *In Cold Blood* over four consecutive issues in the fall of 1965, to a reading public feverishly clamoring for each one. "During its long history *The New Yorker* has printed many important and influential pieces," Clarke writes, "but never, before or since, has it printed one that has been as eagerly anticipated as *In Cold Blood*." When the book came out the following January, the *New York Times Book Review* gave Capote the longest interview in its history. *Life* magazine gave him eighteen pages, also a record for an author, and trumpeted its issue by flashing the words "In Cold Blood" on its giant electronic billboard. "*In Cold Blood* is a masterpiece," proclaimed the *Times Book Review* critic, "agonizing, terrible, possessed, proof that the times, so surfeited with disasters, are still capable of tragedy." The common-man city columnist Jimmy Breslin chimed in: "This Capote steps in with flat, objective, terrible realism. And suddenly there is nothing else you want to read."

Just as *In Cold Blood* was captivating the country, Capote left "the only place to live in New York" and moved back to Manhattan, to a gleaming tower unlike anything in Brooklyn, at 870 United Nations Plaza. "He wanted to be in the thick of things," Oliver Smith told Clarke. "At the time, the U.N. Plaza was very glamorous, *the* place to live in Manhattan." So much for the window boxes, flower-loaded wagons, and cock's crows he'd lovingly described in his essay about the Heights. Within a year he was hosting the legendary Black and White Ball. A black-tie masquerade for five hundred of Capote's closest and most highly placed acquaintances, the event is still often referred to as the party of the century. "It was ostensibly for Kay Graham," Capote's close friend Leo Lerman said. "It was for *Truman*." Other writers found in Brooklyn a refuge from the white-hot flame of Manhattan. Capote *was* the flame.

Even while in Brooklyn, Capote and the storied residents of 7 Middagh Street appear to have shared a point of view that was oriented toward Manhattan, across the water. Although nearly all of them had tried living in Manhattan first, they weren't very interested in breaking ties, nor in delving wholeheartedly into Brooklyn as a place of its own. The house on Middagh Street hosted a whole generation of artists and thinkers, but most were visiting only for an evening. Even the ones who lived there left relatively little trace of their interest in the surroundings, and almost all said good-bye to Brooklyn for good when the Middagh Street experiment fizzled out. So, too, did Capote move on.

He and the Middagh Street crew made sure while they were there, however, to let it be known they were living in Brooklyn. They were early believers in what you might call "Brooklyn cool," a notion that an address in the borough gives you a hip credential as an exile from the more celebrated Manhattan. To them it was a discovery they could boast about, quietly or not, as though it were an obscure novelist or jazz musician. "I live in Brooklyn. By choice." It's a refrain that has echoed through the decades that followed among Brooklyn's literary types. In recent years so many have made that choice that it's become much harder to say that

Brooklyn represents an unsung alternative. But the draw has remained much the same. As with the February House crowd, low rent has often been the initial attraction. A sense of escape from the hustle has also proved alluring, but so, too, has the idea of joining a community of like-minded people, making the escape together.

8.

The Shadow of the War

WILLIAM STYRON AND *SOPHIE'S CHOICE*

ON THE EVENING OF MAY 2, 1949, WILLIAM STYRON WROTE TO his father, "I am writing this letter from my new home in—you wouldn't believe it—Brooklyn." He was twenty-four years old and had yet to publish anything professionally, but he knew he wanted to keep trying. And he had moved to a rooming house in Flatbush, at the southeast edge of Prospect Park, to get some work done. Styron did not stay long—about two months—and he didn't recognize then that anything very consequential had occurred. But his time in Brooklyn was a signal event in his life. *Sophie's Choice*, published in 1979, grew out of Styron's experiences thirty years before in Brooklyn, the novel's principal setting. In a 1980 interview, Styron described the moment in the seventies when he decided to reimagine on the page a time in his past.

> I sensed I had dreamed a vision of a girl named Sophie
> whom I remembered from Brooklyn in the postwar years.
> She was a very vivid image in my mind and in my dream.
> When I woke up I lay there for quite a long time with a
> sense that (and I don't mean to sound fancy or imply that

this was a psychic experience because it wasn't), but I realized I had almost been given a mandate to write this book.

Sophie's Choice begins with a lightly fictionalized account of
the time Styron spent living in Manhattan before he arrived in
Brooklyn, with the protagonist, called Stingo, standing in for
Styron. This period, beginning just after he graduated from Duke
in the wake of World War II, was spent largely in a sweltering room
the size of a bathroom back home in Virginia. The room was in the
University Residence Club in the West Village, whose highbrow
name could not disguise that it "fell short of resemblance to a flop-
house only by the most delicate of degrees." Daytime passed slowly
at a hated publishing job at McGraw-Hill. In the novel Styron re-
creates the drudgeries of the job with panache. Stingo is plagued by
a comically desperate lust and, until he's let go, shows an impossibly pretentious and superior attitude toward his work, unwilling to
make compromises with the lamentable ways of the corporate
world. Assessing woeful unsolicited manuscripts "with a snootful
of English lit.," Stingo explains, "I treated these forlorn offspring of
a thousand strangers' lonely and fragile desire with the magisterial,
abstract loathing of an ape plucking vermin from his pelt." The narrator knows full well his younger version's weaknesses, and that
awareness draws us closer to him. Our ears incline toward the voice.

Styron's eventual firing was merciless, but he saw it as merci-
ful, since it allowed him to devote himself to writing. The man who
sacked him, remarkably, was Edward Aswell, flush with the renown
of editing Thomas Wolfe's final books and publishing Richard
Wright. Styron kindly disguised the boss with a near-anagram: the
Weasel.

In the first chapter of the novel, Stingo and the Weasel get
along like opponents in a custody dispute. The Weasel's incessant
dropping of Wolfe's name drives Stingo mad because, like Styron,
he has "gone through the throes of Wolfe-worship" and has imagined that he would soon be spending "a chummy, relaxed evening"

with the great man's editor, "pumping him for fresh new anecdotes about the master, voicing phrases like 'God, sir, that's priceless!' at some marvelous yarn about the adored giant and his quirks and escapades and his three-ton manuscript." Too bad they hate each other. When the ax falls, Stingo's response is this: "'Up yours, Weasel, you're firing a man who's going to be as famous as Thomas Wolfe.' I did not say this, but the words trembled so palpably on my tongue that to this day I've retained the impression that they were spoken. I think I merely said nothing."

While Stingo is packing up his things that afternoon, the older editor who has been his supervisor, an Irishman called Farrell, comes by for a talk, offering a bit of the rye that is already heavy on his own breath. Loosened by drink, Farrell says to Stingo that he's better off leaving this deadening office to write, and then he tells Stingo he reminds him of his son. "I didn't know you had a son," Stingo replies innocently, and suddenly the tone of the scene shifts into a deeper register: "'Oh, I *had* a son all right!' [Farrell's] voice was suddenly a cry, startling me with its mingled tone of rage and lament. . . . He rose to his feet and wandered to the window, gazing through the twilight at the incomprehensible mirage of Manhattan, set afire by the descending sun. 'Oh, I *had* a son!' he said again." Stingo is gripped with feeling for Farrell as he tells of his only child, Eddie, a young writer of talent and promise who was killed in Okinawa just two years before, one of the last marines to die in the war. Stingo, too, has served in the marine corps, as did Styron, who attended Duke under the V-12 officer-training program. Styron expected an imminent deployment to Okinawa in early August 1945 until the fighting abruptly ended under two atomic clouds. In *Sophie's Choice*, though, Stingo thinks back on the time when he arrived in Okinawa, mere days after Eddie, only to experience a certain regret that he'd missed out on "something terrible and magnificent." That callow romanticism now fills Stingo with shame as he hears "Farrell's brief, desolating story of his son Eddie, who seemed to me immolated on the earth of Okinawa that I might live." Farrell recites a passage from Yeats in lament for his lost soldier and writer, turns to Stingo, and drawls, "Son, *write your guts out*," and then walks out of Stingo's life for good.

The guiding hand of Thomas Wolfe is plain to see in this scene. A moment of high drama comes hard on the heels of the firing that already makes for a momentous day. And the author heightens the intensity of the encounter and the electric charge of the language nearly to the breaking point. (The Yeats bit is particularly iffy.) But Styron, a writer in much better command of his talents than Wolfe, has crucially earned the reader's trust at this point, even in the space of a single chapter. In the opening, Styron consciously used elements of his own life (familiar to many readers) to lend the story authenticity and to make it "seductive," as he explained in an interview: "I had to . . . give the reader—from the very first page—a sense of who was talking, which is a very good dramatic device and an old-fashioned one, but one that if done properly almost never fails." Stingo is relating his experiences at a remove, just as Styron was when he wrote the book in the late seventies. Thirty years have passed since the action took place, we're told, and the narrator now recalls the period with a feeling familiar to all of us: an embarrassment over the folly of youth coupled with a fond nostalgia for the youth that one was. By contrast, Wolfe's work, more autobiographical still, indulged in a self-mythologizing that knew no embarrassment, and he treated his youth with no irony whatsoever.

The novel skips over the stretch in Styron's life after his firing when he continued living in Manhattan and tried to make his start as a writer. Manhattan began to wear on him. *Letters to My Father*, a 2009 collection of his correspondence edited by James L. W. West III, gives insight into Styron's inner life during his twenties. Styron's mother had died when he was fourteen, after battling a crippling cancer throughout his childhood, and he was profoundly grateful for the emotional and financial support of his father. This was a very close bond, perhaps the most important relationship of Styron's life, as his daughter Alexandra told me. When Styron was struggling with his first novel and considering going back to full-time work, his father, not a wealthy man, sent money and advised him to stay the course. The older man gets a loving portrait in *Sophie's Choice*, which Styron was nearly finished writing when his father died.

In one letter from 1948, Styron wrote of Manhattan:

> The novelty has worn off; the city, with all its excitement and grandeur, is a terrible place. The tide swarms on; how people manage the pretense of humanity in such a jostling, surly ant-heap is beyond me. The eyes bend down from the jutting skyscraper—man's material achievement—to gaze in horror on the pawing mess of Broadway at lunchtime and the greasy, muttering squalor of the interior of a subway car—surely the symbol of man's spiritual decay.

While snowed in during a huge storm in late December 1947, Styron devoured Robert Penn Warren's milestone novel of the South, *All the King's Men*, a fictionalized rendering of the Huey Long story. "This, I thought with growing wonder, this was what a novel was all about, this was *it*, the bright book of life, what writing was supposed to be." The beginning of Styron's debut, *Lie Down in Darkness* (1951), which owes a considerable debt to Warren's first chapter, emerged from his pen that week, in a fit of inspiration. But Styron put the book aside after a while, doubting himself, and floundered for quite some time. He spent nine months back at Durham with Duke friends, making little progress on his work. The teacher of a class Styron had taken at the New School, an editor named Hiram Haydn, stepped in when he received a letter from Styron that indicated his distress. Haydn had seen promise in Styron and now encouraged him to return to New York, offering hands-on help. Agnes de Lima, a New School employee and the mother of a fellow student in Haydn's seminar, helped him comb the apartment ads.

Styron never planned on moving to Brooklyn. He didn't go there because he'd heard about those parties on Middagh Street earlier that decade. And fellow southerner Truman Capote hadn't told him about his stay on Clinton Hill, though Styron admired and envied Capote's work and they did come to know each other later. Styron wasn't embarking, either, on a pilgrimage to trace the footsteps of Thomas Wolfe, though he'd read all of Wolfe's work in the space of two weeks and called him "the greatest writer of our time" in a letter to his father from college six years before. But he was following a trend in at least one respect. The opening sentence of *Sophie's Choice* tells the story succinctly: "In those days cheap apartments were almost impossible to find in Manhattan, so I had to move to Brooklyn."

In the novel as in life, Stingo searches the classifieds and soon finds himself surfacing from the subway on a fine day in Brooklyn, in the foreign land outside the Church Avenue station of the BMT line. Taking in a few "intoxicating breaths of the pickle-fragrant air of Flatbush," he walks to a boardinghouse overlooking Prospect Park. Owing to a bargain on navy surplus paint, the large house is entirely pink, outside and in. The rotund owner and den mother of the place, a memorable bit player named Yetta Zimmerman, shows Stingo a room on the ground floor that becomes his home.

Flatbush was an improbable place for Styron to be. He grew up in Hilton Village, Virginia, a quaint, wooded suburb then just outside the city limits of Newport News. Hilton Village was a small town of modest homes built by the U.S. government to house the families of the workers who manned the city's shipyards. Styron's father worked in a white-collar job as a midlevel engineer, a draftsman, at the largest shipyard in the country. Hilton Village was largely Protestant and all white. The only black presence was the domestic help who literally crossed the tracks in the morning to work and returned in the evening. Very few Jewish people lived in the area. Styron's father, a broad-minded and cultured man, taught him to respect those who visited the lonely synagogue just across the way from the Presbyterian church the family attended. But in his youth Styron had little familiarity with Jews, and Stingo recalls filling the vacuum of his childhood ignorance with scary and ridiculous scenarios involving "incense and rams' horns and sacrificial offerings." Now Styron, in his twenties, found himself in Flatbush, "wandering amid the Kingdom of the Jews."

Styron likely had no idea what his new neighborhood would be like when he went to see the boardinghouse, but he quickly realized while settling in that he would not be blending into the scenery. The landlord was one of thousands of Jewish teachers who were being placed in the New York public schools in Jewish areas, as the Board of Education saw them as better able to "socialize" the children. Meeting her and seeing the Jewish names of most of the other tenants gave a hint of what he'd find on the streets outside. Jewish people constituted more than a quarter of New York City's population (while making up about 3 percent of the rest of the nation). And Brooklyn had a greater share of them—over 40 percent—than any other borough. Many were the sons and daughters of immigrants, as Kazin, Fuchs, and Malamud were, but by now more of them had moved up in the social order. Like the neighborhoods of Williamsburg, Brownsville, and Borough Park, Flatbush had become a pocket where Jews had settled in large enough numbers to surround themselves with elements of their culture of origin: synagogues, of course, but also kosher groceries, Yiddish-speaking shopkeepers, low-powered local Yiddish radio stations, *landsmanschaften*, a feeling of quiet on Shabbos. On nighttime walks, thinking about the writing he was and was not doing, Styron smelled the pickles and heard the unfamiliar music of the foreign accents. According to James L. W. West III's *William Styron: A Life* (1998), a valuable source, Styron was baffled by the sight of yarmulkes and had to ask what so many men and boys were wearing on the crowns of their heads.

Far from feeling a fish out of water, though, Styron felt quite content in his new environment. In that first letter to his father he began by explaining his difficulty finding an affordable place in Manhattan. Part of the problem was the postwar housing crunch, Styron knew, but he put it in terms any contemporary New Yorker would recognize: "I suppose that it all involves some terrifically complicated economic theory, but it still strikes me as being a gigantic sort of fraud." Nevertheless, he added, "I am still glad to be in Brooklyn in a clean and decent place."

Styron was living in a very pleasant mini-neighborhood within Flatbush called Caton Park, just one block long and two blocks wide. It is bordered by the rectangular section of Prospect Park called the Parade Ground, to the north, and the grand old homes of the historic Prospect Park South district to the south. Caton Park, developed in the first decade of the twentieth century, consists of about fifty large freestanding homes that are set back from the road on relatively roomy lots.

In another letter to his father, Styron described the surprising peace of the place: "The street is lined with sycamores and elms, the houses all have green lawns, and sometimes—along with the scent of mown grass and burning leaves—I seem not to have ever left Hilton Village. Especially the suburban sort of smells—grass, food cooking, smoke; these are so evocative of memory." In the novel, Styron echoes this description but takes it further, and the passage exemplifies an aspect of the book that is now often forgotten, so burned in the mind are the horrific events recounted later on: *Sophie's Choice* gives us a wonderful evocation of a Brooklyn summer. Here we are in an environment that is unmistakably urban and urbane, and yet the world has slowed down, the blood pressure has dropped, and the pure act of contemplation takes hold, giving rise to the kind of ruminative low-grade melancholy that's more sweet than it is bitter.

> It was such a placid and agreeable view I had of the park, this corner known as the Parade Grounds. Old sycamore trees and maples shaded the sidewalks at the edge of the park, and the dappled sunlight aglow on the gently sloping meadow of the Parade Grounds gave the setting a serene, almost pastoral quality. It presented a striking contrast to remoter parts of the neighborhood. Only blocks away traffic

flowed turbulently on Flatbush Avenue, a place intensely urban, cacophonous, cluttered, swarming with jangled souls and nerves; but here the arboreal green and the pollen-hazy light, the infrequent trucks and cars, the casual pace of the few strollers at the park's border all created the effect of an outlying area in a modest Southern city— Richmond perhaps, or Chattanooga or Columbia. I felt a sharp pang of homesickness, and abruptly wondered what in God's name I was doing here in the unimaginable reaches of Brooklyn.

Despite all the struggles he was having with his writing, Styron could tell his father that "although I'm not exactly ecstatic about the world and life in general, I'm very happy." He had spent the last four or five days almost entirely alone, he said, and yet he did not feel lonely. "At night, after I've worked through the day, I walk up Church Avenue and thence down Flatbush, enjoying every minute of the walk. The faces are all Jewish, all harried and metropolitan, all enormously middle-class; yet as I say it's somehow all of a sudden wonderfully exciting. Maybe it's just forgetting one's self for a minute."

Indeed the area was "enormously middle-class," bearing little relation to the punishing Williamsburg slums that Fuchs described or the grim Brownsville of Kazin's upbringing. Residents had more in common with the Jews on Eastern Parkway whom Kazin called the "*alrightniks*, making out 'all right' in the New World." ("They were still Gentiles to me," he wrote.) Flatbush became a Jewish enclave later than Williamsburg and Brownsville, and it was populated by more who were native-born, more who were there by choice. Newcomers were greeted not by bathtub-in-the-kitchen tenements but by new apartment buildings that had patrician-sounding names and touted "steam heat, electric light, gas, hardwood floors, bathroom and kitchen Spanish tile." New York City's first Sears arrived nearby on Bedford Avenue, a sure sign that this was consumer America. Movie theaters abounded in the neighborhood, the grandest of them the Loew's Kings, seating more than 3,600 in an opulence inspired by Versailles. Although Flatbush suffered in the Depression along with every other place, in 1939 the *WPA Guide* declared, "Flatbush is one of Brooklyn's most desirable residential neighborhoods." Later on, too, the end of the war contributed to a sense of stability and the prospect of growth.

In *Sophie's Choice*, however, Flatbush is not destined to be simply an agreeable setting for Stingo to pursue his wants (in short: women, a novel, acclaim). A couple living in separate rooms upstairs enter the plot comically; Stingo hears their riotous sex overhead, throwing off his concentration. But in time the two will confirm Stingo's vague feeling that in this cheerful pink house there is "something subtly and inexplicably wrong." The woman turns out to be Sophie, a lithe blonde with a lovely Polish accent who steals Stingo's heart right away, reminding him of a young woman he pined for in adolescence who has died. (Shades of *Lolita*.) He meets Sophie by coming upon a severe argument she's having in the hallway with her lover, Nathan, who is subjecting her to a wicked verbal assault. The "despair on her face" draws Stingo's eye, and when Nathan storms off, Stingo comforts her. He notices a number tattooed on her forearm. Unable to help himself, he asks, "Where were you?" In Polish she answers, "Oświęcim." Auschwitz.

The real Sophie whom Styron met in Flatbush was also an attractive upstairs neighbor, and she, too, was Polish and had been tattooed with a number at Auschwitz. She also distracted him, while he tried to write, with her loud and active sex life with the man from across the hall. But the lover was an unremarkable person as far as Styron could tell in brief encounters. Styron went to a party at Sophie's place and they took a few walks together and talked a little bit, but that was that. It seems that Styron didn't think about her much for the next twenty-five years. Here the novel makes a pronounced break away from the autobiographical facts.

In *Sophie's Choice*, Sophie and Nathan are suddenly on delightful terms the morning after their frightful argument. They appear at Stingo's door to whisk their new friend off to Coney Island to bask in the "popcorn, candy apple, and sauerkraut fragrance" by the beach. So begins the triangular relationship that carries the novel. Stingo invites us into his curiosity about this baffling, captivating pair. One is a caring and playful woman literally marked by a dark and mysterious experience of the war; the other is a passionate man with a "keenly honed and magisterial intelligence" whose destructive anger emerges unbidden from an otherwise magnetic charisma. When they are at their most beguiling, Stingo can't help but try to win the affection of these two, even as he becomes disturbed and obsessed by the turmoil of their private dramas.

His mind now in a state of upheaval, Stingo gets down to work in earnest on his first novel, which fits the description of Styron's debut almost exactly. (It's called *Inheritance of Night*, Styron's working title for *Lie Down in Darkness*.) Stingo also hits on an idea for another book, a novel about a slave rebellion that occurred just miles from his hometown; Styron's *The Confessions of Nat Turner*, based on that event, won him the Pulitzer Prize in 1967.

But Stingo's life is overturned that summer as Sophie reveals her past to him little by little as they grow close. They gather together with Nathan in Sophie's room to listen to cherished classical records as a breeze stirs the curtains; the three have drinks together at the Maple Court bar nearby, alongside Gentiles who run the elevators and unplug the plumbing in Jewish Flatbush; and Stingo and Sophie, who works part-time as a receptionist, share long picnics by the lake in Prospect Park and a day at Jones Beach. Eventually, gradually, the voice of the book becomes Sophie's voice, and it takes us back to her terrible wartime memories. Styron leads us into the novel through the familiar travails of a lustful college grad, but soon we are right there inside the consciousness of a Holocaust survivor.

For Sophie, her suffering is made worse for being solitary. Stingo feels like a lonely outsider in the strange land of Flatbush, exiled from the South and from Manhattan, but Sophie's alienation makes his trivial. She has been exiled from humanity. She has come to Brooklyn from a place where all that is good or creative or loving has been crushed into dust, burned into ash.

There are secrets she never brings herself to tell even Nathan, beloved as he is. Meanwhile, a crowd of recent Brooklyn College graduates whom the trio meet up with at Coney Island talk relentlessly about themselves, particularly about the progress of their psychoanalysis. This is a good period detail of the 1940s middle class: penis envy, transference, pre-genital fixation—all the Freudian buzzwords are comically bandied about from beach towels. Sophie doesn't find it funny: "'Those strange creepy people, all picking at their little . . . scabs,' she had complained to me. . . . 'I *hate* this type of'—and here I thought she used a lovely gem of a phrase— '*unearned unhappiness!*'"

Sophie has earned her anguish, but it is not the kind she wants to talk about at the beach. During his relationship with Sophie, Nathan, a voracious reader, has developed an obsession with the genocide, becoming fixated on the Nuremberg trials, spending long hours stoking his anger at the Brooklyn Public Library on Grand Army Plaza. But Sophie tells Nathan he must never ask her about Auschwitz. At a party he brings her to, the radio comes on with a report from the hangings at Nuremberg, and all is quiet. In a rare public reference to the war in the novel, one young Jewish professor does begin speaking, denouncing the executions as "token vengeance," but Sophie flees. She doesn't want to dredge up the awful past, of course, but it's also not clear that anyone but Nathan wants her to.

This is not atypical of the historical and social setting of the novel. Many survivors of the camps who resettled in the United States—often through relocation programs like the one that brought Sophie—found that in America there was little appetite for discussing what they had experienced. In *The Holocaust in American Life* (1999), Peter Novick writes that in the early years after the war, "survivors were told . . . that they should turn their faces forward, not backward; that it was in their interest, insofar as possible, to forget the past and proceed to build new lives." This message, Novick demonstrates, sometimes came from Jewish people and organizations, who did not want to foster an image of Jews as victims and feared a backlash against any appeal for special treatment. In other cases, the obstacle was simply a lack of awareness. Sophie thinks to herself, "That was the strange thing: people here in America, despite all of the published facts, the photographs, the newsreels, still did not seem to know what had happened, except in the most empty, superficial way. Buchenwald, Belsen, Dachau, Auschwitz—all stupid catchwords." Perhaps, she thinks at a different point, for many Americans it was all "part of a drama too far away, too abstract, too *foreign* (and thus too hard to comprehend)."

In the wake of the war, Flatbush's residents were very distant from the shtetl, in place, in time, and in social standing. The name of the game here was to get with the program, move up, get ahead, live the American dream. Why look back when there was so much to look forward to? When you weren't at work or at synagogue, the thing to do was read the *Eagle* or sit on a stoop and listen to the Dodgers. To join the United States and New York City was to join the culture of the new, to believe in the kind of progress that was also a kind of forgetting. Besides, the war was over, and what's more, "we" had won. The horror at the camps—we'd vanquished it, and that was part of the pride of being American.

When V-E Day had arrived, and then, more glorious still, V-J Day, the families of Flatbush were right there among the hundreds of thousands who gathered in Times Square to kiss soldiers and shake confetti out of their hair. The war effort had put an end to what remained of the Depression, and though the national debt had skyrocketed, you could look to the horizon and see prosperity. Europe's major cities and cultural centers had been devastated by the war, but New York not only had escaped physical damage but had lent its strength to the winning side of a global struggle. "The New York that O. Henry described forty years ago was an American city," J. B. Priestly wrote in 1947, the year *Sophie's Choice* takes place, "but today's glittering cosmopolis belongs to the world, if the world does not belong to it." Nothing symbolized the new order of things like the construction beginning that year of the United Nations headquarters on the East Side. Describing the project in 1949, E. B. White wrote, "In its stride, New York takes on one more interior city, to shelter this time, all governments, and to clear the slum called war. New York is not a capital city—it is not a national capital or a state capital. But it is by way of becoming the capital of the world."

A triumphalist narrative, however, has a way of leaving things out—leaving people out. Like Sophie. She has survived the war, but those who were closest to her have not, and with them went much of her soul, as the last quarter of the book makes wrenchingly clear. As autobiographical a writer as he sometimes was, Styron had a talent for inhabiting experiences alien to his own. And the people he inhabited were themselves alien to the societies in which they lived. In *Lie Down in Darkness* he explored the consciousness of a woman falling into madness. In *The Confessions of Nat Turner*, Styron adopted the role, in a first-person novel, of a black slave who led a massacre of whites. A huge controversy followed publication, as black readers and writers protested that Styron had trespassed on their history and created a sensational account that capitalized on racist ideas about sex and violence. While writing *Sophie's Choice*, Styron was aware that he might draw similar fire, that Jews in particular could object that a southern Christian man had tried to make sense of the Holocaust, had "dared to enter this secret temple." What is more, he had chosen to see Auschwitz through the eyes of a victim who was not Jewish. The real Sophie upstairs on Caton Avenue had in fact been Catholic, but Styron's reasons for making the character Catholic were also aesthetic. Very few works of art had addressed the non-Jewish victims of Nazism. There were millions of them, and in Styron's view this unjustly was "not in the public mind."

Sophie's is an extreme version of a postwar experience that was (and is) not always given its proper due. The joy of a new peace, a focus on the heroism of "the greatest generation," and the rebounding American economy obscured the fact that the war left a lasting and often severe emotional mark, even among those who celebrated its outcome. Those familiar words of Walt Whitman capture something essential about Styron's outlook and approach: "Through me many long dumb voices, / Voices of the interminable generations of slaves, / ... Voices of the diseased and despairing." Three decades after Styron left Brooklyn, Sophie's despairing voice, long dumb, came to him in a dream. Then he woke up and began to write down what she said.

9.

Underground Rumbles

NORMAN MAILER

TWENTY-FIVE-YEAR-OLD NORMAN MAILER WAS LIVING WITH his wife in France when his debut novel was published. On a hot June day in 1948, he collected his mail from an American Express office while driving through Nice with his sister and a friend. Going through the stack of cables and letters and clippings in the car, Mailer looked up and said, "Gee, I'm number one on the best seller list." *The Naked and the Dead* swamped its startlingly young author in a tidal wave of fame. The reviews announced the arrival of a major talent, and readers thrilled to a young veteran's front-lines account of the war that had recently shaken the world. America may not have been quite prepared for the horrifying Holocaust stories of a person like Sophie from *Sophie's Choice*, but accounts of the U.S. soldiers who had beaten back the enemies of freedom—that was different. "Everyone was ready," Mailer wrote five decades later, "for a big war novel that gave some idea of what it had all been like—it thrived on its scenes of combat—and it had a best-seller style."

As one of Mailer's heroes, Henry Miller, described his own prose, the writing of *The Naked and the Dead* is "direct as a knife thrust." It provides an unsanitized and vivid picture of the troops who are trying to seize a small island in the Pacific theater. The novel offered up an antidote to the patriotic cheerfulness and bluster that had shaped the public image of what is sometimes called "the good war." The army that fights for a just cause, Mailer reminded us, does not look like pure virtue up close. The exercise of American power both enthralled and repelled him, and that tension ratchets up the energy of the book. Mailer wanted to reproduce the way GIs really lived and talked. He knew that presented a problem and used the word "fug" throughout in place of "fuck," which is distracting and unfortunate, and still the first publishing house to offer him a contract refused to put out the book unless the content was cleaned up further. (Official censorship and lawsuits were a legitimate concern; Miller's books were still banned in the United States and were not legally available until 1961.) *The Naked and the Dead*, picked up by a different publisher at a bargain, did draw fire from the critics for its obscenity and coarseness. But the portrayal of the boots on the ground has an authenticity that gives the novel a gathering force.

While he was churning out his seven-hundred-page debut in fifteen months, mostly in a stifling room in a boardinghouse in Brooklyn Heights, Mailer kept four books on the shelf by his desk. Among them was *U.S.A.*, by John Dos Passos, another war veteran, who had written much of *Manhattan Transfer* while living a few blocks away on Columbia Heights. Critics saw the strong influence, perhaps too strong, of Dos Passos, and Mailer later acknowledged the debt in style and technique. Also on the shelf was *Of Time and the River*. As Mailer well knew, Thomas Wolfe had tortured himself over that epic on the very same terrain, stalking the nighttime Heights, walking across the Brooklyn Bridge and back, finally falling asleep only to see in his dreams the "blazing visions" of his anxieties. Like his contemporary William Styron, later a major rival, Mailer saw a greatness in Wolfe. He admired the southerner's ambition to capture the whole American experience with a vision that came "up from the people." The price Mailer paid for this reverence, he once suggested, was his "occasional overrich descriptions."

When Mailer returned to the States after mounting the best-seller list, money was suddenly not a problem, yet he and his wife rented a room in the same lousy Remsen Street boardinghouse that he had earlier used only as a place to work. He brought a royalties check from his publisher to deposit it at the neighborhood branch of Bankers Trust. The clerk, holding a check worth roughly three hundred thousand dollars in today's terms, peered at the customer's combat jacket and T-shirt. He asked for the name of Mailer's usual clerk at a Manhattan branch and placed a call to verify his identity. Mailer heard him let out a long "Ohhh" before he hung up and congratulated Mailer for writing that book. Or so the story went in Mailer's telling.

Like anyone, Mailer wanted to be admired, but selling two hundred thousand copies in the first year caught him flat-footed. His wife wrote in a letter to friends that Mailer had become something of a local hero, joking that he'd supplanted doctors and lawyers as the model son for Jewish Brooklyn mothers: "'Go to your room, Sonny,' they tell their offspring, 'and write a book like Norman Mailer did.'" Of course the success was satisfying and at first he soaked up the attention, which fed his already formidable ego. But in quiet moments, he later said, what he felt was this: "I must have done something wrong. They shouldn't have liked it."

The reception of *The Naked and the Dead* troubled him because he conceived of it as fiercely antiwar, which many people seemed not to understand. Graver still, the book's success threatened his conception of himself as an oppositional figure, a fighter against all that is easily swallowed by mainstream culture. Now he'd have to fight against himself. And so he did. Mailer battled everyone else, too, and in full view—the bigger the stage, the better. Soon enough he became widely known as a bully, a drunk, and a misogynist. The reading world turned out for each book to debate whether he had fallen on his face or had shown his gift for saying what no one else could see or had the guts to say. He was the leading enfant terrible of the American literary century.

Mailer was raised in a less fancy Brooklyn environment than the Heights, but it wasn't so gritty as he sometimes let others believe. In the first few years of his life, his family moved from Long Branch, New Jersey, where he was born in 1923, to Flatbush, near Cortelyou Road. They fit the demographic profile that made Flatbush what it was when William Styron wound up there after the war: they were Jewish and they were climbing up the ladder, already better off than was the norm in the Jewish enclaves of Williamsburg and Brownsville but not so comfortable as the home owners of Borough Park. Mailer's father, Barney, born in Lithuania, had lived in South Africa and been trained as an accountant before immigrating to the United States. He and his wife, Fanny, benefited from their association with wealthier relatives, particularly Barney's brother-in-law, who had immigrated earlier and done very well for himself. He sometimes took in Norman and his sister in the summers by the beach in New Jersey. He also owned a heating oil company in Brooklyn, and Mailer's parents both worked there for a time, with Fanny outlasting Barney and eventually running the place. She put in long hours taking orders and coordinating deliveries, but she took in enough to have help at home with the kids. Barney had trouble getting jobs throughout the Depression, and, like Alfred Kazin's father in Brownsville, he was greeted each day with the question, "Did you find work?" But in the Kazin family the question had much more urgency. Barney Mailer always dressed impeccably and carried himself with high style and dignity, and many people who knew him would have been surprised to hear that he was ever unemployed.

The family moved to a two-bedroom apartment at 555 Crown Street, in the Crown Heights section of Brooklyn, when Norman was nine years old. It was a step up. Now they were living in the vicinity of Eastern Parkway (the area sometimes went by that name) among the "*alrightnik*" Jews whom Kazin thought of as citizens of another world. The Mailers chose the neighborhood partly because it was even more Jewish than Flatbush. Corner vendors sold Yiddish newspapers like the *Jewish Morning Journal*, the

Forward, and the Communist *Freiheit*. As a Mailer friend recalled it, about twenty synagogues, packed on holidays, lined Eastern Parkway, and "everything in the neighborhood was kosher—the butchers and the delicatessens, everything." By comparison, Flatbush was marred by "cheap *goyim*," Mailer's mother told Peter Manso, author of the juicy *Mailer: His Life and Times* (1985). Fanny had a streak of prickly pride; she argued with Mailer's teacher over a grade, for instance, and years later, when she sensed anti-Semitism while house hunting in Brooklyn Heights, she told off the offender. "I just couldn't leave without telling her she's a bum," she recalled. The adult Norman Mailer could never do that either.

That mediocre grade was an aberration. Mailer was a very fine student. His classmates in the nearby public elementary school, P.S. 161 (still in operation), fit a certain image of the city kid of the pre-television era, particularly the Brooklyn kid. They spent their free time hanging out by the candy store, where you could get an egg cream or a soda mixed on the spot. They played ball in the streets, with each block fielding its own team, and they got into occasional scrapes. The rumor was that Mailer's protective mother kept him from joining much of the fun. In any case he took more of an interest in his studies and his musical instruments. A childhood friend described a genteel atmosphere in the Mailer house, with an emphasis on manners. "None of us obeyed our parents; he did." In his high school years he got interested in sex and went on group outings to the Star Burlesque at a theater on Jay Street in downtown Brooklyn. But he did little else to ruffle the feathers of his parents, who lavished attention on him. When he graduated from eighth grade, the principal announced that he had "the highest IQ we've ever had at P.S. 161."

He went on to Boys' High School, a venerated public institution in a grand Romanesque Revival building at 832 Marcy Avenue in Bedford-Stuyvesant. (The building still stands, though the school merged with another to create Boys and Girls High School in a new location.) Alumni of Boys' High include the composer Aaron Copland, the polymathic science-fiction writer Isaac Asimov, and

Norman Podhoretz. Podhoretz was a few years too young to know Mailer in high school but later they became close friends. Later still, they turned against each other. The rift came when Mailer published a virtuoso essay in *Partisan Review* about Podhoretz's book *Making It* that threw some brutal punches. In the piece, Mailer shows approval for the way Podhoretz's book about the "dirty little secret" of ambition and success had mounted a challenge to the New York literary establishment by subjecting it to scrutiny. The old guard had in fact overwhelmingly hated the book. But Mailer comes down hard on Podhoretz for not pissing off the establishment *enough*, and then proceeds to give it a go himself. Sorry, pal, the essay seems to say, you aren't up to the job: "My old dear great and good friend Norman Podhoretz . . . brings the mind of a major engineer to elucidating the character of complex literary structures but would seek—for such is the innocence of his good heart—to climb the Matterhorn on ice skates." But Podhoretz would not have recognized this bruiser if he'd met him back in high school. Mailer got into some hallway debates but he was not a fighter. He continued to perform in the classroom, and at the age of sixteen he set off for Harvard to join the intellectual elite.

The true outline of Mailer's youth was not what his adult self would have liked it to be. It was too average, too *respectable*. He had behaved too well. Mailer probably would have preferred to claim for himself the childhood of Henry Miller, whom he admired "enormously," to the point of obsession. Near the peak of his career, after winning the Pulitzer and the National Book Award, Mailer took time out for an unprofitable book devoted to Miller, *Genius and Lust*, a collection of Miller excerpts with Mailer's commentary interspersed. He was untroubled, clearly, that both Kate Millett and Gore Vidal had recently denounced him and Miller together, posing the two Brooklyn boys as key emblems of a misogynistic and nasty strain of literature. "There has been from Henry Miller and Norman Mailer to Charles Manson a logical progression," Vidal wrote in the *New York Review of Books*. (Mailer and Vidal— "not a suitable valet for Henry Miller," in Mailer's view—had a famous rivalry, punctuated by kiss-off lines, televised showdowns, and even physical violence.)

If Mailer had stood shoulder to shoulder with Miller, throwing rocks at the south side kids on the streets of turn-of-the-century Williamsburg, if he, too, had clashed with his bourgeois parents and his teachers and dropped out of college after six weeks—that he would look back on and smile. Instead he cringed over an upbringing characterized by love and achievement, the way others feel shame about early poverty and dysfunction. He wanted to become someone different and not look back. In the relatively rare instances when Mailer discussed his youth, either he played up its coarseness or he admitted that he had trouble reckoning with his childhood. "I left what part of me belonged to Brooklyn and the Jews on the streets of Crown Heights," he once wrote. "In college, it came over me like a poor man's rich fever that I had less connection to the past than anyone I knew." In his mid-forties he still felt the sting of this anxiety. Watching himself on-screen in a documentary, he saw not the warrior and radical and "champion of obscenity" he had happily become but instead "a fatal taint, a last remaining speck of the one personality he found absolutely insupportable—the nice Jewish boy from Brooklyn."

At Harvard, Mailer began to cultivate his tough-guy streak. In *Mailer* (1999), a nuanced and superb biography written without his participation, Mary V. Dearborn suggests that in college Mailer needed a new way to get the attention that had come to him automatically back in Brooklyn, where he was the smartest guy around and always had his mother's fawning approval. Now he chain-smoked, tipping his ash into the upturned cuff of his trousers; tried out for a house football team; and spun tales of amorous adventures that his friends found dubious. One of them told biographer Hilary Mills, "I did not, by any standards, see him as sexually precocious, except in his fantasy life. There, my god, yes." Mailer also tried his friends' patience by constantly saying he was just a poor Jewish kid from Brooklyn: "It was his standard riposte, playing the slum child."

Mailer got himself elected to the board of the leading college literary magazine, the *Advocate*, and became embroiled in the aesthetic controversy roiling the publication. The central debate echoed Philip Rahv's identification of two camps in literature, the "pale-faces" and the "redskins," in a very influential essay published in the *Kenyon Review* the same year Mailer entered college, 1939. On campus and in editorial meetings, Mailer sided with the redskin faction, which Rahv argued was best represented by the original bard of Brooklyn, Walt Whitman; Mailer favored vigorous, raw, and often proletarian writing over the refined, intellectual, and polished work of the aesthetes he found precious. He had lately fallen under the spell of Dos Passos, John Steinbeck, and most of all James T. Farrell, whose Studs Lonigan trilogy, set in Chicago, showed him that loners and failures casting about in the sweaty city could be the stuff of the novel.

Although Mailer completed his degree in engineering, writing became his overriding preoccupation. He was something of a self-made writer, as was Thomas Wolfe, another early model of his. Like Wolfe, he began scrawling like mad when he still had much to learn about literature or history. What resulted was sometimes naive and hollow, but it was also unfettered by the kind of critical instinct that can stifle creativity. Mailer was running free. In 1941, at eighteen, he won *Story* magazine's annual prize for the best undergraduate fiction. That got him noticed by an executive at *Time* magazine and a young book editor, Ted Amussen, who later signed up *The Naked and the Dead*.

The campus became more and more consumed by the war in Europe, as students and faculty moved from a predominately isolationist position in '39 toward heated arguments about intervention (mirroring the debates happening at the same time among the crowd on Middagh Street). Mailer didn't seem much interested in the politics of it. He later wrote that in the forty-eight hours after the bombing of Pearl Harbor, "I was worrying darkly whether it would be more likely that a great war novel would be written about Europe or the Pacific." He graduated in 1943, in a ceremony shadowed by thoughts of the draft cards that were soon to follow the diplomas. Half a year passed before he got his notice, for reasons unknown to him, and during that time he did not volunteer; at twenty years old, he harbored fears of battle, he later admitted, which left him nagged by guilt.

In the meantime he lived with his parents, who had just moved to an apartment in a narrow, elegant town house on a lovely block in Brooklyn Heights, at 102 Pierrepont Street. The fact that a summons to war could arrive on any given day contributed to his urgency to write. He rented cheap studio space in an industrial building down by the Fulton Ferry Landing in the shadow of the Brooklyn Bridge, near Whitman's old office at the *Eagle*, and he worked hard. He knew the area had a literary pedigree, and he liked that. Walking down to the studio from the Heights in the morning, Mailer passed within a couple of blocks of the building where Whitman printed *Leaves of Grass*; and the Henry Street apartment Henry Miller shared with June and her lover in the twenties; and February House, where George Davis still presided and where Richard Wright was still living on the bottom floor.

Before leaving for basic training, Mailer married a woman he had met in college, Bea Silverman, and finished a novel he'd written in nine months called *A Transit to Narcissus*, based on his experience working for one week at a mental hospital while at Harvard. Ted Amussen turned down the book, as did about twenty other publishers, with the rejection letters continuing to reach him one by one down at Fort Bragg.

The army sent Mailer to the Pacific theater to join the mission to retake the Philippines. Mailer would have qualified to start as an officer, as was the expected course of Harvard graduates, but he had enlisted intentionally as a private; he didn't want the responsibility of rank, and he thought that this way he had a better chance of seeing action. His developing subversive streak meant that he didn't want anybody keeping him in line, yet he didn't want to play the authority role either. He had "absolutely no use" for officers, an army buddy said. His resentment of the higher-ups would find its way into the pages of *The Naked and the Dead*, where many of them come off very badly, most notably General Cummings. Mailer cycled through two posts early in his time in Asia, each time clashing with a superior. Apparently by request, he was finally assigned to frontline duty on the main island of Luzon, as a rifleman with a unit much like the one in his novel-to-be.

Combat was not heavy, as much of the Japanese force had been beaten back already. Mailer was involved in only "a couple of fire-fights and skirmishes," in his words, less than *The Naked and the Dead* would lead some readers to believe, but he did live under the threat of a Japanese ambush, sleeping in bivouacs and patrolling in awful jungle conditions. He wrote four or five letters a week to his first wife, Bea, and he started asking her to save them, for material. A diary might rot or get lost. His discharge after the war thrilled him. Dearborn writes that Mailer told his second wife that his discharge papers carried the notation "This man does not know how to take orders," next to which Mailer wrote, "Fuck this guy."

⁂

Returning to the States in May 1946, Mailer began work on his World War II novel almost immediately, at twenty-three. He and Bea rented a place that summer in Provincetown, Massachusetts, on Cape Cod, where Mailer would spend a lot of time throughout his life. He worked diligently both there and at his parents' place on Pierrepont Street during the initial months of writing *The Naked and the Dead*. Fanny and Barney now had a neighbor in their building who Mailer knew was a writer. Norman would see the tall man downstairs at the mailboxes and make small talk, but he wasn't much impressed: "I can remember thinking, This guy's never going anywhere. I'm sure he thought the same of me." The neighbor was Arthur Miller.

Soon Norman and Bea took a small two-room apartment with a miniature kitchen at 49 Remsen Street, three blocks away from his parents and a block from 91 Remsen, where Henry and June Miller lived just after getting married and just before getting booted for not paying rent. Mailer felt he needed a separate place to write, and by chance a new friend, the writer Norman Rosten, was vacating for a few months an attic space in a rooming house just down the street. Mailer was living on the fairly tight budget afforded by the GI Bill for returning veterans, but the price was right for the space, at four dollars a week. The building, 20 Remsen Street, stood where Montague Terrace meets Remsen and comes to its end. The stoop was a literal stone's throw from the chaotic Thomas Wolfe apartment at No. 5 Montague Terrace and Auden's old apartment at No. 1.

Much of the labor that went into *The Naked and the Dead* happened in that stuffy and depressing attic. Mailer approached the writing with a professional determination, carefully charting his characters and scenes on index cards and turning out about twenty-five draft pages a week. The insecurities of the typical young, aspiring author were not for him; there was little stewing over whether the novel was any good, none about whether he was cut out for this. "I doubt if ever again I will have a book which is so easy to write," he wrote in his mid-thirties.

In the same essay, from *Advertisements for Myself* (1959), Mailer explained with remarkable candor the personal toll of scoring a big hit with his first novel.

> I spent the next few years trying to gobble up the experience of a victorious man when I was still no man at all. . . . So success furnished me great energy, but I wasted most of it in the gears of old habit, and had experience which was overheated, brilliant, anxious, gauche, grim—even, I suspect—killing. My farewell to an average man's experience was too abrupt.

Mailer felt the pressure of following up his opening act, and he didn't know where to turn for a second novel, partly because his youth did not interest or inspire him: "There was nothing left in the first twenty-four years of my life to write about."

In fact, he did draw from his own past in his next work, though he altered it in the direction of the bizarre. *Barbary Shore* (1951) is Mailer's only book set principally in Brooklyn, though he lived there for the majority of his life. The novel, short by Mailer's standards, takes place contemporaneously in a boardinghouse very similar to 20 Remsen Street. The first-person narrator, Michael Lovett, rents a room there with help from a writer friend, and he begins work on a novel. Lovett believes he was in the war, only he can't be sure because he has somehow been rendered almost entirely amnesiac about his previous life, presumably by the same injury that has left scars and surgical marks on his body. The first sentence establishes the atmosphere of uneasy ambiguity and doubt: "Probably I was in the war."

The summer Brooklyn streets outside are nearly as down at the heel as the boardinghouse itself. Lovett looks toward Manhattan and watches "a dirty moon yellow the water"; a walk across the Brooklyn Bridge yields the sight of a bum collapsing drunkenly; at the foot of the bridge is "a bare little park with concrete paths and a stunted tree" where Lovett hears the sound of the elevated train and thinks of "the long ride out to the end of the line, and the Negro slums along the way where children sleeping on the fire-escape would turn in their slumber as the train passed, moaning a little in acceptance of its fury."

Living in a room neighboring Lovett's is a man who becomes more central in some ways than the narrator. Mailer later called this character, named McLeod, "an intensified version of Charlie Devlin," Mailer's actual neighbor at 20 Remsen. Devlin was an eccentric loner who wrote fiction that was never published, but he had a sharp, sometimes cruel intelligence, and an acute literary judgment that Mailer respected; Mailer hired him to edit *The Naked and the Dead* before he turned it in. (Devlin convinced him to make significant cuts, often giving long, very sardonic accounts of why a passage was all wrong, until Mailer interrupted: "I got it. I agree.")

In *Barbary Shore*, McLeod is set up as a kind of mentor-interlocutor to the narrator. McLeod's way of getting to know Lovett is to interrogate him in a weird conversational style that suggests a real curiosity but also a palpable derisiveness with no evident cause. Lovett is understandably unnerved, but also curious, and so are we, at first. McLeod has a rivalry with the resident of the other room on their floor, Leroy Hollingsworth, who initially seems to be a young bank clerk from a small town, wide-eyed at the big city across the river. Hollingsworth is not who he says he is, though, and neither is McLeod, and neither is a possibly deranged young woman who takes a room downstairs and becomes involved in the story.

Barbary Shore is a very peculiar book. The first two-thirds, though often baffling, sustain our interest in figuring out what exactly is happening. Mailer creates an effectively queasy feeling of disorientation by unhooking the action from ready explanation and familiar signposts. Something called "the little object" figures centrally but is never described; McLeod is said to have roots in a Balkan country that is never named; Trotsky is repeatedly alluded to but also never named. We are in an allegory of sorts, an allegory steeped in anxiety, whether justified or paranoiac, about world-historical forces and massive authorities bearing down on individual lives. It eventually emerges that McLeod was an active and radical member of the Communist Party and that Hollingsworth is an operative of an unnamed government agency reminiscent of the FBI. He has been assigned to unmask McLeod and pry from his clutches a "little object" he may have stolen from the agency. Their verbal showdowns generate a certain drama about who is telling the truth and what Mailer is up to, but eventually the method in the madness becomes only too clear.

McLeod's character may resemble Charlie Devlin's, but his ideas come straight from Jean Malaquais, a radical to whom the novel is dedicated. Mailer met Malaquais in France in the late forties and became intrigued by his combative and prickly personality, which alienated others. Malaquais, who had written a novel praised by Trotsky himself, didn't think highly of Mailer. He would tell him how poorly *The Naked and the Dead* was written (Malaquais translated it into French), and he would argue with Mailer for hours about politics, telling him he was naive. Malaquais recalled to Manso that Mailer "seemed eager, touching, romantic. Also, how do you say?—uncouth? His manners were those of a young Brooklyn boy, not eccentric, not bohemian, with fuzzy notions and no culture, as far as I was concerned. Even then he had this talent for expatiating about philosophers he didn't have the vaguest understanding of." Malaquais represented a new opponent for Mailer to spar with. *The Naked and the Dead* had won nearly everyone over. But here was an exception—here was someone new to impress.

The last third of *Barbary Shore* takes a bad turn. Several chapters are devoted to extended political speechifying by McLeod, standing in for Malaquais, and the novel suffers for it. We wait in vain for signs of skepticism from Lovett, and the contest of will and wit between McLeod and Hollingsworth becomes heavily rigged.

In 1951, critics did not care for McLeod's sermon, nor for the novel, which took a beating that Mailer was not prepared for. Mailer was embracing a maverick form of leftism—both anti-Communist and anti-American—that was popular with almost nobody, Malaquais excepted. Moreover, Mailer, at twenty-eight, had become a devoted follower of Malaquais and many felt he was not politically sophisticated enough to adequately question his views. The writer and editor John Leonard said much later that though he was sympathetic to the book's project, "Mailer—posing as the bad boy—invented himself as though everyone before him, the people who wrote about American culture and society in the thirties and forties, hadn't written, as though they hadn't thought they'd solved certain problems." Irving Howe's review in the *Nation* showed some of the resulting frustration.

> Mailer has come to his radicalism a little late: he does not really know in his flesh and bones what has happened to the socialist hope in the era of Hitler and Stalin, and that is why he can refer so cavalierly to democracy and carry on like a stale pamphleteer. He is sincere and he is serious; I admire his courage. . . . But I can only say that his relation to his material, like his presentation of it, is not authentic. Otherwise he would not seem so sure.

The hatchet jobs poured in: the *Herald Tribune* ("dull, in execution if not conception"); the *New Yorker* ("it has a monolithic flawless badness"); *Saturday Review of Literature* ("I think it is a mistake"); and, perhaps harshest of all, *Time* magazine, a nemesis of Mailer's ("Paceless, tasteless and graceless").

Although Mailer knew the politics of *Barbary Shore* would not be greeted warmly, the book's reception was a rude shock that lasted a long time. He did not expect to see his skill as a novelist be challenged and to lose so quickly the status that his debut had won him. The years that followed were among the darkest of his life; in fact, the whole decade that followed *The Naked and the Dead* may have been his worst. We know Mailer had over fifty more years of literary celebrity ahead of him despite the flop of *Barbary Shore*; he, of course, did not, and he began to "act out," to use the kind of schoolmarmish term he abhorred. Before splitting with Bea, he took up with the mercurial woman who became his second wife, Adele Morales. Her outlandish behavior and penchant for manipulating male attention calls to mind Henry Miller's great love, June. Mailer picked fights just for the sake of it and began a lifelong habit of butting heads with people—literally. (He did it to Vidal in the dressing room backstage before the two authors had a nakedly hostile debate on *The Dick Cavett Show.*) Mailer helped found the *Village Voice* and then wrote bad columns with the explicit goal of being "actively disliked each week." When his 1955 novel, *The Deer Park,* had a hard time of it with the critics, he took out a big ad in the *Voice* featuring quotes from the most cutting reviews. Having heard somewhere that William Styron was spreading a rumor that Adele was a lesbian, he sent Styron a vicious letter that severed their friendship for over twenty years. Looking back in the late fifties, Mailer wrote, "There may have been too many fights for me, too much sex, liquor, marijuana, benzedrine and seconal, much too much ridiculous and brain-blasting rage at the miniscule frustrations of a most loathsome literary world."

That last quotation comes from *Advertisements for Myself* (1959), and it suggests the new self-awareness that helped to make that obnoxiously titled book an extraordinary demonstration of why Mailer mattered. *Advertisements* revealed that somewhere in the destructive bonfire of Mailer's late twenties and early thirties was the inner flame of his true talent. The book is a hodgepodge of material, much of it previously published and some of it poorly written. The valuable elements come mostly in the newly written italicized text that appears between the excerpts. Here Mailer speaks plainly, freely acknowledging his ego, his desire to outrage, and his failings from the first bracing sentence: "Like many another vain, empty, and bullying body of our time, I have been running for President these last ten years in the privacy of my mind, and it occurs to me that I am less close now than when I began." In admitting his mixed opinions of his own career and work, Mailer pulls a very rare maneuver. ("I don't see how I can recommend 'A Calculus at Heaven,'" he writes, introducing his early novella.) Aha, the reader now thinks, if this man realizes he's an arrogant bully and that "obviously *Barbary Shore* was not good enough," then here is a man I can listen to. Partly this is tactical, a canny way of disarming the audience so he can tangle with them once again.

The collection's biggest shocker in literary circles was the short piece, newly published, called "Evaluations—Quick and Expensive Comments on the Talent in the Room." In it Mailer takes up one contemporary fiction writer after another, for a few sentences or paragraphs each, and gives his unsparing assessment. A selection of examples: James Jones, a former close friend of Mailer's, "has sold out badly"; Styron's "mind was uncorrupted by a new idea"; Capote has what it takes, Mailer thinks, but "has shown no evidence that he is serious about the deep resources of the novel"; Kerouac's "rhythms are erratic, his sense of character is nil, and he is as pretentious as a rich whore"; about Saul Bellow, future winner of the Nobel Prize, Mailer says, "I cannot take him seriously as a major novelist." In a typical gesture, he also dismisses with one stroke "the talented women who write today." Mailer's sexism was undeniable, and his writing suffered for his almost total failure to take women seriously.

Seen from one angle, Mailer's drive-by shooting of his peers is an irresponsible exercise that seems as if it could have been written in a heedless night or two. It was like doing a cannonball into a swimming pool full of adults. But the piece is in keeping with Mailer's larger purpose in the book, which is to throw down the gauntlet: I know this is against the rules, but who made these rules, and why should we listen? We all have our private thoughts and conversations, he seems to say, so let's put it out in the open, quick and dirty. In other words, Mailer was writing a blog forty years early.

Another of the book's audacious provocations was "The White Negro," an essay that had aroused controversy when it appeared in *Dissent* two years earlier, in 1957. In this case Mailer introduces the piece without apology: "It is one of the best things I have done." In the essay, Mailer posits that in the age of the death camps, the atom bomb, and fifties conformity, the country has been gripped by an existential fear that now stymies creative and vital instincts. Faced with this grim reality, a new breed of person has arisen, "the American existentialist—the hipster," who holds that "the only life-giving answer is . . . to divorce oneself from society, to exist without roots, to set out on that uncharted journey into the rebellious imperatives of the self. In short, whether the life is criminal or not, the decision is to encourage the psychopath in oneself." In the dichotomy between "the Hip" and "the Square" that Mailer puts forward, "the source of Hip is the Negro." But a certain segment of white people have begun to adopt the Hip attitudes of black life, as a result of a "ménage-a-trois" involving the bohemian, the juvenile delinquent, and the Negro, a marriage in which "marijuana was the wedding ring." (Nice touch, that one.) Whether white or black, the hipster is a kind of mystic in Mailer's vision. He—always he, never she in Mailer—obeys no code derived from his upbringing or past. His only morality is "to be engaged in one primal battle: to open the limits of the possible for oneself, for oneself alone, because that is one's need."

What raised a ruckus in "The White Negro" was not only the offensive assumptions and stereotypes about "the Negro" but

Mailer's attitude and tone. He sounded awfully approving about the antisocial stance he was describing, and he seemed to be sincere in suggesting the merits of "encouraging the psychopath in one-self." In the most controversial passage, Mailer speaks of the "cour-age" of a hypothetical pair of hoodlums who "beat in the brains of a candy-store keeper," thereby "daring the unknown." This was the era of Eisenhower, of suburbanization and wholesomeness and homogenization, of *Leave It to Beaver* and *The Man in the Gray Flannel Suit.* Elvis Presley could be shown on television only from the waist up. A lot of people were unprepared for "The White Negro."

Mailer was consciously testing the limits here, crossing lines, baiting the audience. His writing in "The White Negro" is incau-tious, abstract, and full of suspect generalizations. But the essay wielded influence in intellectual circles by boldly moving into taboo terrain that others were tiptoeing around. Mailer put his finger on something, and his critics would have a harder and harder time denying that fact as time went on. As Mary Dearborn argues, Mailer identified a rebellious agitation—brewing under the surface of the fifties—that would become central to the story of the sixties. The hip sensibility Mailer described, with some modifica-tions over time, was a driving force of the civil rights era, the hip-pie movement, free love, drug culture, and the general breakdown of consensus values. Mailer was digging into fertile ground.

For all his wild punches and loud oratory, Mailer had a gift for sensing the underground rumbles in American life. Even in *Bar-bary Shore*, the central preoccupations were legitimate and prescient. Typically, the way he later described the novel sounds unhinged, but it captures something of the wild anxieties of America in the early Cold War era, when jubilation over victory in World War II was giving way in some quarters to fear of another world war and an atmosphere of political repression: "*Barbary Shore* . . . has in its high fevers a kind of insane insight into the psychic mysteries of Stalin-ists, secret policemen, narcissists, children, Lesbians, hysterics, revolutionaries—it has an air which for me is the air of our time, authority and nihilism stalking one another in the orgiastic hollow of this century."

"Insane insight"—it's a nice turn of phrase, and it succinctly captures what Mailer was all about. Mailer shares with many of his Brooklyn literary ancestors—notably Miller and Whitman—a fascination and affinity with the weirdo elements of society, the people without status, the ones who raise eyebrows, the "psychic outlaws," as Mailer called them. Among his subjects were loner radicals (*Barbary Shore*), murderers (*An American Dream*, *The Executioner's Song*), hunters drunk on testosterone (*Why Are We in Vietnam?*), and prizefighters (*The Fight*). Like Whitman and Miller, he embraced the animalistic, reveling in sex and in the raw human impulses.

Mailer also bore the influence of the "insane insight" of Wolfe, another man who liked to take shots at the high and mighty. Putting forth a Wolfe-like view, he wrote, "A young adventurer reads a great novel in the unvoiced hope it is a grindstone which sharpens his axe sufficiently to smash down doors now locked to him." Showing great respect, Mailer described Wolfe as daring death with the boldness of his attack on the page, "firing the passions which rotted his brain on those long paranoid nights in Brooklyn when he wrote in exaltation and terror on the top of a refrigerator." Mailer also hailed Wolfe, with somewhat less respect, for describing society "like the greatest five-year-old who ever lived, an invaluable achievement."

Mailer was like a five-year-old, too. The phrase "enfant terrible" is fitting, for he often behaved like a tyrannical child—only a child with clout and a drinking problem. When sharply criticized by Kate Millett for his misogyny, Mailer proved her point by writing a dismissive rejoinder that called her "Kate-baby." And that's nothing compared to stabbing your wife with a penknife. It happened at a party that he and Adele threw in 1960 at an apartment they briefly lived in on the Upper West Side. Mailer had invited everyone from high-society types to homeless people and it became a rowdy affair. Mailer got blind drunk and began provoking guests, who grew uncomfortable and started to leave. Dearborn pieces together the events from various accounts of uncertain credibility. With a few guests still there very late, Adele screamed at Norman and he stabbed her in the stomach and the back. Chaos followed, as some cared for Adele while others protected Mailer and still others slipped away, protecting themselves. Adele briefly showed support for Mailer after he was arrested, which eventually helped him get off absurdly lightly for the crime. But that marriage didn't last, and Adele was wife number two out of six for Mailer.

❧

Mailer bought a Brooklyn brownstone at 142 Columbia Heights with his mother, and in 1962 he moved in with his third wife, a woman of aristocratic lineage named Lady Jeanne Campbell. He would keep the place for the remaining forty-five years of his life. For all of Mailer's bad-boy antics, the house bore many hallmarks of the bourgeois life. Early on, he brought in a maid and began major renovations. The address, on a placid street with Manhattan skyline views and a storied literary history, would have been desirable to almost anyone. For Mailer, an added draw was the proximity to his parents. "Here I married this great and powerful writer," Jeanne once joked, "and all we ever did was go to dinner with his mother."

The renovation divided the building into five apartments and raised the roof. That made the top-level apartment's living room two stories high, and the new windows offered a glorious view of the river and Manhattan. In the mid-seventies, facing money troubles, Mailer turned the brownstone into a condominium and sold off the lower three floors. The top-floor space, with the tall ceiling, remained the Mailer headquarters. He had a carpenter friend build a loft near the ceiling to serve as his office. To reach it, Mailer, ever the adventurer, had to scale a crow's nest that led to a catwalk that led to a rope ladder—very pirate-on-the-high-seas.

In this apartment, Mailer raised his children (there were eight in all); wrote untold pages (for a time he kept a studio down the block); ate the same breakfast almost every day, often with his mother; celebrated his fourth and sixth weddings; built a huge model city out of Legos; and eventually brought his mother to live with him and his sixth and last wife, Norris Church Mailer. Norman also hosted fancy affairs at the Brooklyn brownstone, revealing that for all his anger at what he called "the Establishment" with a capital *E*, he had a weakness for glamour. These huge parties included a 1976 anniversary celebration of the marriage of historian Doris Kearns to Dick Goodwin. Among the A-list guests was Jacqueline Onassis, who had visited with Truman Capote one street over more than a decade before. Mailer also threw a soirée in 1965 in honor of the new light-heavyweight champion of the world, José Torres, as well as a fund-raising event for striking Columbia University students in 1968. In 1969, it was in the living room on Columbia Heights that Mailer and the columnist Jimmy Breslin and a coterie of friends and advisers (including Gloria Steinem, oddly) had a first merry meeting to discuss a run for New York City mayor.

Mailer had intended to run for mayor in the 1961 race, but the scandal surrounding the stabbing put an end to that. Not so in 1969, when Mailer shared a ticket with Breslin, under the slogan "No more bullshit." (Unfortunately for the campaign, those words could not appear in papers or on television.) He ran in earnest, not as a stunt, but his platform included such curiosities as turning the city into the fifty-first state and developing a "Vegas East" at Coney Island. Mailer somehow secured about forty thousand votes, despite drunkenly insulting his supporters and staff in a speech at a fund-raiser at the Village Gate bar.

Mailer also became involved in the intrigue surrounding a drug ring that came under large-scale investigation in the early eighties. When a friend of his, Buzz Farbar, got busted in the sting, Farbar agreed to wear a wire and record his conversation with Mailer over lunch at Armando's, a restaurant still in operation at 143 Montague Street in Brooklyn Heights. The federal authorities were targeting the big-name author. Mailer, who might have sensed trouble, said nothing at lunch to incriminate himself. A drug smuggler who knew him told Dearborn that Mailer's Brooklyn apartment was broken into and ransacked in the course of the investigation. It looked like the work of law enforcement: nothing was stolen, and a bag of Mailer's pot was pointedly placed in the center of his bed.

A growing contingent of those around him became concerned about Mailer's attraction to underworld figures. His fascination with transgressive and aggressive acts repeatedly got him into trouble (as in the case of "The White Negro"). In an infamous episode in the early eighties, Mailer helped publish the letters of Jack Henry Abbott, an imprisoned convicted killer he had been corresponding with. Mailer extended a job offer in case Abbott were granted parole. Upon his release, Abbott flew to Kennedy Airport, where Mailer met his flight at 1:00 a.m. They went back to Mailer's place and the two had a late-night talk out on the terrace overlooking Manhattan's skyline. About a month later, Abbott murdered a young waiter with a knife to the chest. During the trial, the press bore down on Mailer, who had to admit, "I have blood on my hands."

If Mailer was too infatuated with violence—and there's not much question that he was—that obsession also lent power to his work. His reported book *The Fight* chronicles the so-called Rumble in the Jungle, the heavyweight battle in Kinshasa, Zaire, between George Foreman and Muhammad Ali. This account, informed by Mailer's longtime love of boxing, produced some of his classic bravura reportage. (His on-screen commentary is a highlight of the dynamite 1996 documentary about this fight, *When We Were Kings*.) Here's Mailer's jazzy riff from *The Fight* on the climactic moment of the bout, when Ali tagged Foreman with a stiff right hand that sent him wheeling to the canvas: "He went over like a six-foot sixty-year-old butler who has just heard tragic news, yes, fell over all of a long collapsing two seconds, down came the champion in sections and Ali revolved with him in a close circle, hand primed to hit him one more time, and never the need, a wholly intimate escort to the floor." In Mailer's thousand-page 1979 book, *The Executioner's Song*, a very lightly fictionalized account subtitled "A True Life Novel" (shades of *In Cold Blood*), Mailer revisited the story of Gary Gilmore, a convicted killer who was put to death by rifle squad in 1977. Written with dispassion in a direct, "straight jailhouse prose," as Larned Bradford put it, the book proved divisive as usual, but it made a mark the size of a crater. Joan Didion's *New York Times* review itself drew a lot of attention. Her praise for Mailer's charting of "that vast emptiness at the center of the Western experience," her own terrain, rang out loudly, as did her closing sentence: "This is an absolutely astonishing book." *The Executioner's Song* won Mailer his second Pulitzer Prize.

The book that won him his first Pulitzer, *The Armies of the Night* (1968), is a work of nonfiction that could also have been called *The Fight*, but in this case a fight against violence. It recounts the October 1967 march on the Pentagon in protest against the Vietnam War. The book cemented Mailer's reputation as one of the leading practitioners of the so-called New Journalism, which borrowed novelistic techniques and took a more personal and subjective approach to reporting. Mailer participated in the march, first giving a poorly received speech while swigging bourbon out of a coffee mug. He later deliberately got himself arrested and briefly imprisoned for "transgressing" a line of military police.

Mailer had adopted an antiwar line earlier than many others on the left. In 1965, a collection of New York intellectuals published an open letter in *Partisan Review* that gave a mixed assessment of U.S. policy in Southeast Asia, opposing the current tack but stating that they "have not heard of any alternative policy" that would bring peace. Mailer's printed reply was another attack on lily-livered literary New York: "Your words read like they were written in milk of magnesia." He added, "The editors ask for a counterpolicy. I offer it. It is to get out of Asia."

Mailer was uneasy about activism and about certain elements of the antiwar contingent, as he makes clear in the very funny opening chapters of *The Armies of the Night*. As in *Advertisements for Myself*, Mailer mixes in a redeeming element of self-mockery throughout the book. But his purpose in *The Armies of the Night* is serious. It is to stand with the motley crowd, the ragged opposition, against "the Pentagon, blind five-sided eye of a subtle oppression which had come to America out of the very air of the century." As Dearborn writes, Mailer's account, entertaining as it was, made readers understand that the ragtag protest movement, largely made up of students, was not to be taken lightly.

A core of ambivalence runs through *The Armies of the Night*, for Mailer is clearly disgusted with the course the United States has taken, but he can't help feeling a swelling pride at taking part in the American tradition of speaking out. What always energized Mailer was a chance to do battle, to show that he was not a timid middle-class Brooklyn boy but a Brooklyn street fighter. In 1952 Mailer said, "Is there nothing to remind us that the writer does not need to be integrated into his society, and often works best in opposition to it?" Fifteen years later, he applied the principle in *The Armies of the Night*, but his opposition grew out of loyalty. In the *New York Times* review, one Brooklyn writer, Alfred Kazin, invoked another, Walt Whitman, to weigh the achievement of a third, Norman Mailer—all of them tied in a tradition of posing a challenge to a country they believed in.

> When a writer gets old enough, like Whitman, one forgets that he was just as outrageous an egotist and actor as Norman Mailer is. . . . I believe that "Armies of the Night" is just as brilliant a personal testimony as Whitman's diary of the Civil War, "Specimen Days," and Whitman's great essay on the crisis of the Republic during the Gilded Age, "Democratic Vistas." I believe that it is a work of personal and political reportage that brings to the inner and developing crisis of the United States at this moment admirable sensibilities, candid intelligence, the most moving concern for America itself.

10.

The Postwar Chill

ARTHUR MILLER, PETE HAMILL, HUBERT SELBY JR.

THE LATE 1940S AND THE 1950S, THE STORY GOES, WERE THE age of the growing American family taking a shiny, bulbous car for a spin on new highways before returning to a new driveway next to a new front yard. The U.S. of A. stepped out of the shadow of World War II and bought a house, went to work with a packed lunch, had babies, and bought so many homes and televisions and backyard grills that the mountain of war debt just couldn't keep up.

But the writers of Brooklyn told a different and darker story. It was in 1951, recall, that Norman Mailer wrote about radicals and an undercover agent in a Brooklyn boardinghouse to capture "authority and nihilism stalking one another in the orgiastic hollow of our century." And six years later came "The White Negro," which detected a gathering subversive urban element at the fringe of a conformist society. Mailer was not the only one to see, in Brooklyn, a vision that did not fit the narrative of the American dream.

Arthur Miller came into his own in Brooklyn in this era as a leading chronicler of American hard times. He had lived in the borough in his teens during the early part of the Depression, and after college he returned and lived primarily in Brooklyn from the late thirties until the mid-fifties. During that period he rose from the relief system to exceptional fame.

Miller's Jewish immigrant father, who had built a very success-ful coat and suit business, saw his finances take a plunge in the late twenties. The family gave up an apartment at 45 West 110th Street, bordering Central Park, and moved to Brooklyn. They wound up in a small house at 1350 East Third Street, where Miller shared a room with his grandfather. This address, on a dead-end street, was less than a mile from where Bernard Malamud was then growing up above his father's store, listening longingly at the window to a piano in a nearby apartment.

The neighborhood, still underdeveloped then, abutted a huge cemetery. It was an area "psychologically divorced" from Manhat-tan, Arthur later said, and even from the rest of Brooklyn: "My neighborhood was bounded by Gravesend Avenue and Ocean Parkway, a matter of six blocks, and from Avenue M over to Ave-nue J. Once you got out of there you might as well be taking a voy-age to Kansas." His mother rarely set foot in Manhattan, but his father took the long trip daily to the Garment District, beginning with a trudge up the steps to the elevated Culver Line (today's F train). All was not well when he returned home. The severe decline of his business, which never really recovered, took a toll on the marriage and on the man's spirit.

Miller graduated from Abraham Lincoln High School in 1932 and worked odd jobs to earn enough to attend the University of Michigan. After finding his footing as a playwright, Miller turned his eyes back to the house on East Third Street in Brooklyn in *Death of a Salesman* (1949) and created arguably the single most iconic American play. Miller's father and, more so, his uncle served as inspirations for his protagonist, but the character embodied a far broader swath of experience. His name, Willy Loman, is now synonymous with the journeyman driven to desperation. Miller made the struggling working man of Brooklyn stand in for every-one caught up in the heartaches of capitalism. The common man, Miller once said, is "as apt a subject for tragedy in its highest sense as kings were," and the everyday men and women who peopled his dramas were all around him during his teenage years in Brooklyn, as he explained in an interview.

> In my neighborhood there were always Swedes, Italians, black people, Jews, Irish. There was quite a mélange. I'm glad I grew up that way. You get a sense of the *moyenne* man—God help us—the man who is the backbone of the country. It never leaves you; you get a good sense of how he views the world.

Death of a Salesman is set in the postwar years, and Willy Loman is a traveling salesman who made his way "on a smile and a shoeshine" for decades. But recently he's been taken off of salary and he is fruitlessly traveling on commission to cities where all the old clients have retired and no one greets him or knows his name. He's taken to talking to himself and having strange visions and worrying his wife. Willy believes in the national gospel of chutzpah and success, but that only makes his own reality less palatable. Denial and a desire to be well liked wage a battle against the painful truth. Wondering where he made a wrong turn, he feels trapped in his Brooklyn house, where the backyard trees have gone and fresh air has disappeared. Everyone else, including Willy's brother, appears to be on the move, infused with a postwar vigor. Willy can't keep up, and the rules of supply and demand show no mercy. To him, only one way out seems possible.

Around the same time he wrote *Death of a Salesman*, Miller was working on a screenplay about corruption in the dockside underworld of Red Hook. Called "The Hook," it was meant to be directed by his close friend and artistic collaborator Elia Kazan, who also directed the original production of *Salesman*. To research the script, Miller got a tour of Red Hook from a friend who was a waterfront lawyer, Vincent Longhi. Miller, then living in Brooklyn Heights, had long been curious about what went on at the crime-ridden docks. But, he said, "I could never penetrate the permanent reign of quiet terror on the waterfront hardly three blocks from my peaceful apartment." Longhi later explained it a different way to author Nathan Ward: "He being an intellectual, who's gonna talk to him? Nobody." In Red Hook, Miller spent time with longshoremen, he said, "tuning my ear to their fruity, mangled Sicilian-English bravura." When he visited Columbia Street for "the shape-up" in the morning, the sight sickened him. Workingmen surged forward to surround the hiring boss as he handed out jobs for the day, according to bribery or whimsy. It struck Miller with a cold realization: "America, I thought, stopped at Columbia Street."

As that statement suggests, Miller was among a number of Brooklyn writers to capture one of the sad ironies of twentieth-century urban American life: in the years following World War II, the United States entered a twenty-five-year period of economic expansion and personal prosperity, but in many ways the rising tide failed to lift the nation's cities. The pattern was intensified in Brooklyn; success in the white-collar service economy stabilized Manhattan and gave a big boost to suburbia, but there was not nearly enough boom in Brooklyn.

The end of the war brought a moment of euphoria in Brooklyn, where much of the population had contributed to the war effort, whether as soldiers or as workers at the factories and docks at home. Because of that tight connection to the war economy, though, the end of war, and the decline of manufacturing more generally, hit segments of Brooklyn society hard. Brooklyn Heights remained a place of relative privilege, and middle-class Flatbush, where Styron spent time, fared reasonably well. But the working class suffered as the industrial engines of the borough wound down.

During wartime, masses of soldiers and equipment had moved through the Brooklyn Army Terminal and the Bush Terminal on their way to Europe, creating jobs and boosting the local businesses that served the troops. More important still, the Brooklyn Navy Yard employed as many as seventy thousand people, over three times as many as Google employs today. The workers included women for the first time—more than four thousand real-life versions of Rosie the Riveter. After the United States entered the war, the yard built more ships than all of Japan did. (The war ended aboard a ship launched from Brooklyn the year before, the USS *Missouri*, where Japanese officials signed the unconditional surrender.) Employees worked in three eight-hour shifts to keep the yard running around the clock and to keep spending money all over the borough. The size of the operation altered the complexion of blue-collar Brooklyn. Miller himself had worked at the yard as a fitter, doing tough labor to make ends meet while he worked on his plays, but for most men this was all there was. Now, in peacetime, jobs like these were on the way out. In the Automats and bars, people talked of another depression.

Miller's Red Hook screenplay ran into political difficulties. In the era of McCarthyism, a Hollywood producer wanted to pose Communism as a villain in the story—a nonstarter. And in 1952, the close friendship between Kazan and Miller, two products of immigrant New York, suffered a huge blow, also related to politics. Miller had not been, like Kazan, a member of the Communist Party, but he was sympathetic to those who were, having known many of them in New York intellectual and artistic circles. After Kazan agreed to name names as a "friendly witness" before the House Un-American Activities Committee, the two men did not speak for a decade.

With "The Hook" dead in the water, Kazan directed a similar tale of crime and comeuppance on the docks in the film *On the Waterfront* (1954), featuring a legendary Marlon Brando lament over the corruption that cost him his big chance: "I coulda been a contender. I coulda been somebody, instead of a bum, which is what I am." Miller, for his part, wrote the 1955 play *A View from the Bridge*, which allowed him to explore again the insular, bare-knuckle world of the Italian longshoremen in Red Hook, a "slum facing the bay" and "the gullet of New York swallowing the tonnage of the world." In the play, a dockworker, motivated by the love of a woman, informs on two illegal immigrant relatives staying in his home. The code of loyalty at the docks runs deep, and he is not forgiven.

Miller lived at a number of Brooklyn Heights addresses,

including 102 Pierrepont Street, where Mailer's parents lived and where the two writers crossed paths in the hall. Before that Miller had lived at 62 Montague Street with his first wife, Mary Slattery. He later owned a house at 31 Grace Court, right behind the boardinghouse, re-created in *Barbary Shore*, where Mailer wrote much of *The Naked and the Dead*. Miller eventually sold it in 1951 to octogenarian W. E. B. DuBois (who had trouble renting in the area because of his race). Miller also lived for years at 155 Willow Street, down the street from Truman Capote's apartment. They knew each other but weren't too chummy. When Miller left Brooklyn in the fifties, he still had decades of an illustrious career ahead of him. His understanding of "the *moyenne* man" from the borough stayed with him.

⁊

Brooklyn's postwar chill touched Pete Hamill's childhood, too. Born in 1935 to immigrant Irish parents and now an icon of New York City journalism, Hamill has become the dean of The Way Brooklyn Was at midcentury. In columns, articles, interviews, in novels like *The Gift*, and especially in his 1994 memoir *A Drinking Life*, Hamill's spare, tough-love prose and his touch with an anecdote make his perspective on the borough's history come alive. Hamill's father, who spent most of his son's childhood on the clock or in bars, worked as a clerk during the war. He often took the night shift at a military supplier in the Bush Terminal. Gaining peace meant losing a job, and "we were suddenly poor," Hamill writes. "The ferocious winter came howling into New York, and so did a new kind of fear, replacing the old fear of Nazis and Japanese." His family lived in three successive apartments in his childhood, all within a few blocks in the southern part of the Park Slope section. Each move represented a step down. The last place, a tenement apartment at 378 Seventh Avenue, remained his parents' home for many years.

Today Seventh Avenue is an upscale thoroughfare, where young professionals take walks on Sunday after brunch and peer at ads in the real estate offices that seem to be on every block. In Hamill's youth, there was an Irish saloon on nearly every block, and all the patrons seemed to know his father. Hamill describes a telling little culture clash involving an early girlfriend of his, named Maureen Crowley. She was also Irish and from Brooklyn, but she was a different kind of Irish and from a different kind of Brooklyn. Her parents were not impressed with Hamill: "The Irish from Seventh Avenue were 'shanty': low, common, often violent and alcoholic. The Crowleys were 'lace curtain'; the father worked for himself, wore a necktie to his job, had moved at least one step past the immigrant generation."

In *A Drinking Life*, Hamill gives revealing details of his childhood like having his worn-out shoes lined with cardboard by his mother, but there's not much self-pity in his account. As in his reporting, he gives you the straight story, with feeling but not sentimentality, and he provides a nuanced portrait of a place and time, very much akin to Daniel Fuchs's "dictionary of Williamsburg." In Hamill's Brooklyn, there is crime, conflict, and chronic need, but there is pride, too—pride in making your way without complaining, in never snitching on anyone, in not being a draft dodger, in being from Brooklyn, in coming from somewhere else but learning to be an American.

"The Neighborhood" (capitalized throughout the book) was the key unit of existence, Hamill writes, a small state unto itself. You knew the woman on Sixth Avenue was cheating on her husband in the military; you knew who held the record for the longest stickball home run, measured by the distance between manhole covers—*he hit it four sewers!*; you knew the name of the bookmaker and the bartender; and if you were voting age, the politicians knew a thing or two about you, too. Brooklyn became a key locus of power in the Democratic machine politics of midcentury New York, and Hamill's family had some experience with what the machine looked like on the local level. One year around Christmas a delivery of coal and a turkey arrived at the house, no payment required. Young Pete asked his father what you're supposed to give in return.

"Loyalty, he said. Always remember the most important thing in life: Vote the straight ticket."

Neighborhood loyalty went hand in hand with a broader allegiance to the borough as a whole. This was more complicated: while on Seventh Avenue your countrymen were everywhere and you knew your neighbor's business, Brooklyn was huge and heterogeneous. But in the forties and early fifties, at least everyone had the *Eagle* and the Dodgers in common. The *Eagle* had a peak daily circulation of three hundred thousand, well larger than the *Boston Globe*'s or *San Francisco Chronicle*'s today. Passed around at home and at diners and bars, the paper told you what was happening beyond the confines of your turf, and the articles gave you something to talk about with strangers. For many people, and not just men, the biggest draw was the sports section, because that's where the Dodgers were priority number one.

If you weren't a Brooklynite then, or perhaps even if you were, it's hard to grasp today just what the Dodgers meant to Brooklyn. Baseball was the working man's game and by far the most popular sport in the city in the forties and fifties. The team gave Brooklyn a national presence and a force to rally around. To this day, older men in Brooklyn will reel off the names of just about every starting player of the Dodger glory days. In their rivalry with the Yankees, the Dodgers were the scrappy underdogs who got their uniforms dirty and didn't care. Many people recall that you could walk down the Brooklyn sidewalks in summer and follow the game by listening to radio after radio through windows open to the street. Ardent fan Marianne Moore would watch the games on the building superintendent's television in the basement before she had her own set. On the evenings of home games, thousands of fans streamed across Prospect Park and down Flatbush Avenue to head to Ebbets Field, men in hats walking hand in hand with their children. A lot of nostalgia now surrounds the Brooklyn Dodgers (and few people mention that attendance waned in the mid-fifties), but an essential truth shows through the gauze: the team crystallized civic pride and fostered the kind of shared experience that makes urban life what it is.

When Jackie Robinson joined the Dodgers in 1947, becoming the first black man in the major leagues, white Brooklyn was divided on the news. But then Brooklyn saw Robinson play, and just about everyone knew what side to be on. The borough's black population, in the thick of Great Migration growth, came out in force to Ebbets Field. Every home game created the rare phenomenon of an integrated crowd all taking joy in the same sight: Jackie Robinson running the bases. Thousands wore pins on their shirts that said, "I'M FOR JACKIE."

In 1955, the *Brooklyn Eagle* folded in the face of a strike. Walt Whitman's paper, a central fixture of Brooklyn life dating back over a century, suddenly stopped landing on the stoop. The publisher, Frank D. Schroth, said in a statement, "Brooklyn, the largest community in America without a voice, will indeed be doomed to be cast in Manhattan's shadow." The citywide newspapers based in Manhattan didn't pick up the slack in Brooklyn coverage, as Hamill has said; arguably they still haven't. (A reborn *Eagle* with a smaller circulation now exists.) The *Eagle* had coined the phrase "Wait Till Next Year" with a 1941 headline when the Dodgers came up just short. When the team at last beat the Yankees in the World Series in 1955, unleashing blissful pandemonium, there was no *Eagle* to announce that next year had finally arrived. And of course the *Eagle* wasn't around to editorialize against the Dodgers' departure in 1957. Walter O'Malley aroused enduring loathing across the borough when he took the team to Los Angeles in search of more revenue. The loss of the Dodgers, though hardly a matter of life or death, provided a ready symbol of Brooklyn's midcentury decline. Note the end of the time span in the title of a wistful 1986 book by Brooklyn native Elliot Willensky: *When Brooklyn Was the World, 1920–1957.* "For a lot of people that was the end of innocence," Hamill wrote twelve years later. "Romantics are always betrayed in the end, and O'Malley did a savage job of betrayal."

The twin losses of a major newspaper and a major league team echoed other changes that chipped away more gradually at the foundations of Brooklyn's cohesiveness. On the one hand, a sense of postwar optimism colored the fifties, and in architecture and real estate, art and commerce, New York City was at the center of it all. Many people who lived in Brooklyn at the time look back on the late forties and fifties with nostalgia: this was the era of hanging out at corner candy stores, dodging trolleys in the street (hence the Dodgers' name), taking a day trip to the beach at Coney Island, playing ball games on the block until Mom or Dad called out from a window that it was time for dinner. Many Brooklyn residents were getting ahead and making big plans.

The problem was that often Brooklyn didn't figure in the plans. Those people who go into reveries about the Dodgers—well, a lot of them live in Florida now. Or Westchester, or New Jersey, or Long Island. In the 1950s, for the first time ever, the population of New York City declined, despite a massive influx of newcomers, including Haitians, Cubans, Puerto Ricans, and black migrants from the South. A vast middle-class emigration to the suburbs was at hand—eight hundred thousand white New Yorkers made the move between 1954 and 1965—with profound consequences for Brooklyn, New York City, and urban America at large.

Starting even before the war ended, the growth of families and government incentives encouraged a move to the suburbs. The GI Bill played a crucial role. It gave veterans access to low-interest mortgages with little to no money down, allowing lifelong renters to put down roots in towns just beyond the five boroughs. This clientele flocked to hugely popular Levittown, New York, which inspired a host of developers to replicate the success. New highways and parkways, many of them the work of Robert Moses, made the city more commuter friendly. Truly wealthy people retained their foothold in Manhattan and pockets of Brooklyn, but the middle- and upper-middle classes started to bail out. In Manhattan, many felt the squeeze of a rising cost of living. In Brooklyn, more often people moved away not because they had too little money to stay but because they had enough to leave.

The outflow had a very damaging effect on the city's tax base, with clear effects in Brooklyn. Who would pay for the social services that the borough needed? And those services were becoming more needed than ever. Even as white-collar employment in Manhattan remained strong and office space increased, manufacturing jobs in Brooklyn were in deep decline by the late fifties and sixties, exacerbated by a trend toward automation. Now the port, for example, could operate on a fraction of the former payroll, and commerce was being lost to New Jersey besides. When Pete Hamill signed on at the Brooklyn Navy Yard as an apprentice sheet-metal worker at age sixteen in 1951, the yard had already shed thirty thousand jobs since the wartime peak. The free fall continued until the Department of Defense closed the place and eliminated the last nine thousand jobs in 1966.

Newcomers arriving in droves found that the kind of work that had always been the first step for immigrants and the poor was drying up. Migrants fleeing the deterioration of Puerto Rico's economy—who were U.S. citizens not subject to immigration rules—came to New York at a dizzying rate; a 1952 estimate put the number at 1,135 per week. In Brooklyn many of them settled around Smith Street, near the Williamsburg Bridge, and in Sunset Park, and then tried to make their way up. But by 1960 Puerto Ricans received 30 percent of the public assistance while constituting just 8 percent of the city population. For black residents, the picture in fast-growing places like Bedford-Stuyvesant, Brownsville, and East New York was similarly bleak. Between 1940 and 1960, Brooklyn's black population more than tripled, bringing it to 371,000, while the borough's overall population declined. By 1960 blacks made up 13 percent of New York City's people and received 45 percent of welfare payments.

The narrative implied by the phrase "white flight" does not make a neat fit with the facts, as Craig Steven Wilder writes. In areas throughout Brooklyn, white residents began packing up for the suburbs before other races had a substantial presence in their neighborhoods. (Brooklyn was still less than 8 percent black in 1950.) With the manufacturing economy stagnating, and the government urging on the suburban ideal, those with the means took the opportunity. In areas losing people every month, landlords dropped the rent and some took in the growing nonwhite contingent when they might not otherwise have done so. (Wilder argues that the arrival of nonwhite residents saved parts of Brooklyn from a complete real estate collapse by bolstering demand for available housing.) In Colm Tóibín's 2009 novel, *Brooklyn*, set in the fifties, the owner of a department store downtown on Fulton Street (then a relatively upscale shopping corridor) makes a similar decision; rather than lose business, she will allow "colored people" to shop at the store. When the first black customers walk in, everyone falls silent and stares.

Racism undoubtedly accelerated the white shift toward suburbia. A store in the New Lots area of Brooklyn put up a sign: "YOU MAY TAKE WATTS, BUT YOU'LL NEVER TAKE NEW LOTS." Some white Brooklynites instinctively equated the arrival of blacks with decline, ignoring those new neighbors who only wanted to work as hard for their children as immigrant families like their own had worked a generation before. And their families had not faced quite so cruel a level of prejudice and even hysteria. Real estate firms took advantage of white fear and black vulnerability simultaneously by "blockbusting." First they deceived white home owners into thinking their block was "turning black" in order to instigate panic-selling by whites at bargain prices. Then they sold at a big markup to blacks, who faced very limited choices in a discriminatory housing market. Soon home values in these neighborhoods fell beneath the new residents' feet as whites lost interest in the territory.

But the forces at play here were more complicated than simple bigotry, as Hamill has pointed out. For home owners, the fear that the value of your house would drop if the racial makeup changed was an unseemly thought but not exactly an irrational one. It was happening throughout the city and the country, whether you felt it was unjust or not. To look at it from a more personal standpoint, if you were a Jew from Brownsville, say, part of what drew you to live there was that it offered synagogues, kosher groceries, Yiddish-speaking shopkeepers—things that made it feel like home, however poor it was. When the neighborhood started changing from Jewish to black—and it did so very, very quickly—the place that had once inspired your loyalty was no longer the same place. The Jewish businesses were shutting their doors, the synagogues emptying out. You had never intended to keep your family in this crumbling tenement forever, and now your friends were all moving elsewhere. Was it racist to decide it was time to go?

౭

When Pete Hamill went back to visit his parents in mid-fifties Park Slope, he saw a world left behind: "The Eisenhower era bragged of the good life for all, a time of abundance and prosperity, but it didn't touch the Neighborhood. The prosperous were gone to the suburbs; among those who stayed, money was still short. Everywhere in the city, factories were closing."

Street gangs made up of teenagers and young men of all colors and creeds had become widespread by this time. In Hamill's part of town, the main force was the Tigers, mostly Irish, who squared off with the South Brooklyn Boys, an Italian crew. Both sides carefully tended their slick hair and wore clean and stylish outfits. Brightly colored zoot suits, with pants that were wide in the middle and pegged at the bottom, marked the wearer as a gangster. The pistol pockets in the seat were an extra reminder. Loitering on corners, the gangs intimidated passersby and committed crimes ranging from the petty to the not so petty. Robbery and theft were common, though Hamill recalls that the code among the local crews forbade preying on easy targets like drunks or old folks. Much of the violence was directed at members of opposing gangs, and Hamill recalls a night in 1950 when a South Brooklyn Boy shot and killed one of the Tigers during a big brawl in Prospect Park. The call went out everywhere: "*They killed Giacomo!*"

Irving Shulman wrote the bible of the gang scene with *The Amboy Dukes*, which Hamill says is "probably the best-read novel in the history of Brooklyn." Published in 1947, it is now out of print and all but forgotten, but the cover of a 1971 edition proclaims "5 million copies sold." The Amboy Dukes is the gang featured in the novel, and it's made up of Jewish boys from tough backgrounds in wartime Brownsville. They like to skip school, build homemade pistols, run schemes, and take girls to their clubhouse. The protagonist, Frank Goldfarb, has a softer side that comes out when he's with his younger sister or his new girl. But he and another Duke get into a confrontation with one of their high school teachers, and it leads them down a ruinous road. The novel gained a reputation as a dirty book, and in fact it has enough of a steady sizzle of violence and sex that it was probably wise for kids to stash it under the mattress. The writing is facile and clichéd and the mechanics of the plot run too smoothly to be credible, but the book is powered by a slickness that suits the material. Shulman slips in some social observation and moral suasion that young readers surely missed in their hunt for the juicy bits. What made more of an impression— and still does—is the stylish urban argot and the portrait of a fierce, underage underworld.

With the arrival of the heroin trade in the fifties, the real gangs in Brooklyn that had earlier been a nuisance grew to be a more serious problem. Youth gangs teamed up with mobsters, or became mobsters themselves, in a very profitable enterprise. Hamill writes, "The streets that once had the most drunks—Twelfth Street, Seventh Avenue, Seventeenth Street—now housed the most junkies. The South Brooklyn wise guys did to the Tigers what they couldn't do with fists, bats, or guns: wasted them and robbed them of their pride." As always, addiction bred the crime—robberies, muggings, forgeries—that netted the cash for another hit. In a 1969 article for *New York* magazine, Hamill looked back with sadness on the changing attitudes of Brooklyn residents who wanted a safety and peace that seemed to be slipping away.

> Those who had escaped the Lower East Side now started talking about escaping Brooklyn. Events seemed to have moved beyond their control. You could do the best you were capable of doing: work hard, hold two jobs, get bigger and

better television sets for the living room, watch steam heat replace kerosene stoves, see the old coal stoves in the kitchens dragged out to be replaced by modern gas ovens, and still people in their teens were found dead in the shrubs of Prospect Park, their arms as scarred as school desks. "We gotta get outa Brooklyn." You heard it over and over in those days. It wasn't a matter of moving from one neighborhood to the next; the transportation system was too good for all that; it was out "to the island" or to California or Rockland County. The idea was to get out.

Last Exit to Brooklyn, the 1964 novel by Hubert Selby Jr., gave the borough's reputation another black eye just when it didn't need one. In its raging pages, Selby takes the Brooklyn dynamics that were driving people out in the fifties and sixties and pushes them to an extreme. The book is set in the area around the Brooklyn Army Terminal, located along the water near the border of today's Sunset Park and Bay Ridge—just the kind of place where the lack of blue-collar prospects was exacting a heavy toll. (Many people have erroneously described the book as taking place primarily in Red Hook.) The novel chronicles a white, predominately Italian underworld peopled with dead-eyed prostitutes, hysterical transvestites, and vicious gangsters. Portions of the book, which is divided into six loosely connected sections, were published in magazines as early as 1957. By the time Barney Rosset of Grove brought out the novel in 1964, a few years after courting obscenity charges by publishing D. H. Lawrence, William S. Burroughs, and of course Henry Miller, an aura of scandal already surrounded *Last Exit*. Soon it was selling a lot of copies, but it was also on trial in English courts, debated in the House of Commons, and banned in Italy. It's not hard to see why. You don't have to be moralistic to find reading the book a stomach-turning experience.

Selby, who died in 2004, once said that he felt a great "hatred of God" while writing *Last Exit*, owing in part to his own misfortunes beginning at a young age. Born in 1928 in Brooklyn, Selby attended

P.S. 107 in Bay Ridge and went on to Peter Stuyvesant High School, but he stayed only one year before becoming an oiler in the U.S. Merchant Marines at fifteen. While stationed overseas he contracted tuberculosis, nearly died in surgery, and spent several years convalescing in various institutions. He came out on the other end with missing ribs, lung problems, asthma, and addictions that ranged from prescribed painkillers to alcohol to heroin.

Selby fell in with a crowd of outsider writers, the most influential among them Gilbert Sorrentino. A born Brooklynite, Sorrentino eventually spread lines of influence widely as a poet, essayist, editor, and writing teacher. He wrote, among numerous formally innovative books, *Steelwork*, a series of disconnected vignettes from his Brooklyn childhood, and the acclaimed cult classic *Mulligan Stew*, a semi-crazed hodgepodge of parodic riffs that picked bones with the literary world. Sorrentino became a key mentor and advocate for Selby. When Selby was in his mid-twenties, he and "Gil" and a few other guys would hang out and get into arguments at an all-night diner on Fourth Avenue and Sixty-ninth Street in Bay Ridge, the Royal, or at the Melody Bar, or in Selby's hundred-dollar busted-up car. All the book talk made Selby want to read what everyone was talking about and try his hand with the pen. Selby and some of Sorrentino's Brooklyn College friends helped Sorrentino start the magazine *Neon* in 1956, and a broader group of writers coalesced and inspired one another in their pursuit of new genres, fresh modes of expression. Among these were Amiri Baraka (then named LeRoi Jones), Edward Dahlberg, and several Black Mountain College poets, such as Joel Oppenheimer, Fielding Dawson, and Robert Creeley.

Last Exit was Selby's debut (among his later works was *Requiem for a Dream*), and Selby might have characterized it as Henry Miller had described *Tropic of Cancer* in its opening pages: "This is not a book, in the ordinary sense of the word. No, this is a prolonged insult, a gob of spit in the face of Art, a kick in the pants to God, Man, Destiny, Time, Love, Beauty." What is both most striking and most hard to take in Selby's novel is not only that it's graphic—it vividly depicts gang rapes and beatings and constant drug abuse—but that the characters, presented without any distancing by the author, are so emotionally cruel. There's little honor among these thieves. One fifteen-year-old girl, ill-used by the guys she knows, starts picking up men and robbing them, beating them up if necessary. In the end she gets abused in turn, in perhaps the worst imaginable way, but before the physical violence comes a different kind of awful moment. After she meets an army officer in a bar, they spend several days together as a couple. For once, someone cares about her for more than one drunken night. When he has to leave for duty, he hands her an envelope as he boards the train. It's a love letter that suggests a future between them, but when she sees there's no money along with the letter, she tosses it before reading to the end. Something inside her has died.

So it is with Selby's other characters, whether they are gangsters; pitiable factory workers on strike who want to believe they're more important than they are ("Strike" is the book's strongest section); or residents of a sorry public housing project where the burned remains of infants are found in the incinerator. Selby resolutely, almost maliciously, refuses to show a way out or allow for any signs of hope. He transforms a tough Brooklyn into a place of his own creation—recognizable, but filtered through experimental prose and through a species of unforgiving surrealism. However distorted was the picture, Selby's book, which proved to be a succès de scandale, helped shape Brooklyn's sixties image as a failing and forbidding urban community; even if you didn't read the book, if you'd heard of it, you knew it was about an urban nightmare, and the word "Brooklyn" was right there in the title.

The apple-pie patriotism and corporate good cheer of American mainstream midcentury culture left out some unsavory truths. The midcentury Brooklyn that its writers have brought to life was a place whose pride did battle with its fortunes, which were coming undone from the nation's as a whole and drifting downward. These writers gave us portraits of people who were left behind by those who stepped up: the salesman in decline, the dockworker clamoring for a day's work, the laid-off man who takes to the bars, the gangster who's stopped thinking about hope. Dark story lines like these tend to linger, and so it would be in Brooklyn in the decades to come. Lasting urban neglect would soon meet with the green shoots of a spotty revival, making for an uneasy mix.

11.

Into the Thickets of Urban Crisis

JONATHAN LETHEM, L. J. DAVIS, PAULA FOX

> *Mongrel by deep nature, the place absorbed the first*
> *scattering of hippies, homosexuals, and painters pretty*
> *ungrudgingly. But with signs of a real-estate boom,*
> *and a broad displacement of the existing population,*
> *the changes were politicized.*

—JONATHAN LETHEM, on 1970s brownstone Brooklyn

IT'S SIXTH GRADE AND YOUR CLOTHES AREN'T RIGHT, YOU'RE not an athlete, you're scrawny, and you're too good at school. And if you're Dylan Ebdus, the protagonist of Jonathan Lethem's autobiographical novel *The Fortress of Solitude*, you've got the added problem of being the wrong color at the wrong time and place.

It's the mid-seventies and you're living in the Boerum Hill section of Brooklyn, though to some people it's still called Gowanus, after the fetid nearby Gowanus Canal. Some of the stately brownstones that line the streets, mostly built in the nineteenth century, are now cheap rooming houses, and others are boarded up and falling apart. You live on Dean Street, and the high-rise Brooklyn House of Detention looms overhead just two short blocks north, on Atlantic Avenue. And a low-income housing project looms two blocks south, off Wyckoff Street. If you're Dylan, you don't want to go near Wyckoff, but really there's nowhere that's a safe haven from getting "yoked."

You're walking back from school, just one block from home, and a group of kids spot an easy mark and surround you. One or another puts you in a headlock and sends your book bag flying. Others dig into your pockets and empty them of money and your bus pass.

> "Yoke the white boy. *Do* it, nigger."
>
> [Dylan] might be yoked low, bent over, hugged to someone's hip then spun on release like a human top, legs buckling, crossing at the ankles. Or from behind, never sure by whom once the headlock popped loose and three or four guys stood around, witnesses with hard eyes, shaking their heads at the sheer dumb luck of being white. It was routine as laughter. Yoking erupted spontaneously, a joke of fear, a piece of kidding.

Worse things have happened, Dylan knows, but still it's not so funny. And it's not so funny to be one of those guys roughing Dylan up, either. Malcolm X, Dr. King, and Bobby Kennedy have all been shot dead, and anyway they're just names to these young kids. They're more familiar with the attitudes and ground-level realities the civil rights era didn't fix. The dysfunction eating away at New York City and Brooklyn, which no one in power has wanted to talk about for a decade or two, is now impossible to ignore.

The forces behind the anger and fear outside Dylan's house in *The Fortress of Solitude* had been growing unchecked in Brooklyn for years. Back when *Last Exit to Brooklyn* was published in 1964, the same year Lethem was born, a crisis was brewing that New York City's leadership was not equipped to handle. America's GDP was still on the march, and the city was still at the center of it, still the financial capital, still the manufacturing capital, still outpacing most U.S. states in retail trade. Still, still, still. But what about the future?

As the historian George Lankevich argues in his book *New York City*, a certain blithe denial reigned among city officials. Job growth was a small fraction of the national average and a growing segment of the population relied on government aid. Racial conflicts were coming to the fore nationwide, including in destination cities of the Great Migration. Major riots broke out in nearby Newark, New Jersey (1967), in Detroit (1967), and in Chicago and Washington (1968, in the days after the King assassination). New York, with its famously close quarters and its tradition of confrontational politics, threatened to become a pressure cooker. Parts of Brooklyn—a place stricken by economic stagnation and home to more black residents than any other borough—seemed to be dry tinder ready for a spark. During a 1964 heat wave, four days of sporadic rioting had broken out in Harlem and Bedford-Stuyvesant after a police officer shot and killed a black boy in Harlem. Yet voters were alarmed enough about crime to overwhelmingly side with the cops: a proposal for a civilian review board to monitor police behavior was struck down, angering minority groups who distrusted police. In retrospect it is perhaps surprising that New York did not have a much larger riot, a fact that many have credited to the leadership from 1966–73 of Mayor John Lindsay, who had a very mixed record in other respects.

Nevertheless, crime was on the rise, and it would rise much higher in the ensuing decades. Living conditions and safety declined around low-income housing projects that had been built with the opposite intention in mind. Slum dwellings had been razed to construct the Walt Whitman and Raymond V. Ingersoll Houses, bordering Fort Greene Park and located where Whitman once lived. They were proudly billed as the world's largest public housing project when they were renovated in the fifties. A *New York Times* reporter gave this assessment of the result (in a news article, not an editorial): "Nowhere this side of Moscow are you likely to find public housing so closely duplicating the squalor it was designed to supplant." Marianne Moore, recall, was living just across the park then. Toward the end of her time there, an elderly woman was mugged and beaten in the subway near Moore's apartment; her neighbor was robbed three times; people sometimes slept on the stoop of her building. She bought a new lock for her door and a can of tear gas but, she reluctantly admitted, she still didn't feel safe. By 1966 she was gone, back to Greenwich Village. She moved only after much urging from family and friends. "It's a terrible thing to be beset by fear," she told the *New York Times* just after her departure. The article's headline is "Brooklyn Loses Marianne Moore" and the reporter writes that she "was sometimes called Brooklyn's last ornament."

Leaving aside "the Manhattan-oriented enclave on the Heights," the late L. J. Davis once wrote, some felt that when Marianne Moore left Brooklyn, "the sun had set forever on its literary life." And yet as Moore was leaving, Davis was one of a group of writers who passed her on their way in. Where one saw decline, others saw opportunity, and Brooklyn's literary life went on.

Davis opted to buy a cheap, neglected house in Boerum Hill in 1965, on Dean Street in fact. "Anyone who chose to move to the neighborhood was in some way crazy," he later said. "I know I was." In several well-received novels written in the late sixties and early seventies and in occasional essays and interviews, Davis paints a rather caustic portrait of the Brooklyn of this era. "Davis is not a writer tender of others' susceptibilities," Paula Fox has written, being polite. In other words, he's mean. He's also exceptionally funny. *A Meaningful Life* (1971), reissued by New York Review Books in 2009, is a very enjoyable novel—if you don't mind some truly uncomfortable reading.

By the late sixties, parts of Brooklyn that were once prosperous had faltered and become unstable. Some educated newcomers, though, were just starting to reenter the picture, hunting for houses with "good bones," hoping to spiff things up. The urban poor and the middle class began to cross paths at the corner store—and not always with a smile. In subtle and not-so-subtle ways, a tussle for the turf was taking shape, and one side had the advantage of a thicker wallet. Davis's novel chronicles the wrenching and halting beginnings of Brooklyn's era of gentrification, a word so politically fraught that to this day it will silence a Brooklyn auditorium full of people wondering who will say the wrong thing. In *A Meaningful Life*, L. J. Davis stands up and says the wrong thing. He spins out his comic tale and pays no heed to the fact that he's stomping around on the fault lines separating races and social classes in America. You spend some time dying of laughter and you spend some time dying for him to change the subject. I suspect that some of Davis's neighbors wanted to burn this book when it came out.

In the novel, Lowell Lake, intelligent but comically ill-equipped for the world, wanders over from Manhattan and into the thickets of urban crisis by buying a huge Brooklyn mansion that's been turned into a rotted, foul rooming house. His marriage has been going badly. He's given up on his novel because of its "overwhelming livid awfulness" and because his nocturnal writing schedule had the drawback that "for all practical purposes, he might as well have been dead." His subsequent job at a plumbing-trade magazine has only left him fearing that he will stay in it forever: "It was surprisingly easy for him to imagine what the rest of life held in store for him, short of Negro rebellion or atomic war. It did not hold much, and he would go through it sort of standing around mutely in tense attitudes reminiscent of Montgomery Clift, not particularly liking what was happening to him but totally unable to think of a single thing to do about it." Finally he finds inspiration in an article he reads: "Creative young people were buying houses in the Brooklyn slums, integrating all-Negro blocks, and coming firmly to grips with poverty and municipal corruption. It was the stuff of life. It was what he was looking for." Lowell's wife, raised in Flatbush, wants no part of moving back to Brooklyn, unless it's the Heights or Albemarle Road, a suburban-looking street near her childhood home. It is not.

The house they buy—or really he buys, sending another wrecking ball into the marriage—is one of a cluster of grand homes near

the border of Fort Greene and Clinton Hill. Most of these were
built and owned in the nineteenth century by the cream off the top
of Brooklyn society: the Pratts, other magnates, pillars of the community. The twenty-one-room mansion that Lowell goes to see—
with ornamental brickwork, terra-cotta panels, a mansard roof,
and a turret—fits right in. But now each room is a home, sometimes
for an entire family. The real estate agent, shady as they come, has
told Lowell and his wife that for less than twenty thousand dollars
the house will be theirs, "delivered vacant." (Any Brooklyn house
hunter is well acquainted with the term, which has an ugly whiff to
it: *Don't worry about the people who live there—we can make them
go away.*) Showing the couple around the house, the realtor acts as
if the residents aren't there. Lowell sees what's cooking on a stove
in one room and blurts out to the tenant, "Soul food, huh?" He gets
a look of "implacable hatred" in response.

As it turns out, Lowell gets stuck with the task of gradually for-
cing out the tenants so he can restore the house. In one case, Lowell
mistakenly disposes of all of a destitute black man's belongings,
thinking they've been abandoned—a cheap old bed and chest, a ratty
mattress and suit—and the man confronts him about it. I wasn't the
only one cringing when Davis read this passage aloud in 2009 at
Fort Greene's Greenlight Bookstore. The scene takes place four decades earlier, but the setting is within a five-minute walk of the store.

With his narrative of unintended consequences, Davis creates
a pressurized microcosm of the central story of brownstone Brooklyn since the time the book was written. In come the expensively
educated bargain hunters, drawn by the lovely real estate and
visions of historical preservation, staking themselves on a faith in
social harmony, carrying with them a little pride, perhaps, in their
willingness to live among families poorer than their own. Out go
the people who called the neighborhood home before the "pioneers" started to "discover" it, now lacking the means to stay on a
block getting fancier by the day.

Davis could not have known when he published this book in
1971 that "brownstoners" like him would help bring about the kind

of dramatic and disruptive change that they have in the decades since. And in fact *A Meaningful Life* doesn't leave you with the suggestion that the tide of the neighborhood is going to rise, though Lowell's experience is perhaps not the best guide. For him, things go wrong, first slowly and amusingly, then quickly and shockingly. The novel eventually casts his whole project and its intentions thoroughly into darkness.

Despite the comedy that continues nearly to the end, *A Meaningful Life* offers up something of a nightmare vision. The Brooklyn streets here are sinister, barren, and frightening, lined by abandoned or burned buildings, full of people leering from the shadows and from windows overhead. Davis describes the sights on one particularly ugly block, where Lowell is being harassed by drunken men as he passes by: "Half the front doors appeared to be off their hinges, all the brownstone facings were flaking in a way that suggested rotting teeth, and naked light bulbs could be seen burning weakly in bare and garishly painted rooms beyond cheap and often ragged curtains hung from sagging bits of string." It's typical that in the midst of this description we get a bit of dark wit, in questionable taste: "The scene was so hyperbolically poverty-stricken that it didn't look real; it looked contrived, like a set for some kind of incredibly squalid version of *Porgy and Bess*."

It's often unclear what the novel's attitude is to the protagonist, since the narration closely tracks Lowell's point of view. Those tempted to make judgments about the author's own attitudes may be surprised to learn from Lethem's introduction to the 2009 edition that Davis adopted two black daughters, who were raised alongside his white children. While Lowell thinks his neighbors are making his life difficult, he is making his own life difficult, too, and the novel eventually lays waste to his notion that he can tackle urban ills and renovate his life by fixing up an old house.

The high-wire risks that are liable to alienate readers are also what make the novel significant. Like Henry Miller and Mailer on his better days, Davis doesn't appear to care whether we like his book or even like him. He's hunting bigger game. The novel explores material that most of America doesn't want to hear about—urgent and ambiguous matters like crime, class, and race that many people were seeking to ignore or "transcend" at the time the book appeared. The bleak comedy lends charm but also ups the ante by creating a discomfort that provokes thought by force. Lethem (who was a friend of Davis's son growing up) discusses the way Davis trained a spotlight on the elephant in the room.

> The dystopian reality of late 60s and early 70s outerborough New York City can be difficult to grant at this distance; these streets, though rich with human lives, were collectively damned by the city as subhuman, crossed off the list. Firehouses and police stations refused to answer calls, whether out of fear, or indifference, or both. . . . How precarious this existence was—morally, sociologically, financially—was never exactly permissible to name outside of L.J.'s books, or at least not with such nihilistic glee.

Perhaps Davis and Lethem exaggerate the local horror, for effect or out of an impulse to share war stories from the bad old days. (Lethem has written of "New Yorkers my age, we who preen in our old fears . . . mythologizing the crime-ruled New York of the seventies.") Many Brooklynites of the era would take issue with the idea that they lived in a "dystopian reality." However, a little-known 1974 nonfiction book called *Fort Greene U.S.A.*, by Barbara Habenstreit, does much to confirm the grim conditions depicted in *A Meaningful Life*. Habenstreit, a resident of Fort Greene for eight years at the time she was writing, carries out a careful examination of the neighborhood. She poses it as a microcosm of urban poverty in America, using statistics and case studies to fill out her account. Bearing a cover illustration of a crumbling block of brownstone, this book is a depressing visit to a not-so-distant past. Although the author shows much more empathy for the poor than Lowell does and gives some committed local social service agencies their due, the overall picture hits hard.

"In Fort Greene, few people leave their houses after dark if they can help it," Habenstreit writes. She describes Myrtle Avenue—which today has its grit but also its French bistro and its hip wine store with art on the walls—as a virtual wasteland. Faced with rampant shoplifting and a dwindling number of customers willing to brave the street, businesses shut their doors in a domino effect. Kentucky Fried Chicken, Habenstreit writes, opened a tiny takeout branch on Myrtle in the early seventies with floor-to-ceiling safety partitions and a closed-circuit camera. The store thus escaped robberies, but the customers did not, as teenagers stood outside and shook people down for their food. The place closed in a year. Those businesses that did remain open relied indirectly on government money: shoppers used their welfare checks, which kept the whole neighborhood economy from collapsing, Habenstreit says. In response to "a drug problem that can only be described as devastating," eighteen methadone clinics operated in the neighborhood. Offenses like purse snatching and vandalism, more so than major crimes, meant that, in her words, "an air of lawlessness prevails on the street."

The situation wasn't quite so severe in nearby Boerum Hill, where Davis and young Lethem lived at the time; a fixer-upper cost a little bit more there. But since citywide and nationwide trends played a large role, the dynamics were much the same, and conditions were still very poor. Davis said of his family, "We got robbed—not mugged, robbed—four or five times, which was not so bad, actually."

In spite of the crime, the writer Paula Fox, born in 1923, came from Manhattan to live in Boerum Hill in 1967, two years after Davis arrived. She also lived on Dean Street, oddly, as did Davis and the Lethem family (who came the next year). It was there that she wrote *Desperate Characters*, before moving three years later to adjacent Cobble Hill, where she still lives.

Desperate Characters, a slim, bleak novel published in 1970, has attracted an illustrious and powerful crowd of admirers (including Alfred Kazin). In its pages Brooklyn's disputed terrain gets a cold portrait, discolored by fear and filtered through the disintegrating fabric of a failing marriage. Recounting one weekend in the life of the Bentwoods, a white, childless married couple in their forties, the book portrays a Brooklyn close to its nadir. Otto and Sophie Bentwood live within walking distance of Brooklyn Heights but inhabit more precarious territory, as the author did at the time. Although Otto's and Sophie's personalities and politics refract the atmosphere differently, they both feel a steadily encroaching sense of threat. The Bentwoods own their town house, appointed with the domestic signposts of the intellectual class. Otto is a lawyer, and his wife, Sophie, the protagonist, is a sometime literary translator who doesn't need to work. They have a Mercedes and a second home on Long Island and live on a kind of oasis block of mostly owner-occupied brownstones. There is one boardinghouse, but the tenants are "very quiet, almost furtive, like the last remaining members of a foreign enclave who, daily, expect deportation."

In the opening scene, a stray cat Sophie has been feeding bites her hand fiercely, triggering a swelling panic she tries to suppress. Otto has warned her that she shouldn't feed the mangy cat. She doesn't want it to be true that it has bitten her—that Otto was right, that it is dangerous to venture outside, even with good motives. The wound drives the novel's suspense as Sophie spends the weekend in a state of dread. It can't be rabies, can it? Things couldn't be that bad, could they?

Around them, the Bentwoods see an atmosphere of delinquency and blight, a landscape where they feel unwelcome and embattled, where they grimly contend with garbage dumped out on the streets, dogs tormented nearby, rocks thrown through their friends' windows. Sophie is bewildered and ill at ease, unsure of what right she has, if any, to judge the community she's chosen. Otto is more confident that he's in the right and tends to paint Sophie as a hysteric. Two more Manhattanites have bought houses nearby on a poorer block than theirs. Sophie asks, "What happens to the people in them when the houses are bought? Where do they go? I always wonder about that." Otto doesn't seem to care. Sophie tells a friend that Otto is "too preoccupied with fighting off a mysterious effluvium he thinks will drown him. He thinks garbage is an insult directed at him personally."

Otto's law partner, Charlie Russel, breaks with him over Otto's lack of interest in serving a needy clientele. (Otto: "You can't imagine the people in the waiting room, a beggar's army.") Charlie, pointing up the street toward downtown Brooklyn, tells Sophie, "There's Family Court. . . . Your husband won't set a foot in there. Too low class. Half my clients spend most of their time in those urine-scented chambers."

Sophie and Otto's childlessness, while rarely discussed, is a significant element of the backdrop. Today Brooklyn is full of couples who go there to raise children, but the Bentwoods go it alone, and Sophie is troubled by a concern that her life—"the quiet, rather vacant progression of the days she spent in this house"—has turned too far inward. "Now I'm at the brink," Sophie thinks, "the extinguishing point." She is beset by the feeling that the world around her is changing too fast to keep her safe.

> There was a siege going on: it had been going on for a long time, but the besieged themselves were the last to take it seriously. Hosing vomit off the sidewalk was only a temporary measure, like a good intention. The lines were tightening—Mike Holstein had known that, standing in his bedroom with the stone in his hand—but it was almost impossible to know where the lines were.

The Bentwoods try to one-up each other morally, which leads nowhere. A man rings their doorbell and asks to use the phone to find out the train schedule from Grand Central to a town upstate, where he says his mother has suffered a stroke. Otto gives him money for the fare, but later tells Sophie he doesn't believe the man. Sophie says:

"But it's not so strange a story, Otto. It's ordinary. And what
if it wasn't true? What is $11?"

"You mean, *they* are not to be held accountable?"

"I didn't mean that. I meant, when you give something,
give it."

The argument peters out, with both showing pangs of social con-
science, as they do elsewhere in the novel (Otto more rarely), but
only enough to feel a gnawing sense of self-reproach. Sophie takes
the subway to Manhattan on the theory that taking a taxi "would
have been self-indulgence, made more obnoxious by the fact that she
could afford one." But neither she nor Otto can always suppress the
alienation and even scorn they feel about "them," who are referred
to as "the slum people."

The country is shifting underfoot—Vietnam is dividing everyone, the city is falling, strangers hate each other—and the Bentwoods don't know which way to turn. As Charlie puts it, they are
"drearily enslaved by introspection while the foundation of their
privilege is being blasted out from under them." Such intimations
and metaphors of violence recur throughout, underscoring a ferocious social upheaval that Fox makes palpable by addressing it
both in miniature and indirectly. Jonathan Franzen has said about
the novel, "I had never read a book before that was about the indis-
tinguishability between an interior crisis and an exterior crisis."

Like *A Meaningful Life*, *Desperate Characters* traffics in uncomfortable truths. Fox won't let us have our avoidances, our unexam-
ined beliefs. In a 2001 interview, she said, "When there's a terrible
murder, people who are interviewed say, 'This has always been a
quiet neighborhood.' That is so dumb and uninformed! The earth is
not a quiet neighborhood. There isn't anyplace that's a quiet neighborhood."

No matter how the Bentwoods look at it, it seems that in their
neighborhood, in their city, a kind of war is on. There might be
friendliness and cooperation and good faith, too, but one shouldn't
pretend there's no battle. On one side the tenants at the boarding-

house look like they "expect deportation," as though they're in a hostile foreign land. On the other "the besieged" hose vomit off the sidewalks while the invisible lines tighten around them. Both sides think they're losing. Both might be right.

⌘

Jonathan Lethem, born in 1964, was a young boy when Paula Fox was writing *Desperate Characters* just down the street. Davis and Fox were writing about the Brooklynites of his parents' generation. In his late thirties, with five novels under his belt, Lethem looked back at his youth in the neighborhood in *The Fortress of Solitude* (2003). Its portrait of the area is less stark than Fox's, more expansive. The core of the book takes place in the seventies, when in many respects New York City declined even further, especially in the outer boroughs. Commission after commission had warned of the city's fiscal state, but not nearly enough action was taken before financial catastrophe came to visit in 1975, arguably the rock-bottom moment for New York. On October 17, New York City's cash needs totaled $477 million, but the balance in all its accounts was a hair less than that. Actually it was $34 million. The city was fifty-three minutes from default when a deal was reached for a short-term fix. But New York needed help from the country, and President Gerald Ford did not want to give it. He took a firm position against any bailout despite warnings of the nationwide ripple effects of a bankruptcy. "FORD TO CITY: DROP DEAD" read the famous agonized cry on the cover of the *New York Daily News*.

State and federal intervention finally averted a city collapse, but painful austerity measures and other consequences followed. During the 1977 World Series, the television broadcast showed an abandoned school on fire near Yankee Stadium. At the time the Bronx had for years been losing as much as four square blocks of housing per week to physical decay and suspicious fires. Speaking over the image of the building ablaze, announcer Howard Cosell said, "There it is again, ladies and gentlemen, the Bronx is burning." One July night in a heat wave in 1977, the year the Son of Sam killer was on the loose, the power went out in the city. Many parts of Brooklyn, particularly Bushwick, Bedford-Stuyvesant, and Crown Heights, were lit up by fires and beset by looting in what Mayor Abe Beame called "a night of terror."

The blackout makes a touching appearance in Lethem's novel. Young Dylan, the main character, is out of town for once, in Vermont courtesy of the Fresh Air Fund, a charity that sends city kids to the country for the summer. He's fallen for the daughter of the family hosting him, so when footage of the blackout chaos in New York appears on the news, he tries to act casual, playing it cool. But that night, Lethem writes, "Dylan lay dreaming awake of the city on fire." For Dylan, the seventies in Brooklyn are not about urban decay, fiscal shortfalls, and the limitations of the civil rights movement. They are the world of his youth, at once frightening and exhilarating, perplexing and charged with meaning. In some ways he is as embattled as the Bentwoods, and more vulnerable. He can never be sure what path to take home, what group of kids might shake him down with no one around to help: "Adults, teachers, they were as remote as Manhattan was to Brooklyn, blind indifferent towers." But the streets as seen through Dylan's and Lethem's eyes are tinged with a reverie and nostalgia entirely absent from *Desperate Characters*. The writing is jazzy, loose, even exuberant, and *The Fortress of Solitude* is suffused with the fumbling excitement of reaching across social boundaries, of forging a relationship to the world on the fly.

Lethem's family, he has written, defined themselves as "artists or potential artists, . . . hippies, protesters, commune dwellers, Quakers, white kids but in public school." His father was a serious and inventive painter, and his mother held odd jobs like piercing ears in Greenwich Village. She destroyed lettuce and grapes in the supermarket because they'd been picked by exploited migrant workers. Both parents were deeply involved in volunteering and liberal activism; they marched against Robert Moses freeways (one of which cut right through the neighborhood next door), against Vietnam, against nuclear power. For them Brooklyn, and specifically Boerum Hill, was a natural place to be. Alongside black and Puerto Rican families and "some new white renovators who'd launched an unsystematic gentrification," five or six houses in the immediate blocks served as communes for young people. Lethem writes, "The neighborhood was a laboratory, a zone of mixing, never defined by one ethnicity or class," and it felt accepting, at least at first. The Lethems were among the same wave of white brownstoners as the Bentwoods, but instead of being shut inside a claustrophobic house, the Lethems threw open the doors—to friends from back in Greenwich Village, to a new crowd from the area, even to other lovers. Where the Bentwoods saw a social ecosystem of trespasses and distrust, the Lethems saw neighbors and potential allies in a new social order.

Lethem clearly modeled Dylan's parents, Rachel and Abraham Ebdus, on his own, with some significant variations. Rachel, a chain smoker of cigarettes and marijuana, insists on sending Dylan to a public school with only two other white students. Otto Bentwood probably wouldn't have approved, any more than Isabel Vendle does in *The Fortress of Solitude*. Vendle, an older white woman who coins the term Boerum Hill in an effort to impart some class by evoking the area's Dutch past, is a kind of grande dame of the neighborhood's slowly whitening face, policing the area to make sure her kind of people set the tone. To her, Boerum Hill is "partial, recalcitrant, corrupt." She wishes "she could slather money over Dean Street entirely, could bribe the man with the car with the painted flames to polish it on Pacific or Nevins instead or just drive it into the Gowanus Canal." Isabel urges her Dean Street neighbor Rachel to consider private school for Dylan—Packer, the Friends School, or St. Ann's—and even offers to help pay for it. "It isn't about money," Rachel answers. "I believe in public school." Rachel also tells her son to call their neighborhood Gowanus, because Boerum Hill is "pretentious bullshit."

Even after Rachel skips town and even as his father holes himself up in his top-floor studio, Dylan takes their optimistic sense of possibility with him to the blocks around their house. There he tries to keep his fear under wraps, finds friends, and plays ball games packed with the drama of childhood defeats and victories in the fading light of wonderfully evoked summer afternoons.

Dylan finds his most crucial ally in a boy named Mingus Rude, who becomes a popular kid about town after he moves in down the block. He's the son of a black man, a washed-up former soul singer for a chart-topping group, and another absentee white mother. Dylan and Mingus grow close, ardently pursuing their pastimes— comic books, stickball, graffiti, pop music, chasing girls, smoking pot—with Mingus leading the way. He is more confident, Mingus, more of a piece with the surroundings and one grade older, at an age when that matters. But they share crucial things, not least the experience of growing up without a mother and of trying to walk a delicate line in an urban environment whose growing pains mirror their own.

> The grid of zones, the huddled brownstone streets between prison and projects, Wyckoff Gardens, Gowanus Houses. The whores on Nevins and Pacific. The high-school kids pouring out of Sarah J. Hale all afternoon, black girls already bigger than *yo mama*, Third Avenue another no-man's-land, the empty lot where *they raped that girl*. The halfway house. It was all halfway, you walked out of your halfway school and tried to chart a course through your halfway neighborhood to make it back to your own halfway house, your half-empty house.

For Dylan there's a critical bond between these two, this "uncanny sporadic pair, their solidarity a befuddlement to passersby," though Mingus's presence later grows more sporadic than Dylan would like. Mingus puts Dylan in reach of the social life he craves among the cool kids who look nothing like him. Mingus gives him cover in the neighborhood when he wants to join the crowd, brings him along one cherished day to a DJ jam session where he's the only white face. Their relationship is made magical when Dylan allows

Mingus to share a ring given to him by a vagrant—a ring that confers supernatural powers. It allows the two boys to fly, to take on the role of a superhero and fight crime. As Dylan felt when he first met Mingus, "Anything was possible, really." Maybe Dylan's mother was on to something real. Maybe all could be made right, and Brooklyn could be a kind of multicultural commune where everyone is welcome and safe.

But Dylan's father, Abraham, can only wonder the opposite when Mingus gets caught mistakenly breaking up a drug sting in Fort Greene while wearing a superhero costume. What Abraham thinks but does not say, never mind getting an answer: "*Is Brooklyn itself a geographical form of insanity?*" Just down the street, Mingus's father is going to pieces, padding around his dark sanctum in a threadbare robe; he and Brooklyn have discovered freebase cocaine. A few years down the road, it'll be crack, which will take hold of Brooklyn's poor neighborhoods like a strangling vine.

The bridge between Mingus and Dylan proves shaky as they move through adolescence, strained by the racial and class dynamics that didn't seem to matter so much back when they were kids—the divisions that Dylan's parents and so many sixties progressives hoped to overcome. Lethem has written of his actual family, "The souring of utopian optimism in the mid-seventies, a culture-historical cliché, was for us true, and personal." Dylan gets into a magnet high school in Manhattan, Stuyvesant, and becomes drawn into a new, more privileged sphere, with mixed feelings about leaving Dean Street and Mingus behind. Then he's off to his first-choice college in Vermont, working hard to pay for tuition. It's an intentional wholesale escape from the Brooklyn streets to a thinly veiled Bennington College (which Lethem attended). Dylan thinks, "If a kid from Gowanus goes to the most expensive college in America maybe he's from Boerum Hill after all. If not Brooklyn Heights."

Meanwhile, Mingus gets mixed up with a tough kid from the projects who hazed and frightened Dylan as a boy, the kind of kid who might have thrown that rock through the window in *Desperate Characters*. Mingus skips school for years at a time, holed up in his room cooking for himself on a hot plate to avoid his only parent, who's upstairs in the kitchen getting high. The boy Dylan once idolized, Mingus gets into harder drugs with intent to distribute, builds up a rap sheet, and winds up at a dead end. Despite Dylan's hard-won escape, his recollections of his Brooklyn childhood keep pulling at him like undertow—as Lethem's own memories have done, it seems. Like many of his Brooklyn forerunners—Henry Miller, Bernard Malamud, Alfred Kazin—he excelled enough at a young age to leave the trials of the place in his wake, but he came back to tell its story.

Lethem's previous novel, his breakthrough hit *Motherless Brooklyn* (1999), depicted a somewhat different slice of borough life in the seventies, eighties, and nineties. Similarly vivid and alive, this brainy detective novel takes place in much the same area, specifically Boerum Hill and the adjoining Cobble Hill and Carroll Gardens, with stop-offs elsewhere. But here Lethem trains his focus on the Italian locals who hold some sway over the territory, even in the face of the arriving brownstoners. A guy named Frank Minna picks out four of the five white kids in an orphanage in a desolate stretch of downtown Brooklyn and takes them under his wing. He's a low-level dealer in stolen goods who later sets up a detective agency that fronts as a taxi service, with the orphans as his worker bees. Minna needs minions for his shady purposes, and the kids need a parental figure. One of them, Lionel Essrog, is an unusual boy and an even more unusual narrator: he has Tourette's syndrome. His words spill out in barrages of clever puns and profanity. Minna, a believer in tough love—with the emphasis on tough—initiates him and the other "Minna Men" into an Italian Brooklyn realm that lines Court Street and the surrounding area.

> Minna's Court Street was the old Brooklyn, a placid ageless surface alive underneath with talk, with deals and casual insults, a neighborhood political machine with pizzeria and butcher-shop bosses and unwritten rules everywhere. All was talk except for what mattered most, which were unspo-

> ken understandings. The barbershop, where he took us for
> identical haircuts that cost three dollars each, except that
> the fee was waived for Minna—no one had to wonder why
> the price of a haircut hadn't gone up since 1966. . . . The bar-
> bershop was a retirement home, a social club, and front for
> a backroom poker game. The barbers were taken care of
> because this was Brooklyn, where people looked out.

No one who really counts on Minna's Court Street has a job in Manhattan. And everyone seems to know everyone else from way back,
because they grew up just around the corner. Older men sit out on
their stoops together, or on lawn chairs on the sidewalk, trading
stories and jibes.

Minna's mother, Carlotta, a taciturn but nurturing woman, is
an "Old Stove," a cook who works in her own apartment making
Italian dishes for people who swing by to pay for a plate of homemade food. Minna is a small-time mobster, but he's gotten himself
into deep trouble involving a couple of aging dons—last names
Matricardi and Rockaforte—who own a brownstone on Degraw
Street. He's knifed in the stomach and killed in the opening
sequence. It's just another Brooklyn murder to everyone but the
Minna Men, who set out to solve the case. *Motherless Brooklyn* is a
zippier but less ambitious book than *The Fortress of Solitude*; in
essence it's a crime novel with a postmodern Tourettic twist. Both
books, though, convey a memorable and textured sense of place. In
Motherless Brooklyn there is less of a focus on race than there is in
The Fortress of Solitude, and social issues play a background rather
than a foreground role, but each novel provides a convincing entrée
into the overlapping cultural networks that defined the Brooklyn
of the time: the world of liberal brownstoners, coming up against
the limits of their ideals; the world of Italians with deeper roots in
the borough; the world of black kids enmeshed in a tightly knit but
restrictive sphere.

Conflict is a steady presence, yes, but through Lethem's eyes
the terrain is distinct from the bleak landscape that L. J. Davis and

Paula Fox portrayed; it's less of a battleground than a mosaic, a mosaic-in-progress that looks different depending on your angle. Where Davis and Fox show the rot at the core of urban America that too often met with a blind eye, Lethem captures a different aspect—also underrepresented—of the story of city life. In his Boerum Hill, always "a zone of mixing," well-heeled newcomers brought tension and ended up effecting some changes that Dylan's family would lament. But Lethem's writing is nuanced enough to avoid casting gentrification in straightforward terms. The evolution of Brooklyn was and remains halting, fragmentary, and uncertain; it resists being slotted into a political narrative. What Lethem brings is an eye for life in the streets—a laboratory of democracy that the suburbs cannot replicate. His work recalls the photography and films of Brooklyn native Helen Levitt, particularly her documentary of 1940s Spanish Harlem called *In the Street*, a fourteen-minute film that illustrates the lyricism and theatrics that transpire every day, on every block. Lethem's novels stand in Walt Whitman's shadow, too, dramatizing the weird tumult and diversity of the American city. Lethem brings out the egalitarian poetry in what happens close to the ground.

12.

A Hint of Things to Come

PAUL AUSTER, A RENAISSANCE IN FORT GREENE

WHEN PAULA FOX AND L. J. DAVIS WERE WRITING ABOUT THE beginnings of the so-called brownstone movement, its future was, at the very least, unclear. As *Desperate Characters* and *A Meaningful Life* suggest, if anything Brooklyn and New York were on the way down in the late sixties and early seventies, as was urban America at large. In 1968, a high-ranking New York official said, "The city has begun to die." Seven years later, it went broke. Crack cocaine, the AIDS epidemic, and the city's highest recorded crime rates were still to come. Brooklyn could have gone the way of Detroit.

Instead it has had a renaissance. This revival has often been traced back to the return migration of white-collar home owners and the brownstone movement, but to link the developments too closely is to imply a history more simple than the real thing. The college-educated renovators began arriving in earnest in the sixties, as Fox, Davis, and Jonathan Lethem's parents did, and in 1971 Davis was already hailing brownstone Brooklyn—and not only the Heights—as a haven for writers. But home restoration and cultural vitality would not be the lead story for a long time to come. Many gave up waiting for Brooklyn to feel safe and prosperous, picking up stakes and leaving it behind. In the 1970s, Brooklyn lost 14 percent of its population and fully a third of its white residents. Violence in New York City reached a new high in 1981. Four years later, the leading cause of death for New Yorkers in their early twenties was homicide. (For ages twenty-five to forty-four, it was AIDS.) And the crime rate in the late eighties and early nineties surpassed the record mark again.

In other respects, conditions improved in the eighties as the city climbed out of its mid-seventies fiscal hole. During the mid-eighties bull market, the New York employment picture brightened considerably. Median family income increased by 29 percent over the course of the decade, compared to 8 percent for the nation as a whole. Mayor Ed Koch, who asked "How'm I doing?" as he made the rounds of the city with a smile, was reelected with 78 percent of the vote in 1985. But as economic inequality increased, the image of Brooklyn as a forbidding place had some basis in fact. In the midst of a downturn in 1991, a Guyanese boy in the Crown Heights section of Brooklyn was killed by a car in a motorcade accompanying the Lubavitcher rebbe, the leader of a Hassidic sect, and several days of race rioting followed, during which a Jewish man was stabbed to death. The Crown Heights riots brought national attention, another scar on Brooklyn's face. Real estate prices in the borough declined by 26 percent between 1989 and 1996. Decades after the brownstoners arrived, it wasn't clear they were winning the day. Brooklyn neighborhoods varied widely and brownstone Brooklyn was spared the worst of the city's ills. But young Dylan's experience in *The Fortress of Solitude*, cowering at night on gentrifying Dean Street, reflects the reality that trouble was never too far away.

This rocky period, though, did not send the literary types packing. In fact, in many cases it kept them around. It drove living costs down far enough to allow artists to flourish. L. J. Davis, for instance, stayed on Dean Street and continued to write. Paula Fox remained in nearby Cobble Hill. In Paul Auster's *Oracle Night* (2003), a writer buys a notebook in the same neighborhood in 1982. "Many writers here in Brooklyn," says the owner of the store, a Chinese man. "Whole neighborhood full of them." Auster himself moved to the area in 1979, when his career was, by his own account, in bad shape, but in the years to follow he gave Brooklyn some wider visibility to readers, a hint of more to come.

Born in 1947, Auster had spent his twenties and early thirties forever hard up while he struggled as a writer and translator and "everything I touched turned to failure." In his absorbing memoir *Hand to Mouth*, he recounts this pre-Brooklyn period, when he and his then wife, the writer Lydia Davis, were often "no more than a short dry spell from real poverty." The account is so full of cruel twists, humiliations, and defeats that one wonders how he kept it together. Having opted out of a life devoted to the pursuit of money, Auster found himself thinking about nothing but the pursuit of money as his wallet ran on empty. He began to consider himself an ex-writer and looked around for any source of income, only that didn't work either: "I had made a total surrender, had capitulated on every point I had defended over the years, and still I was getting nowhere." His marriage broke up and his father died two months later, hitting him hard. But the "terrible irony" was that his father's will gave him some financial breathing room.

When Auster arrived in Brooklyn shortly thereafter, though, he was still virtually unknown. He lived first in Carroll Gardens and Cobble Hill and then moved to Park Slope, where he still resides. His career changed dramatically beginning in the late seventies and early to mid-eighties. In 1982 he published *The Invention of Solitude*, a moving work that's hard to place between memoir and novel, and then he made his breakthrough with the novella *City of Glass* (1985). It's a tale of mistaken identity and risky intrigue that grew out of two phone calls Auster received at his Brooklyn apartment in 1980. The man calling asked for the Pinkerton Agency both times. Auster told him he had the wrong number, but he began to wonder what might have happened if he'd pretended to be a detective for the agency. In *City of Glass*, a New York writer named Quinn (a pseudonym Auster used in college) gets three calls asking for a detective named Paul Auster, and on the third he takes the case—"and at that moment the madness begins," in Auster's words.

City of Glass and its follow-ups *Ghosts* and *The Locked Room*, which together form his best-known volume, *The New York Trilogy*, bear the hallmarks of nearly all of Auster's now copious body of work: a combination of a plot-driven style and straight-ahead prose with some of the classic tropes of postmodernism—blurred genre boundaries, framing devices, a hall-of-mirrors atmosphere, and a casting of doubt on the teller of the tale. Auster shows an abiding and central interest in "the music of chance"—the title of one of his novels. Uncanny coincidences are a consistent thread both in his fiction, sometimes at a cost to credibility, and in his nonfiction (notably "The Red Notebook" and the longer memoirs). When these unlikely events crop up, often at crucial junctures, a reader willing to believe in them can become swept into a way of looking at the world that is both pleasingly accessible and full of a wonderment that can send shivers down the neck. *Life is strange and beautiful*, the work seems to say. *Look around.* The comparison that comes to mind in this respect is John Irving. Both authors have become household names. Auster's reputation has suffered some in recent years but he remains very popular, particularly overseas, where he sells extraordinarily well and where many regard him as a literary lion of the first order. His work has been translated into forty-one languages. In Germany, taxi drivers have asked for his autograph.

Brooklyn makes appearances throughout Auster's work as a locale or a character's hometown, but Auster hasn't devoted too much artistic energy to capturing its particularities. He is not a practitioner of the social novel, and his books have focused more on favored themes and on conceptual and plot-related schemas than on place. Often they resemble parables, with a free-floating quality to the narrative. "The address is unimportant," he writes in *Ghosts*, set in the late forties. "But let's say Brooklyn Heights, for the sake of argument." In that story, the neighborhood's livable scale, its small-town urbanity, plays some role. The protagonist, a private eye named Blue, is able to follow the movements of Black (on behalf of a client called White) while living in a brownstone apartment across the street from Black's, and on the same floor. Blue can trace Black's activities and his comings and goings mostly from the window, or by following him on an errand or a short walk. The neighborhood's past is mentioned—Henry Ward Beecher preaching down the street, Walt Whitman printing *Leaves of Grass* nearby—but this is a background concern in the story, a bait-and-switch identity drama whose mood of queasy disorientation recalls Mailer's *Barbary Shore*, which takes place in the same neighborhood and period.

Oracle Night is set mostly in early-eighties Brooklyn and conveys a bit of the flavor of the place then. The protagonist, a writer who has not been working for some time, lives in Cobble Hill, and his wife has a job in the art department at a book publisher. In the novel, Court Street, a main thoroughfare of the neighborhood, is not grim or threatening, but it has a down-at-the-heel aspect that's gone missing today. (Now you'll find a Starbucks, upscale boutiques, and a recently expanded, light-filled bookstore.) The stationery store where the character buys the notebook is "the only bright façade in a row of shabby, undistinguished buildings." Another shop selling household goods is a dusty hole in the wall with half-empty shelves. Someone breaks into the couple's home and commits a robbery, and the landlord assumes it's "one of them goddamn junkies." But the culprit turns out to be someone the couple knows, and the tale takes a turn into an off-kilter reality where a notebook might have mystical properties and stories always have more stories within them, which might or might not be true.

Two films Auster wrote, *Smoke* and *Blue in the Face* (both 1995), revolve around a cigar shop in Park Slope, at the corner of Seventh Avenue and Third Street, where a novelist named Paul Benjamin, the protagonist, is a regular customer. *Smoke* features an ensemble cast and touches on the crime and drug use that was relatively common in other parts of the borough at the time, but its thematic weight comes not from such material but from those always unsettling moments when chance alters fate. (One creepy anecdote the main character tells, about a skier finding his father's body encased in ice on a mountain, is borrowed from *Ghosts*. The father's body is frozen at about the age the son has reached, making for a frightful mirroring.) *Blue in the Face*, codirected by Auster and full of celebrity cameos, has a more antic and buoyant feel.

In Auster's novel *Brooklyn Follies* (2006), the place is a generally benign backdrop. An older man, estranged from his family after a divorce, picks a now fully gentrified Park Slope as a suitable destination to live out his days. He happens to run into a beloved nephew, who is visited in turn by an unexpected relative, and soon the protagonist is forming a new impromptu family of an unlikely kind. The novel, a rather frictionless tale about the surprising ways the past can loop back and affect the present, goes down like an egg cream. A note of foreboding that appears on the final page is not sufficient to shake the gentleness of the reading experience. The book portrays Park Slope as a pleasant village-within-a-city, diverse, good for people watching and chance encounters, and blandly appealing.

Sunset Park, Auster's 2010 novel that takes place contemporaneously, once more concerns itself with "the imponderables of fate, the strangeness of life, the what-ifs and might-have-beens." The book takes its title from the Brooklyn neighborhood where several of its main characters decide to squat in a forlorn, abandoned house across from the huge Green-Wood Cemetery. It's a time of recession, and the leader of the group has trouble managing the rent on his quirky shop on Park Slope's Fifth Avenue. A roommate of his is also escaping the cost of Park Slope, where she works as a real estate agent on prime Seventh Avenue, just where Pete Hamill's father worked through beers at the pubs. Auster evokes, at moments, the ungentrified Sunset Park, a mishmash of immigrant populations where one of his characters wanders around depressed by "an area without banks or bookstores, only check-cashing operations and a decrepit public library, a small world apart." Ultimately the book is about splintered families, one real and the other makeshift, and the tone of Austerian wonder modulates into some darker notes.

Although he has not delved too far beneath the surface of Brooklyn, Auster has stoked curiosity about its wider literary scene for three decades, since before there was steady talk of such a scene. He joined Davis and Fox as precursors to the literary new-comers of today. Tourists have been known to ask Park Slope residents where they can find Auster and his wife, the writer Siri Hustvedt. And where's that bar from *Smoke* where the novelist hung out? (The interior is the Brooklyn Inn, a Boerum Hill favorite of the publishing crowd.)

Just when Auster was hitting his stride in the eighties, another important cultural development was taking shape in Fort Greene, the brownstone neighborhood where crime drove Marianne Moore away in the sixties and where "an air of lawlessness" in the seventies kept people indoors at night, as Barbara Habenstreit wrote. By the mid-eighties, as Nelson George writes in his memoir *City Kid* (2009), the area was becoming the place to be for a generation of black creative talent. The streets still had a raw edge to them, but George had seen worse.

Born in 1957, he was raised mostly in the Samuel J. Tilden housing projects in Brownsville. In his childhood, the impoverished Jewish community Alfred Kazin knew, a vista of dank little apartment buildings, was becoming an impoverished black community instead, a vista of government-run towers. Toughness reigned. "The motto of Brownsville . . . was 'I'm from the 'Ville. I never ran and never will,'" George writes. But for him the reality was different: "My father ran." George's mother raised him and his sister alone in the projects: "We were just a living, breathing statistic from the infamous Moynihan report on dysfunctional black families." But his mother believed in education, and he spent hours at the same public library where young Kazin had passed his time. George emerged as a pioneering music journalist, covering the rise and fall of Motown and R & B and the dizzying ascent of hip-hop. He had a regular column in the *Village Voice* called "Native Son," in honor of Richard Wright, a formative influence, and he also became a prolific novelist, screenwriter, and filmmaker.

"That where I live!" a young film director named Spike Lee said when George told him in 1985 that he was moving to Fort Greene. George didn't know until years later that his new place at 19 Willoughby Avenue was half a block from the house where Wright lived when he wrote *Native Son*. Artists of all kinds were arriving, passing around word of the cheap rent and the atmosphere of creative ferment, intangible but real. Lee, who had been living in a lousy apartment on Adelphi Street off of Myrtle, made a splash with his 1986 film set in Fort Greene, *She's Gotta Have It*. A home-skillet sex comedy with a singular style, the movie sent ripples that spread far beyond Brooklyn. "Suddenly black nerds were chic," George writes of the effect of *She's Gotta Have It*, adding, "The bookish gal, the scholarly teen, the wannabe historian, the dedicated cinephile, while celebrated during black history month, had rarely been icons. Spike's visibility changed that." Lee's bigger-budget follow-up, *Do the Right Thing* (1989), looks at race and violence through the prism of one sweltering day on a block in Bed-Stuy, and it made an even larger impact. Ethnic tension and crime were pressing matters in Brooklyn at the time; the murder in Bensonhurst of a black man by Italian Americans became a prominent issue in the mayoral campaign the same year the film came out. *Do the Right Thing* gave a picture of the contested streets on a personal level, where emotions ran high. It also launched many film careers into the upper echelons.

Lee became a cornerstone of a local artistic scene in Fort Greene and Clinton Hill that came to include a notable lineup: a number of jazz legends such as Wynton and Branford Marsalis; the writers Thulani Davis, Lisa Jones, Carl Hancock Rux, and in later years Danzy Senna and Touré; the artist Lorna Simpson; the actors Wesley Snipes, Rosie Perez, and Chris Rock; and the musicians Vernon Reid, Daddy-O of Stetsasonic, and Common. At the Brooklyn

Moon Café on Fulton Street, still in operation, audiences watched spoken word and other acts by performers like Mos Def, Saul Williams, and Erykah Badu. The crowd applauded by snapping their fingers so as not to wake the neighbors. As George told me, the place was Brooklyn's answer to Manhattan's Nuyorican Poets Café. Although some novels and poetry emerged from this crowd, the impulse to create channeled itself most commonly into the performing arts. George ascribes the trend in part to an emphasis on collaboration. Participating in one another's work, and feeding off of it, was part of the appeal.

This "golden age," as George has called it, took shape just as New York City was recording all-time highs in crime, in the late eighties and early nineties. A lot of the violence occurred in areas rougher than Fort Greene, but it was no middle-class paradise. The projects on Myrtle Avenue still bred crime—"you didn't fuck with Myrtle," George told me—and drugs remained a destructive local force, with dangerously cheap crack cocaine replacing heroin. Drug pushers stood outside bodegas by the pay phones and worked Fort Greene Park. (One area kid began dealing drugs at age twelve around this time, on the streets near his family's apartment at 226 St. James Place: Christopher Wallace, later known as Biggie Smalls or the Notorious B.I.G.) But again, as George has written, the advantage for the creative crowd was that fear of Brooklyn, particularly among whites, drove rents down far enough for artists to thrive. You could pick up odd jobs here and there and spend the rest of your time working on your labors of love in a nice apartment. The bohemian life was possible. There weren't many restaurants and you had to be careful at night, but to people like George it was a great place to be.

"My friends and I used to joke," he wrote in a recent essay, "that the presence of these crack dealers on select corners 'protected' us from real estate speculators and home-hungry Manhattanites."

That didn't last.

13.

A Literary Capital

THE BROOKLYN OF TODAY

PAULA FOX, L. J. DAVIS, AND JONATHAN LETHEM ALL PUBLISHED novels about the era in the late sixties and early seventies when, in Lethem's words, Brooklyn's "streets, though rich with human lives, were collectively damned by the city as subhuman, crossed off the list." To many it seemed that the borough was nearing collapse. But when Lethem published his novel *The Fortress of Solitude*, it was 2003 and he could show us, as Davis and Fox could not, how things have turned out in brownstone Brooklyn. When his protagonist, Dylan, returns to the scene of his seventies childhood late in the novel, he finds a place so deeply altered as to test belief.

> Abraham had tried to explain it a dozen times, but there was no understanding until I saw with my own eyes: impoverished Smith Street had been converted to an upscale playground. . . . The street would be barely recognizable for how chic it had become, except the Puerto Ricans and Dominicans had stuck around. They were refugees in their own land, seated on milk cartons sipping from paper bags, wheeling groceries home from Met Food, beckoning across

the street from third-floor sills, trying to pretend gentrification hadn't landed like a bomb.

On the streets that once emptied at night, where the trees were
stripped bare, where his money was routinely yanked from his
pockets, Dylan dizzily takes note of the new landscape: "Brickwork
all along the block was repointed, the brownstone lintels and steps
refreshed, the gatework repaired and reblacked—the block was like
a set for an idealized movie that fudged poverty into quaintness."

This is the face of gentrified Brooklyn today, one that any resident or recent visitor can immediately recognize. It's important to
note that the borough still has not only a struggling working-class
element but many families in extreme hardship. A number of areas
are not seeing white-collar growth, and the proportion of the population living below the poverty line, about one in five, is almost as
large as it was thirty years ago—a sobering fact. But more and more
neighborhoods are seeing an influx of the well educated and relatively privileged, many of them moving from Manhattan and others coming straight to Brooklyn from elsewhere in the country and
the world. The college-educated contingent has grown enormously
over the last three decades. This in-migration has had a demon-
strable impact and has altered the image of Brooklyn everywhere.
"It has become a cliché to say that Brooklyn is booming," the author
Suketu Mehta recently wrote. "But the change has become so
broad . . . that it looks for all the world like a difference not just in
degree but in kind." Everywhere you turn you find an article about
a new Brooklyn neighborhood that's "up-and-coming," where
entrepreneurs are answering to a burgeoning desire for more coffee
shops, restaurants, bars, and bookstores. Often these are neighborhoods that most people wanted to get out of as recently as the eighties or even nineties. This fizz of excited talk and activity slowed
during the recent financial crisis, but not by much.

Those early brownstoners who lasted through the uncertain
years have seen their demographic come to set the tone of their

environment, sometimes too much for their own comfort. But in Paula Fox's 2009 piece on L. J. Davis in the *New York Review of Books*, her outlook on Brooklyn and its evolution during her time there is fond.

> I discovered something in the passing weeks and months, the singularity, the charm of the borough: its tree-lined streets and gardens, its distinctive neighborhoods that sometimes changed by the block, and then changed in a different way when the old working-class or slum populations moved out and new ones (from all over the US and Europe too) moved in; young people, house-mad, scraping paint off marble fireplaces and mahogany banisters, overjoyed to leave asphalt Manhattan behind for what was, most importantly for some, an investment, for some a true dwelling, as true as a dwelling can be in a country, in a world, that shifts and slides as if on sand.

For L. J. Davis's protagonist in *A Meaningful Life*, his Brooklyn home-renovation project, his leap into a minefield of race and class, leads only to a realization that "he had succeeded at nothing." But Davis himself stayed put in the Boerum Hill house he bought in 1965 for $17,500, when neighbors thought he was a silly twenty-four-year-old who overpaid. After restoring the town house, he turned his $1.7 million profit in 2007.

The rise of Brooklyn as a creative capital has coincided with a rapid transformation of New York life and an overhaul of the city's image. Since 1990, New York has recorded truly amazing reductions in crime, making it the safest big city in America. In 1990, 2,262 people were murdered in the five boroughs. In 2009, fewer than 500 were killed, the lowest number since reliable recording began in 1963. Burglary and robbery were also about 80 percent below 1990 levels, despite a very poor economy. It's worth slowing down to think about that. The numbers for Brooklyn hold up correspondingly well. An average of under ten cars per day were stolen in the borough in 2009. The 1990 rate was over 122 a day.

In a city whose intellectual class is politically dominated by the left wing, many are loath to credit these successes to the bareknuckle tactics practiced under Mayor Rudolph Giuliani, the Republican who served from 1994 to 2001, when the most dramatic safety gains occurred. Giuliani had an authoritarian style and allied himself closely with the police department. Together, influenced by the "broken windows" theory of law enforcement—which recommends fixing problems when they're small—they cracked down on so-called quality-of-life offenses such as aggressive panhandling and turnstile jumping in order to set a law-abiding tone. The NYPD also used data collection and mapping to target problem areas. Its approach became more harsh and often incurred the wrath of minority groups in particular, especially after several well-publicized cases of police brutality. But those who prized safety above all felt they had reason to be glad of Giuliani's arrival. Those critics who have ascribed the safety improvements to national trends, which were also positive, need to account for the fact that over 60 percent of the nation's reduction in crime in the midnineties occurred within the five boroughs.

Despite pledges to the contrary, Giuliani did not alleviate poverty during his tenure, a very weighty failing, and his habit of alienating people had its costs for the whole city. Mid-nineties nationwide prosperity, though, shined brightly on those at higher income levels, as Wall Street boomed—as did inequality—and new buildings rose. Along with the sense of security and good fortune among white-collar workers came a host of other developments that have proved divisive ever since. New York City has attracted the kind of upper-middle-class residents that were fleeing in prior decades. The effects of that reversal have been numerous and palpable—and often lamented by the upper-middle class itself. Tourists, encouraged by city government, have descended in force. Chain stores have smelled local demand and pounced, at the expense of Mom and Pop. In the most pronounced and visible example of New York's transformation, Times Square, that infamously grimy den of vice, has become a crammed bonanza of big-box retail with a heavy corporate presence. Complaints that under Giuliani and Michael Bloomberg the city has been "homogenized, suburban-ized, and domesticated," in the words of author Sharon Zukin, are a consistent feature of the local talk, especially among subur-ban exiles who say they liked the old New York just fine. Most widely lamented of all, real estate prices have exploded since the mid-nineties, notwithstanding the deflation of the recent hous-ing bubble.

The sheer expense of living in Manhattan has inspired many to take a long look at the relative affordability of Brooklyn. Many of the people who have followed in the Brooklyn-bound footsteps of Davis, Fox, and Auster have been young creative types, just as those three were on arrival—well educated but not high-income, nor even planning to climb the corporate ladder. In the seventies and eighties, Brooklyn represented a very unconventional choice for, say, a subscriber to the *Wall Street Journal* or *Vogue*. Taxi drivers would often refuse to take you there (much more often than they do now). For some who have since moved to the borough, that's part of the appeal, though they might not put it this way. Brook-lyn's whiff of the rough-and-tumble, the "alternative," the anti-thesis of glamour—this has proved to be an often unspoken draw, as it was for the February House crowd. Brooklyn has become independent film to Manhattan's Hollywood.

Basic economics have also played a role here. Those in the arts or the academy or the nonprofit sector who once would have been able to manage the Upper West Side or the Village have sought out the generally cheaper and larger apartments in Brooklyn. Ben McGrath has referred to "liberals of both the Upper West Side and the Park Slope generations," cleverly evoking this shift. A lot of Woody Allen's characters would live in Brooklyn now. Visual art-ists, musicians, and graphic designers abound among the newcom-ers, but a disproportionate number are editors, literary agents, and writers, or some combination of the three. Brooklyn has sup-planted Greenwich Village as the destination for the intellectual or artist who craves the breath of air that comes from a decrease in rent. The pattern adheres to a certain tradition. You can trace it to the wartime residents of 7 Middagh Street, most of whom knew very little about Brooklyn when they came to live together in the beat-up house where they could split the seventy-five-dollar rent. And then there's the first line of *Sophie's Choice*, describing Stingo's arrival in Flatbush in 1947, when he wanted to make a go of being a writer: "In those days cheap apartments were almost impossible to find in Manhattan, so I had to move to Brooklyn."

Checkbook calculations do not fully explain today's Brooklyn literary boom, however. A writer or editor looking to economize would do considerably better moving to Queens, the Bronx, or Staten Island—a fact that is commonly overlooked in discussion of the Brooklyn phenomenon. The grounds for the move to Brooklyn can be practical, aesthetic, and even subconscious. The Brooklyn neighborhoods that have drawn the literary crowd have adhered closely to the ideal streetscape that Jane Jacobs famously described in *The Death and Life of Great American Cities*. Jacobs cited Man-hattan's West Village, where she lived, as her model, but a number of Brooklyn neighborhoods have managed to hew more closely to her vision than the West Village itself. This ideal streetscape incor-porates mixed uses, a diversity of income levels, and locally owned stores, and it lends an individuality to each neighborhood. If you think *Sesame Street*, you won't be far off. The ideal also embraces a human scale to the architecture, such that a person leaning out her window is never far above the treetops. She also knows the people in her building because there are only a handful of apartments, and the man behind the counter at the deli knows her, too—he doesn't have a high-rise full of people as customers. Brooklyn is full of streets like this, where the world outside the door seems somehow comprehensible, even if that's just an illusion.

Writers are readers first, and readers are interested in the story behind what they can see. In Brooklyn, the story of the place is legible and "a feeling for tradition" persists, as it did when Carson McCullers described it in the forties. Its visual icons are not skyscrapers but relics of the nineteenth century: the Brooklyn Bridge and the brownstone. Lovers of literature tend to be sentimental about the past; they are committed, after all, to an art form that requires only a pen, despite all advances in storytelling technology. Perhaps the brownstone neighborhoods of Brooklyn have proven to be the biggest draw because, as Davis wrote, on many streets "the 19th-century city is surprisingly intact and, in parts, it is unusually handsome, with its low skyline and big old trees and rows of sculptured houses of brick and brownstone. Writers seldom live where it is ugly, if they have any choice in the matter."

One factor that has kept these streetscapes relatively unaltered in Brooklyn is that many have been protected through the creation of designated historic districts. The city's Landmarks Preservation Commission was established in 1965 following the destruction of the magnificent old Penn Station, a Beaux Arts masterpiece of monumental scale. This was a heartbreaking loss. "One entered the city like a god," Vincent Scully famously wrote. "One scuttles in now like a rat." The outcry that followed the demolition led to the formation of the LPC, which protects not only individual buildings of note but whole districts. Brooklyn Heights was the first neighborhood in the city to be "landmarked," and the other brownstone neighborhoods in Brooklyn began to follow. Another key reason that much of Brooklyn's architectural character has been preserved is one more irony of urban history: Brooklyn fell on such hard times at midcentury that private real estate developers did not come knocking. If Brooklyn hadn't maintained its forbidding image and the LPC had not come along, Cobble Hill, Fort Greene, and Park Slope, for instance, might be a pincushion of ritzy high-rise towers. But in Brooklyn's dark decades it didn't pay to tear down the old and put up something new and expensive. In Manhattan's prime neighborhoods, it always pays.

Brooklyn is about change, too, but it is not as committed or adept at "Manhattan's amnesiac dance of renewal," as Lethem writes in *Motherless Brooklyn*; you feel instead the "embrace of its long memory." The cultural tradition runs deep, and it is intimately tied to America's story about itself. If you're a writer, even if you're unaware of the Brooklyn roots of many of the authors in this book, you know that there's an American mythology about the borough, suffused with nostalgia though it may be; that a team called the Dodgers epitomized the underdog, integrated baseball, and captured everyone's hearts until it broke them; that kids played ball in the streets amid all the trolleys; that you can find famous hot dogs and a melting-pot beach and boardwalk at Coney Island; that newcomers in thrall to the American idea have come through Brooklyn for generations, perhaps including your own parents or grandparents—up to a quarter of all Americans can trace their family tree through Brooklyn. You also know that no public works project in the world is as potent a literary symbol as the Brooklyn Bridge. There are no epic poems about the George Washington Bridge.

In more recent years, bookish people have thronged into Brooklyn not only because of its literary past but because of its literary present. Some writers, aspiring or established, have come to join the growing crowd of others like them, though they might prefer not to say that. Writing is a solitary and often lonely activity. It entails weighty conversations that take place silently, within the self. Ideally this plays out in "a room of one's own" and in an atmosphere of quiet. Brooklyn has a lot more rooms that fit the bill than Manhattan. They offer a distance from the commercial racket and the high blood pressure of Manhattan, as Brooklyn always has. Writers have recognized that appeal since Whitman did in the nineteenth century.

But when the workday is done, or abandoned, or perhaps never really begun, a typical writer is less interested in solitude. She might want to get coffee with a fellow slave to the page, or meet a friend in the park who will understand the problem she's having in this hopeless chapter, or go to happy hour with the friend and drown that problem in Jameson. These small moments, multiplied many times over, are what create an artistic boom, where lines of literary influence are formed, connections made, ideas exchanged. On a weekend, a writer might want to go to a party with a bookish crowd, where people understand why someone would get a great education and choose such a lousy career, where everyone has read that vicious and exact review. In New York, the Village was once the nexus for these interactions. Today it is Brooklyn.

The writers who have converged on Brooklyn in recent years are generally quite young, and they cover a wide range in background, vision, and technique. The collection of accomplished authors is a great deal more inclusive in gender and ethnicity than the group of prominent Brooklyn authors of the past, and it seemingly grows by the month. To speak only of those who write fiction, it includes Jhumpa Lahiri, Colson Whitehead, Jennifer Egan, Rick Moody, Jonathan Safran Foer, Susan Choi, Nathan Englander, Nicole Krauss, Darin Strauss, Kurt Andersen, Arthur Phillips, Julie Orringer, Rivka Galchen, Keith Gessen, Hannah Tinti, Tim McLoughlin, and Jonathan Ames. Many others could be and probably ought to be added to this list. Still more will emerge, including people who don't even know they're writers yet. Some are surely growing up now in an unfashionable neighborhood far from Manhattan, as Alfred Kazin, Bernard Malamud, and Arthur Miller did.

As writers have arrived, so, too, have other elements of literary culture. While in Manhattan bookstores keep shutting down, in Brooklyn they keep opening up and expanding. The Brooklyn Book Festival, launched in 2006, has grown to be an enormous event, the most prominent of its kind in New York and among the most prestigious in the country. Each year the borough president, Marty Markowitz, proclaims that Brooklyn is "New York's Left Bank," the creative capital of the city and of America. He's an incurable booster, but in this case he is hard to refute. Literary people from elsewhere now sometimes feel the need to take a position on the Brooklyn phenomenon, to perhaps defend the merits of their town, or to wonder, as a Washington, D.C., critic has, "if every damned writer has to do time in Brooklyn." Malcolm

Gladwell has stated, in praise of the Brooklyn-based magazine *n + 1*, "Intelligent thought is not dead in New York. It has simply moved to Brooklyn."

By now, a lot of Brooklyn writers are inclined to roll their eyes at such talk, partly because puncturing hype and enthusiasm is de rigueur, the cultural currency of our time. You'll see Brooklyn and its many literary types come in for skillful skewering on countless blogs, in humor pieces for magazines, on television, and in a witty essay Whitehead wrote for the *New York Times* called "I Write in Brooklyn. Get Over It." You'll see it, too, in cutting social chatter about Brooklynites who carry canvas bags, use laptops in coffee shops, read liberal journals, and commit other such crimes against humanity.

But a lot of people living in Brooklyn now might later look back with nostalgia at the current era of creative ferment. Many literary types in Paris in the twenties had a world-weary attitude about it and scoffed at the idea that they lived in a golden age. Wolfe: "The 'going abroad to write business' is the bunk." Fitzgerald: "Paris had grown suffocating." Someday, though, a Brooklyn writer of today might well write a book in the manner of Hemingway's Paris memoirs, *A Moveable Feast*, or Anatole Broyard's chronicle of postwar Greenwich Village, *When Kafka Was the Rage*. I can't see why we shouldn't hope so.

❧

Given the gathering of literary talent, it seems curious that we have not seen a similar profusion of literature *about* contemporary Brooklyn or even set there. Some have recently delved into the borough's history. Emily Barton and Elizabeth Gaffney explore the Brooklyn of the eighteenth and nineteenth centuries in *Brookland* and *Metropolis*, respectively. The Colm Tóibín novel *Brooklyn* takes place partly in the author's native Ireland and the rest in the Brooklyn of the early fifties, though the particulars of the borough play relatively little role. Edwidge Danticat, who now lives in Miami, writes of Brooklyn in the eighties and touches on more recent years in her work, notably *The Dew Breaker* and the family memoir *Brother, I'm Dying*. She came to Brooklyn in 1981 from Haiti, at age twelve, to rejoin her parents, who had immigrated years earlier. The family lived then in an apartment on a cul-de-sac in Flatbush called Westbury Court, a short walk from where William Styron stayed in 1949, but by then the area was heavily Caribbean rather than the "Kingdom of the Jews" portrayed in *Sophie's Choice*. Danticat, whose writing has earned her a MacArthur Fellowship, remembers seeing much of Brooklyn's vast expanse as a passenger along for the ride in the gypsy cab her father drove for decades.

As for chronicling life in the deeply changed and rapidly evolving Brooklyn of roughly the last fifteen years, a few novels do exist. *Prospect Park West*, a 2009 Brooklyn novel by Amy Sohn, is a light romp that focuses on "the more easily satirized aspects of the neighborhood" of Park Slope, as the author has said. Sohn has some fun with the personal lives of four female members of Brooklyn's liberal bourgeoisie. The markers of their days fit the twenty-first-century stereotypes of the borough's chattering classes to a tee, and the author winks as they appear one after the other: Baby and Me swim classes, playground flirting, Democratic causes, Pilates, the Food Coop, even the overheated online parenting forum.

Joanna Smith Rakoff's *A Fortunate Age* (2009) sets out to do more. Rakoff takes Mary McCarthy's 1963 novel *The Group* as a model and spins out a comedy of manners for gentrifying Brooklyn at the turn of this century. A cohort of friends, young graduates of Oberlin College, have come to New York after a thorough education in liberal principles that rate their parents' suburban lifestyles and occupations as inherently suspect, or at least *really dull, you know?* All creatively and intellectually inclined, they've nearly all decided, rightly, that Brooklyn is the place to find people like themselves. Some have moved to scruffy, hip Williamsburg, where the suffocating canyon of tenements from Daniel Fuchs's *Summer in Williamsburg* is now a landscape dotted with iced coffee and yoga mats. You have to wait in line for brunch. The young woman from the wealthiest background has opted for the leafier Cobble Hill, a

place whose khaki-clad young parents Thomas Wolfe wouldn't recognize. This crowd of friends, who work in publishing, theater,
academia, and music, regularly go out on the town and find themselves flirting with other Brooklyn partygoers who all seem to wear
glasses: "*Is our entire generation going blind?*" Rakoff knows how to
capture a social type, just so, and add a zing of humor. But the novel's attitude toward its characters gives the book trouble. Rakoff isn't
shooting for outright satire, and yet a certain condescension or even
disdain comes through. The kind of people she's describing are, I
think, more interesting than the novel makes them out to be.

In Keith Gessen's debut novel, *All the Sad Young Literary Men*
(2008), a few ambitious and intellectual guys from the Ivy League
make their way through the trying postcollegiate years, grappling
constantly, and often comically, with the cultural climate of the most
recent decades. A number of strong scenes take place in Brooklyn, a
natural setting given the story. At its best the novel manages to be
satirical without being cynical. Gessen, born in 1975, takes his own
generation seriously, which is rarer than it sounds.

Man Gone Down (2007), Michael Thomas's first novel, powerfully conveys the experience of a man who occupies an uneasy
position in the social order of today's brownstone Brooklyn. The
book was rejected by a number of publishers but later won the
prestigious IMPAC Dublin Award. The narrator, who bears much
of Thomas's own experience, is a black man who lives in spruced-
up Cobble Hill or Carroll Gardens, walking those same streets
where gentrification has landed "like a bomb." He moves among
the crowd who see one another at playdates, at the gym, at events
for parents at a progressive private school in Brooklyn Heights—
among those "who'd first rejected their suburban origins then
rejected Manhattan's crush and bustle." His blue-blooded white
wife and his biracial children, he senses, give him an entrée into this
social circle that wouldn't otherwise be granted, despite his accom-
plishments and erudition: "We became a part of the 'us,' that seemingly abstract and arbitrary grouping that is able to specifically
manifest itself: the right school, the right playground, the right

stores and eateries, the right strollers, the right books and movies, the right politics, and the right jobs to bankroll all the rightness and distance them from asking whether it was perhaps all wrong."

For reasons both concrete and emotional, the narrator exists at an alienated remove from this "us." His wife's friends don't know that his father slipped away from the family, little by little, an absent drunk with a sloppy, happy-go-lucky charm that sets his son on edge. His mother sneaked him into good schools in a wealthy suburb when the family was living poor in Boston, but she was a hard drinker, too, and by now she's gone. They don't know he got kicked out of Harvard after a run-in with the law and has battled with drink himself, and they don't know about what happened at camp growing up. Pressing on him heavily now is what needs to happen in the four days in which the main action of the book takes place; while his wife takes refuge with the kids at her mother's place, he needs to come up with thousands of dollars of rent and tuition for the children. And he doesn't have steady work, having flamed out as an adjunct professor. He's back to working construction jobs, renovating the homes of the kind of rich folks he sees at dinner parties. He embodies, in a sense, the push-and-pull beneath the languid, happy surface of a Brooklyn environment that sometimes "feels like a giant set for a sitcom about trendy young people," in Suketu Mehta's words. Thomas makes us see what we might not have seen before. What is more, he makes us feel it. His picture of Brooklyn life is recognizable, but more layered and rich than the one we know. In the tradition of some of the best Brooklyn literature of the past, it challenges the story we've heard and gives us a greater insight into American life through the prism of Brooklyn, where black meets white within one family, where day laborer meets scholar within one man.

❦

A remarkable number of the writers in Brooklyn today have shown real promise and achieved artistic success, whether they have written about the place or not. Jhumpa Lahiri, for instance, who lives in the Fort Greene area, is one of a very few writers to have become an immediate sensation with her debut short-story collection, which reached the top of the best-seller list and won the Pulitzer Prize. In that collection, *Interpreter of Maladies*, in the novel *The Namesake*, and in another collection, *Unaccustomed Earth,* she writes largely about Indian American immigrant families and their American-born children (setting an occasional scene in Brooklyn). She has struck a chord, though, among a swath of readers with no familiarity with that experience at all. Her technique, with major themes often miniaturized or rendered in a minor key, bears the influence of Alice Munro and Mavis Gallant. Lahiri not only has a facility with efficient portraiture and the telling detail; what is rarer, she combines a raconteur's charms with a quiet, sometimes painful intensity.

Jennifer Egan, not yet fifty, has published a story collection, long-form journalism, and four novels, each with an element of real originality: *The Invisible Circus*, *Look at Me*, *The Keep*, and, most recently, *A Visit from the Goon Squad*. Her work is spirited even when the material has a serious emotional weight, as it often does. Egan has become a more inventive writer over the course of her career and has attracted a growing chorus of praise, particularly for *A Visit from the Goon Squad*. The goon squad is time, and the book, which takes its epigraphs from Proust, adopts a fresh approach—part hopscotch, part *Rashomon*—to the old theme of the strange things time does to us all. In the book's intricately connected series of chapters, told from various perspectives, a major character will appear as a minor character elsewhere; you will learn about the past of a person you already know too much about; a character's whole life to come will flash before you in the space of a paragraph. It sounds like a collection of gimmicks, but it feels like more than that.

Colson Whitehead, born in 1969 and a Brooklyn resident since 1994, is a gifted writer who has made a mark from the start with his feel for a multiplicity of voices. His observations hit their spots; his comic touches hum; his sentences feint one way and then go another, leaving you to play catch-up with a smile on your face. Already named a MacArthur Fellow, he has published four imaginative novels that approach race, myth, consumerism, and much else from an angle askew from the ones we've seen: *The Intuitionist*, *John Henry Days*, *Apex Hides the Hurt*, and *Sag Harbor*, the last a coming-of-age book with more than a little autobiography. Whitehead has also written a deliciously quotable little collection of vignettes about New York life called *The Colossus of New York*.

In Susan Choi's three novels, *The Foreign Student*, *American Woman*, and *A Person of Interest*, she shows a willingness to take on the kind of large and pressing subjects that lend an urgency to her fiction: immigration; political activism and violence; technology and terrorism and racial suspicion. In *American Woman*, a left-wing young woman growing disenchanted with 1970s radicalism gets involved in a fictionalized version of the Patty Hearst case. Novels of this kind can go off the rails with so much freight loaded on the story, but Choi provides the kind of quiet insight into the characters' interior lives that political fiction doesn't commonly achieve. The same is true in *A Person of Interest*, whose more complicated narrative combines elements of the Wen Ho Lee affair and the Unabomber case. In the midst of extreme circumstances and pathological motives, the real subject that Choi dramatizes is the complex crosscurrents in the "ordinary" mind.

Nicole Krauss, born in 1974, has published three novels, all of them influenced by foreign experience and largely foreign literary forebears. Her second novel, *The History of Love*, a hall-of-mirrors narrative spanning continents and eras, drew widespread attention, particularly for the singular voice of its characters, one a lonely eightysomething man beset by loss, another an eccentric teenage girl. Krauss's third book, *Great House*, which winds together four widely separated stories that all revolve around the same desk, was a finalist for the National Book Award.

Krauss lives in Park Slope with her husband, Jonathan Safran Foer, born in 1977. Foer has become one of the more well-known and controversial writers in the country. He achieved great sales and acclaim for a book written in his early twenties, *Everything Is Illuminated*, a novel that weaved comedy and narrative high jinks into a story about a place obliterated in the Holocaust. His second novel, *Extremely Loud and Incredibly Close*, brought even more avant-garde tricks to bear and touched fresher wounds: there were symbols, blank pages, illegible mash-ups of text, and a famous/infamous series of images from September 11 arranged as a reverse flip book at the novel's end. The book received some harsh criticism, as the author must have suspected it would. Foer shows no signs of veering off his own curious course.

Rick Moody, who has lived mostly in Brooklyn since 1992, has taken his own share of literary insults, particularly in Dale Peck's 2002 review in the *New Republic* that began, for maximum attention, "Rick Moody is the worst writer of his generation." (Six years later, Moody smacked Peck in the face with a pie as a stunt at a fund-raiser in Brooklyn, smiling for the cameras, so it seems he's a good sport.) Moody, the author of nine books, including *Purple America*, *The Ice Storm*, and *The Diviners*, is not as prominent a figure as he was a decade ago, but he continues to publish big, breathing novels that spew out stories and metastories and backstories and story ideas as if he were handing out money from an overfull artistic wallet. He often explores northeastern family dysfunction, with shades of John Updike and John Cheever, but his style bears more in common with a later generation of brainy writers with an obsessive streak for capturing detail and an avid appetite for culture high and low, like David Foster Wallace. Moody's fiction often presents itself as energetic and quirky, but in the middle of things is a thread of despair—despair about the current state of things, which can feel tired, and about the everlasting state of things, which can be very moving.

With such distinctive writers now living in Brooklyn, surely more will train their narrative focus on the streets they see every day. The person in Brooklyn who sits on the stoop or leans out a window with "eyes on the street," as Jacobs described it, has a great deal to see. The special character of a neighborhood, the town-within-a-city ideal, the threats to that ideal, the struggles and strife, the palpable history, the diversity, the space to think and look at the sky, the social crosstalk that can be lively, harmonious, acrimonious, and absurd—all these are the makings of vivid writing, as the literary history of the borough shows.

Some see the uniqueness of today's Brooklyn as being under threat or on the wane. Whenever a Starbucks opens, or a chain store, or another real estate broker, you hear the refrain: there goes the neighborhood. A culturally vital neighborhood is a neighborhood where a lot of people want to be, and a place where a lot of people want to be is a place that's more expensive. Gentrification has its costs, and they are serious. Whether Brooklyn is becoming a better or worse place to live, though, does not seem the most interesting question for a fiction writer to ask. Brooklyn has been a setting and a subject for great literature about times of happiness and about times of terrible struggle. Sometimes both are occurring at once, and on the same street.

Perhaps a young Brooklyn author might now feel that living in Brooklyn is among the least interesting things about her, because just about everyone she knows seems to live there, too. If the subject now feels somehow parochial, that's an instinct worth fighting. In the literary tradition of Brooklyn, we find the opposite. Whether a talented author is writing about a sweltering ghetto or a leafy enclave, a writer or a grocery store owner, a happy child or a faltering marriage, the true subject encompasses far more than one borough. Even novels that don't seem to be about the place they depict—even the most personal and small-scale stories—tend to open up an unexpected vista onto the world that surrounds the characters. In Brooklyn those surroundings so often open a still larger vista onto the nation, and in the end we comprehend just a little bit better the whole incomprehensible whirl of American life.

Notes

Introduction

1 "paved with mattresses" . . . caved in: L. J. Davis in a public conversation with Jonathan Lethem, Community Bookstore, Brooklyn, NY, March 31, 2009.

2 more people live in Brooklyn: 2009 U.S. Census figures.

2 277 votes: Glenn Thrush, "The Mistake of '98?" *Brooklyn: A State of Mind*, ed. Michael W. Robbins and Wendy Palitz (New York: Workman, 2001), 332.

2 some residents hung black crepe: Ric Burns, James Sanders, and Lisa Ades, *New York: An Illustrated History* (New York: Alfred A. Knopf, 2003), 217.

2 "remote as . . . Tibet": Ralph Foster Weld, *Brooklyn Is America* (New York: Columbia University Press, 1950), 3.

4 "young men were writing": Thomas Wolfe, *Writing and Living*, reprinted in *The Autobiography of an American Novelist*, ed. Leslie Field (Cambridge, MA: Harvard University Press, 1983), 136.

1. The Grandfather of Literary Brooklyn: WALT WHITMAN

7 "Just as you feel": Walt Whitman, *The Complete Poems*, ed. Francis Murphy (New York: Penguin Classics, 2004), 191.

7 To entertain people: David S. Reynolds, *Walt Whitman's America: A Cultural Biography* (1995; repr., New York: Vintage, 1996), 156.

8 He took on the look: David S. Reynolds, *Walt Whitman* (New York: Oxford University Press, 2005), 15.

8 "There was a great boom": Reynolds, *Walt Whitman*, 10.

8 "I found myself": Jerome Loving, *Walt Whitman: Song of Himself* (Berkeley: University of California Press, 1999), 178.

8 "No other book": Malcolm Cowley, introduction to *Leaves of Grass: The First (1855) Edition*, by Walt Whitman (New York: Penguin Classics, 1961), viii.

9 You could stand: Reynolds, *Walt Whitman's America*, 30.

9 In Brooklyn in 1823: *New York: A Documentary Film, Episode 2: Order and Disorder*, directed by Ric Burns.

9 about 60 percent: Edwin G. Burrows and Mike Wallace, *Gotham: A History of New York City to 1898* (1999; repr., New York: Oxford University Press, 2000), 348.

10 born the same year: Reynolds, *Walt Whitman's America*, 23.

10 Whitman's great-uncle: Ibid., 12.

10 That rout: Kenneth T. Jackson, introduction to *The Neighborhoods of Brooklyn*, 2nd ed., by Kenneth T. Jackson and John Manbeck (New Haven, CT: Yale University Press, 2004), xx.

10 "Good God!": Burrows and Wallace, *Gotham*, 237.

10 "The Declaration": Jackson and Manbeck, *Neighborhoods of Brooklyn*, xxi.

10 Between 1790 and 1810 . . . from the river: Burrows and Wallace, *Gotham*, 390–91.

11 Their known addresses . . . Portland Avenue: JoAnn P. Krieg, *A Whitman Chronology* (Iowa City: University of Iowa Press, 1998).

11 Whitman attended: Reynolds, *Walt Whitman*, 5.

11 "No comparable figure": Harold Bloom, introduction to *Leaves of Grass*, 150th Anniversary Edition, by Walt Whitman (New York: Penguin Classics, 2005), xi.

11 At age eleven: Reynolds, *Walt Whitman's America*, 34.

11 Few residents wanted: Ibid., 40.

11 The stodgy and relatively expensive: Ibid., 81.

11 Soon Whitman would enter: Ibid., 45.

12 "O, damnation": Loving, *Walt Whitman*, 41.

12 "situation for grandeur": Walt Whitman, *Walt Whitman's New York: From Manhattan to Montauk*, ed. Henry M. Christman (New York: New Amsterdam Books, 1989), 137.

12 "It may not generally be known": Whitman, *Walt Whitman's New York*, 53.

12 "With much greater attractions": Ibid., 56.

13 "believed in resisting much": Loving, *Walt Whitman*, 29.

13 The poet and aesthete: Reynolds, *Walt Whitman's America*, 106.

13 Part of what spurred . . . both ways: Burrows and Wallace, *Gotham*, 582.

14 By the 1850s . . . in Williamsburgh in 1949: Ibid., 660–61.

14 Immigrants, in large part . . . roughly half in 1855: Ibid., 745–46.

14 Joining the immigrant . . . East New York: Ibid., 728.

15 "I am the poet of woman": Whitman, *Leaves of Grass*, 150th Anniversary Edition, 50.

15 Although he was not a Quaker . . . took root: Ibid., 37–39.

15 The most famous: Ibid., 172.

15 "Beecher's Ferry": Burrows and Wallace, *Gotham*, 729.

15 With his informal manner: Reynolds, *Walt Whitman's America*, 255.

16 "If a whaling ship": Loving, *Walt Whitman*, 102.

16 The paper was steeped: Ibid., 101.

16 "The attitude of great poets": Whitman, *Leaves of Grass*, 17.

16 *"We must plant ourselves"*: Loving, *Walt Whitman*, 110.

16 The owner of the *Eagle* . . . out of a job: Ibid., 111.

17 "his poetry was generally reviled" . . . "to be an art": Ibid., xi.

17 Describing "the greatest poet": Whitman, *Complete Poems*, 746.

17 "I celebrate myself": Ibid., 675.

17 "I am the mate": Ibid., 681.

18 "This is what you shall do": Ibid., 747.

18 "mass of filth": Reynolds, *Walt Whitman*, 13.

18 Boston district attorney: Ibid., 117–18.

18 "Through me many long dumb voices": Whitman, *Leaves of Grass*, 54–55.

18 poetry had restricted itself: Loving, *Walt Whitman*, xi.

19 "The scent of these": Whitman, *Leaves of Grass*, 55.

19 "It is to be hoped": Reynolds, *Walt Whitman's America*, 535.

19 "Walt Whitman, an American": Whitman, *Leaves of Grass*, 54.

19 "the greatest democrat": Loving, *Walt Whitman*, 226.

19 "Crowds of men" . . . "you might suppose": Whitman, *Complete Poems*, 189–90.

20 "How could [this poem] change": Bloom, introduction to *Leaves of Grass*, xvii–xviii.

20 "the vast Gomorrah": Burrows and Wallace, *Gotham*, 707.

21 "lung": Seth Kamil and Eric Wakin, *The Big Onion Guide to Brooklyn: Ten Historic Walking Tours* (New York: New York University Press, 2005), 44.

21 "pull-down-and-build-over-again" . . . "break things!": Walt Whitman, *The Uncollected Poetry and Prose of Walt Whitman*, vol. 1, ed. Emory Holloway (Garden City, NY: Doubleday, 1921), 92–93.

21 "Our city grows so fast": Whitman, *Walt Whitman's New York*, 137.

22 "the greatest American tragedy": Jackson and Manbeck, *Neighborhoods of Brooklyn*, xxi.

22 "Greater than memory": Whitman, *Complete Poems*, 520.

22 "a general laxity": Reynolds, *Walt Whitman's America*, 202.

22 the Dead Rabbits . . . "rule the hour": Ibid., 371.

23 "O year all mottled": Whitman, *Complete Poems*, 268.

23 New York was divided: George J. Lankevich, *New York City: A Short History* (New York: New York University Press, 2002), 113.

23 At the outset . . . "triumphant return!": Reynolds, *Walt Whitman's America*, 407.

23 In 1863, writing: Walt Whitman, "Our Brooklyn Boys in the War," *Brooklyn Daily Eagle*, January 5, 1863.

23 "the commonest average": Reynolds, *Walt Whitman's America*, 439.

23 "the greatest, best": Ibid., 440.

24 "But O heart!": Whitman, *Complete Poems*, 359–60.

24 "essentially non-conventional": Loving, *Walt Whitman*, 443.

24 "I sound my barbaric yawp": Whitman, *Complete Poems*, 124.

2. The Street Was Everything: HENRY MILLER

25 "My concern was always": Henry Miller, *Sexus* (1949; repr., New York: Grove Press, 1987), 19.

25 In a scene . . . "whoremongers": Ibid., 31–32.

26 "the greatest man": George Wickes, "Henry Miller," in *American Writers,* vol. 3 (New York: Scribner's, 1974), 170–92.

26 "In Whitman the whole": Henry Miller, *Tropic of Cancer* (1934; repr., New York: Grove Press, 1994), 239.

26 went on trial: Robert Ferguson, *Henry Miller: A Life* (1991; repr., New York: W. W. Norton, 1993), 348.

26 Brooklyn court issued a warrant: Mary V. Dearborn, *The Happiest Man Alive: A Biography of Henry Miller* (New York: Simon & Schuster, 1991), 282.

27 "We need a blood transfusion": Anaïs Nin, 1934 preface to Miller, *Tropic of Cancer,* xxxiii.

27 "to get off the gold standard": Henry Miller, *Tropic of Capricorn* (1939; repr., New York: Grove Press, 1961), 243.

27 "What is not": Henry Miller, *Black Spring* (1936; repr., New York: Grove Press, 1994), 3.

27 "a really great book": Henry Miller, *Aller Retour New York* (1935; repr., New York: New Directions, 1993), 32.

27 "What was then": Burrows and Wallace, *Gotham,* 697.

28 In the five-day draft riots . . . from attack: Ibid., 888–95.

28 In the depression of 1873: Ibid., 1023.

28 Those who had jobs: Ibid., 1012–13.

28 Middle-class families . . . to put them: Ibid., 970–73.

29 In the 1860s . . . a pioneer: Ibid., 972.

29 The well-to-do . . . *Record and Guide*: Christopher Gray, "When the Pratts Decamped for Manhattan," *New York Times,* November 18, 2010.

29 Less costly housing: Burrows and Wallace, *Gotham,* 972.

30 "uncivilized classes": Ibid., 1033.

30 Some Brooklyn residents: Lankevich, *New York City,* 120.

31 And some Manhattan commercial and political interests: Burrows and Wallace, *Gotham,* 934–35.

31 The bridge's first engineer . . . cost many their lives: Ibid., 935–37.

31 Whitman had predicted: The Academy of American Poets, "Poetry Landmark: The Brooklyn Bridge in New York City," http://www.poets.org/view media.php/prmMID/5754.

31 "to the right the East river": Walt Whitman, *Prose Works* (Philadelphia: David McKay, 1892; Bartleby.com, 2000), www.bartleby.com/229/.

32 Both husband's and wife's parents: Dearborn, *Happiest Man Alive,* 20–22.

32 Henry's original last name: Ferguson, *Henry Miller,* 2. Dearborn has the last name spelled Muller.

32 "Where others remember": Miller, *Black Spring,* 5.

32 In the most insular: Ferguson, *Henry Miller,* 3.

32 Sometimes his parents . . . many of his friends: Henry Miller, *Book of Friends* (Santa Barbara, CA: Capra Press, 1976), 11.

33 He once gave away: Dearborn, *Happiest Man Alive*, 26.

33 "the morgue": Miller, *Black Spring*, 222.

33 On North First Street . . . German songs of his youth: Jay Martin, *Always Merry and Bright: The Life of Henry Miller: An Unauthorized Biography* (1978; repr., New York: Penguin Books, 1980), 8–9.

33 "no one seemed to notice": Miller, *Black Spring*, 4.

33 "some of the gang": Miller, *Book of Friends*, 21.

33 Henry gladly got involved: Ibid., 23.

33 "Our pleasure was": Ibid.

33 Sometimes Alfie Melta: Ibid.

33 "Napoleon, Lenin": Miller, *Black Spring*, 4.

33 "It was a life": Ferguson, *Henry Miller*, 9.

34 Miller described how: Miller, *Tropic of Capricorn*, 118; Miller, *Book of Friends*, 60; and Ferguson, *Henry Miller*, 9.

34 "seemed to be replicas": Miller, *Book of Friends*, 31.

34 "the street of early sorrows": Ibid., 28.

35 He learned very quickly: Dearborn, *Happiest Man Alive*, 27–28.

35 "Jews' Highway": Clifton Hood, *722 Miles: The Building of the Subways and How They Transformed New York* (New York: Simon & Schuster, 1993), 136.

35 Williamsburg was at the vanguard . . . intact ever since: Ilana Abramovitch, introduction to *Jews of Brooklyn*, ed. Ilana Abramovitch and Seán Galvin (Hanover, NH: University Press of New England, 2002), 6. Brooklyn had about 36 percent of New York City's Jews in 2000, according to the Association of Religious Data Archives.

35 "sheenies": Dearborn, *Happiest Man Alive*, 38.

35 "After the Williamsburg Bridge": Henry Miller, *Moloch* (published posthumously, New York: Grove Press, 1992), 223–24.

35 "intolerably Jewish": Dearborn, *Happiest Man Alive*, 42.

36 In his adolescence . . . see her there, he said: Miller, *Book of Friends*, 96–97.

36 furiously blamed: Ferguson, *Henry Miller*, 14.

36 When Henry once broached: Dearborn, *Happiest Man Alive*, 54.

36 "a sign of manhood": Ibid., 48.

36 Beatrice had been educated: Ibid., 56.

36 "lugubrious parlor": Miller, *Tropic of Capricorn*, 279.

37 When Beatrice got pregnant: Dearborn, *Happiest Man Alive*, 60.

37 In his father's tailor shop: Ibid., 51.

37 "He was very much a product": Miller, *Tropic of Capricorn*, 267.

38 "Cosmodemonic Telegraph Company": Ibid., 9.

38 Miller worked out of . . . "every descriptive phrase": Dearborn, *Happiest Man Alive*, 64–72.

38 June Smith: Ferguson, *Henry Miller*, 78.

38 "America on foot": Miller, *Tropic of Capricorn*, 339.

39 Henry married June: Dearborn, *Happiest Man Alive*, 87.

39 far too expensive: Ferguson, *Henry Miller*, 96.

39 "We occupied": Henry Miller, *Plexus* (1953; repr., New York: Grove Press, 1987), 9.

39 "A short walk": Ibid., 12.

40 288 Clinton Avenue: Correspondence with Randy Chase.

40 As he describes it: Miller, *Plexus*, 505.

41 "No more hopes": Dearborn, *Happiest Man Alive*, 99.

41 In the Village . . . Jean Kronski: Ibid., 102–3.

41 (an invented name): Ibid., 104; and Ferguson, *Henry Miller*, 132. Whether June invented the name herself is a matter of dispute.

41 Henry Street near the corner of Love Lane: Dearborn, *Happiest Man Alive*, 106.

42 "Using soiled shirts": Anaïs Nin, *Henry and June: From A Journal of Love: The Unexpurgated Diary of Anaïs Nin, 1931–32* (New York: Harvest Books, 1990), 46.

42 "Dear Val": Henry Miller, *Nexus* (1960; repr., New York: Grove Press, 1987), 153.

42 He broke every piece: Dearborn, *Happiest Man Alive*, 110.

42 at his office: Miller, *Book of Friends*, 79.

44 "in midnight mood" . . . "A dump heap": Miller, *Moloch*, 263–66.

44 "direct as a knife thrust": Dearborn, *Happiest Man Alive*, 131.

45 "This is not a book" . . . "I will sing": Miller, *Tropic of Cancer*, 2.

45 "I have no money": Ibid., 1.

45 "the Paris book: first person": Ferguson, *Henry Miller*, 186.

45 "First I want to be read": Ibid., 215.

46 "Will you get a divorce": Henry Miller, *My Life and Times* (Chicago: Playboy Press, 1971), 159.

46 "the drunks and dead-beats": George Orwell, "Inside the Whale" (1940), in *All Art Is Propaganda: Critical Essays*, by George Orwell, ed. George Packer (New York: Houghton Mifflin Harcourt, 2008), 99.

46 "the task which the artist": Miller, *Tropic of Cancer*, 253.

47 "The man who raises": Ibid., 256.

47 "I had read the most terrible": Dearborn, *Happiest Man Alive*, 155.

47 "the written word loses": Ibid., 190.

48 "a tomb of June": Ibid., 161.

48 "I think they would hang me": Ibid., 198.

48 "I should say": Orwell, "Inside the Whale," 131.

49 "I was so lucid": Miller, *Tropic of Capricorn*, 282.

49 "I am beyond that": Dearborn, *Happiest Man Alive*, 180.

49 He took Nin on a tour: Martin, *Always Merry and Bright*, 308.

49 "New York City would become": Dearborn, *Happiest Man Alive*, 176.

50 "a working-class Proust": Ferguson, *Henry Miller*, 149.

50 "A man writes": Miller, *Sexus*, 17.

50 "Choke on it": Ibid.

51 as Ferguson notes: Ferguson, *Henry Miller*, 333.

51 "SEXUS DISGRACEFULLY BAD": *The Durrell-Miller Letters, 1935–1980*, ed. Ian S. MacNiven (New York: New Directions, 1988), 233.

52 "Writing seems so foolish": Ferguson, *Henry Miller*, 336.

52 Ferguson takes note: Ibid., 2.

53 "Once I wrote": Miller, *Book of Friends*, 28.

3. Out of the Fray: HART CRANE AND MARIANNE MOORE

54 "Rt. Rev. Miss Mountjoy": Clive Fisher, *Hart Crane: A Biography* (New Haven, CT: Yale University Press, 2002), 261.

54 "vapid and pretentious": Marianne Moore, *The Selected Letters of Marianne Moore,* ed. Bonnie Costello (New York: Alfred A. Knopf, 1997), 213.

55 He visited a friend: Paul Mariani, *The Broken Tower: A Life of Hart Crane* (New York: W. W. Norton, 1999), 199.

55 "*The Dial* bought": John Unterecker, *Voyager: A Life of Hart Crane* (New York: Farrar, Straus and Giroux, 1969), 404.

55 "I would never": Ibid.

55 He quipped that: Mariani, *Broken Tower,* 200.

55 "Hart Crane complains": Donald Hall, "Art of Poetry No. 4: Marianne Moore," *Paris Review* (Winter 1961), http://www.theparisreview.org/inter views/4637/the-art-of-poetry-no-4-marianne-moore.

55 Her biographer Charles Molesworth surmises: Charles Molesworth, *Marianne Moore: A Literary Life* (New York: Atheneum, 1990), 220.

55 "so much intuition": Hall, "Art of Poetry No. 4."

55 "one goes back": Quoted in Moore, *Selected Letters,* 214.

56 "No other American": Fisher, *Hart Crane,* 275.

56 "The more I think": Hart Crane, *O My Land, My Friends: The Selected Letters of Hart Crane,* ed. Langdon Hammer and Brom Weber (New York: Four Walls Eight Windows, 1997), 135.

56 "Walt, tell me": Hart Crane, *The Complete Poems and Selected Letters and Prose of Hart Crane,* ed. Brom Weber (New York: Anchor, 1966), 89.

56 "yes, Walt": Ibid., 95.

57 C.A.'s company made candy: Mariani, *Broken Tower,* 24.

57 At fifteen he twice: Ibid., 27.

57 But at seventeen: Ibid., 30–31.

57 He convinced: Ibid., 29.

57 The single-minded pursuit: Unterecker, *Voyager,* 52.

57 "I have had": Ibid., 51.

58 "fetid corpse": Mariani, *Broken Tower,* 65.

58 "the memoranda" . . . "throat and sides": Crane, *Complete Poems,* 27–28.

59 "The blood-dimmed tide": W. B. Yeats, *Selected Poems and Four Plays by W. B. Yeats,* ed. M. L. Rosenthal, 4th ed. (New York: Simon & Schuster, 1996), 89.

59 "I take Eliot": Unterecker, *Voyager,* 272.

59 "Perhaps this is useless": Crane, *Selected Letters of Hart Crane,* 85.

60 "At times, dear Gorham": Ibid., 92.

60 "the picture of health": Fisher, *Hart Crane,* 239.

61 "I have gone": Unterecker, *Voyager,* 355.

61 "the 'arty' middle class": Fisher, *Hart Crane,* 220.

61 Another young writer . . . *Manhattan Transfer*: Susan Edmiston and Linda D. Cirino, *Literary New York: A History and Guide* (Boston: Houghton Mifflin, 1976), 345; and Brad Lockwood, "On This Day in History: September 28: Writer of U.S.A. Trilogy and More," *Brooklyn Daily Eagle,* September 28, 2010, http://www.brooklyneagle.com/categories/category.php?id=38368.

61 "the finest view": Hart Crane, *Letters of Hart Crane and His Family*, ed. Thomas S. W. Lewis (New York: Columbia University Press, 1974), 305.

62 "Imagine my surprise" . . . "been answered": Crane, *Selected Letters of Hart Crane*, 186.

62 "This section of Brooklyn": Unterecker, *Voyager*, 356.

62 "America's first suburb": Kenneth Jackson, as quoted in John B. Manbeck, *Brooklyn, Historically Speaking* (Charleston, SC: History Press, 2008), 95.

62 as far back as 1820: Number 24 Middagh Street, at the corner of Willow Street, dates from 1820 and is the oldest house in the Heights. Ibid., 100.

62 The tracks were demolished . . . "cynosure of Paris": Francis Morrone, *An Architectural Guidebook to Brooklyn* (Layton, UT: Gibbs Smith, 2001), 59–61.

64 "As I looked up": Paula Fox, "Light on the Dark Side," *New York Review of Books*, December 3, 2009.

64 A series of additions: Caroline H. Dworin, "Trying to Recapture the Glory Days, Up in the Old Hotel," *New York Times*, April 3, 2009.

65 "Hell's Half Acre": Leonard Benardo and Jennifer Weiss, *Brooklyn by Name: How the Neighborhoods, Streets, Parks, Bridges, and More Got Their Names* (New York: New York University Press, 2006), 51.

65 "Sands Street at night": John Kobler, *Capone: The Life and World of Al Capone* (Da Capo Press, 2003), 24.

65 "Whitman before him": Mariani, *Broken Tower*, 32.

66 When Crane was seriously drunk: Edmiston and Cirino, *Literary New York*, 345.

66 "roll in the gutters": Mariani, *Broken Tower*, 47.

66 New York City's mayor: Lankevich, *New York City*, 157–59.

67 "New York is truly": Langston Hughes, "The Fascination of Cities," *Crisis* 31 (January 1926), 138–40.

68 "Upon the steep floor": Hart Crane, *The Collected Poems of Hart Crane*, ed. Waldo Frank (New York: Liveright, 1933), 104.

68 "Everytime one looks": Crane, *Letters of Hart Crane and His Family*, 312.

69 "this Pollyanna": Mariani, *Broken Tower*, 300.

69 "The bridge as a symbol": Unterecker, *Voyager*, 447.

70 "Tomorrow afternoon": Ibid., 554.

70 He ended up: Mariani, *Broken Tower*, 308.

70 The first piece of mail: Unterecker, *Voyager*, 554–55.

70 he was walking one day . . . "ten years back": Fisher, *Hart Crane*, 388.

70 In a few weeks: Ibid., 390.

71 One night . . . why live?: Mariani, *Broken Tower*, 313–14.

71 Making the final changes: Fisher, *Hart Crane*, 421–22.

71 Waiting for the book: Mariani, *Broken Tower*, 347.

72 "Thee, across the harbor" and all subsequent quotations from *The Bridge* in Crane, *Collected Poems*, 3–58.

73 "a kind of ode": Crane, *Complete Poems*, 252.

73 "to handle the beautiful skeins": Mariani, *Broken Tower*, 233.

74 "lack of intelligibility": Unterecker, *Voyager*, 619–20.

74 "Your vision": Ibid.

74 A review Tate wrote: Ibid., 621–22.

74 Crane penned: Ibid., 622–23.

75 "The periodicity of his excesses": Crane, *Complete Poems*, 277.

75 Crane got drunk . . . over the rail: Mariani, *Broken Tower*, 419–21.

76 "The catering to dissipation": F. Scott Fitzgerald, "My Lost City," in *Writing New York: A Literary Anthology*, ed. Phillip Lopate (New York: Washington Square Press, 1998), 576.

76 "Dear Family": Moore, *Selected Letters*, 54.

77 Jim Thorpe: Molesworth, *Marianne Moore*, 90.

77 "black frenzy": Moore, *Selected Letters*, 37.

77 "there are times": Marianne Moore, *The Complete Prose of Marianne Moore*, ed. Patricia C. Willis (New York: Viking, 1986), v.

78 As Charles Molesworth notes: Molesworth, *Marianne Moore*, 111.

78 There emerged: Ibid., 103.

78 "Not so far as I know": Hall, "Art of Poetry No. 4."

78 "an amazing output": Molesworth, *Marianne Moore*, 122.

78 "had met no writers": Hall, "Art of Poetry No. 4."

78 In fact, at twenty-three: Molesworth, *Marianne Moore*, 83.

79 "an astonishing person": Alfred Kreymborg, *Troubador* (New York: Boni and Liveright, 1925), 238–39.

79 "I was . . . greatly impressed": Moore, *Selected Letters*, 4.

79 some suitors—seven: Ibid., 82.

80 "a crude, undignified": Ibid., 186.

80 At the time that Dreiser: Bill Morgan, *Literary Landmarks: A Book Lover's Guide to New York* (New York: Universe, 2003), 24.

80 "My candle burns": Edna St. Vincent Millay, "First Figs," reprinted in Edna St. Vincent Millay, *Early Poems* (New York: Penguin Classics, 1998), 51.

81 "Plague House": Molesworth, *Marianne Moore*, 231.

81 "seems much more": Ibid., 138.

81 "I like New York . . . in one boat": Moore, *Selected Letters*, 123.

81 "when you / See a light": Marianne Moore, "Callot-Drecol-Cheruit-Jenny-Doucet-Aviotte-Lady," reprinted in *The Poems of Marianne Moore*, ed. Grace Schulman (New York: Penguin, 2005), 129.

81 "Poetry": Ibid., 135.

81 "with all my heart": Moore, *Complete Prose*, 436.

82 "without doubt": Donald Hall, *Marianne Moore: The Cage and the Animal* (New York: Pegasus Books, 1970), 57.

82 It did not fall: Molesworth, *Marianne Moore*, 209.

82 "try to meet the challenge": Henry Farnham May, *The End of American Innocence: A Study of the First Years of Our Own Time, 1912–1917* (New York: Columbia University Press, 1992), 297.

82 "I must tell the truth": Moore, *Selected Letters*, 208.

82 "At a time when": Hall, *Marianne Moore*, 31.

82 "New York": Moore, *Poems of Marianne Moore*, 146.

83 In a 1922 letter: Molesworth, *Marianne Moore*, 155.

83 At one point Sigmund Freud: Moore, *Selected Letters*, 212.

83 "intensity" . . . "conforming to anything": Hall, "The Art of Poetry No. 4."

84 "God how I hate you": Moore, *Selected Letters*, 213.

84 "You have a vivid": Ibid., 494.

84 "Judging by our experimental writing": Moore, *Complete Prose*, 344.

84 She took exception: Moore, *Selected Letters*, 404.

84 "I knew some of the poems": Moore, *Complete Prose*, 360.

84 seeing Charlie Chaplin: Moore, *Selected Letters*, 236.

85 where he was stationed: Ibid., 251.

85 Miller was probably visiting: Ferguson, *Henry Miller*, 165–67.

86 Italianate and Anglo-Italianate row houses: Gerard L. Wolfe, *New York: A Guide to the Metropolis*, rev. ed. (New York: New York University Press, 1983), 459.

86 Washington Park became one of the most: Wolfe, *New York*, 453.

86 liked to play tennis: Molesworth, *Marianne Moore*, 296.

87 "seemed to her decorous": Ibid., 247.

87 "Anonymity": Moore, *Complete Prose*, 540.

87 "a city of churches" . . . "each leaf": Ibid.

87 "although he attracted attention": Ibid., 557.

87 she attended talks: Ibid., 543.

88 The Brooklyn Institute had grown: *The WPA Guide to New York City: The Federal Writers' Project Guide to 1930s New York* (New York: New Press, 1995), 453.

88 "eminent stationer": Moore, *Complete Prose*, 547.

88 largely written: Molesworth, *Marianne Moore*, 256.

88 "seem to come": Hall, *Marianne Moore*, 77.

88 "When an author writes": Moore, *Complete Prose*, 340.

88 "'Society' is intolerable": Moore, *Selected Letters*, 494.

89 "The *Poetry* award": Ibid., 255.

89 "I confess": Ibid., 283.

90 "In Distrust of Merits": Moore, *Poems of Marianne Moore*, 252–54.

90 "It is just a protest": Hall, *Marianne Moore*, 111.

90 "much more aware": Moore, *Complete Prose*, 588.

90 "I don't approve": Hall, "The Art of Poetry No. 4."

90 "The Camperdown Elm": Moore, *Poems of Marianne Moore*, 358.

90 so he could write it up: The resulting article was "The World Series with Marianne Moore," *Harper's*, October 1964, 50–58.

91 even on Johnny Carson's *Tonight Show*: Jeredith Merrin, "Marianne Moore and Elizabeth Bishop," in *The Columbia History of American Poetry*, ed. Jay Parini and Brett Candlish Miller (New York: Columbia University Press, 1993), 348.

91 "a kind of declawed": Ibid.

91 "Brooklyn has given me pleasure": Moore, *Complete Prose*, 547.

4. A Long Way from New York: THOMAS WOLFE

92 If one of his stubby pencils . . . the writer's feet: Many details drawn from David Herbert Donald, *Look Homeward: A Life of Thomas Wolfe* (Cambridge, MA: Harvard University Press, 2003), 284, 253.

93 sixty-five dollars a month: Ibid., 253.

93 "You have crucified": Ibid., 217.

93 "I know this now": Ted Mitchell, ed., *Thomas Wolfe: An Illustrated Biography* (New York: Pegasus Books, 2006), 81–82.

94 "one of the greatest": Donald, *Look Homeward*, 248.

94 "Life is not worth" . . . "EXCUSE LETTER": Ibid., 243–44.

94 "It would be hard": Ibid., 211.

94 "saw the passionate fullness": Thomas Wolfe, *Look Homeward, Angel* (1929; repr., New York: Scribner, 1995), 17.

95 "terrible will": Ibid., 57.

95 She opened a boardinghouse: Donald, *Look Homeward*, 11.

95 "the full delight": Wolfe, *Look Homeward, Angel*, 166.

95 "sank deeper year by year": Ibid., 197.

95 "over-excited verbosity": Donald, *Look Homeward*, 243.

95 "There is no possibility": Harold Bloom, "Passionate Beholder of America in Trouble," *New York Times*, February 2, 1987.

96 Notices everywhere: Andrew Turnbull, *Thomas Wolfe* (New York: Scribner's, 1968), 149.

96 so over-the-top that: Ibid., 145.

96 The British writer . . . "for this bird": Ibid., 150.

96 "a 'writer' was": Thomas Wolfe, *The Story of a Novel*, reprinted *Autobiography of an American Novelist*, 108–9.

96 "Less than any other": Donald, *Look Homeward*, 145.

97 "Like many another young person": James Dickey, foreword to Thomas Wolfe, *The Complete Short Stories of Thomas Wolfe*, ed. Frances E. Skipp (New York: Scribner's, 1989), xi.

97 "I can't help it": Thomas Wolfe, *The Selected Letters of Thomas Wolfe*, ed. Elizabeth Nowell and sel. Daniel George (London: Heinemann, 1969), 171.

98 a record of launching careers: Turnbull, *Thomas Wolfe*, 46.

98 "I simply can't" . . . "and so on": Ibid., 50.

98 "niggling and over-refined": Wolfe, *Writing and Living*, reprinted in *Autobiography of an American Novelist*, 113.

99 "I have wanted": Turnbull, *Thomas Wolfe*, 86.

99 "The chemises": Thomas Wolfe, *You Can't Go Home Again* (1940; repr., New York: Harper Perennial Modern Classics, 1998), 210.

99 "the literati": Donald, *Look Homeward*, 229.

99 He got together with F. Scott Fitzgerald . . . outraged Wolfe: Turnbull, *Thomas Wolfe*, 158; and Wolfe, *Selected Letters*, 160.

100 "Dear Jack": Wolfe, *Selected Letters*, 122.

100 "the 'going abroad'": Ibid., 169.

100 "No one has ever": Ibid., 173.

100 "Most of the people": Ibid., 171.

100 Soon he decided: Donald, *Look Homeward*, 252–53.

101 "NEED NO HELP NOW": Ibid., 252.

101 "Brooklyn is a fine town": Ibid., 254.

101 "may seem to you": Wolfe, *You Can't Go Home Again*, 377.

101 "George Webber has": Ibid., 379.

102 "Shipwrecked men" ... "why?": Wolfe, *Writing and Living*, reprinted in *Autobiography of an American Novelist*, 135.

102 "Young men were writing": Ibid., 136.

102 had been the Mercantile Library: Morrone, *An Architectural Guidebook to Brooklyn*, 145.

103 Department stores ... and the Fox: Ibid., 3–5, 11, 16.

103 "Sailors from a hundred": *WPA Guide*, 463.

104 "It's a good place": Wolfe, *Complete Stories*, 262.

104 the public Red Hook Houses: *WPA Guide*, 466.

104 "When you enter": Turnbull, *Thomas Wolfe*, 183.

104 "Suddenly I would see": Wolfe, *Story of a Novel*, 32.

105 "shacks, tenements" ... "prehistoric eggs": Wolfe, *You Can't Go Home Again*, 378–79.

105 "saw, lived, felt": Wolfe, *Story of a Novel*, 60.

105 "All the underdogs": Mitchell, *Thomas Wolfe*, 169.

106 "Both came too late": Ibid., 288.

106 "no ordered narrative" ... "superior to his hunger": Wolfe, *Story of a Novel*, 36–37.

106 "It was a black time" ... "my own work": Ibid., 59–60.

107 "utter, naked need": Ibid., 54.

107 "favorite sport": Wolfe, *You Can't Go Home Again*, 325.

107 "he had no part": Ibid., 456.

107 Wolfe had no bank account: Donald, *Look Homeward*, 283.

107 he began to sell off: Ibid., 275–76.

107 moved into an even cheaper apartment ... books and clothes: Mitchell, *Thomas Wolfe*, 168; and Donald, *Look Homeward*, 289.

108 "My spirit quivered": Turnbull, *Thomas Wolfe*, 199.

109 became enraged: Donald, *Look Homeward*, 301.

109 "What he was doing": Ibid., 302.

109 "numberless touches": Turnbull, *Thomas Wolfe*, 200.

109 "blazed the pinnacles": Wolfe, *You Can't Go Home Again*, 391.

109 Perkins, a mainstay: Donald, *Look Homeward*, 303–4.

109 an interview in the *New York Herald-Tribune*: Sanderson Vanderbilt, "Thomas Wolfe Cuts 2nd Book to 450,000 Words," *New York Herald-Tribune*, February 18, 1935, reprinted in Mitchell, *Thomas Wolfe*, 168–69.

109 attracted unwanted visitors: Donald, *Look Homeward*, 310.

110 "I have lived here long enough": Ibid., 307.

110 As America receded: Wolfe, *Story of a Novel*, 82.

110 "MAGNIFICENT REVIEWS" ... "WITH LIGHT HEART": Donald, *Look Homeward*, 313.

110 garnering the most votes: Ibid., 354–55.

110 "had been a North Carolina book" ... "Whitman could rival": Turnbull, *Thomas Wolfe*, 206–7.

111 "Oh God!" ... "has known it": Thomas Wolfe, *Of Time and the River* (1935; repr., New York: Scribner, 1999), 323–34.

111 "the impossible anguish": Donald, *Look Homeward*, 458.

111 "DEAR TOM": Ibid., 326.

111 On a gloriously sunny day . . . Fourth of July: Ibid., 326–28.

5. *The Longest Journey:* DANIEL FUCHS, BERNARD MALAMUD, ALFRED KAZIN

113 "One of the longest": Norman Podhoretz, *Making It* (New York: Random House, 1967), 3.

115 "I beat myself into shape": Lee Siegel, "The Fixer-Upper," *New York Times*, December 9, 2007.

115 He was one of six . . . on a stool: Daniel Fuchs, *Contemporary Authors Autobiography Series*, vol. 5 (Gale Group, 1987), 59–62.

115 "sweaty dinginess": Daniel Fuchs, *Homage to Blenholt*, in Daniel Fuchs, *The Brooklyn Novels: Summer in Williamsburg, Homage to Blenholt, Low Company* (Boston: David R. Godine, 2006), 364.

115 He would see bums . . . the opposite direction: Fuchs, *Contemporary Authors*, 61–62.

116 "from 'good' families": Alfred Kazin, *Starting Out in the Thirties* (Ithaca, NY: Cornell University Press, 1989), 12.

116 "moved the streets": Ibid., 15.

116 Although Roth was a Communist: Daniel Mendelsohn, "The Last Minstrel," *New York Review of Books*, December 15, 2005.

116 "a hundred other ghettoes": Michael Gold, 1935 author's note to his *Jews Without Money* (New York: Carroll & Graf, 2004), 10.

116 "The worst example": Quoted in Gabriel Miller, *Daniel Fuchs* (Boston: Twayne Publishers, 1979), 21.

117 "I was determined": Fuchs, 1961 preface to *The Brooklyn Novels*, xiv.

117 "I had 'ideas'": http://www.blacksparrowbooks.com/titles/fuchs.htm.

117 old women peddle pretzels: Fuchs, *Brooklyn Novels*, 78.

118 "a dictionary of Williamsburg": Ibid., 11.

118 "a closed-in canyon": Ibid., 919.

118 "the exact point": Ibid., 600.

118 "cumulatively a counterhistory": Boris Fishman, "A Cigarette and a Window," *New Republic*, May 7, 2007.

118 He came from Russia: Philip Davis, *Bernard Malamud: A Writer's Life* (New York: Oxford University Press, 1997), 12.

119 "He used to get up": Ibid.

119 "It was not very good": Ibid., 14.

119 "nobody starved": Ibid.

119 "There were no books": Daniel Stern, "Bernard Malamud: The Art of Fiction No. 52," *Paris Review* 61 (Spring 1975), http://www.theparisreview.org/interviews/3869/the-art-of-fiction-no-52-bernard-malamud.

119 Malamud helped save: Davis, *Bernard Malamud*, 5.

119 a scene re-created: Bernard Malamud, *Dubin's Lives* (New York: Farrar, Straus and Giroux, 2003), 68.

119 But he couldn't: Davis, *Bernard Malamud*, 5.

119 Eugene dropped out: Ibid., 25–27.

120 "and when I was convalescing": Stern, "The Art of Fiction No. 52."

120 his parents may have used: Davis, *Bernard Malamud*, 32.

120 in 2009 the school had: National Center for Education Statistics, http://nces.ed.gov/.

120 "mother of high schools" . . . in 1896: *WPA Guide*, 494.

120 in Malamud's era, enrollment: Davis, *Bernard Malamud*, 34.

120 "I felt, my God": Ibid., 22.

121 "in the awkwardness of their speech" . . . "perhaps it did": Irving Howe, *World of Our Fathers* (New York: Harcourt Brace Jovanovich, 1976), 252–53.

121 "It was not for myself alone": Alfred Kazin, *A Walker in the City* (1951; repr., New York: Harcourt, 1969), 21–22.

122 "a half-acknowledged shame": Howe, *World of Our Fathers*, 262.

122 "There was a kind of treason in it": Podhoretz, *Making It*, 4.

122 "close to a waste": Davis, *Bernard Malamud*, 48.

123 "there was nothing to go back to: Kazin, *Starting Out*, 14.

123 In 1940 . . . no pay: Davis, *Bernard Malamud*, 50–51.

123 "Brooklyn you are the universe": Ibid., 31.

124 He found it . . . "Emerson to Whitman": Robert Giroux, introduction to *The People and Uncollected Stories*, by Bernard Malamud (New York: Farrar, Straus and Giroux, 1989), x.

124 "like a Jewish Brooklyn version": Davis, *Bernard Malamud*, 160.

124 "a map of the world": Joshua Cohen, "A Life Torn Between Myth and Fact," *Forward*, November 2, 2007.

124 *The Assistant* sold: Davis, *Bernard Malamud*, 114.

124 Bellow took to calling them: Alfred Kazin, *Alfred Kazin's America: Critical and Personal Writings*, ed. Ted Solotaroff (New York: HarperCollins, 2003), 255.

124 "its unions": Alfred Kazin, "A Single Jew," *New York Review of Books*, October 9, 1997.

124 "The Thirties were not just": Arthur Krystal, "The Worst of Times," *Harper's*, November 2009, 72.

125 "I feel that every day": Bernard Malamud, *The Assistant* (1947; repr., New York: Farrar, Straus and Giroux, 2003), 43.

125 "Interests me what you can learn here": Ibid., 40.

125 "almost without understanding why" . . . "both ways": Bernard Malamud, *Talking Horse: Bernard Malamud on Life and Work*, ed. Alan Cheuse and Nicholas Delbanco (New York: Columbia University Press, 1996), 6–7.

126 minority groups were staging: Michiko Kakutani, "A Talk with Saul Bellow," *New York Times*, December 13, 1981.

126 "Who cared?": Sam Tanenhaus, "Hello to All That," *Slate*, August 16, 2003, http://www.slate.com/id/2081610/.

127 Kazin had walked: Kazin, *Starting Out*, 7–10.

127 as Jed Perl has argued: Jed Perl, "The Troubadour Intellectual," *New Republic*, March 26, 2008.

127 256 Sutter Avenue: Richard M. Cook, *Alfred Kazin: A Biography.* (New Haven, CT: Yale University Press, 2007), 4.

127 "the margin of the city": Kazin, *Walker in the City*, 10.

127 "dead land": Ibid.

127 The Kazins joined the migration: Cook, *Alfred Kazin*, 4.

127 "When I was a child": Kazin, *Walker in the City*, 8.

128 The wave of new residents: *WPA Guide*, 498.

128 A dizzying conversion . . . 95 percent Jewish: Abramovitch and Galvin, *Jews of Brooklyn*, 6.

128 "it belonged to people": Kazin, *Walker in the City*, 43.

128 More than seventy Orthodox synagogues . . . 2.19 square miles: *WPA Guide*, 498–500.

128 The Kazins . . . after his father died: Cook, *Alfred Kazin*, 4–5.

128 worked as a house painter . . . there was not: Kazin, *Walker in the City*, 38.

129 She had been a seamstress: Cook, *Alfred Kazin*, 4.

129 "the loneliest man in the world": Ibid., 5.

129 Young Alfred . . . with his mother: Ibid., 6.

129 "To anyone who grew up": Alfred Kazin, "Writers in the Radical Years," *New York Times*, March 23, 1980.

129 "It was never learning": Kazin, *Walker in the City*, 17.

129 "Anything less than absolute perfection": Ibid., 21.

130 "spawning more gangsters": Gerald Sorin, *Nurturing Neighborhood: The Brownsville Boys' Club and Jewish Community in Urban America, 1940–1990* (New York: New York University Press, 1992), 22.

130 Brownsville was radical enough: Wendell E. Pritchett, *Brownsville, Brooklyn: Blacks, Jews, and the Changing Face of the Ghetto* (Chicago: University of Chicago Press, 2003), 36.

130 Daniel Bell: Cook, *Alfred Kazin*, 15.

130 "everyone else I knew": Kazin, *Starting Out*, 4.

130 "I could swim out": Kazin, *Walker in the City*, 120.

130 "The radical ambience": Cook, *Alfred Kazin*, 24.

131 "saw New York" . . . "to remind me of Brownsville": Kazin, *Walker in the City*, 11; and Cook, *Alfred Kazin*, 18.

131 He loved the America: Cook, *Alfred Kazin*, 18.

131 Eighty-five percent . . . enrollment: Ibid., 21.

131 "I looked to literature": Kazin, *Starting Out*, 5.

131 "The thing was there": Davis, *Bernard Malamud*, 32.

132 "The brilliance of this young couple": Cook, *Alfred Kazin*, 42.

132 two-room apartment at 150 Remsen Street: Ibid., 52.

132 Kazin read and wrote: Ibid., 54.

132 Kazin was at work . . . "It's not true!": Ibid., 56.

133 "I felt what I have never felt": Ibid., 51.

133 But as Malamud's daughter, Janna Malamud Smith: Janna Malamud Smith, *My Father Is a Book: A Memoir of Bernard Malamud* (Boston: Houghton Mifflin, 2006), 139–40.

133 "heavy Brownsville voice": Cook, *Alfred Kazin*, 32.

133 nursed a long and bitter grudge: Ibid., 318–19.

133 Meanwhile, a plainly dressed Malamud: Davis, *Bernard Malamud*, 160.

134 "It is easier to shun materialism": Adam Kirsch, "Dear Dirty Old Brooklyn," *New York Sun*, November 1, 2006.

134 "I could never walk": Kazin, *Walker in the City*, 172.

6. *The Great Migration:* RICHARD WRIGHT

135 Richard Wright would rise at six o'clock: Hazel Rowley, *Richard Wright: The Life and Times* (2001; repr., New York: Henry Holt, 2002), 154.

135 4 percent: Harold X. Connolly, *A Ghetto Grows in Brooklyn* (New York: New York University Press, 1977), 75.

136 35 percent: 2005–2009 American Community Survey, U.S. Census.

136 "Now the most powerful": James Baldwin, "Many Thousands Gone," reprinted in *Richard Wright's Native Son: A Critical Handbook*, ed. Richard Abcarian (Belmont, CA: Wadsworth, 1970), 126–27.

136 originally bore the title "American Hunger": This title was eventually given to the portion of the original manuscript that was not included in *Black Boy* and was published only after Wright's death. This portion covers the period after his move to Chicago, which concludes *Black Boy*.

136 "Hunger stole on me": Richard Wright, *Black Boy: A Record of Childhood and Youth* (1945; repr., New York: Perennial Classics, 1998), 14.

137 Twenty-five years passed . . . "to a crude and raw past": Ibid., 34.

137 grandparents were slaves: Rowley, *Richard Wright*, 1.

137 "swarmed with rats" . . . plates of food: Wright, *Black Boy*, 59.

138 his schoolmates . . . "devil's work": Rowley, *Richard Wright*, 34–35.

138 "Dick, you're black": Wright, *Black Boy*, 183.

138 "what kind of life": Ibid., 164.

138 "I was building up in me": Ibid., 169.

138 "The locomotive of my heart": Ibid.

139 In the months before publication . . . "than an embrace": Rowley, *Richard Wright*, 286–88.

139 "That moment in the black rural South": Nicholas Lemann, *The Promised Land: The Great Black Migration and How It Changed America* (1991; repr., New York: Vintage Books, 1992), 41.

140 "a black person could go anywhere" . . . "The Attitude": Ibid., 40.

140 living with several others . . . several families: Ibid., 52–53.

140 "The safety of my life": Wright, *Black Boy*, 233.

141 the Great Migration's prime period . . . in world history: Lemann, *The Promised Land*, 6.

141 In those three decades: Ira Rosenwaike, *Population History of New York City* (Syracuse, NY: Syracuse University Press, 1972), 141–42.

141 White home owners established: Janice L. Rieff, Ann Durkin Keating, James R. Grossman, eds., *Encyclopedia of Chicago* (Chicago: Chicago Historical Society, 2004), http://encyclopedia.chicagohistory.org/pages/1761.html.

142 "Who would complain": David Bradley, introduction to Richard Wright, *12 Million Black Voices* (New York: Basic Books, 2002), x.

142 This held true in New York City: Craig Steven Wilder, *A Covenant with*

Color: Race and Social Power in Brooklyn (2000; repr., New York: Columbia University Press, 2001), 162.

142 Twenty-four unions: Bradley, introduction to Wright, *12 Million*, xi.

142 "The only difference": Rowley, *Richard Wright*, 58.

142 "a taunting sense": Richard Wright, "How Bigger Was Born," reprinted in Richard Wright, *Native Son* (New York: Harper Perennial, 2005), 442.

143 "What happens": Langston Hughes, "Harlem," *Montage of a Dream Deferred* (New York: Henry Holt, 1951), 71.

143 Among nonfiction writers . . . people more like him: Rowley, *Richard Wright*, 60.

143 "I rode in zero weather": From a draft of *Black Boy*, quoted in ibid., 67.

144 In the autumn of 1933 . . . later published Wright: Ibid., 74–76.

144 Abe Aaron . . . "lost my job over him": Ibid., 77.

144 "antagonism or distrust": Wright, *Black Boy*, 62.

145 the most prestigious job: Rowley, *Richard Wright*, 109.

145 "No theory of life": Ibid., 117.

145 "Most of the young artists": Ibid., 121.

145 not a single public high school: Ibid., 128.

145 "parasitic and mannered" . . . "who do clever tricks": Ibid., 136.

146 "dreadfully repetitive": Ibid., 139.

146 "quite conservative politically" . . . "let you down": Ibid., 141.

146 only black member of the "Atlanta Six": Ibid., 94.

147 When they were arrested: Ibid.

147 "I'm staying in Brooklyn": Ibid., 148.

147 "the full weight of his anger": Howe, "Black Boys and Native Sons," *Dissent*, Autumn 1963, reprinted in *Richard Wright's Native Son*, ed. Richard Abcarian, 137.

147 "contained no spiritual sustenance": Wright, "How Bigger Was Born," *Native Son*, 454.

148 "Whenever I thought": Wright, *Black Boy*, 37.

148 "I found that I had written": Wright, "How Bigger Was Born," *Native Son*, 454.

148 "he knew that they were suffering": Wright, *Native Son*, 10.

148 He is known: Ibid., 49–50.

149 the "Jungle": Connolly, *A Ghetto Grows in Brooklyn*, 122.

149 Fort Greene had won him over: Correspondence with Hazel Rowley, October 2009.

149 the New Deal–created Home Owners' Loan Corporation . . . resulting financial boycott: Wilder, *Covenant with Color*, 185–93.

150 Wilder tells us: Ibid., 180.

151 "steel himself": Rowley, *Richard Wright*, 289.

151 "The average moral-minded American": Ibid.

152 "Lawd, I'd rather be a lamppost": Ibid., 52.

152 By 1970, 43 percent: Connolly, *A Ghetto Grows in Brooklyn*, 186.

152 As late as 1962 . . . only one chapter: Lemann, *The Promised Land*, 130–31.

152 When the federal government: Ibid., 148.

153 the landlord on Lefferts Place: Rowley, *Richard Wright*, 167.

153 Wright joined the Newtons again: Ibid., 226, 555.

153 "It was a really eerie thing": 1963 interview with Poplowitz by biographer Constance Webb, quoted in Rowley, *Richard Wright*, 230.

153 Ellen came from difficult . . . on Fulton Street in Brooklyn: Rowley, *Richard Wright*, 231–32.

154 "somebody had had a *black baby*": Ibid., 266.

154 who had published his story "Almos' a Man": Constance Webb, *Richard Wright: The Biography of a Major Figure in American Literature* (New York: G. P. Putnam's Sons, 1968), 194.

154 89 Lefferts Place: They moved there in mid-August 1943, according to Rowley, *Richard Wright*, 282.

154 "terribly still": Ibid., 280.

154 "I think it is significant": Ibid., 289.

7. The Birth of Brooklyn Cool: "FEBRUARY HOUSE" AND TRUMAN CAPOTE

157 Sherill Tippins gives an engaging account: Sherill Tippins, *February House: The Story of W. H. Auden, Carson McCullers, Jane and Paul Bowles, Benjamin Britten and Gypsy Rose Lee, Under One Roof in Wartime America* (New York: Houghton Mifflin Harcourt, 2005).

157 Anaïs Nin dubbed: Ibid., 164.

157 Davis served . . . for Davis's section: Ibid., 13–16, 31.

157 "a sit-up-and-take-notice book": Clifton Fadiman, "Books: Pretty Good for Twenty-two," *New Yorker*, June 8, 1940, quoted in ibid., 5.

157 McCullers snapped to attention . . . at cheap restaurants: Tippins, *February House*, 9–23.

158 They considered the countryside: Ibid., 31.

158 The house had been converted: Ibid., 36.

158 a reputedly rich old woman: Ibid., 64.

159 Seventy-five dollars a month: Ibid., 36.

159 But he was quite fond . . . short of money: Ibid., 38.

160 1 Montague Terrace: Humphrey Carpenter, *W. H. Auden: A Biography* (New York: Houghton Mifflin, 1981), 278.

160 "Really, it's all as quiet here": Alfred Kazin, *New York Jew* (Syracuse, NY: Syracuse University Press, 1978), 151.

160 "For the first time": Carpenter, *W. H. Auden*, 282.

160 "This house has": Ibid., 278.

160 He had thought it would be in reach . . . homosexuality was illegal: Tippins, *February House*, 38–39.

160 in the spring of '39 he fell hard: Carpenter, *W. H. Auden*, 257–59.

161 The rent was the same: Tippins, *February House*, 39.

161 "The surest way": Carpenter, *W. H. Auden*, 279.

161 "Sorry, my dear": Ibid., 306.

161 The young man was the . . . "have found my happiness": Ibid., 257–60.

161 Davis launched into: Carson McCullers, "Brooklyn Is My Neighborhood," *Vogue*, March 1941.

162 "George naked at the piano": Tippins, *February House*, 70.

162 "Dear Harry": Ibid., 71.

162 "as vivacious as a country fair" . . . "want to go to Sands Street": McCullers, "Brooklyn Is My Neighborhood."

162 At Tony's Square Bar: Tippins, *February House*, 78.

162 "we've got a roast": Christopher Sawyer-Lauçanno, *An Invisible Spectator: A Biography of Paul Bowles* (1989; repr., London: Paladin Books, 1990), 225.

163 detachment seemed . . . became a consistent presence: Tippins, *February House*, 93–96.

163 The Manns . . . than their father did: Colm Tóibín, "I Could Sleep with All of Them," *London Review of Books*, November 6, 2008, 3–10, http://www.lrb.co.uk/v30/n21/colm-toibin/i-could-sleep-with-all-of-them; and ibid., 18–19.

163 Gypsy Rose Lee . . . World's Fair: Tippins, *February House*, 79–81.

163 "I wasn't naked": Ibid., 84.

164 She moved to 7 Middagh Street: Ibid., 86–87.

164 "Where am I?": Ibid., 99.

164 "whirlwind of laughter": Ibid., 116.

164 Davis invited him over: Ibid., 109.

164 "to handle Negro characters": Ibid., 26.

164 The dinner party he missed . . . before it was published: Ibid., 109–11.

165 "Ideas vibrate": Ibid., 142.

165 On one of her visits . . . cotton mill town in the South: Ibid., 156–58.

165 "mooned in the alley": McCullers, "Brooklyn Is My Neighborhood."

165 Middagh Street took its name: Tippins, *February House*, 65.

166 "Comparing the Brooklyn I know": McCullers, "Brooklyn Is My Neighborhood."

167 had spent relatively happy times: Virginia Spencer Carr, *Paul Bowles: A Life* (2004; repr., Evanston, IL: Northwestern University Press, 2009), 26.

167 "The only trouble": Ibid., 65.

167 renting two rooms: Ibid., 120.

167 Even while living: Ibid., 134.

167 now in the famous Chelsea Hotel: Ibid., 140.

168 "an obscene and lecherous man": Ibid., 129.

168 Paul took Gypsy Rose Lee's room: Tippins, *February House*, 165.

168 Paul and Jane brought: Ibid., 165–66.

168 Auden became close to Jane: Carr, *Paul Bowles*, 152.

168 Paul got angry . . . four months after moving in: Ibid.

169 "one of the finest": John Ashbery, "Up from the Underground," *New York Times*, January 29, 1967.

169 Within sight of the house: Lorraine B. Diehl, *Over Here!: New York City During World War II* (New York: Smithsonian/HarperCollins, 2010), 43.

169 Brooklynites who lent their support: Ibid., 52.

170 Auden was bereft ... horrified at what he had done: Tippins, *February House*, 216–17.

170 "It's frightening how easy": Carpenter, *W. H. Auden*, 311.

170 The twenty-three-year-old Oliver Smith: Tippins, *February House*, 172, 184.

170 moving into the parlor floor and basement: Webb, *Richard Wright*, 195.

170 Anaïs Nin, who had gotten ... his wife, Lotte Lenya: Rowley, *Richard Wright*, 270.

171 "Middagh was a white man's street": Ibid., 268.

171 "not a proper environment": Webb, *Richard Wright*, 196.

173 a blond young stranger ... in 1945: Gerald Clarke, *Capote: A Biography*. (1988; repr., New York: Carroll & Graf, 2005), 83–85.

173 a rooming house at 17 Clifton Place: Ibid., 125.

173 "As you can see": Truman Capote, *Too Brief a Treat: The Letters of Truman Capote*, ed. Gerald Clarke (New York: Random House, 2004), 39.

173 "the single worst person": Clarke, *Capote*, 41.

174 "Truman regards the trip to Brooklyn": Paul Bigelow letter, quoted in Clarke, *Capote*, 126.

174 sold in 2005: Public records, viewable at http://www.city-data.com/.

174 "In despair one views" ... "some elements of Brooklyn": Truman Capote, *Portraits and Observations: The Essays of Truman Capote* (New York: Random House, 2008), 17.

174 Capote cruelly portrays ... "all of them": Ibid., 18–19.

174 Richard Wright had been living: He had been at 89 Lefferts Place until mid-September 1945, according to Rowley, *Richard Wright*, 321.

175 "look rancid" ... "an altitudinous society": Capote, *Portraits and Observations*, 22.

175 "the less contrived" ... "eating at its palisades": Ibid., 23.

175 Even before the publication date: Clarke, *Capote*, 130–31.

175 Clarke suggests that George Davis: Ibid., 90.

175 Clarke writes that Davis was silent: Ibid., 157–58.

176 "guillotine tongue": Capote, *Portraits and Observations*, 235.

176 "a hell of a household": Ibid., 255–56.

176 He and McCullers ... book contract: Clarke, *Capote*, 96–98.

176 spent several months in 1949: Ibid., 196–99.

176 spent a few months in Tangier: Ibid., 199–201.

176 He referred to her: Capote, *Portraits and Observations*, 256.

176 "Oliver Smith has *produced* a show": Tippins, *February House*, 251.

176 He once said that *West Side Story*: Ibid.

177 Capote said it had twenty-eight rooms: Capote, *Portraits and Observations*, 236.

177 Built in 1839: Norval White, Elliot Willensky, and Fran Leadon, *AIA Guide to New York City*, 5th ed. (New York: Oxford University Press, 2010), 608.

177 was recently available: Jason Sheftell, "Truman Capote's 11-bedroom Brooklyn Heights mansion on the market for a Brooklyn-record $18M," *New York Daily News*, May 9, 2010.

177 they came to visit their friend . . . "I should have some of them": Capote, *Portraits and Observations*, 236–37.

177 Smith was already turning: Clarke, *Capote*, 296.

177 Brinnin remembered: John Malcolm Brinnin, *Truman Capote: Dear Heart, Old Buddy* (New York: Delacorte Press, 1986), 16.

177 He had Jackie Kennedy over: Clarke, *Capote*, 297.

178 "is as tart as a grand aunt": Norman Mailer, *Advertisements for Myself* (1959; repr., Cambridge, MA: Harvard University Press, 1992), 465.

178 "I live in Brooklyn": This and all subsequent quotations from this essay, Capote, *Portraits and Observations*, 233–45.

178 "the only place to live in New York": Clarke, *Capote*, 297.

179 It was also in 1959: Ibid., 317.

179 "During its long history" . . . "you want to read": Ibid., 360–67.

180 "He wanted to be": Ibid., 367.

180 "It was ostensibly": George Plimpton, ed., *Truman Capote: In Which Various Friends, Enemies, Acquaintances, and Detractors Recall His Turbulent Career* (New York: Anchor, 1998), 249.

8. *The Shadow of the War*: WILLIAM STYRON AND *SOPHIE'S CHOICE*

182 "I am writing this letter": William Styron, *Letters to My Father*, ed. James L. W. West III (Baton Rouge: Louisiana State University Press, 2009), 79.

182 "I sensed I had dreamed": Hilary Mills, "Creators on Creating: William Styron," reprinted in James L. W. West III, ed., *Conversations with William Styron* (Jackson: University Press of Mississippi, 1985), 236.

183 "fell short of resemblance": William Styron, *Sophie's Choice* (New York: Vintage Books, 1992), 11.

183 "with a snootful": Ibid., 5–6.

183 the Weasel: Ibid., 17.

183 "gone through the throes" . . . "three-ton manuscript": Ibid., 17–18.

184 "'Up yours, Weasel'": Ibid., 21.

184 While Stingo is packing up . . . has served in the marine corps: Ibid., 22–26.

184 as did Styron . . . two atomic clouds: James L. W. West III, *William Styron: A Life* (New York: Random House, 1998), 123.

184 Stingo thinks back . . . good: Styron, *Sophie's Choice*, 24–26.

185 "I had to": Mills, "Creators on Creating: William Styron," 236.

185 perhaps the most important relationship: Alexandra Styron, in discussion with the author, February 11, 2010.

186 "The novelty has worn off": Styron, *Letters to My Father*, 65.

186 "This, I thought": William Styron, *This Quiet Dust: And Other Writings* (New York: Vintage Books, 1993), 269.

186 The teacher of a class: West, *William Styron*, 165.

187 "the greatest writer of our time": Styron, *Letters to My Father*, 12.

187 "In those days cheap apartments": Styron, *Sophie's Choice*, 3.

187 "intoxicating breaths": Ibid., 34–35.

187 He grew up . . . the city's shipyards: West, *William Styron*, 22–23.

188 "incense and rams' horns": Styron, *Sophie's Choice*, 176.

188 "wandering amid the Kingdom of the Jews": Ibid., 4.

188 the Board of Education saw them: Abramovitch and Galvin, *Jews of Brooklyn*, 130.

188 Jewish people constituted: Rosenwaike, *Population History*, 152.

188 kosher groceries: Adina Back and Francis Morrone, *Flatbush Neighborhood History Guide* (Brooklyn: Brooklyn Historical Society, 2008), 47.

188 baffled by the sight of yarmulkes: West, *William Styron*, 168.

189 Caton Park, developed in the first decade: Jackson and Manbeck, *Neighborhoods of Brooklyn*, 122.

189 "The street is lined": Styron, *Letters to My Father*, 12.

189 "It was such a placid and agreeable view": Styron, *Sophie's Choice*, 39.

190 "although I'm not exactly ecstatic": Styron, *Letters to My Father*, 81.

190 "*alrightniks*" . . . "Gentiles to me": Kazin, *Walker in the City*, 9.

190 "steam heat, electric light": Back and Morrone, *Flatbush Neighborhood History Guide*, 47.

190 Movie theaters abounded: Ibid., 48.

191 "Flatbush is one of Brooklyn's": *WPA Guide*, 492.

191 "something subtly and inexplicably wrong" . . . Auschwitz: Styron, *Sophie's Choice*, 48–54.

191 The real Sophie: Michel Braudeau, "Why I Wrote *Sophie's Choice*," reprinted in *Conversations with William Styron*, 246; and West, *William Styron*, 169.

192 "popcorn, candy apple": Styron, *Sophie's Choice*, 134.

192 "keenly honed": Ibid., 160.

192 Styron's working title: West, *William Styron*, 151.

192 the three have drinks: Styron, *Sophie's Choice*, 196.

193 a crowd of recent Brooklyn College: Ibid., 135–41.

193 "token vengeance": Ibid., 358.

193 "survivors were told": Peter Novick, *The Holocaust in American Life* (New York: Mariner Books, 2000), 83.

194 "That was the strange thing": Styron, *Sophie's Choice*, 154.

194 "part of a drama": Ibid., 350.

194 "The New York that O. Henry described": Quoted in Shaun O'Connell, *Remarkable, Unspeakable New York: A Literary History* (New York: Beacon Press, 1997), 233.

195 "In its stride, New York takes on": E. B. White, *Here Is New York*, quoted in Kenneth T. Jackson and David Dunbar, eds., *Empire City: New York Through the Centuries* (New York: Columbia University Press, 2005), 685.

195 "dared to enter this secret temple": Braudeau, "Why I Wrote *Sophie's Choice*," 251.

195 "not in the public mind": Michael West, "An Interview with William Styron," reprinted in *Conversations with William Styron*, 232.

9. Underground Rumbles: NORMAN MAILER

197 On a hot June day . . . "best seller list": Peter Manso, *Mailer: His Life and Times* (1985; repr., New York: Simon & Schuster, 2008), 118.

197 "Everyone was ready": Norman Mailer, introduction to *The Naked and the Dead*, 50th Anniversary Edition (New York: Picador, 1998), xi.

198 fifteen months: Mailer, *Advertisements for Myself*, 91.

198 Mailer kept four books: Manso, *Mailer*, 101.

198 As Mailer well knew: Norman Mailer, *Cannibals and Christians* (New York: Dial Press, 1966), 108.

198 "blazing visions": Wolfe, *Story of a Novel*, 61.

198 "up from the people": Mailer, *Cannibals and Christians*, 97.

198 "occasional overrich descriptions": Manso, *Mailer*, 101.

199 He brought a royalties check . . . in Mailer's telling: Mary V. Dearborn, *Mailer: A Biography* (New York: Houghton Mifflin, 1999), 66.

199 roughly three hundred thousand dollars: Differing accounts on Mailer's part make the actual amount uncertain.

199 " 'Go to your room, Sonny' ": Dearborn, *Mailer*, 67.

199 "I must have done something wrong": Ibid., 63.

200 In the first few years of his life: Manso, *Mailer*, 14–16.

200 Barney Mailer always dressed impeccably: Ibid., 16.

200 two-bedroom apartment . . . more Jewish than Flatbush: Dearborn, *Mailer*, 14; and ibid., 18.

200 Corner vendors . . . "the delicatessens, everything": Manso, *Mailer*, 26.

201 "cheap *goyim*": Ibid., 18.

201 "I just couldn't leave": Ibid., 95.

201 They spent their free time . . . in downtown Brooklyn: Manso, *Mailer*, 25–31.

201 "the highest IQ": Dearborn, *Mailer*, 17.

202 "My old dear great and good friend": Norman Mailer, "Up the Family Tree," *Partisan Review*, Spring 1968, reprinted in Norman Mailer, *Existential Errands* (Boston: Little, Brown, 1972), 175.

202 admired "enormously": Mailer, *Existential Errands*, 262.

202 "There has been from Henry Miller": Gore Vidal, "In Another Country," *New York Review of Books*, July 22, 1971.

202 "not a suitable valet": Dearborn, *Mailer*, 302–3.

203 "I left what part of me belonged": Norman Mailer, "Responses and Reactions," *Commentary*, December 1962.

203 "a fatal taint": Norman Mailer, *The Armies of the Night* (1968; repr., New York: Plume, 1994), 134.

203 "I did not, by any standards": Hilary Mills, *Mailer: A Biography* (New York: Empire Books, 1982), 47.

203 "It was his standard riposte": Manso, *Mailer*, 63.

204 Mailer favored vigorous . . . the stuff of the novel: Dearborn, *Mailer*, 26–28.

204 students and faculty moved: Ibid., 33.

204 "I was worrying darkly": Mailer, *Advertisements for Myself*, 28.

205 Ted Amussen turned down the book . . . Fort Bragg: Mills, *Mailer*, 74–76.

205 he didn't want the responsibility: Ibid., 75.

205 "absolutely no use": Manso, *Mailer*, 80.

206 he was finally assigned: Mills, *Mailer*, 77.

206 "a couple of firefights": Ibid., 78.

206 He wrote four or five letters . . . rot or get lost: Manso, *Mailer*, 90.

206 "This man does not know how": Dearborn, *Mailer*, 45.

206 "I can remember thinking": Manso, *Mailer*, 99.

206 took a small two-room apartment: Dearborn, *Mailer*, 51.

207 four dollars a week: Manso, *Mailer*, 156.

207 Mailer approached the writing: Dearborn, *Mailer*, 53.

207 "I doubt if ever again": Mailer, *Advertisements for Myself*, 92.

207 "I spent the next few years" . . . "of my life to write about": Mailer, *Advertisements for Myself*, 92.

208 "a dirty moon" . . . "in acceptance of its fury": Norman Mailer, *Barbary Shore* (1951; repr., New York: Vintage International, 1997), 118–22.

208 "an intensified version": Manso, *Mailer*, 158.

208 Mailer's actual neighbor: Ibid., 106.

208 "I got it. I agree": Ibid., 107.

209 "seemed eager, touching": Ibid., 113.

210 "Mailer—posing as the bad boy": Ibid., 158.

210 "Mailer has come to his radicalism": Irving Howe, "Some Political Novels," *Nation*, June 16, 1951, quoted in Manso, *Mailer*, 159.

211 The hatchet jobs: Manso, *Mailer*, 159–60.

211 "actively disliked" . . . cutting reviews: Louis Menand, "It Took a Village," *New Yorker*, January 5, 2009.

211 Having heard somewhere: Dearborn, *Mailer*, 134.

211 "There may have been": Mailer, *Advertisements for Myself*, 17.

212 "Like many another vain, empty, and bullying body": Ibid.

212 "I don't see how I can recommend": Ibid., 28.

212 "obviously *Barbary Shore*": Ibid., 105.

212 "Evaluations—Quick and Expensive Comments": All quotations from ibid., 463–67.

213 "It is one of the best things": Ibid., 335.

213 In the essay, Mailer posits: All quotations from ibid., 337–58.

214 As Dearborn argues: Dearborn, *Mailer*, 130.

214 "*Barbary Shore* . . . has in its high fevers": Mailer, *Advertisements for Myself*, 94.

215 "psychic outlaws": Ibid., 355.

215 "A young adventurer": Mailer, *Cannibals and Christians*, 97.

215 "firing the passions which rotted his brain": Ibid., 108.

215 "like the greatest five-year-old": Ibid., 97.

215 Dearborn pieces together the events: Dearborn, *Mailer*, 159–64.

216 Early on, he brought in a maid: Ibid., 176.

216 "Here I married this great and powerful writer": Mills, *Mailer*, 30.

216 he kept a studio down the block: Ibid., 30.

217 These huge parties included: Ibid., 24–25.

217 Mailer also became involved in the intrigue: Dearborn, *Mailer*, 370–75.

217 A drug smuggler who knew him: Ibid., 372.

218 "I have blood on my hands": Ibid., 362.

218 "He went over like a six-foot sixty-year-old": Norman Mailer, *The Fight* (1975; repr., New York: Vintage International, 2007), 208.

219 "straight jailhouse prose": Mills, *Mailer*, 430.

219 "that vast emptiness": Joan Didion, "'I Want to Go Ahead and Do It,'" *New York Times*, October 7, 1979.

219 a collection of New York intellectuals ... "get out of Asia": Dearborn, *Mailer*, 218–19.

219 "the Pentagon, blind five-sided eye": Mailer, *Armies of the Night*, 113–14.

220 "Is there nothing to remind us": Dearborn, *Mailer*, 95.

220 When a writer gets old enough: Alfred Kazin, "The Trouble He's Seen," *New York Times*, May 5, 1968.

10. The Postwar Chill: ARTHUR MILLER, PETE HAMILL, HUBERT SELBY JR.

222 The family gave up an apartment: Martin Gottfried, *Arthur Miller: His Life and Work* (Cambridge, MA: Da Capo Press, 2004), 5, 12.

222 "psychologically divorced" ... "a voyage to Kansas": Edmiston and Cirino, *Literary New York*, 337.

222 "as apt a subject for tragedy": Arthur Miller, "Tragedy and the Common Man," in *The Theater Essays of Arthur Miller*, ed. Robert A. Martin (New York: Viking, 1978), 3.

223 "In my neighborhood there were": Edmiston and Cirino, *Literary New York*, 337–38.

223 "on a smile and a shoeshine": Arthur Miller, *Death of a Salesman* (1949; repr., New York: Viking Press, 1966), 138.

223 "I could never penetrate" ... "Sicilian-English bravura": Nathan Ward, "How Arthur Miller Found His 'View,'" *Wall Street Journal*, January 27, 2010.

224 "America, I thought": Arthur Miller, *Timebends* (1987; repr., New York: Harper & Row, 1988), 147.

224 more than four thousand real-life versions: Jennifer Egan, "Reading Lucy," in Chris Knutsen and Valerie Steiker, *Brooklyn Was Mine* (New York: Riverhead Books, 2008), 24.

225 a Hollywood producer wanted: Gottfried, *Arthur Miller*, 176–80.

225 the close friendship: Ibid., 200–202.

226 Hamill's father: Pete Hamill, *A Drinking Life* (1994; repr., Boston: Back Bay Books, 1997), 15.

226 "we were suddenly poor": Ibid., 63.

227 "The Irish from Seventh Avenue": Ibid., 11.

227 "The Neighborhood" ... husband in the military: Ibid., 60–61.

227 One year around Christmas ... "the straight ticket": Ibid., 68.

228 The *Eagle* had a peak daily circulation: Ibid., 66.

228 Baseball was the working man's game: Eric Homberger, *The Historical Atlas of New York City* (1994; repr., New York: Henry Holt, 2008), 154–55.

229 Thousands wore pins: David McCullough, *Brooklyn: And How It Got That Way* (New York: Dial Press, 1983), 176.

229 "Brooklyn, the largest community in America": Tara George, "The Last Days of the Eagle," in Robbins and Palitz, *Brooklyn: A State of Mind*, 373.

229 The citywide newspapers: Peter Golenbock, *In the Country of Brooklyn* (New York: William Morrow, 2008), 419.

229 The *Eagle* had coined the phrase: McCullough, *Brooklyn*, 175.

229 "For a lot of people": Pete Hamill, "Brooklyn: The Sane Alternative," *New York*, July 14, 1969.

230 eight hundred thousand white New Yorkers: Lankevich, *New York City*, 197.

231 manufacturing jobs in Brooklyn: Ibid., 192–93.

231 When Pete Hamill signed on: Hamill, "Brooklyn: The Sane Alternative."

231 Migrants fleeing the deterioration: Lankevich, *New York City*, 188–89.

231 In Brooklyn many of them settled: Hamill, "Brooklyn: The Sane Alternative."

231 But by 1960 Puerto Ricans: Lankevich, *New York City*, 197.

231 Brooklyn's black population more than tripled: Rosenwaike, *Population History*, 141.

231 By 1960 blacks made up: Lankevich, *New York City*, 197.

231 less than 8 percent black: Rosenwaike, *Population History*, 133.

232 Wilder argues that the arrival: Wilder, *Covenant with Color*, 212.

232 "YOU MAY TAKE WATTS": McCullough, *Brooklyn*, 212.

232 Real estate firms took advantage: Rieff, Keating, Grossman, eds., *Encyclopedia of Chicago*, http://encyclopedia.chicagohistory.org/pages/147.html; and Hamill, "Brooklyn: The Sane Alternative."

233 "The Eisenhower era bragged": Hamill, *Drinking Life*, 209.

233 In Hamill's part of town . . . "best-read novel in the history of Brooklyn": Ibid., 96–97.

234 With the arrival of the heroin trade . . . "robbed them of their pride": Ibid., 187.

234 "Those who had escaped": Hamill, "Brooklyn: The Sane Alternative."

235 he felt a great "hatred of God": James R. Giles, *Understanding Hubert Selby, Jr.* (Columbia: University of South Carolina Press, 1998), 2.

236 Born in 1928 in Brooklyn: James R. Giles, "Hubert Selby, Jr.," in *Dictionary of Literary Biography*, vol. 227: *American Novelists Since World War II, Sixth Series*, eds. James R. Giles and Wanda Giles (Columbia, SC: Bruccoli Clark/Gale Group, 2000).

236 While stationed overseas: Giles, *Understanding Hubert Selby, Jr.*, 7–8.

236 he and "Gil" and a few other guys: Hubert Selby Jr., "Gilbert Sorrentino," *Review of Contemporary Fiction* (Summer 1981), 48–51.

11. *Into the Thickets of Urban Crisis:* JONATHAN LETHEM, L. J. DAVIS, PAULA FOX

239 "Mongrel by deep nature": Jonathan Lethem, *The Disappointment Artist* (2005; repr., New York: Vintage, 2006), 92.

240 "Yoke the white boy": Jonathan Lethem, *The Fortress of Solitude* (2003; repr., New York: Vintage, 2004), 83.

241 As the historian George Lankevich argues . . . relied on government aid: Lankevich, *New York City*, 205–15.

241 Yet voters were alarmed enough: Ibid., 203.

241 They were proudly billed: Harrison E. Salisbury, "'Shook' Youngsters Spring from the Housing Jungles," *New York Times*, March 26, 1958, 1.

241 renovated in the fifties: Morrone, *An Architectural Guidebook to Brooklyn*, 169.

241 "Nowhere this side of Moscow": Salisbury, "'Shook' Youngsters," 1.

242 Toward the end of her time there . . . "Brooklyn's last ornament": Michael Stern, "Brooklyn Loses Marianne Moore," *New York Times*, January 20, 1966.

242 Leaving aside "the Manhattan-oriented enclave": L. J. Davis, "Brooklyn a Rival of San Francisco as Home of Writers," *New York Times*, September 26, 1971.

242 Davis opted to buy: Eric Konigsberg, "For a Brooklyn Tale, and Its Author, a Second Chance at a First Impression," *New York Times*, April 5, 2009.

242 "Anyone who chose": Jonathan Lethem, introduction to *A Meaningful Life*, by L. J. Davis (New York: New York Review Books, 2009), ix.

242 "Davis is not a writer": Fox, "Light on the Dark Side."

243 "overwhelming livid awfulness": L. J. Davis, *A Meaningful Life* (1971; repr., New York: New York Review Books, 2009), 79.

243 "for all practical purposes": Ibid., 60.

243 "It was surprisingly easy": Ibid., 80.

243 "Creative young people": Ibid., 87.

244 "delivered vacant": Ibid., 101.

244 "implacable hatred": Ibid., 111.

245 "Half the front doors" . . . "squalid version of *Porgy and Bess*": Ibid., 182–83.

245 Davis adopted two black daughters: Lethem, introduction to *A Meaningful Life*, ix.

246 "The dystopian reality": Ibid., viii–ix.

246 "New Yorkers my age": Lethem, *Disappointment Artist*, 53.

247 "In Fort Greene, few people": Barbara Habenstreit, *Fort Greene, U.S.A.* (Indianapolis: Bobbs-Merrill, 1974), 137.

247 Kentucky Fried Chicken: Ibid., 6.

247 "a drug problem": Ibid., jacket copy.

247 eighteen methadone clinics: Ibid., 154.

247 "an air of lawlessness": Ibid., 137.

247 "We got robbed": Eric Konigsberg, "For a Brooklyn Tale, and Its Author, a Second Chance at a First Impression."

248 "very quiet, almost furtive": Paula Fox, *Desperate Characters* (1970; repr., New York: W. W. Norton, 1999), 12.

248 "What happens to the people": Ibid., 5.

249 "too preoccupied with fighting off": Ibid., 89.

249 "You can't imagine the people": Ibid., 8.

249 "There's Family Court": Ibid., 35.

249 "Now I'm at the brink": Ibid., 43.

249 "There was a siege going on": Ibid., 154.

250 "But it's not so strange": Ibid., 99–100.

250 "would have been self-indulgence": Ibid., 74.

250 "drearily enslaved by introspection": Ibid., 39.

250 "I had never read a book before": Melanie Rehak, "The Life and Death and

Life of Paula Fox: An Unexpected Literary Resurrection," *New York Times*, March 4, 2001.

250 "When there's a terrible murder": Ibid.

251 On October 17, New York City's cash needs: Lankevich, *New York City*, 219.

251 the Bronx had for years been losing: Ibid., 209.

252 "a night of terror": "The Blackout: A Night of Terror," *Time*, July 25, 1977.

252 "Dylan lay dreaming awake": Lethem, *Fortress of Solitude*, 171.

252 "Adults, teachers": Ibid., 83.

252 "artists or potential artists": Lethem, *Disappointment Artist*, 97.

252 they marched against Robert Moses freeways . . . "never defined by one ethnicity or class": Ibid., 91.

253 "partial, recalcitrant, corrupt": Lethem, *Fortress of Solitude*, 62.

253 She wishes "she could slather money": Ibid., 24.

253 "It isn't about money": Ibid., 18.

253 "pretentious bullshit": Ibid., 51.

254 "The grid of zones": Ibid., 78.

254 "uncanny sporadic pair": Ibid., 135.

255 "Anything was possible, really": Ibid., 57.

255 "*Is Brooklyn itself*": Ibid., 235.

255 "The souring of utopian optimism": Lethem, *Disappointment Artist*, 97.

255 "If a kid from Gowanus": Lethem, *Fortress of Solitude*, 270.

256 "Minna's Court Street": Jonathan Lethem, *Motherless Brooklyn* (1999; repr., New York: Vintage, 2000), 55.

258 "a zone of mixing": Lethem, *Disappointment Artist*, 91.

12. A Hint of Things to Come: PAUL AUSTER, A RENAISSANCE IN FORT GREENE

259 "The city has begun to die": Lankevich, *New York City*, 205.

259 in 1971 Davis was already hailing: Davis, "Brooklyn a Rival of San Francisco as Home of Writers."

260 fully a third of its white residents: Wilder, *Covenant with Color*, 178.

260 Violence in New York City . . . it was AIDS: Lankevich, *New York City*, 232–33.

260 Median family income: Edward Glaeser, "Do Mayors Matter?" *New Republic*, February 25, 2011, http://www.tnr.com/book/review/do-mayors-matter.

260 Real estate prices in the borough: Daniel Massey, "Past Indicates Little on Home Price Future," *Crain's New York Business*, March 11, 2009.

260 "Many writers here in Brooklyn": Paul Auster, *Oracle Night* (2003; repr., New York: Picador, 2004), 7.

261 "everything I touched": Paul Auster, *Collected Prose: Autobiographical Writings, True Stories, Critical Essays, Prefaces, and Collaborations with Artists* (New York: Picador, 2005), 153.

261 "no more than a short dry spell": Paul Auster, *Hand to Mouth: A Chronicle of Early Failure* (New York: Henry Holt, 1997), 101.

261 "I had made a total surrender": Ibid., 123.

261 "terrible irony": Ibid., 127.

261 a pseudonym Auster used: Ibid., 48.

262 "and at that moment the madness begins": Auster, *Collected Prose*, 262–63.

262 translated into forty-one languages: Paul Auster, *Sunset Park* (New York: Henry Holt, 2010), end matter.

262 In Germany, taxi drivers: Adam Begley, "Case of the Brooklyn Symbolist," *New York Times*, August 30, 1992.

262 "The address is unimportant": Paul Auster, *The New York Trilogy: City of Glass; Ghosts; The Locked Room* (New York: Penguin, 1990), 163.

263 "the only bright façade" Auster, *Oracle Night*, 3.

263 "one of them goddamn junkies": Ibid., 173.

264 "the imponderables of fate": Auster, *Sunset Park*, 34.

264 "an area without banks or bookstores": Auster, *Oracle Night*, 132.

265 "The motto of Brownsville": Nelson George, *City Kid: A Writer's Memoir of Ghetto Life and Post-Soul Success* (2009; New York: Penguin, 2010), 20.

265 "we were just a living, breathing statistic": Ibid., 31.

266 "That where I live!": Ibid., 210.

266 "Suddenly black nerds were chic": Ibid., 216.

267 "My friends and I used to joke": Nelson George, "Strangers on His Street," *New York Times*, April 3, 2009.

13. *A Literary Capital:* THE BROOKLYN OF TODAY

268 "Abraham had tried to explain it": Lethem, *Fortress of Solitude*, 424.

269 "Brickwork all along the block": Ibid., 431.

269 living below the poverty line: American Community Survey 2005–2009, U.S. Census.

269 the college-educated contingent: For data to 2000, see "Brooklynites: Interactive Graphic," *New York Times*, June 19, 2005, http://www.nytimes.com/packages/html/nyregion/20050619_BROOKLYN_GRAPHIC/index.html.

269 "It has become a cliché": Suketu Mehta, "The Great Awakening," *New York Times*, June 19, 2005.

270 "I discovered something": Fox, "Light on the Dark Side."

270 "he had succeeded at nothing": Davis, *A Meaningful Life*, 214.

270 $1.7 million profit: L. J. Davis, interview with the author, February 2011.

270 In 1990, 2,262 people were murdered: New York Police Department figures.

270 the lowest number: Evan Buxbaum, "New York Marks Fewest Murders Ever," cnn.com, December 30, 2009.

270 Burglary and robbery . . . 122 a day: New York Police Department figures.

271 over 60 percent of the nation's reduction in crime: Fred Siegel, *The Prince of the City: Giuliani, New York, and the Genius of American Life* (San Francisco: Encounter, 2005), 149.

272 "homogenized, suburbanized, and domesticated": Sharon Zukin, "How the City Lost Its Soul," *Playboy* (April 2010).

272 "liberals of both the Upper West Side": Ben McGrath, "The Untouchable," *New Yorker*, August 24, 2009.

274 "the 19th-century city is surprisingly intact": Davis, "Brooklyn a Rival of San Francisco as Home of Writers."

274 "Manhattan's amnesiac dance": Lethem, *Motherless Brooklyn*, 179.

277 "Intelligent thought is not dead": *n+1* promotional copy.

277 a witty essay Whitehead wrote: Colson Whitehead, "I Write in Brooklyn. Get Over It," *New York Times*, March 2, 2008.

277 "Paris had grown suffocating": Malcolm Cowley, *Exile's Return: A Literary Odyssey of the 1920s* (1934; repr., New York: Penguin Classics, 1994), 240.

278 The family lived then in an apartment: Edwidge Danticat, *Brother, I'm Dying* (2007; repr., New York: Vintage, 2008), 112.

278 "the more easily satirized aspects": Steven Kurutz, "A Park Slope Novel Seems a Little Too Real," *New York Times*, September 9, 2009.

279 "*Is our entire generation*": Joanna Smith Rakoff, *A Fortunate Age* (2009; repr., New York: Scribner, 2010), 107.

279 "who'd first rejected their suburban origins": Michael Thomas, *Man Gone Down* (New York: Black Cat, 2007), 121.

279 "We became a part of the 'us'": Ibid.

280 "feels like a giant set": Mehta, "Great Awakening."

Works Cited

Abramovitch, Ilana, and Seán Galvin. *Jews of Brooklyn*. Hanover, NH: University Press of New England, 2002.

Auster, Paul. *The Brooklyn Follies*. New York: Henry Holt, 2005.

———. *Collected Prose: Autobiographical Writings, True Stories, Critical Essays, Prefaces, and Collaborations with Artists*. New York: Picador, 2005.

———. *Hand to Mouth: A Chronicle of Early Failure*. New York: Henry Holt, 1997.

———. *The New York Trilogy: City of Glass; Ghosts; The Locked Room*. New York: Penguin, 1990.

———. *Oracle Night*. 2003. Reprint, New York: Picador, 2004.

———. *Sunset Park*. New York: Henry Holt, 2010.

Back, Adina, and Francis Morrone. *Flatbush Neighborhood History Guide*. Brooklyn: Brooklyn Historical Society, 2008.

Baldwin, James. "Many Thousands Gone." In *Richard Wright's Native Son: A Critical Handbook*, edited by Richard Abcarian. Belmont, CA: Wadsworth, 1970.

Benardo, Leonard, and Jennifer Weiss. *Brooklyn by Name: How the Neighborhoods, Streets, Parks, Bridges, and More Got Their Names*. New York: New York University Press, 2006.

Bradley, David. Introduction to *12 Million Black Voices*, by Richard Wright. New York: Basic Books, 2002.

Braudeau, Michel. "Why I Wrote *Sophie's Choice*." In *Conversations with William Styron*, edited by James L. W. West III. Jackson: University Press of Mississippi, 1985.

Brinnin, John Malcolm. *Truman Capote: Dear Heart, Old Buddy*. New York: Delacorte Press, 1986.

Burns, Ric, dir. *New York: A Documentary Film*, Episode 2: *Order and Disorder, 1825–1865*. 1999. New York: PBS DVD Gold, 2001.

Burns, Ric, James Sanders, and Lisa Ades. *New York: An Illustrated History*. New York: Alfred A. Knopf, 2003.

Burrows, Edwin G., and Mike Wallace. *Gotham: A History of New York City to 1898*. 1999. Reprint, New York: Oxford University Press, 2000.

Capote, Truman. *Portraits and Observations: The Essays of Truman Capote*. New York: Modern Library, 2008.

———. *Too Brief a Treat: The Letters of Truman Capote*. Edited by Gerald Clarke. New York: Random House, 2004.

Caro, Robert A. *The Power Broker*. New York: Alfred A. Knopf, 1974.

Carpenter, Humphrey. *W. H. Auden: A Biography*. New York: Houghton Mifflin, 1981.

Carr, Virginia Spencer. *Paul Bowles: A Life*. 2004. Reprint, Evanston, IL: Northwestern University Press, 2009.

Clarke, Gerald. *Capote: A Biography*. 1988. Reprint, New York: Carroll & Graf, 2005.

Connolly, Harold X. *A Ghetto Grows in Brooklyn*. New York: New York University Press, 1977.

Cook, Richard. *Alfred Kazin: A Biography*. New Haven, CT: Yale University Press, 2007.

Cowley, Malcolm. *Exile's Return: A Literary Odyssey of the 1920s*. 1934. Reprint, New York: Penguin Classics, 1994.

———. Introduction to *Leaves of Grass: The First (1855) Edition*, by Walt Whitman. New York: Penguin Classics, 1961.

Crane, Hart. *The Collected Poems of Hart Crane*. Edited by Waldo Frank. New York: Liveright, 1933.

———. *The Complete Poems and Selected Letters and Prose of Hart Crane*. Edited by Brom Weber. New York: Anchor Books, 1966.

———. *Letters of Hart Crane and His Family*. Edited by Thomas S. W. Lewis. New York: Columbia University Press, 1974.

———. *O My Land, My Friends: The Selected Letters of Hart Crane*. Edited by Langdon Hammer and Brom Weber. New York: Four Walls Eight Windows, 1997.

Danticat, Edwidge. *Brother, I'm Dying*. 2007. Reprint, New York: Vintage Books, 2008.

Davis, L. J. *A Meaningful Life*. 1971. Reprint, New York: New York Review Books, 2009.

Davis, Philip. *Bernard Malamud: A Writer's Life*. New York: Oxford University Press, 1997.

Dearborn, Mary V. *The Happiest Man Alive: A Biography of Henry Miller*. New York: Simon & Schuster, 1991.

———. *Mailer: A Biography*. New York: Houghton Mifflin, 1999.

Dickey, James. Foreword to *The Complete Short Stories of Thomas Wolfe*. Edited by Frances E. Skipp. New York: Scribner's, 1989.

Diehl, Lorraine B. *Over Here!: New York City During World War II*. New York: Smithsonian / HarperCollins, 2010.

Donald, David Herbert. *Look Homeward: A Life of Thomas Wolfe*. Cambridge, MA: Harvard University Press, 2003.

Edmiston, Susan, and Linda D. Cirino. *Literary New York: A History and Guide*. Boston: Houghton Mifflin, 1976.

Egan, Jennifer. "Reading Lucy." In *Brooklyn Was Mine*, edited by Chris Knutsen and Valerie Steiker. New York: Riverhead, 2008.

Federal Writers' Project. *The WPA Guide to New York City: The Federal Writers' Project Guide to 1930s New York*. 1939. Reprint, New York: New Press, 1995.

Ferguson, Robert. *Henry Miller: A Life*. 1991. Reprint, New York: W. W. Norton, 1993.

Fisher, Clive. *Hart Crane: A Biography*. New Haven, CT: Yale University Press, 2002.

Fitzgerald, F. Scott. "My Lost City." In *Writing New York: A Literary Anthology*, edited by Phillip Lopate. New York: Washington Square Press, 1998.

Fox, Paula. *Desperate Characters*. 1970. Reprint, New York: W. W. Norton, 1999.

George, Nelson. *City Kid: A Writer's Memoir of Ghetto Life and Post-Soul Success*. 2009. Reprint, New York: Penguin, 2010.

Giles, James R. *Understanding Hubert Selby, Jr.* Columbia: University of South Carolina Press, 1998.

Giroux, Robert. Introduction to *The People and Uncollected Stories*, by Bernard Malamud. New York: Farrar, Straus and Giroux, 1989.

Golenbock, Peter. *In the Country of Brooklyn*. New York: William Morrow, 2008.

Gottfried, Martin. *Arthur Miller: His Life and Work*. Cambridge, MA: Da Capo Press, 2004.

Habenstreit, Barbara. *Fort Greene, U.S.A.* Indianapolis: Bobbs-Merrill, 1974.

Hall, Donald. "Art of Poetry No. 4: Marianne Moore." *Paris Review*, Winter 1961. http://www.theparisreview.org/interviews/4637/the-art-of-poetry-no-4-marianne-moore.

———. *Marianne Moore: The Cage and the Animal*. New York: Pegasus, 1970.

Hamill, Pete. *A Drinking Life*. 1994. Reprint, Boston: Back Bay Books, 1997.

Homberger, Eric. *The Historical Atlas of New York City*. 1994. Reprint, New York: Henry Holt, 2008.

Hood, Clifton. *722 Miles: The Building of the Subways and How They Transformed New York*. New York: Simon & Schuster, 1993.

Howe, Irving. *World of Our Fathers*. New York: Harcourt Brace Jovanovich, 1976.

Hughes, Langston. "The Fascination of Cities." *Crisis* 31, January 1926, 138–40.

———. "Harlem." In *Montage of a Dream Deferred*, by Langston Hughes. New York: Henry Holt, 1951.

Jackson, Kenneth T., and David Dunbar, eds. *Empire City: New York Through the Centuries*. New York: Columbia University Press, 2005.

Jackson, Kenneth T., and John Manbeck. *The Neighborhoods of Brooklyn*, 2nd ed. New Haven, CT: Yale University Press, 2004.

Kamil, Seth, and Eric Wakin. *The Big Onion Guide to Brooklyn: Ten Historic Walking Tours*. New York: New York University Press, 2005.

Kazin, Alfred. *Alfred Kazin's America: Critical and Personal Writings*. Edited by Ted Solotaroff. New York: HarperCollins, 2003.

———. *New York Jew*. Syracuse, NY: Syracuse University Press, 1978.

———. *On Native Grounds*. 1942. Reprint, New York: Harcourt Brace, 1995.

———. *Starting Out in the Thirties*. 1965. Reprint, Ithaca, NY: Cornell University Press, 1989.

———. *A Walker in the City*. 1951. Reprint, New York: Harcourt, 1969.

Knutsen, Chris, and Valerie Steiker, eds. *Brooklyn Was Mine*. New York: Riverhead Books, 2008.

Kobler, John. *Capone: The Life and World of Al Capone*. Da Capo Press, 2003.

Kreymborg, Alfred. *Troubadour*. New York: Boni and Liveright, 1925.

Lankevich, George J. *New York City: A Short History*. New York: New York University Press, 2002.

Lemann, Nicholas. *The Promised Land: The Great Black Migration and How It Changed America*. 1991. Reprint, New York: Vintage Books, 1992.

Lethem, Jonathan. *The Disappointment Artist: Essays*. 2005. Reprint, New York: Vintage, 2006.

———. *The Fortress of Solitude*. 2003. Reprint, New York: Vintage, 2004.

———. Introduction to *A Meaningful Life*, by L. J. Davis. New York: New York Review Books, 2009.

———. *Motherless Brooklyn*. 1999. Reprint, New York: Vintage, 2000.

Loving, Jerome. *Walt Whitman: Song of Himself*. Berkeley: University of California Press, 1999.

MacNiven, Ian S., ed. *The Durrell-Miller Letters, 1935–1980*. New York: New Directions, 1988.

Mailer, Norman. *Advertisements for Myself*. 1959. Reprint, Cambridge, MA: Harvard University Press, 1992.

———. *The Armies of the Night*. 1968. Reprint, New York: Plume, 1994.

———. *Barbary Shore*. 1951. Reprint, New York: Vintage International, 1997.

———. *Cannibals and Christians*. New York: Dial Press, 1966.

———. *Existential Errands*. Boston: Little, Brown, 1972.

———. *The Fight*. 1975. Reprint, New York: Vintage International, 2007.

———. *The Naked and the Dead*. 50th Anniversary Edition. New York: Picador, 1998.

Malamud, Bernard. *The Assistant*. 1947. Reprint, New York: Farrar, Straus and Giroux, 2003.

———. *Dubin's Lives*. 1979. New York: Farrar, Straus and Giroux, 2003.

———. *The Magic Barrel*. 1958. Reprint, New York: Pocket Books, 1972.

———. *Talking Horse: Bernard Malamud on Life and Work*. Edited by Alan Cheuse and Nicholas Delbanco. New York: Columbia University Press, 1996.

Manbeck, John B. *Brooklyn, Historically Speaking*. Charleston, SC: History Press, 2008.

Manso, Peter. *Mailer: His Life and Times*. 1985. Reprint, New York: Simon & Schuster, 2008.

Mariani, Paul. *The Broken Tower: A Life of Hart Crane*. New York: W. W. Norton, 1999.

Martin, Jay. *Always Merry and Bright: The Life of Henry Miller: An Unauthorized Biography*. 1978. Reprint, New York: Penguin Books, 1980.

May, Henry Farnham. *The End of American Innocence: A Study of the First Years of Our Own Time, 1912–1917*. New York: Columbia University Press, 1992.

McCullers, Carson. "Brooklyn Is My Neighborhood." *Vogue*, March 1941.

McCullough, David. *Brooklyn: And How It Got That Way*. New York: Dial Press, 1983.

Merrin, Jeredith. "Marianne Moore and Elizabeth Bishop." In *The Columbia History of American Poetry*, edited by Jay Parini and Brett Candlish Miller. New York: Columbia University Press, 1993.

Millay, Edna St. Vincent. "First Figs." In *Early Poems*, by Edna St. Vincent Millay. New York: Penguin Classics, 1998.

Miller, Arthur. *Death of a Salesman*. 1949. Reprint, New York: Viking Press, 1966.

———. "Tragedy and the Common Man." In *The Theater Essays of Arthur Miller*, edited by Robert A. Martin. New York: Viking, 1978.

———. *Timebends*. 1987. Reprint, New York: Harper & Row, 1988.

Miller, Gabriel. *Daniel Fuchs*. Boston: Twayne Publishers, 1979.

Miller, Henry. *Aller Retour New York*. 1935. Reprint, New York: New Directions, 1993.

———. *Black Spring*. 1936. Reprint, New York: Grove Press, 1994.

———. *Book of Friends*. Santa Barbara, CA: Capra Press, 1976.

———. *Moloch*. New York: Grove Press, 1992.

———. *My Life and Times*. Chicago: Playboy Press, 1971.

———. *Nexus*. 1960. Reprint, New York: Grove Press, 1987.

———. *Plexus*. 1953. Reprint, New York: Grove Press, 1987.

———. *Sexus*. 1949. Reprint, New York: Grove Press, 1987.

———. *Tropic of Cancer*. 1934. Reprint, New York: Grove Press, 1994.

———. *Tropic of Capricorn*. 1939. Reprint, New York: Grove Press, 1961.

Mills, Hilary. "Creators on Creating: William Styron." In *Conversations with William Styron*, edited by James L. W. West III. Jackson: University Press of Mississippi, 1985.

———. *Mailer: A Biography*. New York: Empire Books, 1982.

Mitchell, Ted, ed. *Thomas Wolfe: An Illustrated Biography*. New York: Pegasus Books, 2006.

Molesworth, Charles. *Marianne Moore: A Literary Life*. New York: Atheneum Books, 1990.

Moore, Marianne. *Complete Poems*. New York: Penguin, 1967.

———. *The Complete Prose of Marianne Moore*. Edited by Patricia C. Willis. New York: Viking, 1986.

———. *The Poems of Marianne Moore*. Edited by Grace Schulman. New York: Penguin, 2005.

———. *The Selected Letters of Marianne Moore*. Edited by Bonnie Costello. New York: Alfred A. Knopf, 1997.

Morrone, Francis. *An Architectural Guidebook to Brooklyn*. Layton, UT: Gibbs Smith, 2001.

Nin, Anaïs. *Henry and June: From A Journal of Love: The Unexpurgated Diary of Anaïs Nin, 1931–1932*. New York: Harvest Books, 1990.

———. Preface to *Tropic of Cancer*, by Henry Miller. 1934. Reprint, New York: Grove Press, 1994.

Novick, Peter. *The Holocaust in American Life*. New York: Mariner Books, 2000.

O'Connell, Shaun. *Remarkable, Unspeakable New York: A Literary History*. New York: Beacon Press, 1997.

Orwell, George. "Inside the Whale." In *All Art Is Propaganda: Critical Essays*, by George Orwell, edited by George Packer. New York: Houghton Mifflin Harcourt, 2008.

Plimpton, George, ed. *Truman Capote: In Which Various Friends, Enemies, Acquaintances, and Detractors Recall His Turbulent Career*. New York: Anchor Books, 1998.

Podhoretz, Norman. *Making It*. New York: Random House, 1967.

Pritchett, Wendell E. *Brownsville, Brooklyn: Blacks, Jews, and the Changing Face of the Ghetto*. Chicago: University of Chicago Press, 2003.

Rakoff, Joanna Smith. *A Fortunate Age*. 2009. Reprint, New York: Scribner, 2010.

Reynolds, David S. *Walt Whitman*. New York: Oxford University Press, 2005.

———. *Walt Whitman's America: A Cultural Biography*. 1995. Reprint, New York: Vintage Books, 1996.

Rieff, Janice L., Ann Durkin Keating, and James R. Grossman, eds. *Encyclopedia of Chicago*. Chicago: Chicago Historical Society, 2004.

Robbins, Michael W., and Wendy Palitz, eds. *Brooklyn: A State of Mind*. New York: Workman Publishing, 2001.

Rosenwaike, Ira. *Population History of New York City*. Syracuse, NY: Syracuse University Press, 1972.

Rowley, Hazel. *Richard Wright: The Life and Times*. 2001. Reprint, New York: Henry Holt, 2002.

Sawyer-Lauçanno, Christopher. *An Invisible Spectator: A Biography of Paul Bowles*. 1989. Reprint, London: Paladin Books, 1990.

Selby, Hubert, Jr. *Last Exit to Brooklyn*. New York: Grove Press, 1964.

Shulman, Irving. *The Amboy Dukes*. 1947. Reprint, New York: Pocket Books, 1971.

Siegel, Fred. *The Prince of the City: Giuliani, New York, and the Genius of American Life*. San Francisco: Encounter, 2005.

Smith, Janna Malamud. *My Father Is a Book*. Boston: Houghton Mifflin, 2006.

Sorin, Gerald. *Nurturing Neighborhood: The Brownsville Boys' Club and Jewish Community in Urban America, 1940–1990*. New York: New York University Press, 1992.

Stern, Daniel. "Bernard Malamud: The Art of Fiction No. 52." *Paris Review*, Spring 1975, http://www.theparisreview.org/interviews/3869/the-art-of-fiction-no-52-bernard-malamud.

Styron, William. *Letters to My Father*. Edited by James L. W. West III. Baton Rouge: Louisiana State University Press, 2009.

———. *Sophie's Choice*. New York: Vintage Books, 1992.

———. *This Quiet Dust: And Other Writings*. New York: Vintage Books, 1993.

Thomas, Michael. *Man Gone Down*. New York: Black Cat, 2007.

Tippins, Sherill. *February House: The Story of W. H. Auden, Carson McCullers, Jane and Paul Bowles, Benjamin Britten and Gypsy Rose Lee, Under One Roof in Wartime America*. New York: Houghton Mifflin Harcourt, 2005.

Turnbull, Andrew. *Thomas Wolfe*. New York: Scribner's, 1968.

Unterecker, John. *Voyager: A Life of Hart Crane*. New York: Farrar, Straus and Giroux, 1969.

Webb, Constance. *Richard Wright: A Biography*. New York: G. P. Putnam's Sons, 1968.

Weld, Ralph Foster. *Brooklyn Is America*. New York: Columbia University Press, 1950.

West, James L. W. III, ed. *Conversations with William Styron*. Jackson: University Press of Mississippi, 1985.

———. *William Styron: A Life*. New York: Random House, 1998.

West, Michael. "An Interview with William Styron." In *Conversations with William Styron*, edited by James L. W. West III. Jackson: University Press of Mississippi, 1985.

White, Norval, Elliot Willensky, and Fran Leadon. *AIA Guide to New York City*. 5th ed. New York: Oxford University Press, 2010.

Whitman, Walt. *The Complete Poems*. Edited by Francis Murphy. New York: Penguin Classics, 2004.

———. *Leaves of Grass: The First (1855) Edition*. New York: Penguin Classics, 1961.

———. *Prose Works*. Philadelphia: David McKay, 1892. Reprint, Bartleby.com, 2000. www.bartleby.com/229/.

———. *The Uncollected Poetry and Prose of Walt Whitman*. Volume 1. Edited by Emory Holloway. Garden City, NY: Doubleday, 1921.

———. *Walt Whitman's New York: From Manhattan to Montauk*. Edited by Henry M. Christman. New York: New Amsterdam Books, 1989. This book consists of a series of essayistic newspaper articles published in the Brooklyn *Standard* beginning in 1861 under the title "Brooklyniana."

Wickes, George. "Henry Miller." In *American Writers*, vol. 3, 170–92. New York: Scribner's, 1974.

Wilder, Craig Steven. *A Covenant with Color: Race and Social Power in Brooklyn*. 2000. Reprint, New York: Columbia University Press, 2001.

Wolfe, Gerard L. *New York: A Guide to the Metropolis*. Rev. ed. New York: New York University Press, 1983.

Wolfe, Thomas. *The Autobiography of an American Novelist*. Edited by Leslie Field. Cambridge, MA: Harvard University Press, 1983.

———. *The Complete Short Stories of Thomas Wolfe*. Edited by Frances E. Skipp. New York: Scribner's, 1989.

———. *Look Homeward, Angel*. 1929. Reprint, New York: Scribner, 1995.

———. *Of Time and the River*. 1935. Reprint, New York: Scribner, 1999.

———. *The Selected Letters of Thomas Wolfe*. Edited by Elizabeth Nowell and selected by Daniel George. London: Heinemann, 1969.

———. "The Story of a Novel." 1936. Reprinted in *The Autobiography of an American Novelist*, by Thomas Wolfe. Edited by Leslie Field. Cambridge, MA: Harvard University Press, 1983.

———. "Writing and Living." 1938. Reprinted in *The Autobiography of an American Novelist*, by Thomas Wolfe. Edited by Leslie Field. Cambridge, MA: Harvard University Press, 1983.

———. *You Can't Go Home Again*. 1940. Reprint, New York: Harper Perennial Modern Classics, 1998.

Wright, Richard. *Black Boy (American Hunger): A Record of Childhood and Youth*. 1945. Reprint, New York: Perennial Classics, 1998.

———. "How Bigger Was Born." Reprinted in *Native Son*, by Richard Wright. New York: Harper Perennial, 2005.

———. *Native Son*. 1940. Reprint, New York: Harper Perennial, 2005.

———. *12 Million Black Voices*. 1941. Reprint, New York: Basic Books, 2002.

Yeats, W. B. *Selected Poems and Four Plays by W. B. Yeats*. 4th ed. Edited by M. L. Rosenthal. New York: Simon & Schuster, 1996.

Acknowledgments

I would first like to acknowledge and thank the many novelists, biographers, historians, and journalists whose work made this book possible. As Edwin G. Burrows and Mike Wallace have written, "A synthesizer, looking back, sees a thief's shadow." A number of writers generously gave their time in addressing my questions, including, in alphabetical order, Elizabeth Blackmar, Randy Chase, Gerald Clarke, the late L. J. Davis, Mary V. Dearborn, Nelson George, Roger Jackson, Stephen Marino, Charles Molesworth, the late Hazel Rowley, Janna Malamud Smith, Alexandra Styron, Sherrill Tippins, Touré, Greg Trupiano, Mike Wallace, and James L. W. West.

I owe thanks to Larry Weissman and Sarah Bowlin, and to David Patterson, Marjorie Braman, David Shoemaker, and Evan Johnston. I want to acknowledge friends who gave valuable feedback and advice: Jordan Mintzer, Michelle Orange, Jana Prikryl, Gary Sernovitz, Meline Toumani. Special thanks go to Barbara Epstein, John Andersen, and J.H.

Very special thanks to my parents, Guy Hughes and Mary Joe Hughes, who taught me what it is to devote yourself to reading and thinking and writing. I miss you, Dad.

Finally, so much gratitude to my confidante, editor, companion, and great love, Adelle Waldman.

Index